BODY PROBLEMS

M. WOLFF

BODY PROBLEMS

What
Intersex
Priest
Sally Gross
Teaches Us
About
Embodiment,
Justice, and
Belonging

Duke University Press
Durham and London 2025

© 2025 DUKE UNIVERSITY PRESS. All rights reserved
Project Editor: Bird Williams
Designed by Courtney Leigh Richardson
Typeset in Freight and Avenir by Westchester Publishing Services

Library of Congress Cataloging-in-Publication Data
Names: Wolff, M. (Michelle) 1983- author.
Title: Body problems : what intersex priest Sally Gross teaches us about embodiment, justice, and belonging / M. Wolff.
Description: Durham : Duke University Press, 2025. | Includes bibliographical references and index.
Identifiers: LCCN 2024050710 (print)
LCCN 2024050711 (ebook)
ISBN 9781478032045 (paperback)
ISBN 9781478028789 (hardcover)
ISBN 9781478060987 (ebook)
Subjects: LCSH: Gross, Sally, 1953-2014. | Gross, Sally, 1953-2014—Religion. | Discrimination against intersex people—South Africa. | Intersex people—South Africa—Biography. | Intersex people—Political activity—South Africa. | Human rights workers—South Africa—Biography. | Intersex people—Civil rights—South Africa. | Racism in medicine—South Africa.
Classification: LCC HQ77.98.G76 W654 2025 (print)
LCC HQ77.98.G76 (ebook)
DDC 306.76/85092—dc23/eng/20250212
LC record available at https://lccn.loc.gov/2024050710
LC ebook record available at https://lccn.loc.gov/2024050711

Cover art and frontispiece: Passport photo of Sally Gross. From GALA Archive.

CONTENTS

| | Introduction | 1 |

| I | **BODY PROBLEMS** | 11 |

| | 1 Context | 15 |
| | 2 Adulthood | 29 |

| II | **PROBLEM BODIES** | 47 |

	3 Religious Bodies	51
	4 Medical Bodies	65
	5 Bodies of Paperwork	87
	6 Bodies of Land	99

| III | **AGITATING BODIES** | 115 |

	7 Transnational Activism	119
	8 Community Building in South Africa	137
	9 Costs of Activism	149

| IV | **BODILINESS** | 165 |

	10 Clearings	169
	11 Breaks	173
	12 Sutures	191
	13 Resonance	213

Postscript	233
Acknowledgments	245
Notes	247
Bibliography	299
Index	309

INTRODUCTION

When your body becomes a problem—and trans bodies are nothing if not problems, institutionally speaking—it also becomes the space where possible solutions get worked out, and this process can intensify anxieties around appearance. —HIL MALATINO, *Trans Care*

Many of us have been told our bodies are problems. People of color. Women. Queers. Fats. Crips. Indigenous folks. Our bodies are met with suspicion and violence. Political and religious groups form institutional bodies that shore up power and stability by deflecting attention away from their exploitative and unjust procedures. We discover that the price of belonging to a community is to reject parts of ourselves.

Rather than accept our bodies as problems, we could interrogate these institutional bodies that operate as systems of regulation. W. E. B. Du Bois introduced the notion of *double-consciousness* in his book *The Souls of Black Folk*. He described being both Black and American as a constant struggle against being torn in two. "To the real question, How does it feel to be a problem? I answer seldom a word."[1] Given that the stakes are so high, how might we bravely unmask the lie that our bodies are problems and thereby expose unjust systems within regulating bodies?

There is an ironic twist to identifying injustice within systems: we become problems to them.[2] The process itself is circular. We have been told that our bodies are problems, but the inhospitality of institutions is the real issue. In pointing that out, however, we opt into becoming problems for those governing bodies. When we choose to become this type of problem, one with agency that purposefully unveils injustice and inequity, we introduce breaks. While at times painful and frightful, breaks make space for the pieces of ourselves that we have been told to cut off. They create room for reassemblage sutured into wholeness. When political and religious bodies transform because of provocation, our bodies are no longer problems, and we are no longer troublesome for pointing out systemic flaws.

What becomes of bodies, individual and regulating, after a break to corrupt systems?[3] What does the subsequent space that fissures open allow for? We get a glimpse of possibilities in Toni Morrison's novel *Beloved*. Morrison sets the scene in a tree clearing where Baby Suggs serves as a pastor to other enslaved people. "Baby Suggs, holy, followed by every black man, woman and child who could make it through, took her great heart to the Clearing."[4] In this scene, Suggs invites everyone back into their bodies. To the children who have been reduced to utilitarian value through slave labor she instructs, "'Let your mothers hear you laugh,' . . . and the woods rang."[5] She directs the men to dance and the women to cry. Baby Suggs restores joy and grief. She attends to brutalized bodies. She preaches: "We flesh; flesh that weeps, laughs; flesh that dances on bare feet in grass. Love it. Love it hard. Yonder they do not love your flesh. They despise it . . . they do not love your neck unnoosed and straight. . . . She stood up then and danced with her twisted hip."[6] A religious leader, Baby Suggs consecrates her affirmation through dance. It is a religious event in the clearing.[7] Breaks allow space for all bodies to resonate within ongoing relations.

In the clearing, individual bodies are not problems. They are present to aches, affect, and history across relationships. This is not a dualist desire for a life free from the frailties of human flesh. Nor is it a longing for an eschatological future not yet realized. Through writing fiction, Morrison opens our imaginations to the possibility of embracing the fullness of our bodies in the here and now, even if only for a few hours in a clearing of the woods. When a religious body dignifies Black life, it moves against the grain of systemic racism that treats Black people as disposable. Compared to individualistic self-care, collectively embodied worth is more radical. We resonate with one another and our environs.[8]

To Morrison's vision of bodily affirmation, we may also heed calls to resist anthropocentrism and recognize our bodily value as integrated within both biological and social ecologies. When Morrison writes that the woods rang with the children's laughter, we might begin to interpret a multiplicity of meaning by taking a cue from Mari Joerstad.[9] Joerstad recognizes that references to actions of nonanimal nature in the Hebrew Bible are sometimes metaphorical but argues that there are also instances in which we might understand the woods as "persons" with whom humanity can have good or bad relations. Her use of "person" is intentionally provocative. When Indigenous people respect bodies of land and water, too often it is mischaracterized by colonizers as nature worship. But it is not the case that humans who honor their environment necessarily venerate it, or elements of it, *as* God.

What I am suggesting here is that we expand our vision of bodies beyond individuals and even collectives to include environments. The significance of a turn to environmentalism ought not to be limited to a single issue. Instead, it is a consequence of advancing social justice in any form. The exploitation of land often parallels racism and patriarchy. Capitalist greed exacerbates these. To be antiracist and egalitarian entails caring for the earth. The deeper we dig into the contributing factors upholding inequity, the more apparent interlocking systems become. Liberation from the lie that our bodies are problems is not an affirmation of the autonomous individual. Deep belonging is nurtured within a broader vision beyond regulating bodies. We are most beloved within diverse ecologies of good relations.

In her analysis of Morrison's *Beloved*, womanist ethicist Emilie Townes writes about the statistical correlation between poverty, people of color, and pollution.[10] Her corpus has aided me in understanding evil as systemic rather than individual, toxic waste sites as a contemporary form of lynching, and the theological imperative to love necks "unnoosed and straight."[11] Townes understands love as "a theo-ethical and political act."[12] Townes demands that society evidence the value of people through policies. She and queer theologian Marcella Althaus-Reid help change our understanding of body problems as actually institutional bodies regulating individuals and the need for agitating bodies to work tirelessly for clearings wherein we might resonate as beloved.[13] This insight provides a framing through which I share intersex scholar-priest activist Sally Gross's story and illuminates my aim: to galvanize justice-oriented action via religiosity for embodied resonance.

Sally Gross

This is the first book-length publication on Sally Gross (1953–2014), an intersex scholar-priest and activist. Despite her many accomplishments that shaped public policy, Sally died impoverished. The Apartheid Museum commemorates her for participating in the African National Congress and for having founded Intersex South Africa (ISSA); however, until now, her devotion to her Jewish heritage, Christian communities, and Buddhist practices remained unanalyzed.

Sally is a helpful companion for shifting our perspective on body problems. Her body was treated as a problem from the moment she was born. It continued throughout her life, with her premature death confronting loved ones with the question of what to do with her many bodies—her physical body, her body of work, her body of possessions. Sally suffered demands to contort her body into something institutional bodies could tolerate but eventually realized that those institutions might need to change to accommodate individual bodies. Instead of disciplinary instruments, institutional bodies could cherish individuals as invaluable to collectives. Sally's ardent desire was to be known and accepted entirely, in the fullness of her complexity. Her story displays both the pragmatism and limitations of working within versus dismantling corrupt systems.

Conventional categories never quite fit Sally because she embodied multiple identities. She was not squarely female or male; she was intersex—a fact that she learned at age forty while serving as a Catholic priest at Blackfriars, a Dominican order in England.[14] Sally did not claim to be either Jewish or Christian; rather, she integrated her Jewish identity with Buddhist practices and Christian community. Sally held citizenship in three countries and agitated as an activist in each. Religious, civil, and medical institutions struggled to categorize her body because bureaucracies tend to insist upon legible taxonomies in exchange for goods and services. The pain of rejection fueled her efforts to make systemic change. At great personal sacrifice, Sally devoted her life to helping others experience what she never did—unconditional belonging.

Sally's shift to holding unjust political and religious bodies accountable would result in her becoming a "problem," a threat to their power and authority.[15] Despite numerous setbacks and tragedies, Sally's story also offers glimpses into the possibility of initiating breaks and entering clearings where a communal body resonates with individual bodies. Life together need not entail indignation. Her dream—to belong as her complex self—is appealing and worthwhile. What this might mean for us in our present moment is a bittersweet invitation to join others in instigating breaks and rejoicing in clearings, however fleeting. Community flourishing requires diversity. A thriving ecology, material and social, must break from colonial constraints. The aim is not autonomous individualism; it is good relations.

Sally presents a laudable example of bravery and a cautionary display of the hazards of working within unjust systems. Sally was among the first generation of intersex activists.[16] Consequently, LGBTQI+ activists in South Africa express their debt to her for the inroads she made in political policy changes and for boldly bringing intersexuality into popular discourse.[17] Sally assiduously utilized all the resources available to her within institutions to advocate for herself and others. Despite her accomplishments and the commonality of her biological occurrence, intersexuality remains relatively unknown and misconstrued. She reached the limits of collaborating with institutions aimed at regulating Black, brown, disabled, female, neurodivergent, queer, and poor bodies. At times, Sally acknowledged her culpability for participating in unjust systems.[18]

Sally's experience confronts each of us with the difficulties of social justice work—choosing to become a problem to institutions. Making institutions, policies, and procedures into tools for self-defense is necessary for maintaining life. Some intersex activists oppose any collaboration with medical professionals or religiosity. I advocate for a multipronged approach because, despite drawbacks, initiating breaks and creating clearings, even if temporary, is worthwhile and life-giving. We need not choose between working within systems or destroying them altogether. It is important to transform laws to protect underserved people and also for activists and theorists to interrogate the limitations of collaborating with medical, religious, and political institutions. Sally's pathbreaking efforts to improve standards of health care, her integration of religiosity, and interventions in public policy did not shield her from harassment, poverty, or loneliness. Intersex people continue to need advocacy, but that does not mean her efforts were unremarkable and did not save lives.

Sally's particular story highlights broader social and political injustices that persist today. Though she was thoroughly singular, a significant number of LGBTQI+ religious people and activists share in Sally's painful experiences.[19] I offer my perspective on her story, hoping that it will prompt us to reflect on the harm we inflict on ourselves and others through communities shaped by binary categories. Like Du Bois, we can refuse to respond to the question of what it is like to be a problem. We might follow Baby Suggs's invitation into clearings where the fullness of bodies is honored. Sally's story emboldens us to initiate breaks that make space for clearings where belonging is defined by the resonance of diverse ecologies. These moves—to reject the notion that our bodies are problems, to choose to become a problem to disciplinary bodies by agitating and initiating breaks, to create clearings where diverse bodies resonate—shape the arc of the book. Alongside the numerous activists she mentored, we might also be motivated by Sally to participate in challenging regulating bodies, to make clearings such that all sutured bodies are, as Emilie Townes put it, beloved.

We will journey alongside Sally in this ongoing, cyclical process. You might wonder about her dates and locations, which will be answered later in the book. Some questions will remain unanswered. As we cycle through her life many times over, examining various aspects of her experiences, an organic type of knowing will emerge—not one organized with timelines or maps, but something closer to how you get to know a person over time.

By increasing our capacity to embrace complex people like Sally, we will better cope with our own unruly excess. On some level, we intuit that we also are more than the limited identity markers offered to us—gender, race, religion, nationality, class, and so on. Embracing dynamic wholeness as opportunities for connection with others amid clearings is a religious and political act. We might even realize that humanity is not the center of collective bodies but rather a member of a broader ecology, spiritual and material.

Theories and Methods

In 2015, I traveled to my place of birth, South Africa, to conduct research on the sexual politics of religion. At the Gay and Lesbian Memory in Action archives (GALA), I first read Sally's personal correspondence. I was simultaneously enamored of and grief-stricken by her letters to and from her confidant, Father Timothy Radcliffe. The two shared an affection for one another strained by the Roman Catholic Church's response to her intersex status. Since then, I returned to the GALA archives twice, in 2016 and again in 2018. In addition, I went to the Douai Abbey in England, which contains the Blackfriars archives. Funding from Augustana College allowed me to interview Sally's friends and comrades in Cape Town and Johannesburg and her former brethren, friends, and comrades throughout England. Because Sally's network spans nearly every continent, I also conducted in-depth interviews via video calls, primarily with intersex activists worldwide. The COVID-19 pandemic prevented me from completing a research trip to Brooklyn, New York, in the summer of 2020, where I had hoped to connect with the Orthodox Jewish community that Sally wrote about having visited. At the end of 2021, I went to the synagogue Sally visited while she was secretly a Catholic priest. I have also been in continual communication with Sally's closest living relative, her brother Raymond (Ray) Schmidt-Gross, who shared family artifacts and gave me access to material on Sally's computer hard drive. On multiple occasions, Ray has reviewed drafts of this manuscript to correct errors and confirm boundaries respecting the privacy of the Gross and Schmidt-Gross families. With special permission from the Blackfriars and the GALA archivist, this book includes quotations and citations of restricted material.

What follows is the synthesis of hundreds of pages of Sally's correspondence, academic lectures, church sermons, photographs, writings, talks, and documents; video, online, and print journalist reports on Sally and her work; and over forty in-depth Institutional Review Board–approved interviews.[20]

The people I interviewed most often described Sally as brilliant, kind, difficult, lonely, and fat. They pointed to the trauma of being pushed out of ministry as the most significant life event upon which Sally dwelt.[21] She was able to forge a new ministry as an activist and, through that, meaningful friendships, but ultimately, she was a severely lonely person after leaving the Dominican order. Sally was difficult to work with because she disrupted harmful regulating bodies, but her principles and stubbornness also needlessly injured friends and colleagues. The five common descriptors listed above tell us something about Sally but perhaps much more about the communities within which she lived.

Upon learning Sally's tragic story, people often want to blame an individual—a particular family member, clergy person, or activist—for her plight. It is tempting to oversimplify Sally's life into good- versus bad-faith actors. I contend that it was not any one person who rendered her impoverished and isolated. How this mother of intersex activism died prematurely is in large part due to institutional structures that were unable to make sense of her body.[22] This position will certainly frustrate readers searching for a simple storyline with one-dimensional actors—friends or foes of Sally.[23] Some of her friends express regret about how they responded to Sally due to their unfamiliarity with intersexuality. They claim that they would conduct themselves quite differently today and, unfortunately, Sally bore the brunt of their ignorance. In what follows, I will try to present the painful reality of what took place while also acknowledging the remorse expressed by the people I interviewed.

Philosopher Albert Memmi describes his failed attempt to write a novel about a romantic couple as an escape from his broader interest in global politics: "I discovered that the couple is not an isolated entity, a forgotten oasis of light in the middle of the world; on the contrary, the whole world is within the couple. For my unfortunate protagonists, the world was that of colonization."[24] Rather than learning about Sally as an individual person *or* for her broader political significance, both of which the reader will see are remarkable, I consider them within a feedback loop. The private world is too often presumed to be the women's sphere of influence, whereas the public is that of men. Perhaps Sally's literal intersexuality configures binaries so that we understand the spheres and genders as mutually shaping one another and, therefore, inextricable. Anecdotes about Sally are inseparable from her political interventions.

Sally's relationship with gender classification was complex and dynamic. Naming herself might have been a rhetorical act of survival rather than expressing a fixed identity; she leveraged terminology in response to context and audience.[25] Throughout this book, I use Sally's chosen name and pronouns, but before she takes the name Sally, I simply refer to her as "S." (For clarity, I use *Sally* here.) This is to honor her efforts to obtain legal documents in this name and to signal that she was a person who was not definitively male and yet entered male-only spaces to participate in male-only traditions. It also serves as a temporal marker because I organized the four parts thematically rather than chronologically. Flashbacks to the time before Sally took her name are emphasized using *S.*, whereas flash-forwards to after she took her name are flagged with *Sally*.

One Catholic priest reminded me that Sally's "bodiliness," a term she was fond of, was always at the forefront of her interactions. The body matters literally and figuratively. Access to citizenship and the priesthood demanded definitive gender categories of her, but her intersexuality troubled classifications. Sally's intellectual insights are inseparable from her embodied experiences; her logic, politics, and prayers cannot be divorced from her corporeality. Sally herself was fascinated with the question of bodies. For example, her doctoral thesis at Oxford University focused on the topic of resurrected bodies.[26] When she became an intersex activist, Sally held to the conviction that intersex anatomy was not a problem so much as unaccommodating societies were. Her attention to bodies befits the framing of *Body Problems*—that individual bodies are wrongly deemed problematic by regulating social bodies and that in choosing to become a problem to those, we initiate breaks to enjoy complete belonging to diverse ecologies.

Part Summaries

The four parts of this book cycle through Sally's story in sequential loops, sometimes micro chronologies that are revisited more than once per part, and are presented in the following thematic pattern: body problems, problem bodies, agitating bodies, and bodiliness. Part I moves through the arc of her life and confronts her tragic end. Subsequent parts return cyclically to the details of her life, in greater depth on the wrongdoing she suffered and the remarkable interventions she made from within institutions. Because Sally moved across many countries, often within the same year, I call your attention to these themes rather than to a sterile timeline or map. Although these parts cannot contain an embodied life, a rich portrait of Sally will gradually emerge. Note that one chapter deals with suicidal ideation, which I have flagged and bracketed for readers who wish to pass over that content. The book elsewhere contains quotations and discussions that include references to violence, discrimination, abuse, slurs, and harassment. While these are often not described in graphic detail, they might be harmful to sensitive readers.

Part I introduces the concept of "Body Problems" as a framework for attending to Sally's body as a site of harm. It recounts various versions of "What is it like to be a problem?," a question posed to Sally by religious and political disciplinary bodies. This part considers Sally's literal flesh, demonstrating simultaneously that this is inextricable from various social bodies that regulate her. Her body is continually formed, read, and written upon. Often, these forces attempt to slice and compartmentalize her into legible and manageable subsets. Her body is marked as too fat, improperly masculine, and only contingently white as Jewish. This part provides background into Sally's political context and social formation. Sally offers a mirror to us. Perhaps we can relate to the experience of our bodies being treated as problems and empathize with the pain of being reduced to one dimension of ourselves.

Part II, "Problem Bodies," shifts our perspective on the source of the problem—away from ourselves and toward the regulating bodies that manage us. These include but are not limited to religious bodies, medical bodies, bodies of paperwork, and bodies of land. In these chapters, I detail Sally's priesthood in the Catholic Church (1981–93), her misdiagnosis as transgender, the subsequent paperwork she navigated to conceal and then reveal her female role, and her turn to racial justice work in South Africa. To shift away from understanding individual people as problems so as to interrogate the processes of regulation by unjust systems requires courage. Revealing the ugly truth is painful work. Those like Sally, who are willing to confront institutional inequity bravely, endeavor to advocate for themselves and transform harmful systems into more just collectives.

Part III, "Agitating Bodies," explores activism and the purposeful choice to become a problem to governing bodies by exposing injustice and inequality. Sally agitated throughout her life in diverse religious and political contexts. Participation in activism promises neither security nor success. The costs for her courage were social and material: She died lonesome and impoverished.

Unfortunately, Sally's ultimate destitution is not uncommon. To instigate change is to forfeit the privileges that are awarded to docile bodies. Despite her premature death, a more hospitable communal life is worth agitating for, I think.

Last, part IV, "Bodiliness," returns to the cyclical process of initiating breaks to make space for clearings and sutures that restructure regulating bodies. The aim is for all bodies to flourish within religious and political ecologies, which I characterize as *resonance*. The setting for bodiliness is a clearing. The events that take place include breaks and sutures. The aim is resonance. By resonance I mean to signal both the musical sound of vibration and a collective effort to establish responsible relationships. These multidimensional, layered metaphors connect through the clearing scene in Toni Morrison's novel *Beloved*. Instead of orienting the reader, part IV generates creativity. Through motif, readers gain a sense that, rather than a biography about Sally or her historical context, we have been learning about our context. Imaginations are stoked by religiosity to envisage sociality otherwise.[27] The form parallels the content.

Sally was fond of the neologism *bodiliness*, making it a fitting term to describe the aims of agitating. It is a bittersweet invitation to join in intersex activism while also acknowledging the limitations of Sally's approach. While she fought tirelessly for systemic justice, Sally did so within the law. Be it religious or secular polity, she worked within established parameters that proved incompatible with her complexity. Some more radical activists and theorists might conclude that her story exposes the futility of working within inherently unjust systems and the need to tear these down entirely before constructing new alternatives. Part IV celebrates her work within religious institutions to advance diverse ecologies and includes some of her accomplishments in changing laws and policies. In the postscript, I examine Sally's limitations, describe the ongoing challenges that intersex activists face, and encourage readers to increase religious literacy and participate in agitating for justice.

I

BODY PROBLEMS

All organisms are emergent multispecies aggregates and communities. . . . Queer theory for lichens suggests that we have never been individuals, and that attention to this can have positive biomedical consequences. —DAVID GRIFFITHS, "Queer Theory for Lichens"

On August 22, 1953, in Cape Town, South Africa, Mildred and Henry Jacob Gross (hereafter Jack) anxiously awaited the doctors' assurance that their firstborn child was healthy.[1] Each time they asked, medical staff exchanged uncomfortable glances. Finally, someone mustered a curt explanation: the baby might die of dehydration. Mildred and Jack were afraid and confused. How could a baby die of dehydration in a hospital?[2] It seemed like a flimsy diversion. What was the fuss about? The baby survived. Overwhelmed by gratitude, Mildred and Jack did not press the issue. They wrapped S. in a blanket and took their baby home.

Eight days later, it was time for the baby's ritual circumcision, or *bris milah*. It happened to be a Saturday, the Sabbath. Friends and family gathered. Mildred entered and handed her baby to the *kvatters*—male and female messengers. The sandek, Jack's representative, sat nervously; his task was to

FIGURE I.1 Gross at seventeen months old. From GALA archive.

hold the infant still while the mohel conducted the ceremony. Jack handed over the surgical knife.

The mohel made the blessing: *Blessed are you L-rd our G-d, King of the universe, Who has sanctified us with His commandments and commanded us concerning circumcision.*

Head reverentially covered, the mohel bent over S. and squinted at the genitalia. Initially unsure of how to make the incision, he resolved to forge ahead. It was not a typical cut, but the mohel reassured himself that it would likely heal satisfactorily. He had been able to draw blood, but he could not cut around the penis to remove the foreskin. Witnesses exchanged whispers as the minutes stretched on. Though flushed, the mohel persisted. He had not left his house carrying his tools on the Sabbath for anything less than to fulfill the commandment to circumcise.[3]

Jack winced. He couldn't help but shift with discomfort as his child shrieked.

Jack: *Blessed are you L-rd our G-d, King of the universe, Who has sanctified us with His commandments and commanded to enter him into the Covenant of Abraham our father.*

Witnesses: *Just as he has entered into the Covenant, so may he enter into Torah, into marriage, and into good deeds.*

The mohel dipped his finger into the cup of wine and placed the drop into S.'s mouth. He announced the baby's name, dipped his finger in the wine again, and placed it in S.'s mouth. The difficult part was over. Now the family could celebrate. Their baby was healthy and circumcised.

A few days later, something was clearly wrong: S. was not healing properly. Mildred and Jack phoned the mohel, who reiterated his instructions that S. had special recovery needs.

The parents insisted: *You need to come here and look.* The mohel returned to fiddle with S.'s wounds.

Decades later, after S. took the name Sally and a female role, her father seethed with rage. How could the mohel have been so stupid? According to Jack, he should have realized that S. was a girl and not attempted the circumcision. However, S. clarified that she had not been born male or female; she was born intersex. About these events, she wrote, "This sets the context of my life history."[4]

1. Context

Israel and South Africa are national bodies shaped by religion. They influenced the reception of S. as well as her transnational movement. Israel was formed in 1948, after World War II and the Holocaust, in which Jewish people were systematically ghettoized and murdered. That same year, apartheid, a racist system that legislated segregation and economic inequity, was instituted in South Africa. Its architects deployed Christian theology and biblical texts to validate and reinforce its programs. South Africa's Public Safety Act (1953) allowed declaring a state of emergency to override extant laws and imposed rigid penalties upon people who protested discriminatory laws. Israel and South Africa forged an alliance. Israel had been a state and South Africa's National Party had instituted apartheid for five years by the time S. was born.

From 1948 to 1954, Prime Minister D. F. Malan became the first head of the South African government to visit Israel, which initiated cooperation among Zionist South Africans and Israelis.[1] South Africa and Israel collaborated to construct gold and diamond values globally. In the decades that followed, South Africa became increasingly isolated from the global market due to trade embargoes and apartheid boycotts. However, by working through Israel, both countries were able to garner capital.

As a Jewish South African, S. understood her body to be only conditionally designated white. Her exposure to Christianity was limited to men dressed as Father Christmas in the sweltering heat of Johannesburg Decembers and fake snow in shop windows. At seven years old, she learned a bit about Easter when, as she put it, a much older boy asked whether she was Jewish. When she confirmed, he punched her in the face "for killing Christ."[2] During the National Party's rise to power, Jewish South Africans feared they might be designated "non-white" and become subject to restrictions that "Coloured" and Indian South Africans had to submit to. (Coloured was a legal category for members of multiracial ethnic communities or, more broadly, as people of color in South Africa during Apartheid. Today, some South Africans continue to ascribe to this racial identity.)

In this liminal space, Jewish South Africans were compelled to permit or, better, endorse Apartheid policy. Some Jewish leaders actively resisted Apartheid, such as Ray Alexander Simons and Hilda Bernstein.[3] S. contributed a chapter to the book *Intellectual Traditions in South Africa* about these trends, and the chapter was published posthumously. In it she details an active Jewish left that shifted in the aftermath of World War II, because, "South African Jews feared that they would be consigned to concentration camps by the new government, expelled from South Africa, at best, or, at worst, subjected to a programme of extermination."[4] According to S., the majority of Jewish South Africans opposed the National Party but feared the loss of their "white" status should they publicly challenge it: "This qualified inclusion was implicitly conditional upon the community not challenging the racial and political status quo."[5]

In one of her drafts, which was not included in the published version, S. summarizes the effects of a radicalized minority and acquiescing majority ascribing to "an ideology of 'survivalism.'"[6] The published version concludes that there were two responses to Apartheid in the Jewish community: "The radicalisation of a minority, often rejected by the community in consequence and consisting largely of non-Jewish Jews, was one. The other response, of the organised community, was of an often ambivalent acquiescence. It was largely anxiety-driven—although zealous collaboration with apartheid, exemplified by [Percy] Yutar, was the exception."[7] While it is obvious why most people are willing to uphold and abide by discriminatory policies in exchange for safety, it became clear over time that S.'s temperament disallowed it. The dissonance she experienced when political bodies problematized individuals or select cultural and racialized bodies never dissipated.

The formation of state bodies entails the management of individual bodies. Early to mid-twentieth-century Germany and South Africa share infamy for their overt efforts to disenfranchise and terminate entire racial and ethnic groups. However, their methods and legacies are not isolated aberrations. As a transnational figure, S. would find similarities across four continents. No government was free of harmful policies aimed at specific population sectors. S. participated in pockets agitating for justice because each legislative body privileged some group over another. It perplexed her that most people are willing to participate in unjust systems for self-preservation.

Nuclear Family

In June 2019, Sally's brother Ray emerged from his Massachusetts basement carrying a weathered cardboard box. We settled down to sift through crackling envelopes and photo albums spread the length of his dining room table. It was his first time looking through the contents since their parents died. Together, Ray and I assembled a gestalt of S.'s family context.

The Gross home was shaped by gendered nationalism and the imperial market.[8] Jack was a cantankerous man and consequently struggled to maintain employment. He frequently fought with coworkers, which resulted in the burden of income falling squarely on Mildred, who worked as a typist. Theirs were gendered bodies: Jack, a muscular Jewish soldier, and Mildred, a tender musician. In a newspaper photo, Mildred smiles modestly. The caption praises her bronze medal achievement for piano playing.[9] Mildred sang opera and played the piano or symphony records. She gave birth to Ray when S. was twelve and instilled in her children a lifelong love of music.[10]

Jack had carefully preserved every medal and government paperwork documenting his military service.[11] In these photographs, Jack poses with showmanship. In one, a comrade balances standing atop Jack's shoulders. In another, Jack holds himself in a handstand on a chair, wearing a swimsuit. He was a proud man who embodied a particular moment in religious and political history.

A former member of the Hashomer Hatzair, a Socialist-Zionist youth movement, Jack adamantly supported the Soviet Union and even considered Stalin's Russia a second homeland in the 1940s. He served in the South African army in North Africa during World War II and went to Palestine in 1945. There, Jack became a minor commander in the Palmach, an elite fighting force of the Haganah, the underground army of the Jewish community

FIGURE 1.1 Photograph of siblings S. and Ray, 1966. Courtesy of Ray Schmidt-Gross.

Yishuv during the British Mandate for Palestine (1921–48). After World War I, the League of Nations mandated that the British declare and establish territories of Palestine to be "the national home for the Jewish people."

Upon Israel's emergence as a state, the Palmach dissolved, and the Haganah went from being a paramilitary to the Israel Defense Forces. Jack founded a Hashomer Hatzair kibbutz, or collective agricultural community, called Shoval in the Negev region. Zionists strategically established these settlements in Palestine to establish a Jewish presence throughout the region. Jack became one of the first junior officers in the Israel Defense Forces. Although not a medical doctor, he served as chief medical officer for the southern Negev.[12] Near the end of 1949, Jack returned to South Africa to visit his family. It was during this trip that he met Mildred. The two married and chose to stay in South Africa because Mildred was hesitant about moving to a kibbutz. After leaving the kibbutz, where his confrontational personality served a valued purpose, Jack struggled to find his place in South Africa.[13]

Often, Jack's politics were mistaken for self-indulgent petulance. At thirty years old, S. described Jack's rigidity:

> My father has always had a huge 'chip on his shoulder.' . . . [He] sometimes quit good jobs, telling his bosses how to run the show and how stupid they were, and how much better he could do it, and was consequently being fired or walking out. He usually did the latter. My mother held a steady job as a secretary, and worked hard to earn our daily bread. . . . We more often than not lived from hand to mouth by white South African standards. We were always moving from flat to flat. . . . Our all time low came when we spent a year in a seedy, flea-ridden hotel in a rather sleazy area of Johannesburg. By the time I was ten, we must have moved flats about twelve times. This nomadic experience meant that there was very little continuity of relationships in my life.[14]

S.'s paternal grandfather once explained to S. that Jack's fervor was not all belligerent temperament; he was motivated by a thirst for justice. Jack often expressed his disdain with employers and resigned regularly over issues of principle, which might have inspired S.'s ability to take firm, though costly, stances. Jack once worked as an administrative assistant at the Vredehoek Synagogue. Upon learning that the cleaner was not paid living wages, he challenged the board. When the board refused to raise the man's salary, Jack resigned. Protests like these left the family unable to pay rent on their flat, which led to S.'s nomadic upbringing. She became accustomed to accepting the monetary cost of fighting for equity.

The Gross household churned with complex emotions. Jack was volatile, and Mildred turned to her children for emotional support. According to Ray, she would complain bitterly about her marital problems but would not consider leaving Jack. Mildred and S. were careful to be wary of Jack and tended to stay out of the house, whereas Ray was more confrontational. Jack would throw plates and slap Ray. Sometimes, their Black maid intervened on Ray's behalf. Despite these difficulties, Mildred was a loving presence. When she was not playing music for the children, she would often read to them or play children's games.

The siblings had very different approaches to navigating relationships with their father, symbolized by their divergent game strategies. When Ray was about ten, S. taught him to play the Chinese game Go. S. would deliberate for long stretches of time before settling on her next move, whereas Ray plunged headlong, relying on intuition. The asymmetry flustered S. and tickled Ray. Although she did not come to Ray's aid directly when Jack's temper heated, S. would invite Ray out for a meal at Wimpy's and walk around town. Their shared discontent forged an exhilarating relationship. Around that time, S. also taught Ray about socialism and South African politics. Sometimes, S. would lean a ladder against Ray's window in the middle of the night, and the siblings would excitedly roam the neighborhood disseminating Communist pamphlets, which was illegal then. Ray reminisced that if a police officer spotted them making a drop at a bus stop, they were prepared to make a clean getaway.[15]

As adults, the siblings spent hours analyzing their markedly different relationships with their father. Ray found Jack unbearable.[16] S. and Ray each dealt with Jack in their own way, which would later translate into notably different opinions on the state of Israel. The siblings were willing to agitate differently: Ray against his father and S. against xenophobia. Initially, Jack had persuaded S. that Zionism was a response to anti-semitism and the best of several evils.[17] In a surprising number of ways, S. would closely align with Jack's principled approach and consequently suffered similar social ostracization and economic loss, though for different causes.

Because the Gross nuclear family lacked wealth and endorsed oppositional politics, they found themselves marginalized by their extended family in both Jewish and South African contexts.[18] Jack's brothers were avid supporters of the right-wing Revisionist movement, which Jack and Mildred viewed as, if not outright Fascism, then dangerously close to it. S.'s godparents had fled Nazi Germany, where they had been Communist Party members.[19] To entertain the mere discussion of communism was radical in Apartheid South Africa, where the National Party had declared the South African Communist Party (SACP) illegal in 1950. The SACP had advocated for Black South Africans to govern the country. The Suppression of Communism Act (1950) was deployed against efforts to end Apartheid. After the Communist Party's banning, some members joined the African National Congress and others aligned with the Soviet Union. The ANC began in 1912 as a Black nationalist organization and spearheaded resistance to the Apartheid policy of racial separation and discrimination. The ban on the ANC was not officially lifted until 1990.

As such, the Gross family were outsiders within South Africa and their own family. Being Jewish marked them as conditionally white, and yet their openness to communism estranged the Grosses from blood relatives. They navigated precarity in between worlds, not fully belonging to any one land, state, religion, or family. Economic instability was the most concrete display of tension, which would characterize most of Sally's life well into adulthood. She learned from Jack that some causes were worth suffering for and that there were multiple approaches to effectively galvanizing social change—both confrontational and circuitous.

Gender Dysphoria

S. describes experiences of "gender dysphoria" not in terms of self-loathing but rather through experiences of social scripts as impositions over and against her nature. She attended South Africa's first Jewish day school, King David, as a child.[20] During the summer months, she took swimming lessons that instilled a sense of purpose in her body. Sometimes, she was teased for lacking aggression but generally does not remember having been bullied. If her father was right that boys and girls were innately different, S. wondered why she found it difficult to conform to male stereotypes.[21] In a letter, she explained:

> I have suffered from what is known as "gender dysphoria" since the age of eight or nine. It has been particularly acute in times of great stress, but it has never left me. As a child I believed that I was essentially a girl and that I had somehow been born with a male body. There was no-one I knew to whom I could confess this: it was a guilty secret, and my childhood was a sustained attempt to live out a role which was radically at odds with my self-perception.[22]

Later, she claimed that her questions about gender began even earlier: "I had some sense from very young, perhaps four or five years old, that something was awry. I had some sense that it was in the area of gender, though I had no sense it was to do with plumbing [laughs]. There's just something so curious about my plumbing."[23]

It is difficult to distinguish between S.'s actual childhood questions and her adult reflections. It seems that it took time to differentiate her sense that she was not a cisgender man from being homosexual or transgender. About her gender exploration, she wrote:

> For years I would fall asleep asking God to let me wake up the next morning with a girl's body so that the need for secrecy could be removed. In my teens, I thought that this might be a sign that I am gay—a painful speculation, since the milieu in which I lived was horribly "homophobic." . . .
>
> It puzzled me that I was not at all attracted to males, while I found girls attractive—although I did not perceive them as sexual objects

either. Surreptitious glances at books on sexual deviation also led me to wonder whether I was a transvestite of some sort. Again, this possibility seemed at odds with the fact that the thought of cross-dressing as such did not turn me on: what I wanted was to **be** female physically, not to be a male who sometimes wore female clothes.[24]

S. resolved to live a male role. Pinpointing an exact moment of self-knowledge might be an exercise in storytelling rather than uncovering the truth.[25] It is as though she entertained the question posed to Du Bois: When did you realize that your body is a problem? Regardless of whether S. had a distinct sense of her intersexuality at any point during her youth, she certainly made a concerted effort to understand her body and its relation to communal bodies at age forty, an endeavor to which we will return.

Not long after her bar mitzvah, S. expressed interest in intensive rabbinical study at a yeshiva. Perhaps her temperament would be well suited to that intellectual environment. To avoid being a problem, S. kept her gender questions to herself. Ignoring suffering in one aspect of her life gave liberation to another—an intellectual life. It was a mode of survival within a continual navigation of contextual community. By prioritizing her religious studies, she attempted to shelve uncertainty about gender and sexuality. Sally would later claim:

> As a boy of six or seven, my parents once told me that I was presented to a Jewish priest on the thirty-first day after my birth, and that they had to redeem me by paying a sum of money (the value of five sela'im or shekels of the sanctuary, which equal 102 grammes of pure silver according to one of my prayer-books). Neither of my parents are of priestly or Levitical descent, I was not delivered by Caesarean section and was the first child born of my mother. The Law of Moses therefore required that I be redeemed as a first-born Israelite son. I asked them what would have happened had my father refused to cough up the money, or had he been unable to afford it. . . . My father replied, with a twinkle in his eye, that the priest would have taken me and would probably have put me in a Rabbinical college. I liked the thought of Rabbinical College for some reason, and remember thinking that it was a pity that I **had** been redeemed.[26]

Even though it would interrupt her secular education, her parents put S. on a plane to the United Kingdom, and from May 1967 to 1968 she studied at a yeshiva in Gateshead, England.[27]

Yeshiva

The yeshiva was a large brick building in the coal mining town of Gateshead, just across the Tyne River from Newcastle. The surrounding neighborhood comprised several blocks of a few hundred Jewish family households that observed the Sabbath strictly (*shomrei Shabbos*). Orthodox communities had formed around the globe postwar, but Gateshead boasts having been an exclusive community since 1887. Some of S.'s all-male classmates had uncut hair at the temples (*payos*), and all were eager to learn from renowned Orthodox Jewish scholars.

It took time for the student body to ignore the passing trains and to adapt to the scholarly rigor. Below the dorm was a dining room, where kosher food was served after being prepared in a basement kitchen. The main feature of the building was the hall used for study and prayers. Students sat on wood benches for twelve hours a day, learning the Torah and praying. Their white shirts grew gray from the coal-smoke-filled air. Books served as the most extravagant flourish throughout the building. On the Sabbath, they lit candles the customary eighteen minutes before sunset. The school's austere architecture and intense rhythm stressed reliance on divine providence and a commitment to achieving spiritual goals without physical or material encumbrances.[28]

The rabbinical college was born from concern about assimilation. According to Miriam Dansky, Jewish immigrants dismayed by the anglicization of local Jews formed places for prayer and a kehillah in direct dissociation from the neighboring community of Newcastle, located across the Tyne River. Zachariah Bernstone set up a synagogue in Gateshead near the end of the nineteenth century, and by 1929, Rabbi Dovid Dryan had established a yeshiva behind the synagogue. Heads of school Harav Nachman, Dovid Landynski, and Havav Eliezer Kahan had escaped religious persecution in Communist Russia. Orthodox Jewish refugees from the Third Reich settled in the town of Gateshead, which became a citadel for Orthodox intellectualism, and Holocaust survivors set the yeshiva's traditional tone. Dansky describes an ethos that integrates a disciplined Germanic approach to the Lithuanian methodology of Torah study, philosophical *mussar*, and uncompromising *Yiddishkeit* (Jewishness).[29] In 1941, the Kollel HaRabbonim was founded for the study of the Talmud and rabbinic literature, and soon it became a boarding school and seminary. Nearby, a seminary for women attracted those interested in marrying men with rabbinical status. Establishing their own licenses to slaughter, marry, teach, and so on became opportunities to distinguish this Orthodox community from assimilated English Jews. Gateshead was a world apart.

Founder of the Gateshead community, Reb Dovid Baddiel became legendary for his generosity coupled with his insistence on firm boundaries. For him, the steel bridge between Newcastle and Gateshead symbolized the geographical proximity and distinction between the two communities. Reb Baddiel often paid the bridge's gatekeeper on Fridays so Jews could cross without paying the toll and return in time for Shabbat. Dansky writes,

> Entered an obviously lapsed Jew, sauntering up to the bridge, cigarette in mouth. Loudly he claimed no less than free passage ... for it was well known that Mr Baddiel paid for all Jews to cross on the Sabbath. The gatekeeper sized him up for a long moment, and then replied. ... Mr Baddiel only paid for God-fearing Jews who observe the Sabbath-day. But you're smoking. For the likes of you, he didn't pay. ... [The gatekeeper's] recognition of the demarcation line drawn by Mr Baddiel and his fellow-founders was unhesitating, and it is for the drawing-up and maintenance of these unequivocal boundaries that Mr Baddiel, amongst others, will be best remembered.[30]

Despite her largely secular upbringing, the study of Divine Law—Talmud Torah—was for S. a religious duty. More than textbook study, it involved the transmission of Torah tradition, which is mainly oral, from sages to disciples. Despite the grueling pace, S. reveled in Jewish religious law and was a self-motivated learner. She fell into a strict rhythm. Before each session, she recited the prayer *Our Father, merciful Father who is compassionate, grant our hearts understanding to comprehend and to discern, to hear, to learn, to teach, to observe, to practice and to fulfill all the teachings of your Torah with love.*[31] S. remembers this time as the beginning of her intellectual life; she was able to wrestle with religious arguments by asking questions and reasoned debate rather than rote learning.[32]

Surprisingly, S. was expelled from the school. Without explaining the circumstances, she bluntly states, "I practically had to escape. It was tantamount to kidnapping."[33] Unfortunately, her brother Ray was too young to understand or remember the specifics of this departure. Perhaps the yeshiva's separatism described above rubbed her the wrong way. We cannot know. The yeshiva sparked in S. a lifelong interest in religious study, but it was also the first of a series of communities in which she seemed not to fit.[34]

Asexuality

In 1969, S. returned to South Africa to rejoin her family, who were then living in Cape Town. There she enrolled in another coed Jewish school, Herzlia Highlands.[35] Proudly Zionist, Herzlia was situated near the slopes of Devil's Peak on the northern edge of Table Mountain. There, she succumbed to pressure to perform a particular kind of masculinity by taking up karate and becoming skilled at Okinawan Goju-Ryu. She approached her training with characteristic intensity, attending classes several times a week to apprentice. Combative training enabled her to suppress questions about gender and instead align herself with the Zionism that her father espoused. "This was also an endeavor to furnish myself with the opportunity to prove to myself that I was male," she reflected. "It was for this reason, I am sure, that I took up karate and that I considered training to become a karate instructor. When I was at school (and was still an ardent Zionist), it also led me to contemplate the possibility of a period in the Israeli army as a career-officer."[36] S. disciplined her body, not just her mind.

By her mid-teens, S. could not help but notice the effects of puberty on her peers, and she felt out of place. An explanation for her unique disposition eluded her. Boys her age were becoming interested in sex, and she wondered why she wasn't enthralled with the thought of intercourse and whether she was gay or asexual. Her research into the deleterious effects of supposedly improper family dynamics—which S. recognized as putative—also ran counter to her traditional, patriarchal family structure. During her high school years, S. recalls having stolen surreptitious glances at books on sexual deviation. However, none of the classifications described her experience.

Celibacy proved desirable. As an adult, she would write:

> Something which was a bit of a puzzle during my adolescence was that I did not develop sexual attractions—although I found girls and women attractive aesthetically, and indeed sometimes identified more internally with girls and women than with boys and men, albeit without any sense of being a girl trapped in a boy's body, I was not attracted sexually to boys or men either. It bothered me a bit. I eventually realised and came to accept that I am asexual, one of nature's celibates, and it has not bothered me in and of itself since I was an adolescent.[37]

S. wondered what celibacy might mean for an Orthodox Jew and whether she could be a rabbi without getting married or having children. She wanted to become a rabbi but was disinterested in matrimony and reproduction.[38] Self-discipline could not stoke sexual desire within her. The dissonance between her embodied experience and prescribed gender roles inhibited S.

While still in school, S. read about a South African designated male at birth, who at eighteen began living as a female without the aid of cosmetic surgery. She sat in awe contemplating this possibility: "I recall my admiration for the courage of this person, and indeed wondered whether I ought not to do something similar once I was no longer subject to parents. In the event, worrying about the effect that such a development would have on my parents restrained me, though it left me with a sense of considerable grief for the loss of childhood and the need to alienate myself from my own self-perception."[39] S. later worked to liberate younger generations from such turmoil.

Through reflecting upon her childhood experience as an adult, Sally came to understand the relationship between racism and sexism in Apartheid South Africa. It was simultaneously personal and political. Social scripts inform one's sense of self. In a job application, she wrote:

> From a very early age, I had a sense that something connected with my bodiliness and related to gender was awry, though I had no idea what it was. The discomfort and confusion associated with this was considerable. As I grew older, it became clear to me that the discomfort was caused, in no small measure, by gender-stereotyping and a constriction of roles which was a piece with racial oppression under apartheid of all kinds. A major motivation for my commitment to struggle against apartheid was the wish to contribute towards a new dispensation in South African in which neither racial oppression nor gender oppression would be countenanced, in which diversity would be welcomed and celebrated, and in which children born as I was could grow up free of the stigmatization and socially imposed pain which I experienced in childhood and adolescence.[40]

Sally translated her experiences into empathy for others. She understood that the pain she experienced under patriarchy was embroiled with racism under Apartheid. At the time, S. shelved the fantasy of life in a female role and put on maleness. Through practice, she hoped she could convince herself of her maleness.

Near the end of high school, S. won a national essay competition organized by Zionists. The prize was a six-week study tour of Israel. Painfully aware that she was likely to be drafted to serve in the Apartheid military, she forfeited a return ticket and stayed in Israel to study. There, she had what may have been her only sexual encounter. While S. was traveling to the university by bus, a slightly older woman took notice of her. The woman lived in a block of flats adjacent to the student hospital, and on one occasion, she invited S. to accompany her on the rooftop. In an interview, S. described the experience: "We engaged in some proper groping and I was utterly and completely clueless. It is the one and only time I've engaged in proper kissing. Down there, absolutely nothing. I enjoyed the cuddling and groping but I was wondering when something was going to happen. [shakes her head no] It was pleasant human contact, but that was about it."[41] Despite the flattery of being desired sexually, S. did not experience genital arousal:

> It has never been in the cards that there would be any genital whatsit with women. I realized at that point I wasn't wired for sexual relationships. I could imagine a situation of friendship. I enjoy hugging men and women equally, but there is nothing particularly sexual about it. It is an expression of a degree of intimacy, but it's not for me about a sexual engagement or sharing in intercourse; it is simply an expression of affection or friendship without sexual connotations. Not that in our world there is anything free of sexual connotations, but there is not that genital whatsit.[42]

According to one friend, "She was very open in answer to my probing questions so when I asked her . . . she [reported] never [having] had any sexual feelings of any kind."[43] Perhaps it seems evident that S. was asexual, but it took her some time to recognize and articulate that.

2. Adulthood

By the late 1980s and early 1990s, S. found an intellectual community as a Catholic priest, though the question of gender did not subside. I describe her journey from South Africa to Israel, and then to the priesthood in the United Kingdom, in later chapters. S.'s religious identity, like her biology, defied conventional categories.[1]

During this time, S. taught moral theology in South Africa for part of the year and in England for the rest. Literally split between two continents, she found that her gender and interreligious commitments repeatedly proved to be an insurmountable concern for those around her. "It was likely that I would be put forward for Priorships and the like, and felt that I was bound to take stock so as to ensure that the Order's plans for me did not founder on neglected business as it were," she explained. "I therefore brainstormed about areas of possible tension, and something which emerged more clearly than I had been able to see before was that the issue of my bodiliness was a nettle I needed to grasp as a matter of urgency."[2]

How many of us, like S., experience the body as a nuisance to be sorted out? Once we begin the extraction process, we find the problem much larger than imagined. There is not a nettle in the flesh to be excised but rather a cultural body forcefully pressing onto and injuring the individual—our pain springs from being contorted into ill-fitting frames because ours is unruly,

FIGURE 2.1 Photograph of S. in Dakar, Senegal, for an African National Congress meeting in 1987. From GALA archive.

unmanageable flesh. Perhaps our resistance is a precursor to expansive, long-lasting reprieve.

After her years of dabbling in growing and dyeing her hair, S. writes about the relationship between the personal and social:

> While in South Africa in 1992, I felt compelled for the sake of my religious vows and my Christian commitment, as well as for my own sake and that of my Order, to essay an "audit" of my life. There were always tensions between my Christian commitment and my intense sense of Jewish identity and yearning for fellowship as a Jew with other Jews, the history of the Church being what it has been; and this was an element in the audit. A further element was gender. Since early childhood I have suffered from a profound form of what is known technically as "gender dysphoria syndrome" relative to my natal gender-classification. I had endeavoured to cope with this for some thirty years by an attempt at denial and sublimation. Trying to think through the issues as dispassionately and honestly as possible, it became clear that the endeavor to deny and sublimate had been a driving-force behind many of my

actions and decisions, and that it had also been central to my conversion to Christianity. This did not, of-course, rule out the operation of grace; but all of this made it clear that I had, for the sake of my vocation, in fairness to my brethren, and for my own sake, to seek to face the issue of gender-identity squarely.[3]

Embracing the social justice directive of religious traditions animated S. to transform the world around her. Although she struck some as too much of a liability due to her outspoken nature, she moved in radical activist circles and used her priestly authority to facilitate demonstrations of civil unrest. Nevertheless, she could not partition her gender from these activities.

Working in the South African seminary, S. felt lonely, in part because of her unsuccessful efforts to cultivate a relationship with the Jewish community. When she disclosed that she was teaching at a Catholic seminary for part of the year and living in a Dominican house the rest of the time, it raised doubts about her identification with Judaism. She assured various rabbis that she was Jewish but began to feel inhibited about divulging her status as a Catholic priest. With time, she came to recognize the parallels between her gender and interreligious commitments. She writes:

> My fear of rejection was too great and my longing for contact was too intense. Each encounter left me with the sense of immense pain at my alienation from other Jews and from things Jewish, a sense of loss which seemed almost too much to bear.... What might come as more of a surprise is that I realised, mulling over the often fraught relationship between my attachment to Judaism and my Christian commitments, that a different and even more fraught issue undergirds my life-history and needs to be confronted as a prior condition for everything else that I proposed to do. This is the issue of gender identity.[4]

Attempts to come to terms with this wedge between herself and other South African Jews initiated S.'s reflection upon why she had entered the Dominican Order in the first place.

The time had come. "The decision to confront the issue of my bodiliness was a decision to confront what I feared the most," S. explained, "and what I had tried to run from in many different ways.... At that stage I rather naively thought I'd see someone with some expertise in this area and after a couple of sessions I could get on with the rest of my priestly life, full stop. [Laughter] It wasn't as simple as that."[5] To be sure, she had begun this inquiry long before.

A decade prior, the Women's Theology Group at Blackfriars had welcomed S.'s exploration of gender. At the group's request, S. first presented a paper on female gender roles in a seminar in March 1982 titled "Towards a Theology of Humankind, Part I." It is noteworthy that in this presentation, prior to exploring life in a female role, she publicly disclosed her unease with identifying as male, because it verifies her later claim that she never kept these questions a secret from the Order. Later, she would obtain a letter from the Master of the Order confirming that S. "shared [her] concerns with him in 1982 with great frankness, and in no way attempted to mislead the Order by concealing a problem."[6]

In her paper, she argued that patriarchal hegemony alienates both men and women from their true selves by reducing them to masculine and feminine stereotypes. Gender stereotypes manifest themselves in economic relationships, which the state reinforces. In theological terms, S. attributed patriarchy to sin and the Fall. In her telling, advancing the kingdom of God entails reconciling and integrating humanity by dismantling gender discrimination in both the church and society. Her conclusion illuminates a burgeoning attempt to integrate her understanding of economic and political justice with gender concerns: "On both the theological and political levels, bringing gender discrimination into question and striving to do away with it, threatens to destroy the whole of which it is part, 'the kingdom of the world,' class-society, the capitalist mode of production. Solving the problem of the part at root implies a transformation of the whole."[7]

The following year, Daphne Nash of the Women's Theology Group invited S. to present a complementary paper on male gender roles. In this work, S. explored a Marxist concern of what is required to build a truly human society despite our shared fragmentation due to alienation from our labor. Angela West, S. recalled, persuaded her to make the second paper autobiographical. Excited and fearful of this opportunity, S. explained her gender dysphoria as a logical consequence of her bourgeois childhood, which included canons of male behavior, precisely because it lacked the flexibility of play. She remembers the immense difficulty she had with writing a personal paper. It was a challenging yet fruitful exploration into integrating embodied experience and intellectual scholarship.[8]

In this more personal reflection on masculinity, S. described to the group at Blackfriars the role of gender in her family:

> My father seems to have suffered from a sense of being a failure "outside." He compensated for this by becoming an absolute dictator

at home. As a child, I absorbed a strong ideology of my father as the "man" of the house, that is, as the dominant male. My mother was continually put down as incompetent, good only at spending my father's hard-earned money. She was in fact the bread-winner, while he was more often than not out of work. Another component of this ideology was the proposition that only my father held common-sense.[9]

S. portrayed Jack as someone who persistently found fault with mother and child. She explained that he would lash out "into vile temper tantrums and would shout at the slightest provocation. I remember him finding fault with a plate of food once. The food was unsavoury, or hadn't been warmed up properly, or the like. It landed or splattered against the dining-room wall.... In summary: the structure of my family in my childhood was strongly authoritarian. My father, who set himself as the epitome of all masculine virtue, dominated."[10] According to S., although Jack failed to fulfill several gender stereotypes, he still understood himself to be manly and sought to impart this view to his children. She reflected upon the harm of patriarchy among men:

> I was brought up on the myth. I also learned that boys were fighters by nature. Boys were meant to be aggressive, unlike girls, who were sweet and placid. As male, I was expected to fight back if bullied at school. Since I was physically weak, I was indeed bullied and teased mercilessly. Ironically, while I was expected to be aggressive at school, I had learnt as a boy that rage and aggression did not pay at home. The slightest manifestation of aggression at home was likely to bring down the full wrath of my father. As a result, I was simply incapable of doing anything other than internalising my own aggression outside. If I were teased and bullied, it was through some fault of my own, and what would otherwise have become aggression on my part turned into guilt. I would therefore typically react by turning the other cheek.[11]

In addition to disclosing objectionable accounts of Jack's attempts to indoctrinate S. into masculinity, she suggested to the group that according to his logic, she was female:

> I had female traits, according to this schema. It ineluctably followed that I was fundamentally a biological female, but that I had somehow been born with an inappropriate body, with a veneer of masculinity. After all, my inner "real" self was female, whether I liked it or not.... I lived in constant fear that someone would discover that I was really

a girl. At the same time, I used to pray at night that God would somehow work a miracle, and that I would wake up the next morning with a female body. That way, I wouldn't have to go on pretending that I was male, nor would I have to cope with the guilt of not measuring up to unreal standards which I couldn't match up to. It goes without saying that this "gender-agony" was the result of stereotyping, and had little to do with "biology" as such.[12]

During this lecture, S. divulged her discomfort with male roles: "I saw myself as being formally male but in fact female, and I too was unable to admit to this."[13] She attributes her reluctance to harmful gender stereotypes rather than to a more complex vision of sex classification.

S. later revealed in a letter to friend Father Timothy Radcliffe, "I was less than candid in some respects. The tenacity of the sense of dysphoria, together with recent neuro-physiological evidence in an analogous domain, suggests that it has its roots in fetal development. I gather that a number of researchers in the field have come round to this view."[14] This statement is an important admission because self-descriptions of gender identity formation are not impervious to tropes or social pressure. Later, in a documentary, S. would claim, "I tried an analysis of that within the dynamics of my family, which I think that I got wrong, but it almost persuaded me [that I was transsexual]."[15]

The paper was well received, and only one participant pushed back. Nevertheless, S. sank into a malaise, wondering whether she could reflect only stoically on her gender identity. Her expression of joy took the form of her self-proclaimed eccentric appearance.[16] She was thrilled the first time she participated in the liturgy with long, orange hair. Before God, her brethren, and the laity, she had begun to reveal parts of herself.[17] Although some exchanged unsettled expressions, no one formally reprimanded her. S. was hopeful that she could one day be loved and accepted in authentic form.

Blackfriars Archives

Archives are fraught repositories where problem bodies are often misrepresented, if not subject to erasure.[18] The Blackfriars archives are no exception. S. felt that her Jewish identity, to which I will add body size and penchant for technology, was a barrier to full entry into the Catholic community. Several Blackfriars told me not to bother traveling to Douai Abbey, where the Blackfriars' house papers are stored in an archive. Curious, I used multiple forms of public transportation to get to the abbey. The last bit entailed a winding uphill walk, where I paused to photograph a charming stone church with trimmed bushes and mist-swept headstones. Upon my arrival at the abbey, Abbot Geoffrey Scott showed me to the library. He introduced me to Father Aidan Nichols, the previous archivist, who happened to be there doing his own research.

Aidan explained how all the documents were organized but, like many others, stressed that I would not find anything. A significant portion of the collection had not yet been cataloged, and anything on S. was likely sealed in the London archives. Portraits of Carmelite nuns looked down on us as I took notes on what proved to be useful information about the collection and the difference between the Book of Constitutions, *Catalagus*, and Code of Canon Law. For example, the *Directory of the English Province of the Order of Preachers* details every person in the Order, including their title and location. With this I was able to confirm S.'s rank and whereabouts and also sleuth out documents filed under different names.

Aidan was correct that there was no box or folder dedicated to S. Yet I was able to locate her account of a visit to Crown Heights, Brooklyn, a historically Jewish neighborhood in New York City, under her Jewish name.[19] I also happened upon a photo album of the Oxford house members dating from 1981–88. A family album of sorts, the collection shows mundane scenes of the brethren eating in the refectory, working at their desks, washing dishes, and ironing clothes.[20] There is a campy aesthetic to the album. Photographs are labeled with names, locations, and dates.

They begin with scenic shots of lush greenery cut by a stream. Four friars in street clothes walk beside one another down a dirt road. Three are in step, their hips swinging to the left with an arm flung back, heads tilted. There is an ease to their excursion. In another shot, three of them lie on their stomachs, gazing with childlike wonder off a rock ledge surrounded by water. In the next photo, Timothy Radcliffe reclines on a towel at the water's edge in what appears to be a black Speedo, his sinuous limbs and slender back reflecting the sunlight. A mop of curly hair hugs his face, which turns over his right shoulder as though caught mid-sentence. An Aquinas scholar, Father Herbert McCabe, poses on his motorcycle in a different photo. Finally, I came to S. sitting in a parlor with priests and nuns, some in their habits and others in plain clothes. She and Mark Dowd were novices at the time. It is followed by a headshot of Mark with a gentle, flirtatious smile. A later photograph shows S. as an ordained priest, wearing sandals, trousers, a zipped sweater over a white shirt, and her hair to her shoulders.

Leafing through the yellowed clinging plastic sheets, I could sense how attractive this community might have been to young men seeking lifelong companionship. A document titled "The Nature and Rules of Blackfriars Community" asserts,

> Community life as inspired by St. Augustine's Rule was very important for the Dominicans from the beginning. This was partly because it is natural for humans to live and work together, and in particular for Christians to live, work and pray together. And partly it was because our study and preaching must grow out of our life of prayer, in which we celebrate in the Liturgy the saving events we preach, and out of our common attempt to live the Gospel and to study it in the tradition of the Order, and must be helped by a sharing of jobs and responsibilities.[21]

In addition to religious reasons for joining an Order, were a young man sexually attracted to men or asexual, he might have found refuge in religious life. In retrospect, it seems possible that people like S. might have longed for respite from the pressure to ascribe to the traditional masculine gender roles of Orthodox Judaism. She writes about her interest in the Order: "It could offer some sense of meaning and fulfillment, and a way to achieve intimacy, to and for people who, like me, are asexual (and this has no necessary or probable connexion with physical intersexuality, transsexuality or the like), provided that this celibacy is not seen as in any way superior to a stable sexual relationship."[22] The Dominican Order offered a spiritual family among men. Rather than face homophobia and isolation, men with same-sex attractions or asexuality could form deep friendships within the Order and be revered rather than reviled by laypeople.

Another page has just one photo, cheekily zoomed in on a man's bare legs, cropped tightly between the soles of his shoes and meager inseam of shorts. The caption reads, "During 1987, in the Blackfriars Community, there was a marked growth in the popularity of physical exercise...."[23] If true, this might have marginalized S., who was considered overweight by her brethren. Perhaps she experienced her body as a barrier to the bonding that her brethren forged through exercise. At Westminster Abbey, S. later preached:

> Physical fitness and health are actively encouraged; athletes are role models; physical beauty is sought and cultivated.... Popular ideals of physical beauty are sometimes so narrow, and the pressure to make recalcitrant bodies conform to them is sometimes so great, that many lives have been blighted and some have been lost. You will

have gathered that I am thinking of *anorexia nervosa* and other such disorders. These disorders involve the rejection, because of a popular ideal, of aspects of one's bodiliness.[24]

S.'s exercise involved cycling. Several sources whom I interviewed mentioned S.'s mountain bike with a chuckle. At first, this seemed to me a negligible detail, but it came up often enough that I began to wonder why it might be significant. There was an implication that seeing a fat person ride a bicycle was humorous. While I am unsettled by the possibility that their laughter is fatphobic, it tells us something about what she might have faced. If the brethren shared an interest in fitness, as the Oxford priory photo album notes, she could have stood out as a fat person. A few brothers laughed at the memory of S.'s claim that her doctor had prescribed a Walkman. Listening to books on tape while walking was her solution to a doctor's suggestion to lose weight. Her efforts to incorporate physical activity into her daily routine suggest that S. might have struggled to conform her body to the community's ideal form.[25]

The Douai Abbey archives included detailed accounts of the Blackfriars' Cambridge House, which I describe in more detail in later chapters. Entries vary from meeting minutes to personal diary entries, depending on the chronicler. From one year to the next, the weather, travels, and events like apple picking are noted. The visitors and activities of lay residents, including women, are also documented. Various tasks for upkeeping the home and conducting regular services were assigned. On May 12, 1992, S. was entrusted to research a headphone system for the TV, which she was later authorized to purchase, but then postponed the purchase to work on a proposal for resiting the satellite dish for the television. Her penchant for technology never waned.

The brethren informed me that money was tight. Each man lived on approximately £5,000 a year, approximately US$15,000 in 2024. S. often made personal requests for expensive technology and gadgets. These included a second bicycle, a flight simulator, a new computer, a headphone system for the television, and so on. Her desire did not ebb in the years to come, which makes me wonder if those purchases were a vain attempt to secure material tokens of self-worth.[26] There is a classist element to the criticisms of how S. spent money.[27] While it might seem logical that someone with little financial means refrain from purchasing expensive technology, underlying this assumption is a moralistic meritocracy in which poor people like S. are deemed unworthy of such luxuries. Coupled with laughter, no matter how well-meaning, these comments stung.

Entries also included an account of S. having engaged in a heated debate with visiting clergy, including a friend of the current and previous pope (Popes John Paul II and I), over ecumenism and the ordination of women.[28] In addition to logging who did what in church services, the Cambridge House Chronicle includes multiple entries about S. being assigned to teach in Cedara, South Africa, but only briefly mentions when she took medical leave to explore life in a female role.[29]

My impression when meeting the present-day brethren was that they are a warm and welcoming community. S. is remembered by contemporary friars through storytelling and a sense of community history. They have understandably mixed feelings about her. Those who personally knew S. shared nearly entirely positive, at worst neutral, sentiments. Most of them appear to have had a cordial, if somewhat remote, relationship with her.

The generation of brethren who never met S. but are privy to candid discussion expressed some grumpiness about how events unfolded and S.'s culpability in being laicized, though never in much detail.[30] The friars attested to their prolonged efforts to accommodate and care for S.'s particular circumstances. Some brethren felt she was given even more leeway than the average brother and subsequently wondered why S. felt discriminated against. I suspect that beyond her fondness for expensive technology, S. craved profound commitment from her brethren—not to be tolerated but actively embraced. Whiffs of anti-semitism during her novitiate and a feeling of being held at arm's length shook her trust in their fidelity to her.

According to S., her brethren also did not take her health concerns seriously. In 1985, S. suffered from life-threatening hemorrhaging. She sought medical help to deal with the bleeding and faintness, but her doctor refused to believe that S. had accurately described her symptoms. The doctor suggested that the faintness was due not to anemia from blood loss but to a viral infection that would sort itself out. Discouraged, S. set out for London to research a paper for the International Defence and Aid Fund for Southern Africa. There, her spells of faintness became prolonged and more frequent: "I very nearly died after two or three years of haemorrhaging.... By then I realised that I was dying, though I did not know what the cause was; but it was painless and gentle, and held no terrors for me. I had done everything I could to try to obtain treatment for the medical problem, and, if no more could be done that was fine by me. I had a good inning, I felt, and would be happy to drift away."[31] Perhaps her brethren wrongly attributed her discomfort to her weight. Body size is sometimes moralized, and medical fatphobia is a well-documented phenomenon; gluttony is considered a vice among some Catholics and is also unfortunately disparaged in secular culture, while weight loss is too often celebrated as though it were a victory of self-control to be rewarded with praise. If the Order had enthusiastically taken up exercise as described in the Oxford album, S.'s illnesses might have been minimized or misattributed to her weight.

Upon returning to Oxford, S. saw another doctor, who insisted she go to the hospital immediately. Rather than taking an ambulance, S. made her way there on foot. Tests confirmed her suspicion that she had become severely anemic. She wrote about her brush with death:

> It transpired that prolonged bleeding had reduced my haemoglobin level by two thirds, and that I would indeed have died with the next few days had I not received treatment.... To my great embarrassment, I lost consciousness standing.... I would have died of heart-failure within a very few minutes had they not got a line into me: I was dying quickly at that stage, and I knew it. Again, the prospect of death held no terrors for me.[32]

More than a decade after the incident, she wrote, "When I was ill in bed, communion was never on offer at that time; and when I was hospitalised to stop haemorrhaging and had to have a massive blood transfusion, coming within seconds of death from congestive heart failure because my vascular system 'shut down' in consequence of shock, no-one visited or enquired about my health, and the comfort of the sacraments was pointedly not on offer."[33] It is unclear whether her Jewishness and weight factored into the lack of visitors. What is certain is that S. discussed her heartache that her brethren did not visit her in the hospital or surround her with emotional support.[34]

The incidence of hemorrhaging has uncanny parallels to tropes about Jewish men menstruating and intersexuality, which are germane to S.'s unease among her Catholic brethren. Daniel Boyarin describes the trope of Jewish men supposedly menstruating:

> One of the most tenacious of anti-Semitic topoi—that Jews are a third sex: men who menstruate.... The explanation of this myth is to be found in the consistent representation of male Jews as female in European culture, largely because of their circumcision, which was interpreted as feminizing (Geller, "Paleontological View"). In Viennese slang of Freud's time, the clitoris was called "the Jew" and female masturbation was "playing with the Jew" (Gilman, *Freud* 38–39). If Jewish men are a kind of women, or even women *simpliciter*, then it is

hardly surprising that they menstruate; moreover, if a primary cause of the theory of their femaleness is their circumcised penises, an operation that causes genital bleeding within which the bleeding is in fact a primary motif, when the basis for myths of Jewish male menstruation seems clear.[35]

S. was not literally menstruating, but her health scare eerily echoes the stereotype that Boyarin describes. Elsewhere Boyarin details Talmudic narratives about obese rabbis with large penises as a figure for celebrating indecorous discourse.[36] Intersex scholar Morgan Holmes also notes an association between Jewishness, intersexuality, and pornotroping: "Meanwhile, the trouble with clitoral hypertrophy was not only that one's patient might be a sodomite—a vague term that could denote almost anything as long as it was *unspeakable*,—but also that she would too closely resemble both the Jewess and the African 'Hottentot Venus.'"[37] Boyarin's and Holmes's scholarship suggests that Jewish men are hypersexualized when signified by large penises and desexualized when associated with intersexuality. Both stereotypes function to feminize male Jewish bodies. The excess of fat bodies and absence of foreskin mark male Jewish bodies as supposedly improperly masculine; it is at once too much and not enough to be recognized as male.

While I doubt any Blackfriars with whom S. cohabitated were aware of these stereotypes, Emilie Townes persuasively demonstrates that myths and stereotypes maintain covert power through everyday humor.[38] Taken together, the insights these scholars offer affirm S.'s felt discrimination. In my reading, she senses something amiss, which Townes terms the Fantastic Hegemonic Imagination. That is, ethnic discrimination need not operate in grand displays of violence, though it sometimes does; the root issue, as Townes identifies it, is the ongoing, covert perpetuation of falsehoods that essentialize people groups because these infiltrate entire populations and fortify systemic injustice. The sort of intimate friendship that S. desired from her brethren was hampered by her body—perhaps considered too fat, improperly masculine, and Jewish.

Ideation

Please note that I have limited my discussion on the topic of suicidal ideation to this section so that readers can choose whether to read it. While conducting my research, I debated whether to include this element of S.'s brain health. Would it be unseemly to include? Is it dishonest to ignore?

Instead of chronologically weaving her dreadful experiences throughout the book, which might surprise readers with harmful content, I have decided to partition them here. This is intended not only to empower readers to choose to skip engaging the topic because they perhaps are already painfully acquainted with it, but also to openly acknowledge the high stakes for impressing upon people that their bodies are problems.

The most deleterious effects of Sally's body being treated as a problem were the moments when she became overwhelmed by the lie that her body was a problem. When political or religious bodies impress upon an individual that they are not worthy of recognition or acceptance, the effects are dire. Incommensurable access to security and support compounded until it was unbearable. She intellectually knew that these were systemic problems, and she hoped for a world more hospitable to biological diversity.

Initially, when Sally began living in a female role, she described what I would term *gender euphoria*. Her brain health improved. The complexity of her inner joy in conflict with a lack of warm reception was difficult to articulate: "The enormity of it all struck me while I was standing beside the railway line," she writes, "and that was when I realised that there was so much pain beneath the surface underneath the defences, despite my own sense that I was coping fairly well in current role, that it could easily lead me to [harm] myself. I am not asserting that I felt suicidal—to the contrary."[39] Aligning her gender presentation with her gender identity was a positive experience. She clearly states that she did not feel suicidal. When those around her did not share her delight, however, Sally was flooded with thoughts of self-harm.

The problem, as Sally herself understood it, was not her body; it was the limited imagination of collective bodies. The first time Sally mentioned feeling suicidal, she did not offer details.[40] It seems to have resulted from the trauma of believing an attempt was made on her life while seeking asylum in Botswana. Another excruciating experience of trying to sort out her gender identity prompted Sally to contemplate stepping in front of the train she ultimately boarded at Finsbury Park Station.[41] During her foray into living in a female role in 1993, the stress of pursuit by tabloid reporters so frightened her that she mentioned resorting to death by suicide.[42] A few months later, when the discovery of her intersexuality resulted in Sally's expulsion from common life at Blackfriars, she wondered if the church might have preferred she had not survived her hemorrhaging episode.[43] She wrote, "All precipitated a serious depression."[44] Sally quoted Psalm 69:1 in Hebrew to express her inability to persevere: "Save me, O God, For the Waters have threatened my life."

Mental illness might have factored into Sally's stress response; however, it would be a disservice to her to limit our understanding of what she faced in her individual body. Sally astutely explained the effects of not being legible as a person in the legal sense as the loss of rights: "As someone who was beyond the pale, an outcast and outlaw, I had absolutely no rights and was denied information about steps taken in relation to my situation."[45] She borrowed from Orlando Patterson the term *social death*, which refers to the social status of persons who are treated as less than human, to describe her experiences of exclusions from the community in a 2013 presentation:

> I was dead in social terms, and promises to the dead are not binding. Because I was alive physically, however, I was deemed to have limitless obligations. In this shadow-existence, the conventional reciprocity of rights and duties broke down. As one who was socially dead, I had no moral rights—least of all to life—but was deemed to have duties. It was acceptable to seek to push me to suicide, and had the legal order permitted, it would have been acceptable to have taken my life more directly.[46]

Sally suggests that her suicidal ideation did not spring from within but rather resulted from disenfranchisement. Fear of contagion, she suspected, motivated her expulsion from the community: "What was done to me was moved by the perceived need to protect others from the highly infectious miasma which I was held to embody."[47]

Are intersex bodies marked for wearing out?[48] Alongside Sally's insights into social death, we might also consider the concept of "slow death" and "debility."[49] Jasbir Puar argues that suicide represents an escape from slow death: "In this nonlinear temporality, for it starts and stops, redoubles and leaps ahead, [Lauren] Berlant is not 'defining a group of individuals merely afflicted with the same ailment, [rather] slow death describes populations marked for wearing out.' That is, slow death is not about an orientation toward the death drive, nor is it morbid; rather, it is about the maintenance of living, the 'ordinary work of living on.'"[50] Debility, or slow death, as Puar describes it, is profitable for capitalism. Her analysis suggests that Sally's ongoing suicidal ideation could have been a longing to escape slow death. This locates the production of Sally's intersexuality and her experiences of dehumanization within social and political networks rather than within an individual body. The various breaks Sally suffered, each attempt to divide her rich multiplicity, were slow and pervasive. When social bodies harm individuals by labeling them as flawed, the stakes are dire. The solution, then, is not up to individuals; collective bodies are obligated to interrogate and adjust such that they facilitate clearings where bodies are appreciated.

Sally wanted to transform institutions for the good of such persons marked for wearing out. She wrote in a job application letter about the need for coalition building:

> [My experience] has made me intensely aware of the way in which different forms of oppression—racial, class-based, the oppression of women, the oppression and abuse of children and infants, and the stigmatization and violence against those who biological sex is ambiguous—are linked inseparably, and I have been involved in struggles against all of these. Personal experience has taught me that these struggles for human rights and dignity are interconnected and cannot be waged effectively in silos.[51]

Puar's insight uncovers the unbearable convergence of Sally's financial debt, pathologization, suicidal ideation, and debility that culminated in a slow social death turned literal premature death.[52] Sally's untimely death was not inevitable.[53] She enjoyed life as Sally. For this reason, she worked tirelessly to transform collective bodies such that they would be more hospitable to intersex persons.

Death by Poverty

On Valentine's Day of 2014, activist Deborah Ewing messaged attorney Jennifer Williams on Facebook. Their mutual friend Sally Gross had missed a Skype date, which was out of character. Jennifer phoned Sally, but there was no answer. Neighbors reported having seen no activity for at least two days. Sally's cats appeared agitated, and eventually, Jennifer decided to call the police.[54] The last known communication anyone had with Sally was on February 11, 2014. She was found dead in her home three days later. The exact date and time of her death is unknown. According to Jennifer, Sally was found on the floor of her office, phone clasped in her hand.[55] An ambulance took her to the morgue, where Sally's brother Ray Gross and friend Eugene van Rooyen identified her body a few days later.

Her younger brother Ray recalled that although he had seen dead bodies, Sally's state was particularly difficult to take in. It is an image indelibly branded into his memory.[56] The autopsy report indicates massive heart failure. The coroner attempted to be polite by talking around her gender, but

Ray asserted that she is Sally.[57] He recalled the coroner offering to do gender confirmation surgery on her corpse, which Ray told me that he declined.

Ray was not sure whether Sally wanted to be cremated or buried and struggled to settle on arrangements. Typically, Jewish burials occur as soon as possible—within twenty-four hours or at most three days.[58] Ray stole glances back at the body-shaped stain on the floor of her office where she died: "It was the room where the essence of Sally was most strong. Being there was not easy. I was talking aloud to her, having full conversations continuing the dialogue that we had been having prior to her passing."[59] He described their last conversation: "We'd been talking about what comes after death and why it wasn't something to be feared. We viewed it as a different kind of existence, not in terms of personality, but the energy goes somewhere. We both had a strong sense of not feeling a grave was needed. It's better to be remembered by ideas and concepts rather than [material] things."[60] Ray settled on cremation.

Sally's ill health and immobility had led to a mountain of disorderly mail, food delivery packets, and receipts. Friend Pam Sykes speculates that Sally was overwhelmed and retreated room by room until she was confined to sleeping in her study. Sykes recalls the difficulty of sorting everything amid grieving. Should this document go to the archive or in the trash? What was important to preserve, and what was merely a consequence of Sally's failing health? Sifting through Sally's possessions was understandably formidable.

An image of Sally came to Sykes's mind during our interview: shoulders pushed back, cane propped in front, Sally's enormous intellect swallowing the room. This person who could have been a world-class theologian, Sykes regretted, was reduced to humiliation and squalor. She wondered why Sally gave up her privilege as a white South African for religious life and then activism. "I don't know how she got toilet paper," Sykes pivoted. "Those are precisely the questions we don't ask about great thinkers because there is always a woman in the background taking care of that stuff for them."[61]

How did this mother of intersex activism die alone and without notice for an indeterminate amount of time?[62] While some might point to her ample body as the problem—as if her physical size caused her illnesses and fatality—I cannot help but wonder how different her outcome would have been if political and religious bodies had embraced her as a gift and cared for her accordingly. Sally's physical body and her body of paperwork wearied loved ones. How were her brother and friends to care for these bodies? They were not mere shells of Sally's being, nor were they the fullness of her presence. To dignify them, they had to be cleared from the rubbish. It is my position that Sally died of poverty. Despite her invaluable contributions to society, she died prematurely. Sally built up a protective shield of papers and laws by working within and transforming institutions, but perhaps what she needed was a clearing—a clearing amid her own paperwork to make room for unruly bodies.

Crip Theory

What you want, who you are, how you feel are all brought into being over time and in relation to others, and those thoughts and feelings are repeatedly inscribed, creating powerful circuits that organize a sense of embodied self. Such is human interdependency that my self-regard depends on your regard for me. —CHRISTINA CROSBY, *A Body Undone*

The body is not a thing, it is a *situation*: it is our grasp on the world and the outline for our projects. —SIMONE DE BEAUVOIR, *The Second Sex*

Are our bodies truly problems, or are the governing bodies that deem us unruly and unfit the problem? Disability experts ask whether the individual or their environment is faulty. Sometimes, a wheelchair user is treated as problematic, whereas inaccessible architecture escapes criticism. Intersex infants might be diagnosed as requiring normalization surgery to fit either male or female categories, but instead, social and political space could be made to celebrate biological diversity.[63] When Crosby writes, "my self-regard depends on your regard for me," it suggests that the onus is not solely on us to affirm ourselves. Rather, dignity and value are imparted socially and politically. If some bodies are marked for wearing out and others for flourishing, an individual in the first category can only survive for so long. Something that Sally learned, though it took her a long while, was the unsustainability of accommodating harmful regulating bodies. To hide parts of herself in exchange for conditional acceptance and access to resources proved untenable.

This first part of the book attends to Sally's various experiences of being wrongly told that her body was a problem. It gives an overview of Sally's transnational, intersex, and interreligious life. Part II exposes the actual problem bodies—religious, medical, documental, and political—before exploring the value of agitating bodies that forge clearings. In the wake of World War II and the Holocaust, Sally was distressed by Zionism and Apartheid. Sally learned the worthwhile costs of adhering to principles from her parents but disliked their expressions of gendered nationalism. Growing up, she waded through the confusion of asexuality and her undiagnosed intersexuality. She sought intellectual and religious community at a Jewish yeshiva and later in a Catholic Order. On the one hand, religious life appealed to her as an asexual, intersex person. However, among Catholics, she experienced antisemitism, and with Jews, she observed racial discrimination. Being fat and disabled contributed to her experience of being made to feel that her body was a problem. Institutional bodies attempted to regulate her unruly flesh. The fortitude required to refuse to accommodate unjust systems negatively affected her brain health. Ultimately, Sally died prematurely, alone, and impoverished. She entered the world in a body marked as a problem through no fault of her own. Sally then left the world, having chosen to become a problem to regulating institutions. Her story stirs our imaginations. What might a community look like wherein all bodies are beloved?

II

PROBLEM BODIES

My argument about trans specificity is at its most emphatic here, and I argue that sex is analogized to property or understood metaphorically as property in much literature, but sex is treated as material property in transpeoples' dealings with medical and state bureaucracies and functions specifically as state property rather than private property for transpeople in a way that it does not for the normatively gendered.
—GAYLE SALAMON, *Assuming a Body*

People do not tend to think of sex and gender as church or state property because we would prefer to believe these are private matters disconnected from public life. And yet, our bodily features establish access to rights and services. Institutional bodies regulate and manage individual bodies with such frequency that we hardly seem to notice. Everyday actions that, on the surface, appear unrelated to polity establish patterns of privilege and disenfranchisement. Redlining is mistaken for coincidence. Limited access to reproductive health care is a consequence of supposedly immoral sexuality. Who, or perhaps more importantly what, are statutes of limitations for sexual assault and low age of consent laws protecting? Initially, Sally set out to learn her sex and gender identities through conventional therapy and clinics, as though those are discoverable through psychoanalytic reflection and the medical gaze. In other words, within the limitations of her historical context, she thought her sex and gender to be private matters that would be made plain through inquiry.

When Sally explored what she fondly called her "bodiliness," it resulted in manifold confrontations. Political and religious bodies presumed to know her body better than she could ever know herself. The limitations of medical practitioners at the time resulted in an initial misdiagnosis and treatment plan. They assumed Sally was transgender and sought to aid her medical and social transition into femaleness. It was not conceivable to her professional support system that a gender nonbinary person was employable. It took time for Sally to realize that her intersex diagnosis was distinct from yet related to transness. From this experience, she learned that the medical management of flesh troubled her.

Helper after helper urged Sally to adhere to a box—a category for herself—in exchange for support. Some offered new boxes to her, as though one might be better than another because it was bigger or different. Choosing male or female roles and cisgender or transgender identities shuffled her from one form of bodily regulation to another. Sally needed time and space to nurture the fullness of her complex self, but her cooperation with regulatory bodies rendered her fraught with gender agony. What was lacking, and what she needed, was a clearing.[1]

Gender agony stems from stereotyping rather than biology. It is an agony we feel when told that our bodies are problems. This is the pain of being reduced to less than the fullness of ourselves. We are disciplined to make ourselves docile and straightforward. The consequence is a loss of home and safety. We learn to hide from both ourselves and others. Gender agony is a strictly curated garden, lacking clearings and sustainable biological diversity. This agony explains why Sally left communities. It is not clear, however, how she chose to join new ones. I suspect that, on a pragmatic level, her decisions had more to do with urgency to secure shelter than strategic long-term careers goals to which a more privileged person might have access.

In part II, we see multiple sites of institutional, regulating bodies—religious, medical, legal, and territorial—that cast Sally's body as a problem when, in fact, they were problem bodies. Religious groups and nation-states demonstrate the importance of sex as *their* property through detailed laws and policies. Initially, Sally sought belonging within these institutional bodies. Later, she agitated to change them. Clearings, however, are needed to allow diverse ecologies to flourish. Instead of folding ourselves into legible and manageable labels, we might pose questions and interrupt structures to initiate breaks.

"Religious Bodies" focuses on Sally's time as a Catholic priest. She entered the priesthood believing herself to be male but at forty years of age discovered her intersexuality. In a tradition that ordains only men, this was a problem. Even prior to the question of her gender, Sally sensed anti-semitism among her brethren. She also faced body size and possibly neurodivergence discrimination. In sum, the institution of the Catholic Church proved harmful to her body, and she would not recover from feeling pushed out by her spiritual family. These were instances in which she felt that categories were imposed upon her. Compartmentalizing religions from one another, as well as genders, races, and nations, never sat right with Sally. Later I will engage her Jewish and Buddhist commitments in more depth.

"Medical Bodies" unpacks the challenges of an intersex diagnosis. Medical experts strongly encouraged her to transition to female. Similarly, the Dominican order also struggled to grasp the distinction between intersexuality and transgenderism. Medical categories are invaluable to institutions because they facilitate the management of bodies. Historically, medical practitioners have imposed so-called corrective surgery on intersex infants to make them more definitively male or female. Here, I will cover some of the research on the harmful effects of these interventions as well as the immense stakes for Sally as a clergyperson living in a religious community.

"Bodies of Paperwork" focuses on the power of discourse and documentation to make bodies legible. Laws, medical documents, newspapers, even personal letters and emails shape bodies. Sally fought to have her identity documents, degrees, and certificates reissued in her new name because these granted her access to legal rights and privileges. She worked within systems to advance social justice, which proved both helpful and harmful. Her efforts demonstrate the benefits and drawbacks of working within institutional conventions to advocate for marginalized persons.

"Bodies of Land" addresses Sally's complex relationship to place as a social and political project. As displayed in her reactions to Zionism and Apartheid, she disliked invoking God-given rights to promised lands in Israel and various colonial sites. Sally was a person who was sometimes granted privileges and, at other times, experienced the pain of having her privileges revoked. What is admirable about Sally was that she did not seek self-advancement but rather sought to change institutions to promote more just systems for all marginalized persons. Her work at the Land Claims Commission pursued restitution and reparation for colonized persons displaced from their land. The work had political, religious, and ecological dimensions. As she sought to establish good relations among diverse persons, she came up against a shortcoming—her own unrealized privilege as a middle-aged, white, educated person that created tension with colleagues. Their judgments against her non-Christian beliefs and disabled fat body added to the complexity of her work relationships.

This part is broadly chronological. It focuses on 1981–94, which were pivotal years for Sally. We begin with her time as a Catholic priest in England, then attend to her misdiagnosis as transgender and year of medical leave in 1993; next, we consider the paperwork involved in concealing and then marking her name and gender change, and, last, we cover her turn to racial justice work in South Africa. All four facets—religious bodies, medical bodies, bodies of paperwork, and bodies of land—are technologies aimed at domesticating Sally's flesh through categorization and regulation. It took repeated lessons for Sally to realize that her individual body was not a problem; instead, unjust institutions that sought to regulate her flesh were the problem. With the latter perspective, Sally eventually became more of an activist agitator, initiating breaks and providing sutures such that clearings would make space for diverse communal life—ecological good relations. From her example, we might become emboldened to question whether our bodies are problems. She might help us name regulating institutions as problem bodies.

3. Religious Bodies

S. joined a Catholic community as a Jewish person who practiced Buddhist meditation.[1] In her physical body, she sat at the intersection of multiple religious bodies. She had hoped that making a home at Blackfriars would allow her to integrate these, but ultimately, religious institutions made binary demands upon her body that she could not endure. Note that this chapter focuses on her time in the Catholic Church, and I will return to her Jewish and Buddhist commitments in more depth in later chapters, as well as how her activism brought her to baptism in the Catholic Church in 1976.

In 1981, the Blackfriars order in Oxford accepted S. to the novitiate. Living in a community promised a religious family supportive of her activism. She believed that the Blackfriars were at the cutting edge of the Catholic Church after Vatican II because they were willing to engage in dialogue with Marxists and supported the liberation of Northern Ireland. Clerical clothing was worn liturgically but otherwise infrequently. "It didn't seem punitive or restrictive. It seemed like a kibbutz—a collective—and I liked that," S. explained.[2] At Blackfriars, S. remained involved in the solidarity movement by chairing the Oxford Anti-Apartheid Group and founding Oxford Academics Against Apartheid.

St. Dominic founded Blackfriars, also known as the Order of Preachers, in 1216. The friars and their houses were called Blackfriars due to the black

FIGURE 3.1 Photograph of S. as a priest. From GALA archive.

capes (*cappa*) brethren wore over their white habits.³ According to their website, "The Dominican Friars' way of life forms men who are contemplative and studious, but also charitable and outward-looking, and highly skilled at public speaking: the very model of the Christian teacher."⁴ These friars are itinerant preachers, "who are thus called to make the world [their] cloister."⁵ St. Albert the Great and St. Thomas Aquinas shape intellectual life at the priory. Blackfriars' ties to South Africa date back to 1916, when Father Bede Jarrett was responsible for sending friars to Southern Africa. Father Jarrett also started the journal *Blackfriars*, now known as *New Blackfriars*.

The portal to the Blackfriars Oxford property is a small, unassuming archway off a busy road in the city center. It leads to a chapel on the right and a priory on the left. Together, these frame a courtyard. Unlike the Franciscan or Benedictine orders, which have monasteries that set clerics apart from society, the Dominican Blackfriars live in priories. Franciscan churches tend to be simple in design to indicate clerical vows to poverty, whereas the Benedictine order is typically ornate to celebrate the splendor of God. Dominicans achieve an elegant simplicity that does not shy away from ornate tapestries yet favors plain stone structures and wood furniture. Some priories are mixed not only in terms of lay and clerical residents but also various genders. At the Oxford priory, however, there are only men.

Upon arriving, S. was assigned a room. The bed, bookshelves, and desk would meet her basic needs, and the paned windows promised continual natural light. A staircase partitions the residential quarters from meeting rooms. Beyond the meeting rooms is the library. Wood bookcases stand alert as soldiers, one after another. Sturdy beams cut across lofted ceilings. Down the center, a desk-high bookcase doubles as a writing surface and storage for library cards. To the right, windows interrupt bookcase-lined walls. At the far back, a wood staircase zigzags to a second story of bookcases and a banister-lined catwalk along the left and back. From the wood chevron-patterned floor to the well-lit lofted ceiling, it is a visual feast.[6]

The Oxford community did not have nuns brought in to cook and clean, nor did the brethren have the means to hire a cook. Instead, they took turns sharing this labor. I note this because nuns serve priests in some Catholic communities. Perhaps this difference facilitated holy friendships across genders. In the refectory, brethren prepared meals and ate together at least once a day. It is a long room with bold black-and-white checkered flooring. The friars sat across from one another at rectangular wood tables. Their 9:30 a.m. service was quite lively, and lay members of the church often joined them for lunch. Brethren entered brotherhood with one another but also into friendship with lay Catholics. Through these interactions with the laity, S. developed a lifelong friendship with Frances Flatman, wife to Anglican priest Martin Flatman.[7]

Frances converted to Catholicism first, and with time, Martin shifted from the Anglican to the Catholic priesthood. Their marriage vows remain intact, they explained to me.[8] It is an intriguing quirk of the priesthood. Frances had lived in South Africa from ages three to thirteen just as Apartheid took hold (1948–58). When her parents returned to England, she felt a sense of significant loss. S. connected with Frances over leftist politics and felt more at home with the Flatmans than among some of her brethren. She would join Frances to picket Barclays Bank, protesting its investments in South Africa during Apartheid. If S. disagreed with one of Father Martin's sermons, she would send him a painfully detailed account of how to improve his homilies as though evaluated according to a standard of scholarship rather than pastoral care.[9] She also prepared one of their sons, Samuel, for reception in the church.[10] The Flatmans were some of the few friends whom S. would introduce to her parents.

When S.'s parents flew from Israel to visit, Jack had throat cancer and was learning to speak from his diaphragm. Her Jewish parents sat uncomfortably at the refectory table among Catholic clergy and laity, wondering how their former yeshiva boy had landed in a Christian religious community. The next day, S. asked Frances if her family could dine at the Flatmans' home because she thought her parents might feel more at ease there. They obliged, and Frances observed how S. fit within her family. Both S. and Jack were outspoken and principled. Like Mildred, S. was gentle and loved music.

In 1981, two novices entered the order alongside S. After a novice's first year in Blackfriars, all the priory brethren and the council vote on their acceptance. If voted in, the novice takes simple (meaning temporary) three-year vows. After those three years, another vote takes place. If voted through, the novice is then invited to take solemn (meaning lifetime) vows. During chapter meetings, S. observed a tension between the older brethren and the younger brethren who had solemnly professed more recently. In her view, the latter resented the former's control over the priory. S. explained, "On the whole, the senior counsel was actually progressive, theologically liberal, or indeed even left wing. Some of the younger people were more conservative and wanted to flex muscles and question the propriety of Dominicans going out on protests on American nuclear bases and getting arrested."[11] At the end of her time in the order, she connected this generational shift to her own situation, writing, "The harshness I have experienced is connected with a sea-change in the Church at large, the growth of a deeply uncharitable neo-conservatism in this country at least, and probably throughout the West."[12]

None of the Blackfriars brethren I interviewed confirmed her impression of a neoconservative shift. Unfortunately, the eldest Blackfriars I contacted were quite ill and declined interview invitations. S.'s friend and superior, Father Timothy Radcliffe, discussed ongoing debates about priestly obligations to obey the law, suggesting that there were matters of disagreement. In retrospect, S. realized that as a middle-aged person, she might have provoked controversy, saying, "I was identified with the older people. I'd been involved in anti-Zionist organizations, I was passionately committed to the struggle against apartheid in South Africa, I had been a communist and I had not renounced Marxist economics. You had people who didn't feel like that, so I became an issue. Apparently, a hardy perennial also, had been: was I really a Christian, ever? I didn't know this. The senior people were saying yes; the younger people evidently were saying no."[13] It was not a requirement for S. to renounce her Jewishness when she became a Catholic priest.

As I discuss further below, she still felt animosity toward her interfaith commitments.

The chapter voted in her two fellow novices for three years, but on S., they were split and settled upon a compromise. She was to make another simple (temporary) vow for a year and then face another vote.[14] In an interview, S. explained, "The prior provincial was furious, but he didn't have the power in terms of the constitutions to override the vote. I was in a state of shock because nothing that had been said had prepared me for this possibility."[15] Years after the fact, she characterized the controversy as bold anti-semitism: "Not the least of these was a strong antipathy, among some towards Jews like me, to put it bluntly. I was nearly voted out toward the end of my novitiate because of this, and I understand that a hardy perennial at chapter meetings until I was voted in for solemn profession was the vexed question as to whether I was truly a Christian."[16]

At the time, S. felt betrayed. She had not been aware that her presence was quite so controversial. At night, she tossed and turned, wondering whether she should leave. Timothy encouraged S. to see it through. The following morning in the kitchen, one of her brethren, a psychiatrist, looked grim-faced. She cracked a joke that shifted his mouth into a grin and then felt reassured that it would be all right. Until then, she had not been in the mood to joke.

Surprisingly, soon after the other two novices made their professions, they left the order. One entered a romantic relationship with a former Dominican brother, and another left after having an affair with a married woman. "It was ironic," S. said. "I was the easy case (shrugs)."[17] She speculates that after the two other novices left the order, no one had the gall to vote against her a second time. From her perspective, the injustice was that her Jewishness was a bigger concern than her fellow novitiates' failure to uphold vows of celibacy. The Blackfriars reject this interpretation of events. Regardless, what constitutes a holy Christian body—one's gender, sexuality, faith, economics, or politics—remains contested within Christian communities.

This episode was one of many in which S. followed explicit rules and then was perplexed by a wary reception from others. The unwritten rules that shape social networks were a persistent mystery to her. Most community members, whether in the Catholic Church or a government organization, fail to notice or pragmatically cope with the dissonance between official procedures and actual practices. The public face of groups presents unity and agreement, while individuals privately do as they like. But S. found inconsistency insufferable. Her fortitude might be mistaken for bravery because most people find the rewards of community far outweigh the pain of adhering to official rules. I suspect that her constitution simply would not allow her to act otherwise. S. lived by adhering entirely to all explicit policies and made her way from within. As I see it, the logic of her position is that one avoids being reprimanded on official grounds and can leverage that very system to advocate for what is just. Hers was a lifelong lesson on the limitations of working within systems.

Religious vows in the order do not automatically entail becoming a priest. Two types of male Dominicans live in permanent vows—priests and lay (cooperative) brothers, who are academic scholars. It was once the case that the lay brothers served the priests, but that practice had since dissolved among the Blackfriars. Some within the order did not appreciate the shift in boundaries. After S. was voted in for lifetime vows, she was put forward for ordination as a deacon, the first of three degrees of Holy Orders—deacon, priest, and bishop. After completing her degree at Oxford, she was put forward for the second: the priesthood.

Notably, S. described her ordination as less significant than her participation in the negotiations that ended Apartheid. She was ordained in 1987, one day after returning from Dakar, Senegal. There, she had been one of sixteen elite representatives of the African National Congress who met with a group composed mainly of Afrikaners and Thabo Mbeki, now the former president of South Africa.[18] Laughing, she recalled the essay she had to write before ordination in which she argued that the New Testament holds there is *one* priest, not a multiplicity of priests: "Ordination for me was not actually a big deal.... The big deal for me was being in community.... Evidently there were some struggles in the early church, and women were knuckled out.... Ironically, I argued that the notion of a priestly caste is actually alien to the New Testament."[19] This argument that only Jesus is a priest granted her entry into the priesthood.

Here is another instance in which S. turned the doctrines of the church against itself. She could not bring herself to maintain a distinction between official policy and private practice. Instead, she cited the biblical canon to advance egalitarianism. Her method was to confront religious persons with the very ideals they claim to hold sacred and point out that they are compatible with progressivism. After ordination, she taught moral theology and ethics at Oxford. She was later assigned to the Cambridge priory, where she became a sub-prior and a British citizen by naturalization and remained active in the ANC.[20]

Companionship

Despite feeling like an outsider, Sally formed close, lifelong friendships at Oxford and Cambridge. She and Father Timothy Radcliffe wrote numerous letters to one another over the years. Their correspondence displays an affectionate bond fortified by their shared faith. In the beginning, they exchanged playful jokes and personal anecdotes. "I shall reply with a similar letter, rather stream of consciousness, and purely written as a friend, someone who does care for you, rather than as THE MASTER!" Timothy quipped.[21] Timothy encouraged and supported Sally through the twists and turns of her gender exploration. "My intention in writing is to thank you for your friendship and your kindness," Sally wrote, "and to assure you of my continued love for you—for what it is worth—regardless of everything that has happened. Your letters to me throughout this extremely fraught affair have been models of *menschlichkeit*."[22]

By the mid-1990s, Timothy's letters arrived less frequently, and he redirected the conversation in support of Father Malcolm McMahon and church polity. While Father McMahon struggled to grasp the specificity of intersexuality, he felt certain that it was incompatible with Catholic priesthood and that Sally ought to be laicized. "I really do believe, though," Timothy wrote, "that Malcolm is acting in a way that is utterly honourable and in the sincere conviction that this is best.... Certainly I have no evidence for Malcolm wishing in any way to drive you out of the Catholic Church or to prevent you finding other ministries in which your talents could be used."[23] Considering the intensity of his travel schedule, it is clear that Timothy made concerted efforts to support Sally through her emotional ups and downs. His letters were often encouraging and religiously grounded. It is worth quoting his initial response to Sally at length here:

> Might it not be that you bear within your body something of the drama that Christ who is not only neither Jew nor Gentile, or [sic] rather who is *both*, and who is also neither male nor female, but *both*. Within your own self, within your identity you seem to live out the drama of that passage of Christ. Might that not be a deeply priestly thing to do? I have a deep belief in God's providence, that in a curious way and by paths that we could never anticipate, we are led by God to places in which finally we can live fruitfully even the pains of our past. Could it be that God in His curious way, led you towards a role in which jewish [sic] and gentile, male and female identities could be lived out as a

sign of the Kingdom and of all our futures? Maybe in a quiet way, God is living out a preaching in you. You may wish to kick God and scream against him, but may not this deep ambivalence become, somehow and when it has found its right expresion [sic], something in which to rejoice? Might we not imagine one day, you and I, really believing that all this is not just a source of pain—though it may *be* an abiding source of pain and hurt until you die—but also be known and experienced as something in which there can be rejoicing and celebration, and image of Christ in whom all is one.

... Might it not be providential that God has plomped you precisely into the middle of this odd group that is the Dominican family! That you belong not just with a group of men but with women too. Might it not be the case that you have an unexpected freedom to live with all sorts of groups and communities, of women too. That being a Dominican means that you have a certain freedom, without embarrassment, to share in the lives of communities of women and see what that is like. Might not God have been jolly cunning, since where else might you have found the possibility to go and live with a group of women, wearing almost the same clothes, and be unquestionably at home? ... Be assured, my dear, dear [former name], you and I will together share the hugely funny of all this. And not *just* in the Kingdom either![24]

Timothy offered helpful biblical and theological insight into Sally's gender exploration. He signed off this initial response letter by reminding Sally of the baptismal formula in Galatians 3:28: "One of the things that I have always loved about you is your great, deep laugh, which is neither male nor female, neither Jewish nor Gentile, but is certainly human and enormously free!"[25] It was a scripture that she would return to many times over while trying to make her intersexuality and interreligious commitments intelligible.

Peter Hunter, another friend, began as a Cambridge student whom S. met at a Blackfriars Mass. He was born in Durban, South Africa, where he spent the first nineteen years of his life. Peter left the country to avoid arrest for refusing to serve in the army. Once he learned that S. was a fellow South African, the two sat for hours discussing politics. The early 1990s was a time of dramatic transition from Apartheid to democracy in South Africa, and there was no shortage of current events to contemplate, including the release of Nelson Mandela from prison. Peter was awestruck by S.'s knowledge of the Hebrew Bible. A deep friendship began that would last the rest of S.'s life.

In 1996, S. returned to the Oxford house to work on her doctoral thesis and found herself locked in a debate with Peter.[26] How could she justify transitioning theologically? Peter asked: *Is not being male or female part of the essence of what it means to be human?* Sally thought of her doctoral thesis on bodily resurrection. She had been contemplating the theological meaning of our physical bodies for years. Surely, she could persuade her dear friend Peter that her biology was compatible with his definition of a human being. Rather bluntly, Peter asserted: *Cats have four legs. Human beings are male or female. It doesn't rule out that some cats might have more or less legs, but when they do it signals that something has happened and requires explanation. Likewise, human beings are generally male or female.*[27] Sally's eyes lowered. She knew that Peter was engaging her in a good-faith debate. Typically, the two bonded in such scenarios even when unsuccessful in persuading one another. They thrived in intellectual combat. Peter could see that her heart was breaking before his eyes. Although the two loved knowledge and truth, this exercise was deeply personal and embodied. It meant that the conversation was taking place on two levels; it was both theological and personal. The stakes were high. Sally collected herself and tried again: *There is a biological reason for me not wanting to be identified as male or female.* Peter stood his ground: *As much as I don't want to hurt you because you are my friend, I cannot agree with your logic.*[28] The harshness of this discussion is an unfortunate by-product of some theological schools of thought.

Leave

Sally presented to Father Malcolm McMahon a letter from Timothy softly illuminating the discovery of her intersexuality. She suspected that he anticipated very different news—perhaps that she had impregnated a woman.[29] Malcolm struggled to grasp the distinction between intersexuality and transsexuality.[30] The two evidently spoke past one another. Sally tried to explain her congenital biology and her asexuality.[31] She had been wrongly designated male at birth, and Sally labored to explain that hers was not a problem in need of any surgical intervention. But Malcolm could not help but think of her in terms of being transgender and of that somehow relating to sexual desire, which is, unfortunately, a common confusion.[32]

Because Sally prided herself on being compliant with rules and regulations, she stressed that no wrongdoing had occurred. "It hurt particularly because I had been at pains not to breach order discipline, to my own detriment, and it seemed cruel to me to bind me hand and foot and then to put the boot," she explained to Timothy in a letter. "I had bent over backwards to do everything the Province had asked of me, and yet a decidedly hostile move seemed to have been initiated or was being prepared behind my back at its own leisure and without any possibility of a 'come-back.'"[33] She had not broken her vows nor had a crisis of faith; she merely discovered an anatomical anomaly and disclosed it to her superiors, hoping to continue some manner of ministry. Years later, S. would express that she feared coerced institutionalization. She claimed that despite her best efforts to educate Malcolm on intersexuality, he reacted severely, and she sincerely dreaded psychiatric confinement.[34] It is not clear where Sally got the idea that Malcolm would consider institutionalizing her or why she felt it to be an immediate concern. She brings this fear up multiple times in different contexts, suggesting that her anxiety was genuine, but does not offer evidence that Malcolm was contemplating such a scenario.

After waiting a few weeks, Sally heard back from Malcolm. She alleges that he granted her leave to explore her gender in distant Eastbourne, but under suffocating terms—namely that she must not communicate with friends or family.[35] Years later, Sally maintained her position that Malcolm had dealt harshly with her: "Eventually I was given permission, but under swinging restrictions: I was not allowed to let any of the brethren who didn't already know, just one or two knew, or any of my friends or family know what the hell was going on. All sorts of restrictions and conditions."[36] None of the brethren I interviewed confirmed Sally's account of such demands. Most expressed doubts that Malcolm would have reacted so harshly, and Malcolm claims not to remember the details of what happened.[37] Near the time of these events, Sally wrote to Timothy, "My life in Eastbourne was constrained by religious obedience: there were 'ground-rules' imposed upon me by Malcolm, which I was bound by obedience to accept although some of them made my life exceedingly difficult."[38] She clarifies: "Only a handful of people—including my former religious superior and the previous Pope himself—were the ones who took decisions about the way in which my situation was to be handled. Most of my brethren were kept in ignorance and, when information was given out, it was misleading."[39] It is difficult to corroborate her account, but it is clear that Sally did not waver from her version of events.

It became evident to Sally that the ease with which she had accessed sites of privilege when presenting as male was waning. In the past, her asexuality, anti-apartheid and anti-Zionist politics, and interreligious commitments posed obstacles to fully belonging to a home and community, be those political or religious. Now Sally felt the sting of yet another demand for conformity: her gender. The consequences of presenting as female would be immense.

Gossip

On Sunday, July 15, 2007, Sally sent a ten-page, single-spaced mass email addressed to "friends." She acknowledged that she was in poor health and felt compelled to take stock of her life, which included informing friends of her current status. The first concern she raised was that she might continue to be the subject of gossip and resentment in some Catholic clergy circles. She wrote, "Accusations are the more hurtful when their subject knows **that** they are but is not allowed to know **what** they are. Accusing whispers spread all the more and do all the more real damage when their exact content is kept from the one who is accused [of sinning] and she is thus denied any possibility of answering them."[40] Sally took umbrage at the suggestion that she defected from the Catholic Church and turned to ultra-Orthodox Judaism or that she breached her vows and was excommunicated. According to Sally, these rumors spread to Dominicans in both South Africa and Israel. She also reports to have caught wind of the suggestion that she had "sex change" surgery and blamed Malcolm for her difficulties.[41] Sally interpreted these events through her suspicion of anti-semitism.[42]

Sally made a compelling argument that the life of her Christian faith required the nourishment of Catholic fellowship, and years without companionship led to the death of her faith. She explained that her Christian faith was genuine and crucial to her Jewish identity. Sally entered the order with a strong sense of vocation. For her, religion was a matter of life and death: "I believe that those who refused to enter into dialogue in the interest of the preservation of my Christian commitment refrained from dialogue largely because they realised that faith had been fundamental to my survival. They were absolutely right: when it succumbed, eventually, part of me died with it in a sense."[43] She went on to assert that her Jewish identity, therefore, became tenuous with the death of her Christian commitment because the two were interrelated.

Sally pointed to Malcolm specifically as having been at pains to mischaracterize her as transsexual rather than intersex due to instruction by the Congregation for the Doctrine of Faith concerning gender dysphoria and reassignment surgery as mental illness and grounds for expulsion. The endocrinological tests confirmed that she should have been classified as female based on intersexuality. The order rejected her offer to submit to a physical examination by a medical professional of their choice, Sally believed, because it would have weakened a mental illness case against her. Sally concluded the email starkly: "The message is that there is no place in the body of Christ for compassion for the intersexed.... When one is intersexed, and when powerful and influential voices around one make it clear that they regard one as less than human and monstrous by reason of one's being intersexed, at a deep level it is difficult not to internalise this."[44] One might counter that she saw an opening within canon law for intersexuality but not transsexuality.

Clearly, Sally was an ally to trans people and, in some ways, might be understood as trans herself. The parsing of details here concerns her desire to work within institutional rules rather than upending them. It is a method for self-preservation about which we might be critical. She makes her case so intensely, and her brethren respond quite differently than when they consider her trans, that it could appear transphobic. From a theological perspective, Blackfriars hinge certain doctrines on embodiment such that surgical intervention might trouble them more than a congenital occurrence. Regardless, discomfort in learning about her experience is a valuable indication that hospitable policies are needed.

Father Richard Conrad of the Blackfriars Oxford replied to her email the following day, expressing regret to hear of Sally's resentment. He gingerly explained that their first impression was that she was biologically male and wanted to transition to female, and they only later came to understand intersexuality. He wrote empathetically, "I have often worried over the way in which laws and 'public procedures' can be 'blunt instruments' and don't always fit the actual 'stuff' of human situations."[45] Some sources say he was one of her closest friends in the order. Unfortunately, he declined interview invitations for this book.

What hurt most was her inability to participate in clerical ministry. Sally described her love for the vocations of preaching and teaching. By all accounts, she excelled at these. A conventual life with the Dominicans still beckoned her, though it was clear that her intersexuality was incompatible with the priesthood. Frustrated, Sally grumbled about having been punished for her honesty and integrity on that matter. Had she been hypocritical, perhaps her material needs would have been cared for. According to Sally, she knew of priests who kept their intersexuality a secret. One in particular, she recalled, was raised as female but, as a teenager, lived as male. He, and others like him with ambiguous genitalia, feared that the revelation of this truth would be life-shattering. An unknown source shared with Sally that had she kept her anatomy a secret and worn women's clothing under her habit and in her private room, she could have stayed in the order. This suggestion demonstrated a lack of understanding that distressed her. In her words, she was not cross-dressing; she was intersex. Moreover, she refused to embrace a double life.[46] That dissonance was incompatible with her temperament.

4. Medical Bodies

In the mid-1990s, S. began to explore her gender. There is a social demand for medical diagnoses, which are epistemological claims. Medical experts funneled S. into transgender therapy and recommended genital reassignment surgery, which is still performed on intersex infants today. Like church, government, and family, medical institutions traditionally understand people as male or female and confront ambiguity by conforming bodies to one or the other. In a 2012 documentary, S. reflected:

> What flummoxes me is that no one asked me to pull down my drawers. There was never an inspection of my genitalia. Never. It was weird. I had known for sometime that all that was needed was to look at my genitalia and a hell of a lot would have been clear. Maybe it was a blessing because perhaps there would then have been pressure to succumb to "normalization" surgery, which I would have wanted like I want a bloody hole in my head. In retrospect, it would have blown my life apart.[1]

While this statement suggests that her intersexuality was visibly apparent, S. offers a less-than-linear account of her self-awareness concerning a biological anomaly. As mentioned earlier, it is difficult to distinguish her childhood memories from demands to impose a through line to frame her self-reflection.

In the same interview footage, she claims she knew from age four or five.² About a doctor's examination, she implied that any sign of abnormality was glossed over:

> When I was about nine or ten years old I fell down a flight of stairs, was knocked out—concussed. My mom took me to the pediatrician who gave me a very careful examination. At the end, he said that there was nothing broken, etc. There's just one thing. And then he had a second thought. I think that it was probably the genitalia. He might have thought that if he commented on it that it would cause hell in the life of this family. The child is being reared as male; it's not caused a problem. Let sleeping dogs lie.³

Concerning her military service in Israel, S. alleges, "I had to strip down to underwear and passed one doctor who pulled it open and peered. The colonel didn't say anything to me about the genitalia, but he started to prepare me for being rejected . . . it was clear that what was there was ambiguous. He didn't want explicitly to say, and he didn't want me branded."⁴

To be sure, for some, intersexuality is externally visible. For others, there might be internal ovaries or testes. S. pointed to test results for her hormonal range as an indication of her intersexuality. Regardless, there is something garish about demanding physical evidence for her intersexuality. At the time, S. wanted professional counseling but was presumed to need sex reassignment surgery. In 1993 she explained, "I spoke to my doctor, who made enquiries and wrote a letter of referral to the gender identity clinic at Charing Cross hospital. This appears to be the only gender identity clinic within the NHS, and my expectation was that I would be able to obtain expert counselling there. . . . I was also informed that they had requested funding for the whole process of gender-reassignment, while what I sought at this stage was no more than basic counselling."⁵ In the process of pursuing medical counsel, she describes the appeal of experimentation:

> I sought disparate advice from radically opposed perspectives in order to be able to gauge my situation as cautiously and comprehensively as possible. . . . The alternative, which involved the possibility of an experimental change of gender role as a method of discernment, seemed preferable; and the specifics of my situation were such that this possibility seemed to offer the only viable way to enable me to see whether the condition was ultimately containable or whether it demanded a change of gender role *tout court*.⁶

Despite her interest in exploring her gender, she conclusively rejected a Freudian analysis of her misgivings, as well as any pressure to have surgical intervention. She describes having seen psychoanalyst Bernice Krikler, "Piers" in Oxford, Richard Woods, and Rick, a therapist working with patients experiencing gender dysphoria in a sexual dysfunction clinic in the United States.[7] Psychoanalysis, she wrote, "presented me with the prospect of living out a life of immense pain and confusion, relieved occasionally by talking to someone but that was it. What Fran [Springfield] was offering was some way to discern fairly quickly, by means of some sort of real-life test, right or wrong. This makes much more sense, an action place and a practical program for discernment which would settle it one way or another."[8] I will say more about Fran soon.

Eventually, S. found a phone number for services for persons with gender dysphoria. It is not clear that this was in fact, the policy, but she certainly interpreted the unit to require she appear in strictly female clothing:

> It transpired that the unit does not offer any counselling, and it seems that for a person like me who is gender dysphoric to come for an appointment at the unit wearing male clothing and without make-up is considered poor form and more-or-less guarantees an abrupt end to any attempt to deal with the issue of one's gender dysphoria through the NHS. Any type of trousers counts as male clothing, and wearing trousers gets one back to square zero. This did not sound at all like the help that I needed at this stage![9]

S. explicitly stated that she had no interest in pursuing surgery; what she wanted was therapy to aid her in living an open and honest life. She alleges that even counseling was only available to trans persons who demonstrated commitment to surgical intervention: "I could be given an appointment only if I was assured of full funding for gender-reassignment surgery, something I [most] certainly did not seek. I therefore have to seek counselling elsewhere. Contrary to my expectations, seeking a couple of sessions of counselling to 'pull the thorn' turned out to be anything but simple—it opened a veritable Pandora's Box and tore my vocation and life comprehensively apart."[10] At every turn, it seemed, institutions that were meant to help instead mislabeled her transgender and enforced an expectation to conform to the binary extremes of either male or female form.[11] She described her bind: "One was expected to live as female. I was in religious life; I was a priest. I had no particular wish to cross-dress. I had no wish to live a life which wasn't whole and open. I had no wish to have any kind of double life.... I did not realize that the referral was for a process leading to surgery. I just wanted some advice.... The expectation was that you get full funding for a whole process leading to and through gender reassignment surgery."[12] Frustrated, she reflected that medical experts, "told me—misleadingly—that there was no significant difference, therapeutically, between transsexuality and intersex."[13] Next, I will explain how and why Sally was initially misdiagnosed as transgender.

Fran

S. was referred to Fran Springfield, the acting administrative director of the Gender Dysphoria Trust in Eastbourne and the first nurse specializing in gender counseling in the United Kingdom. Her partner Norma answered the phone. While chatting, S. learned that Norma had previously served as a marine pilot, and she had captained one of the largest oil tankers in the world while working in the Persian Gulf. She made S. an appointment to see Fran the next day. As a convert to Catholicism, Norma kindly waived the usual fee. It was an enormous relief to S.[14] She reserved judgment despite her initial discomfort with the enthusiastic reception of the transgender community.

On a cold February day, S. met with Fran.[15] She hoped Fran would be able to sort out her gender dysphoria so she could return to priestly duties with a singular focus. Palms sweating and heart racing, S. knocked. A mezuzah hung diagonally on the doorpost, easing her nerves. The door opened, and she introduced herself to Norma and Fran. After a lengthy discussion about S.'s predicament, Fran urged S. to get a chromosomal scan. She suspected that S.'s testosterone levels were exceptionally low and that there might be a chromosomal basis for it. If that were the case, Fran recommended that S. begin taking small doses of estrogen. Fran assured S., "I have no doubt that there is a woman inside of you. When you feel ready, give her a name."[16] Immediately, the name "Sally" sprang to mind.

Sally's time with Norma and Fran was bewildering and thrilling. Though an empathetic listener, Fran did not provide the quick fix that Sally sought. Sally did not know what to make of it all: "I was somewhat dazed at another level: the 'lesbian' relationship between Fran and Norma, the possible impact on Fran's twelve-year-old son, the sense that I was being told that I was wanted 'on board.'"[17] On the one hand, Sally felt pressure to embrace transitioning to female. On the other hand, she could not resist the opportunity to explore her gender. Intrigued by the suggestion that her discontent might be attributable to her biology, Sally made an appointment for a blood test. She described her ambivalence: "Something in me left reassured by the fact that there was relief, that I was not alone and that there were people who had coped, however oddly. There was also a sense of grief at the lost childhood and the fact that I did not open the issues in my early twenties. Part of the grief was also for what I could lose on the path that Fran offers, and part of it was for what I would lose by **not** following it."[18] As much as experimenting with a female role would entail cost, it would not compare to what she had already lost—and would continue to lose—by not doing so.

After their meeting, Sally stood pensive at Finsbury Park Station. In the damp cold, as she waited for a train to Cambridge to resume her priestly duties, a sea of strangers commuting from their homes to work in London called to mind Fran's hypothesis. As the train squealed to a halt, Sally grabbed hold of its handle and pulled herself aboard. She wrote to one of her confidants, Father Timothy Radcliffe:

> I had a most lachrymose journey back to Cambridge, standing in a crowded train frightened by my sense of the power of the subterranean currents within myself, envying the people around me who were not born with this disorder. At the back of the carriage a man and a woman laughed, and the woman rested her head on the man's shoulder. I envied the woman's chromosomal and physical femininity and her apparent ease with herself, and mourned the way in which the gap between my self-perception, the hard realities of my physiology and gender role, have made it impossible for me to experience that ease and apparent intimacy.[19]

Tears streamed down her neck and onto her shirt. She would find refuge in, not from, her body, though not without suffering.

Upon returning to the Cambridge "mixed up" house (detailed later), Sally confided in a few brethren. They were sympathetic, though she suspected they could not absorb the fullness of what she was contemplating. One brother stressed the considerable risk of scandal. Sally also reached out to some laywomen in the community, who offered their support. But Sally desired utter transparency. The pressure to continue as usual eroded her sense of home with them as a place of safety, as she recalled communication with her priestly brother: "I had taken Aidan [Nichols] into my confidence—apart from his considerable kindness." She wrote further that "I had to justify a request for money for travel—and he had been supportive."[20] About David (presumably Sanders), another priestly brother, Sally alleges, "He proved sympathetic, though I suspect that he does not really understand what it means and could mean. He was understandably anxious that I maintain secrecy as far as possible, and I was ambivalent about this."[21] The imperative to be surreptitious about her exploration bothered Sally. She described her misgivings:

> I have not harmed anyone, and [this] does not appear to entail any moral turpitude. An endeavour such as mine is not shameful, and any sense of guilt associated with it is clearly neurotic. Much of the exercise is connected with an attempt to accept myself, much of the plan is a direct product of an attempt to hide, deny and repress, and of the massive proportions of the split which has resulted. I do not want to be any more secretive and conspiratorial about this matter than is absolutely necessary, particularly in my own home.[22]

"Nonetheless," she conceded, "David has a point: I recognise the considerable risk of unfair and unwarranted scandal. I have not felt the need to tell either Conrad or Marcus, nor have I shared this with the lay-community with the exception of Helen and Margaret."[23] But ultimately, she expressed her discomfort with the secrecy, "The sense I have to be at pains to hide my deepest fears and hopes, to act as if it is simply 'business as usual,' has been erosive of my perception of the house as my home and as a place of safety."[24] The cost for authenticity and wholeness was steep.

When her dear friends Kim and Carole visited, they expressed concerns that Sally might have resolved to transition. They were suspicious of Fran. One pressed Sally to turn instead to Jungian analysis. The other suggested that Sally had a narrow understanding of masculinity that, if broadened, could resolve her problem.[25] Sally quoted Carole's letter that followed their visit: "The idea of having medical treatment (hormones) before you have opened up the question, is **unethical** and can only close off choices for you. But it will give you a kind of security because you won't have to go through the questioning process with all its ambiguity."[26] Because she valued their friendship deeply, these words left Sally's mind in turmoil. "Something else I also did was to speak to the Lecturer in Pastoral Studies at the House of Studies in Oxford," she reported. "He was a trained psychoanalyst, and I asked him to assess me impartially to be able to offer confidential expert advice to the Prior Provincial. . . . The advice he sought would seem to have been exclusively legal and canonical."[27] Another friend, a psychotherapist, put her at ease. Though he did not discourage her from returning to Fran, he connected Sally with therapist Bernice Krikler. Like Sally, Krikler was a Jewish South African. Krikler encouraged Sally to pursue therapy but not surgery.[28]

Sally waited for the first set of chromosomal test results over the next weeks. She wondered what it might mean if Fran's hypothesis were vindicated by medical testing. Perhaps she was not a man in need of a cure. If she was biologically unusual, maybe Sally was female. Her head was spinning. Was this a time for caution or bravery? Sally attempted both. It was terrifying that even asking these questions meant that she could not return to life as before. She felt torn between leaping fully into the transition to female and occupying an ambiguous space. The envelope finally arrived in her postbox. Sally unfolded the papers and began scouring the information contained within. Male levels of testosterone range from 13–30, and female from 0.5–2.5, and her levels sat comfortably in the middle of the female range. Her prolactin level was also within the female range. She wondered if that explained why she lactated ever so slightly on occasion.[29] Sally's cheeks turned hot. She would not have joined the order had she known she had these endocrinological abnormalities. Perhaps celibacy had allowed her to remain unaware of her morphological anomalies. Regardless, the results confirmed to Sally that her mind and body indicated that she was not definitively male. The material evidence in her hand meant no one could wish that away.

Returning to gender counselor Fran, Sally inquired about her options. Fran offered her standard advice for transgender clients: "What helped was to find tokens, other ways of expressing femininity. For many people this was not enough to come to terms with their femaleness. She even mentioned one client who contrives to live as a woman, in a place where the client is not known in male role, for a limited period each year. My situation posed real challenges, because most if not all of the things she normally advised were not possible, which meant that a way to cope would have to be invented as we went along."[30] Sally explained her confusion over the diagnosis and treatment recommendation: "I therefore had some sense that intersex was involved, though the only concepts I had in relation to intersex at the time were from the pathologising perspectives of the 'experts,' who told me—incorrectly—that the therapeutic implications of intersex were exactly the same as those for transsexuality, and who sought to regiment me into a transsexual trajectory."[31]

Fran successfully guided Sally to a medical explanation for her unease but wrongly prescribed Sally a transition to female. It would take years for Sally to locate herself within the intersex community rather than the trans community. The two are distinct yet related. Transition indicates some sort of change from cis- to transgender. It can take social and medical forms. To be intersex is to be designated neither definitively male nor female at birth.

An intersex person might also be trans but not necessarily. And vice versa. Not all intersex people are trans, and not all trans people are intersex. The difficulty of distinguishing one from the other demonstrates the limitations of our categories to precisely communicate the complexity of embodied life. Trans people have become hypervisible, while intersexuality remains relatively unknown in mainstream media. Scholars have noted that reactive violence against trans people corresponds to increased visibility.[32] Furthermore, 2024 was the fourth consecutive record-breaking year for a total number of anti-trans bills considered in the United States. While intersex people have suffered nonconsensual "normalizing" surgery, trans people, especially children, have been denied access to such medical treatment. This speaks to the embroiled relationship between intersex and trans communities. Later in life, Sally worked to increase intersex visibility to destigmatize the experience and secure legal rights. Should this movement succeed, we might anticipate a similarly harsh backlash against intersexuality.

It became clear to Sally that Fran did not grasp her living situation in the order. If Sally were to explore life in a female role, she would need to take time away from her brethren. Perhaps taking a few months in Eastbourne would allow her the space to discern a path between Fran's fervor and the church's recalcitrance. Her doctoral thesis advisors, Kathy Wilkes and Janet Soskice, were unequivocally supportive of this time away.[33] Emboldened by their support, she describes having resolved to brave the unknown for the sake of authenticity: "I want to seek personal integration, whatever that means and whatever it takes . . . whether as a woman or as a man, Dominican or not, is perhaps a preliminary to the questions, something which affords one the ease to open them up, and to do so with zest and in a spirit of adventure. God knows where it will lead me, but perhaps God wills that I should find His good news for me in the pain and confusion."[34] That night she recited Psalm 23 to comfort herself:

> The Lord is my shepherd,
> I shall not want.
> He makes me lie down in green pastures;
> He leads me beside quiet waters.
> He restores my soul;
> He guides me in the paths of righteousness
> For His name's sake.
>
> Even though I walk through the valley of the shadow of death,
> I fear no evil, for You are with me;

Your rod and Your staff, they comfort me.
You prepare a table before me in the presence of my enemies;
You have anointed my head with oil;
My cup overflows.
Surely goodness and lovingkindness will follow me all the days of
   my life,
And I will dwell in the house of the Lord forever.[35]

Sally prayed that this Lenten penance would lead to an Easter.[36] She did not specify what she meant by this metaphor. We might speculate that she turned to scripture and prayer for endurance through the difficulty of gender discernment and hoped to remain in a religious community, even if in a new and different way.

Sally sat in her Eastbourne flat, overflowing with mixed emotions. She wondered what her year away from the order might bring. The thought of introducing herself as Sally both thrilled and frightened her. She wanted companions on her journey. Her first thought was to phone her Dominican brethren at Blackfriars, but she restrained herself. As she understood it, the agreement with Malcolm was to protect the Catholic Church from scandal by not making contact. She braced for her first visit to the supermarket as Sally. Checking her makeup in a mirror, she tucked some hair behind one ear and then untucked it, pulled her purse strap over her shoulder, and readjusted her twisted dress. Learning to put on makeup and dressing as a woman was a nuisance, but if this was just part of a process for discernment, then she was willing to try. Allison, her landlord's wife, was a hairdresser and gave Sally styling tips.[37] Sally took a deep breath, unlocked the door, and stepped out. Just up the stairs, there was a spectacular 180-degree ocean view. The nearest bus stop was across the road, Royal Parade. An absence of quizzical glances built her confidence with each step.

After successfully collecting her groceries and having them rung up at the till, Sally's heart suddenly sank. She reached for her checkbook. Across the top read her previous name. Her cards even included the title "Mister." Should she pretend they were her husband's? Would it be better to explain? Would the clerk even notice? It all felt overwhelming. She just wanted to complete this ordinary task.

Upon returning to the flat, Sally reflected on the uncomfortable experience. A tension headache plagued her. Though terrifying, she decided to continue practicing daily routines in a female role. She explained her resolve despite ambivalence: "I didn't like the process of having to learn to put on make-up. Wearing clothing, okay. What was at issue was a wholeness of life. If that was part of the package, then that was it. As soon as I realized that it was a learning process, I needed to have a thick skin, it was kind of okay. In a sense, presenting as female did less violence to me than presenting as male. But the truth is, I'm a person. I'm me."[38] More than anything, Sally wanted to be known as a human being. Her confidence grew bit by bit. A man held the door open for her. She gave a smile of thanks as she scurried forward. Another offered to help her carry parcels, and she politely declined. A woman on the bus gave her a knowing glance as she folded herself to accommodate more passengers. Despite the inconveniences of presenting in a female form, Sally felt seen. She was not playing a male role or feeling out of sorts. She described the sensation as a duck that has fallen into the water.[39]

Each morning, Sally turned to Christ in prayer with an intensity she had previously not known. She recalled feeling his presence more profoundly than ever. Challenges arose like frightful beasts, and she leaned upon God for courage and strength. It was an unfamiliar intimacy, as if Christ were closer to her than she was to herself. In a time when she was remote from family and brethren, Christ's presence made life tenable. She wore a crucifix wherever she went to remind her of the commitment to which she cleaved. The image helped her to make sense of the deep pain she suffered.[40]

Fran Springfield introduced Sally to psychiatrist Russell Reid, who was trained by infamous researcher John Money. Seeking to bolster his hypothesis that gender identity is entirely socially constructed, Money used what are today considered unethical research methods, especially his twin studies. Money took this thesis to the extreme when he encouraged a family to raise one of their twin boys as a girl after the child suffered a botched circumcision.[41] Intersex scholar David Rubin writes about Money, "For people with intersex characteristics, whose bodies Money read as improperly sexed, *gender role* became a way for Money to produce and, as we will see, to literally fashion the sex they were 'supposed' to have been all along.... His work on intersex helped to popularize the view that gender is central to the sexual health of persons in general."[42] Hil Malatino explores "the disciplinary, regulatory function of gender that emerges from John Money's work and proliferates throughout the entirety of the medical apparatus designed to treat intersex and trans folks."[43] Shockingly, doctor Jorge Daaboul admits, "all of us trained in the tradition of Money/Wilkins followed their recommendations. We lied to the parents of intersexed children and we lied to the children and subjected intersex individuals to 'corrective' surgery."[44]

Money's detrimental impact on the health and well-being of generations into the present day is difficult to overstate.

Fran, too, was influenced by the ideas that then held sway. When she counseled Sally, Fran explained to me that it was long before intersexuality or genderqueerness were understood. Today, Fran regrets advising Sally to embrace a female identity, though she remembers when transitioning seemed to be the only option. According to Fran, it was virtually impossible to stay employed in that time if one was neither distinctly male nor female. Fran even provided carry letters for her trans patients that they could show to police officers if accused of dressing in disguise to mask criminal activity. For these reasons, she had pressed Sally to experiment with a female role. It was clear to Fran that Sally's survival depended on conforming to the binary.

Sally wanted wholeness and well-being as a person, regardless of gender. Money's framework emboldened medical professionals and therapists to impose a gender binary onto patients. The effect was a diagnosis and treatment that redirected Sally into new regulatory systems of medical institutionalism. Rather than finding refuge in a place of safety or home where she could live openly as her whole self, she was invited into alternative dichotomies that persisted in severing her from her whole self. Many of us who have been told that our bodies are problems can relate to Sally's desire for dignity and value regardless of categories—such as gender—that too often social bodies understand to define humanity.

Like Sally, Fran was Jewish, and she, too, would become disabled. One night, upon returning home from London to Eastbourne, Fran boarded a train, after which a group of drunk men physically assaulted her. She woke up covered in blood with a spinal injury and no memory of what occurred. For some reason, footage from security cameras did not exist or was irretrievable, so the men were never apprehended. They did not rob her of any of her belongings. Today, Fran uses a wheelchair and serves as cochair of Disability Labour. She was awarded the Labour Excellence award in 2018 for her service to the Union Party.[45]

Fran recalls first knowingly interacting with a trans person while working in a nursing home. There was a transwoman with AIDS whom the staff seemed to be avoiding. Confused about her name and pronouns, Fran popped into her room and introduced herself. After a lengthy conversation, the patient burst into tears: "You're the first person who has spoken to me as a human being."[46] She explained to Fran that she had contracted AIDS through sex work, which she had undertaken to raise funds for reassignment surgery. Fran returned to visit with her patient to listen and learn. She became incensed with medical personnel who did not address their patient with the correct name or pronouns. "Nurses should treat every person with dignity and respect!"[47] After that experience, Fran committed herself to serving the trans community.

Unfortunately, Fran could not preserve any patient records from the time she treated Sally due to being intermittently unhoused. However, Fran was able to recall that when Sally struggled to get a prescription for estrogen, that was when she connected her with psychiatrist Russell Reid.[48] After he prescribed the 50 milligrams of Estradiol, Sally struggled to cover the cost. Fran took it upon herself to mail three-month supplies of estrogen to Sally. She remembers the Dominican Order as being generous with Sally. They paid for her rent, books, and necessities. She suspected, however, that Sally might have been an embarrassment to the order. Fran thinks Sally suffered from an endocrine disorder, indicated by her tendency to put on weight. Like others, Fran observed that Sally needed to be more astute regarding finances. Fran would later walk Sally through making legal complaints against a tabloid reporter, discussed later. Her case affected later changes to tabloid reporting, although it did not turn out well for Sally.

Fran was accommodating and supportive to Sally and many others. Nevertheless, in the present day, she likely would have approached Sally's predicament differently. Her regret occasions pause. Perhaps, rather than seeking new identities exclusively from among those society recognizes as healthy, we might reinterpret those options as conditional and wrongly requiring individuals to cut off parts of themselves to fit in. The sort of belonging that Sally desired was expansive and adaptive. A true sense of belonging reorients our understanding of health, so we see that it is closely linked to wholeness.

Betwixt

With one foot in each world, that of the priesthood and experimenting with a female role, Sally was strained. Throughout 1993, Father Malcolm McMahon periodically traveled three hours from Oxford to Eastbourne to meet with Sally. After introducing Malcolm to her landlord, John, and his wife, Allison, Sally walked him down to her flat below. There, he observed a terrace, sitting room, computer, kitchen, and toilet, which indicated to him that all her needs were met.[49] Today, much to my surprise, given Sally's harsh account of Malcolm, he recalls that he considered her a friend saying he enjoyed their lunches together and walking by the sea.[50] Given the social and psychological stressors, he expressed to Sally his wonder that she was doing well. From Sally's perspective, his conclusion communicated a lack of investment in her well-being.

A dissonance mounted between his sense that he went above and beyond his duties and her belief that he was hardly doing enough. When she confronted him on precisely what she had done wrong, Sally alleges that Malcolm muttered something about mutilation and canon law. She defended herself by explaining the intricacies of her medical condition. Malcolm was out of his depth. She introduced him to her therapist, Fran Springfield, and Fran's trans partner, Norma. All of this was a far cry from the gender roles he had observed in a working-class neighborhood of midcentury North London as a child, not unlike the depiction in the television program *Call the Midwife*, he tells me. Little of what Sally was doing made sense to him, least of all her logic. Of course, this was a time long before concepts of trans, intersex, or nonbinary were understood even by specialists.

On one visit, Malcolm agreed to take Sally to purchase clothing. Upon entering the shop, he realized Sally wanted to buy women's underwear. He swallowed his pride as onlookers puzzled over the relationship between him, in a clerical collar, and Sally, an unconvincing woman. After paying for her undergarments, the two lunched. Malcolm ignored quizzical glances when she went to the lady's toilet. Again, he wondered what their waiter and other diners made of their relationship. It did not matter. He had a duty to fulfill. Even though Sally could be exasperating, she was still a part of the order. He would return regularly to check in on her and buy necessities. Despite his confusion, he sensed this was where Sally needed to be. Before he left for the train, Sally asked if it would be possible for her to get hair removed from her face. Hair removal treatment was an unnecessary extravagance, Malcolm asserted.[51]

Timothy Radcliffe informed Sally that Fathers Malcolm and Peter [Hunter?] would be coming to Eastbourne to conduct an interview. He assured her, "I will try to get through to you in advance a copy of the questionnaire. I shall have to ask you the questions in Peter's presence; it is recommended that Peter tapes the interview, then transcribes it and sends a copy to you for you to suggest changes and clarification—so there will be plenty of opportunity to eradicate misunderstandings and misrepresentations."[52] She later noted, "Notionally, this was called 'helping me with my petition,' but it was in fact just giving the Order the assistance it wanted with a process in which my own input and feedback was minimal."[53] This exchange illuminates the divergence in Sally's goals and interpretations of events from those of the church. She seemed to think that all her efforts were to secure a position wherein she could continue to live and minister within the order, however creative the format. On the other hand, Malcolm understood her to no longer be compatible with the priesthood and worked to have her laicized. In her meeting with Malcolm and Peter, she detailed Fran's recommendation: "The clinical regime for the treatment of my condition involves the taking of female hormones and living consistently in [a] female role.... A year at minimum is the recommended period for the real-life test. All of this is done under medical supervision. I have to see a consultant psychiatrist regularly for this reason; and I also see a specialised gender counsellor frequently."[54] She attempted to clarify the distinction between intersexuality and transsexuality: "I am intersexed—an hermaphrodite or pseudo-hermaphrodite—rather than transsexual in the strict sense of the term.... It is not in question that I was profoundly gender dysphoric; and more than eight months of life in female role leaves little room for doubt that an attempt to return to [a] male role would be a disastrous mistake."[55] I believe she emphasized the distinction because she hoped to remain within the order.

Sally made it clear to them that she was experiencing no crisis of faith or vocation, had committed no breach of vows, and had no desire to leave the order. Peter could not hide an expression of shock when she described her ambiguous genital phenotype. She offered to submit to a physical examination by an expert should the order require evidence of her claims. The two shook their heads, indicating that would not be necessary. Sally sighed with relief. It would have been terribly humiliating, but she was willing to do whatever the church required. Malcolm explained that they needed a life history focused on her gender and a letter to the pope requesting dispensation on the grounds of incompatibility with religious life. In the jurisprudence of the Catholic Church's canon law, a dispensation exempts someone from the immediate obligation of law. In other words, it licenses what would be illegal were it not permitted by authority. Sally gave Malcolm a few photos of herself in a female role. He contained his reaction and simply asked if she would like him to include them in his paperwork to Rome. Typically, it takes a year or two to process dispensation papers, he explained, but these would push things along quickly. Assuming it would help her case, she agreed to his proposal. She later shared with Father John Orme a letter from her doctor concerning her atypical anatomy and endocrinology and its implications: "No surgery of any sort is on the cards. Reconstruction surgery would seem to be ruled out by reason of my anatomy, quite apart from my own reluctance to submit to gratuitous surgery which would create further complications."[56] Notably, this is the only instance in which I have seen Sally redact identifying information. Presumably, with names redacted, evidence supporting her case could not be used against her brethren, suggesting her priority to protect others.

Overall, the documentation indicates that Sally was cooperative with the order. Later, her interpretation would sour, and she would reframe the interview as an interrogation:

> I gave the Order everything it requested: a life-history focusing on issues of gender, a letter to the Pope regretfully requesting a dispensation from priestly obligation on the grounds of incompatibility of way of life, and the names and addresses of those responsible for my medical care. I was interrogated formally at my flat, and emphasised, in the material I was asked to write and provide and in the interrogation itself, that I remain celibate by choice and by congenital constitution, and that I neither wanted nor would I welcome a dispensation from celibacy. I made it clear that no crisis of vocation was involved, that I wished in principle to remain a religious were that possible.[57]

Initially, Sally asked if she could join the nuns connected to their order, but Malcolm was skeptical she would be accepted. Pressed, Malcolm suggested Sally join an order in Nijmegen, Holland. About this visit, she wrote to Timothy that when they had invited her to receive Communion, she declined for fear that it would be inappropriate. "Somewhat to my dismay, I found myself quietly convulsed with weeping, and the tears forced themselves through my closed eyes in spite of my efforts to hold them back. I can almost hear you saying, half-seriously and half-ironically, that tears are a gift! Gift or no, it was downright embarrassing at one level, and decidedly cathartic at another level."[58] David van Ooijen discussed the possibility of Sally visiting for six months to complete her dissertation. He expressed to her that the community embraced her wholeheartedly. She feared that it would not be financially feasible because she would lose her benefits and guaranteed housing in the United Kingdom. Shorter visits would be illegal. It did not seem viable, but she hoped Malcolm might sort out another option.

Malcolm left the interview with the feeling of having been emotionally manipulated, while Sally felt dismissed. From Malcolm's perspective, he had done right by Sally compared to the ex-priests who had begun as novices with Sally, because they had left willingly. Though he dutifully saw to Sally, she never felt his endorsement on a gut level.

Later, Sally would suspect him of having masterminded pushing her out of the order. She explained to Timothy, "I hope that I have made it clear that my motives for collaborating with the Order in the making of the case, well before I was strictly bound to make any such moves, was pre-emptive and the product of the probability of force *majeure*. The effect of it all has in many respects been uncomfortably like the hostile dismissal I sought to prevent; and I have in effect been booted out of the Order."[59] None of the brethren whom I interviewed confirmed her impression. Those privy to the information, though, declined interview invitations. The available evidence indicates that, although Malcolm was bound by canon law, was harsh with her, and regrets some of what he said and did, it is unlikely that he single-handedly expelled her from the order. It is more probable that he and others struggled to understand intersexuality as compatible with clerical community life, and they may have expedited her laicization.[60] It does not excuse the harm she suffered, but it does point to medical and religious institutional regulation as problematic bodies rather than to individual persons.

Intersex Care

Considering intersex adults' attestations to the damage medical practitioners inflicted on them as children, it became apparent to Sally that new standards of health care were vitally needed. The problem occurs "when doctors see a clash between a child's body and the social body, and they choose to address the clash by changing the child."[61] The evidence that early medical intervention benefits intersex patients is lacking. Unequivocally, many intersex persons report immense injury suffered at the hands of medical practitioners who exhibit patients' bodies to one another in person and through photographs.[62] As mentioned, John Money infamously argued that gender is a social construction and, therefore, malleable. Within his school of thought, doctors ought to make surgical interventions when a child is young. Sally and other intersex activists worked to overturn Money's stronghold on the medicalization of intersexuality. Here, I integrate Sally's work with the insights of both intersex and religious studies scholars for a deeper understanding of her multipronged approach to intersex activism.

Sally collaborated with medical practitioners Milton Diamond and Keith Sigmundson to formulate an alternative treatment protocol. "The paradigm is firmly in place—doctor is God in many areas," Sally explained. "But there is a great pocket of people who are questioning. I pushed the Human Rights Commission to begin a process on the issue of regulation that can be pushed further. I would love to be able to get into government to push that harder because my sense is that it can be pushed. The lever is the issue of human rights."[63] As a result of learning from Sally and other intersex activists, Diamond and Sigmundson stress the ongoing need for long-term follow-up of intersex persons to determine how to improve future protocols.

The Intersex Society of North America and the Intersex Society of South Africa assert that surgical intervention should be enacted only as a last resort to preserve life or health.[64] Sally offered her assessment of treatment protocols entailing surgical intervention on infants and children: "The outcome is often great physical trauma, sexual difficulties and terrible psychological trauma which blights lives." She continues, "It is clear that the harm causes disproportionate to any benefit, and that the harm cannot therefore be said to the unintended consequence of the treatment. Were the treatment necessary for the preservation of health or life, by contrast, it would be a completely different matter."[65] Sally then endorsed the article that followed her presentation to medical practitioners on the need for the standard protocol of treatment for intersex infants and children, dated January 22, 2008: "Following the publication in 1997 of Diamond's and Sigmundson's paper about the 'John/Joan' case, Diamond and Sigmundson were challenged to formulate an alternative to the standard protocol of treatment.... [They] emphasise the need for widespread and systematic long-term follow-up in order to establish an adequate empirical basis for interrogation of protocols of treatment."[66] Sally readily collaborated with medical practitioners and scholars in her intersex activism. Today, though, intersex activists are ambivalent about the merits of working with health-care providers.[67]

The primary reason some intersex activists have pivoted away from working within medical bodies is that it maintains a power structure wherein intersex infants and children remain vulnerable. Suzanne Kessler of the Division of Natural Sciences at the State University of New York published an article outlining how families might cope with the ambiguity of intersexuality. Kessler argues, "The doctors talk as though they have no choice but to respond to the parents' pressure for a resolution of psychological discomfort, and as though they have no choice but to use medical technology in the service of a two-gender culture."[68] Sally cited Kessler when interviewed by Stephen Coan for a three-part article for the *Natal Witness* in 2000. She agreed with Kessler that too often, medical professionals misinform the parents about their intersex children's need for a surgically assigned sex. Even the most conscientious best guess could prove wrong, so it should be up to the child to wait until adulthood to choose for themselves. Legal scholar Julie Greenberg reports that the National Endowment for the Humanities funded a project titled "Surgically Shaping Children," in which experts in a variety of disciplines unanimously condemned the performance of cosmetic genital surgery on intersex infants and children until they can meaningfully participate in decision-making. "Most doctors and parents, however, oppose a moratorium on infant genital cosmetic surgeries and believe that surgical alteration is in the best interest of a child born with an intersex condition.... Most parents still consent to surgery."[69] Improved protocols are not disruptive enough to initiate a culture shift that embraces the naturally occurring biological variety of genders among human beings.

Previously, I have argued that cure rhetoric is a technology of religious, political, and medical communities to manage individual bodies in service to institutional bodies.[70] Sally was attuned to medical impulses to cure intersex bodies as often being not in the interest of the patient but rather an attempt at gender regulation.[71] Jewish studies professor Julia Watts Belser unveils historical, imperial regulation of bodies under the auspices of cure.[72] The other side of this logic is that intersex bodies have the potential to upset governing bodies. Belser writes about the disruptive social significance of intersexuality: "The midrash treats the gender-ambiguous body as evidence of destruction, a form of social unmaking that has unbound the cultural markings of gender from the flesh."[73] In addition to political bodies fearing the disruptive potential of intersex persons, Ann Fausto-Sterling adds to this discourse, "If intersexuality blurred the distinction between male and female, then it followed that it blurred the line dividing hetero- from homosexual."[74] Intersex bodies unsettle people, in part, because they call sexuality into question rather than allowing people to presume binary biology and heterosexuality. Intersex bodies cannot be left untouched, because their existence and flourishing call into question the stability of national and social bodies.

Perhaps this offers insight into why someone might ardently oppose female genital mutilation while also supporting intersex disambiguation surgery on infants, however problematic this is.[75] The former exposes overt social and political management of genitals, whereas the latter quietly acquiesces to medical authority that reshapes bodies into docile forms. Nonbinary bodies threaten social and political order by exposing the construction of sex differences. According to Greenberg, intersex activists have attempted to collaborate with feminists who oppose female genital cutting (FGC) due to shared experiences of unnecessary, harmful genital cutting, but "anti-FGC feminists have excluded intersex concerns from their agenda."[76] What was once presumed to be natural is found to be an ongoing production, hence the fear of intersex persons. David Rubin contributes a transnational feminist analysis to these debates on genital mutilation: "The intersex surgery/FGM analogy instantaneously discloses and effaces the asymmetries of contemporary transnational power relations.... The factors that determine whether a procedure, bodily regimen, or corporeal way of life is considered healthy are themselves culturally, politically, and economically overdetermined."[77]

The push for early and thorough intervention is an expression of social anxiety about disabled and gender-ambiguous flesh, not a medical imperative. George Annas's "'monster' approach" to ethics points to disgust as agitating the medical practitioner's drive to intervene when they encounter infants with ambiguous genitals.[78] Ellen Feder summarizes the logic of producing personhood via surgery: "(Babies with atypical sex anatomies) are monsters, and we're going to make them human; after we make you human, the rules of human ethics will apply."[79] I will return to a reframing of monster as monstrance in the final chapter.

While sometimes effective, collaboration with regulating bodies risks perpetuating other forms of coercion. Medicine readily intervenes to regulate intersex youths' bodies but gatekeeps the same procedures from trans youth. Often, intersex infants require no medical intervention because they are not diseased, ill, or endangered, whereas trans youth require treatment that is denied to them. Jules Gill-Peterson demonstrates in her 2018 book *Histories of the Transgender Child* how transgender medicine is inextricable from intersex medicine, though the two people groups are managed differently by doctors. The procedures that trans patients seek were developed through nonconsensual surgeries and interventions enacted upon intersex patients.

And what about the role of religion? Feder reminds readers that, soon after World War II, there was immense pressure on Jewish people to assimilate. She writes at length about doctors' disgust projected onto children with atypical genitalia and links this to anti-semitism:[80]

> In the years after the revelation of the horrors of the Holocaust, [philosopher Eva] Kittay writes, "normality was deeply sought and deeply desired." The desire for normality was a kind of desperate and encompassing desire.... Internalizing this message despite or because of her differences as an immigrant, a Jew, and someone whose life was marked by her parents' horrible suffering, [Eva] Kittay remembers, "I desired above all to be normal, to be like everyone else, to hide the pain of abnormality."[81]

It is not clear to me if Feder is suggesting that intersexuality is more prevalent among Jewish persons. However, she does indicate that the social conditions at the time of Sally's birth might have been marked by pressure to assimilate to social standards of normativity. Like Sally, Feder's intersex case study, Andie, was circumcised, but unlike Sally, Andie was subjected to multiple genital surgeries in the years to come. Andie's story contextualizes the fear of difference that might prompt life-threatening prejudice within post–World War II societies, especially for Jewish persons. It is noteworthy that Sally did not identify as an intersex person who had been subjected to medical "normalizing" procedures because she distinguished these from her having been circumcised in accordance with Jewish custom. Certainly, there are advocates, Jewish and not, who understand circumcision to be harmful. Health insurance providers that classify circumcision as an elective procedure do not cover the cost. Consequently, some parents opt for a mohel and others forgo the procedure.

Feder became particularly interested in the fact that Andie's doctors were Orthodox Jews and speculated about the possibility that observance of Jewish law might have played a role in their treatment decisions. "The medical record [Andie] retrieved as an adult demonstrates that her doctors were cautious about surgical normalization."[82] Feder speculates that this conservative medical treatment plan might have been informed by Jewish law, namely the Halakhic obligation for husbands to provide *onah*—a broad term that includes sexual pleasure—for their wives. She explains:

> I wondered if it was possible that Andie's Orthodox physicians had engaged in a kind of Halakhic reflection regarding the "dilemma" presented by her body that was also an *ethical reflection* on her role—and theirs—in her treatment. The Halakhic proscription against bodily mutilation may well have provided some basis for caution in the performance of surgery in the absence of medical necessity. But there is also the distinctive place that ensuring a women's pleasure, including erotic pleasure, occupies as an integral component of the fulfillment of a husband's duties under Halakha. Might we find in her doctor's approach a model or framework that could provide resources in ethical decision making today?[83]

Andie's pediatric endocrinologist had died by the time Feder was having these thoughts, but Feder was able to speak with his brother, who denied religion would have influenced his diagnosis. Despite Feder's hope to glean an ethic of health care informed by Judaism, she found herself confronted with his insistence that religion ought properly to be relegated to the private sphere and admitted to a limited understanding of the *onah* tradition.

Elizabeth Reis also stresses the impact of World War II on medicine and Jewish people. In the wake of Germany's atrocious medical experimentation on Jews, the Nuremberg Code of 1947 set a new standard for researchers and physicians alike to obtain voluntary consent from patients.[84] Although three developments could have improved intersex medical care—the Nuremberg Code, the Declaration of Geneva, and a 1957 court case involving informed consent—Reis argues that "recent efforts to raise nonbinary children notwithstanding, the gender binary still constitutes 'normal,' a seductive standard to which most parents and physicians aspire," which adversely affects intersex persons.[85] In 2017, Edmund Horowicz published his argument for a shared decision-making approach to support the welfare of intersex children by placing them as the primary decision-makers.[86] He reports that, at present, both domestic English law and international law do not protect intersex children or their human rights.[87]

In addition to curbing aggressive surgeries, Sally prioritized educating the public about intersexuality to ease the isolation and shame that intersex persons suffer. The first draft of South Africa's Civil Union Bill (2006) placed intersex people in a predicament because those in intimate relationships were technically neither heterosexual nor same-sex couples. Consequently, intersex persons were more susceptible to isolation. Though she never pursued marriage, Sally elucidated the stakes: "In an urban context, being intersexed also makes it far more likely than otherwise that one is on the margins, alone and desperate and lonely. In these circumstances, being able to make a life in companionship with someone else is crucial to psychological survival and, at times of crisis or illness, can make the difference between surviving and going under."[88] It is hard to read this without recalling Sally's mental health struggles when she felt cut off from her clerical brethren. Sally supported marriage for the purpose of survival, which is markedly distinct from appeals to human rights rhetoric. To advocate for intersex persons' marriage was not, for Sally, to elevate that form of community above others. It was one of the many forms of disenfranchisement that intersex persons suffer and that Sally sought to redress.

According to Ellen Feder, medical interventions are the cause of isolation rather than prevention of it: "It's the treatment aiming to correct or conceal these conditions—that is, to 'normalize' their bodies—that resulted in their experience of 'isolation, stigma, and shame.'"[89] Historically, medical practitioners have frequently imposed surgical, hormonal, and psychological treatments upon intersex children without their consent. These same options are denied to trans youth. Taken together, this suggests that the institutional aims are to prioritize medical authority. Doctors and parents jump headlong into shaping intersex bodies into male or female but then refuse to support trans youth whose mental and physical health depends on such treatments.

Sally bumped between religious and medical bodies—institutions that sought to manage her flesh. Each problematized her body. She was inter-religious, conditionally white, and intersex. As she questioned the assumption that any of those attributes were problematic, it remained unclear to Sally whether these regulating social bodies were problems resolvable from within their structures or if they required dismantling. First, she would cloak herself in bodies of paperwork as a means of self-preservation before agitating for institutions to change.

5. Bodies of Paperwork

Disability is created by building codes and education policy, subway elevators that don't work and school buses that don't arrive, and all the marginalization, exploitation, demeaning acts, and active exclusions that deny full access and equality to "the disabled." —CHRISTINA CROSBY, *A Body, Undone*

In insisting that the letter on the birth certificate is the arbiter of sex, irrespective of one's genitals, sex becomes the property of a document rather than a body, a maneuver that I have explored in detail elsewhere. —GAYLE SALAMON, *The Life and Death of Latisha King*

Bureaucracy is a body of nonelected government officials or an administrative policymaking group notorious for paperwork. Rules, hierarchy, and procedures characterize it. Newspapers, medical forms, and legal documents make bodies legible. They write upon and shape bodies. Even personal correspondence in letter writing demonstrates ongoing efforts to name individual bodies and their place within collective bodies.

Regardless of whether she was emailing a friend or building a legal case, Sally understood the power of paperwork. After taking the name *Sally*, she had her identity documents, school degrees, and certificates reissued. These were hard-won accomplishments that ultimately did not resolve the pain she experienced as an intersex person. The papers written by and about Sally matter because they marked whether or not she mattered—her personhood, humanity, or lack thereof—and consequently determined her access to rights and privileges. Christina Crosby, quoted above, reveals that disability is a production of unjust paperwork. Gayle Salamon underscores the processes of ownership via documents. To varying degrees of success, Sally leveraged the power of paper in social, legal, and religious spaces to de-problematize her body. It was the seam both that confined her and that she pulled out of place to make room for new possibilities.

Tabloid

Sally forewarned Malcolm of possible press inquiries: "I left two messages on the answer-phone of the Dominican Prior Provincial to let him know that it was possible that the gutter-press was out hunting and to ask him to phone me urgently, and informed others who had a need to know. There was an oppressive sense of an impending storm."[1] The order tasked Father John Mills with managing public relations.[2] Mills's legacy in journalism is well documented; however, regarding this particular issue he fumbled several times.[3] Mills's documentation of conversations with reporters indicates that he was more forthcoming than Sally desired and sometimes misinformed the press with imprecise descriptions.[4]

Nine months into Sally's leave in Eastbourne, Father Mills wrote a letter marked "CONFIDENTIAL" to all the superiors in the United Kingdom "about: [Sally's former name]."[5] In it, he instructed each superior to designate a person at their religious house to handle press inquiries. It included a succinct account of Sally's biography, a list of topics to avoid, and a script of sample questions and answers. The suggested answers used he/his pronouns and contained misinformation.

It proved impossible to deter the press's attention. Her story was easy to sensationalize. A reporter named Stuart Qualtrough of *The People* went to great lengths to obtain information about Sally for a tabloid article. He titled his piece "Priest in Sex Swap" (1994). "A former Roman Catholic priest has confessed to wanting to become a woman," he wrote, "and is already living as one."[6] Qualtrough described Sally as a man with a booming voice wearing women's clothes and makeup. Sally took umbrage that Qualtrough wrongly suggested she was "really a man . . . living as a woman although I am not one and could never really be one."[7] Although Qualtrough was not the only reporter to leak Sally's story to the public, his egregious misrepresentation prompted Sally to issue legal complaints against him.[8]

At that time, Sally was in a precarious position. She was struggling to find work, was seeking medical care for physical disabilities and psychological support, and, having been dismissed from the order, was separated from her family and faith community. Qualtrough might not have grasped the grave risk that publishing Sally's story posed to her social and physical life. His article threw into question any tenuous claim she might have had on the Catholic Church for emotional and financial support. Her encounters with Qualtrough led to an intense downward psychological spiral for Sally. Presumably triggered by post-traumatic stress disorder from being nearly killed in Botswana, described in part III, Sally's lengthy letters to her legal counsel as well as to the defendant, even after all claims and appeals were denied, suggest that the tabloid articles reignited overwhelming concerns that her physical life was in danger, which in turn eroded her mental health.

A central reason for the press's interest in Sally was the public interest in women being ordained priests in the Catholic Church. Initially, the province's answer to whether, under canon law, Sally could function in extremis as a priest was to insist that Sally was anything other than male according to both canon and civil law. Sally thought this misrepresented her gender. Nearly a year after the article was published and Sally had been seeking legal recourse, she labored to explain why she was not technically a female priest. Even in severe circumstances especially at the point of death, she could not and would not perform any priestly function. This required explanation because typically, a male priest who is laicized can still act in extremis, but because, by definition, womanhood is incompatible with the priesthood within the Catholic tradition, it meant that she never was validly a priest. "The official position of the Roman Catholic Church is that women cannot be ordained to the priesthood **validly** and that there cannot, by definition, be such a thing as a woman priest."[9] This is another example of Sally's rigid adherence to technicalities.

On September 4, 1996, Sally wrote to Mills about his errors, stressing that transsexuality is a misclassification of her condition and her designation as female under civil law. Sally consistently appealed to bureaucratic technicalities as a method of self-preservation. Even though she cognitively knew these were systemic problems and hoped for a world more hospitable to biological diversity, Sally struggled to stave off self-harm ideation. A few days prior, she had written to her confidant Timothy.[10] Delayed by travel again, he replied with the encouraging suggestion that her ambiguity is part of who she is, and it is most central to her identity. "I was really sorry to hear of your terrible encounter with the press," he wrote. "I also give thanks to God that you exist.... You are a child of God and destined for the Kingdom."[11]

In her subsequent legal complaints, Sally laboriously recounted her version of events and provided a point-by-point commentary on each sentence of Qualtrough's article. The meticulous dossier included appendices and footnotes, a letter to the editor of *The People*, the breached Code of Practice, her commentary on how the story was obtained, photocopies of the article and her passport, personal medical information, and documents produced at the request of the Dominican Order. Sally also offered evidence of her "gender dysphoria" from childhood, a research paper on trans women being authentically female regardless of surgical intervention, and information on the congenital endocrinological and genital basis for her being female and having been misclassified at birth. She highlighted every inaccuracy in Qualtrough's timeline and events. The result was a large body of paperwork.

Sally argued that the story "involves prejudicial or pejorative reference to" her intersexuality, which was not in the public interest and therefore did not justify "the breaches of privacy, the misrepresentation and subterfuge, the harassment or the discrimination."[12] Needless to say, the complaint itself is exhausting. Sally alleged that Qualtrough violated clause 1 of the Code of Practice, "Accuracy"; clause 8, "Harassment"; clause 7, "Misrepresentation"; clause 18, "Privacy and the Public Interest"; clause 4, "Accuracy"; and so on. Locations, dates, and information contained in the article were incorrect. Mike Jempson, executive director of PressWise and advocate for Sally, wrote to the complaints director, "I doubt that you will have received so detailed and comprehensive a complaint (apart perhaps from the documentation associated with the *Business Age* story about the Queen's wealth), and I trust that this will help speed rather than delay adjudication in this case."[13] Her legal team counseled Sally to simplify her materials because the explanations were long and tiresome—an unruly excess.

The Press Complaints Commission's correspondence was drawn out and meandering. One letter suggests that claims are typically adjudicated within four weeks; however, Sally wrote back and forth with the commission for a year.[14] Len Gould, editor of *The People*, maintained that there had been no wrongdoing. Despite her frustration, Sally pressed on.

Sally submitted letters from medical professionals to verify her intersexuality. Dr. K. E. Leeson wrote, "This is to confirm that there is a question of intersex anomaly in the above patient. This is suggested by the low appearance of the external genitalia and the very low testosterone level that was recorded prior to commencement of oestrogen."[15] Fran attested, "Had this situation been evident at birth (and Ms Gross had been born at the present time) it is almost certain that she would have been assigned female at birth and undergone corrective surgery to confirm this. It is therefore my considered opinion that her South African documentation should be altered to reflect her female identity."[16]

To accurately represent herself within the order, Sally wrote to John Mills, "It has been pointed out to me that the indications are indicative of gonadal dysgenesis, and it is the view of both the people who have examined me that the gonadal structures are not what they were taken to be when I was born. It is highly likely that they are mixed."[17] Considering that Sally had already lost her clerical position in the church, there was no reason for her to feign intersexuality. And yet, church and state pressure to make her body legible prompted her to endure what she describes as humiliating medical exams to prove biological abnormality. These actions reveal her desperation—she thought her life hung in the balance if she did not clear her name.

On May 8, 1997, Joanna Low of the Press Complaints Commission wrote to Sally with the commission's assessment that the evidence against Qualtrough and *The People* was insufficient.[18] The Press Complaints Commission is not compelled to follow formal procedures or case law. Because of its informality, persuading the commission to change its decision would be very difficult. Herein lay Sally's ongoing frustration. She would adhere to policies and procedures as a method of self-protection. However, the persons within institutions often do not adhere to such procedures with rigorous consistency. Ever tenacious, Sally appealed the commission's decision. Sue Roberts, also of the Press Complaints Commission, replied that because there was no new evidence, they would not reconsider her complaint.[19] Even after her complaint and appeal were both rejected, Sally seemed compelled to continue pressing the issue. She detailed her persistent distress to her counsel and the defendant.[20]

For her part, it seems that if Sally could not persuade them with evidence, she would appeal to pathos.[21] Her catastrophic thinking suggests instability, mainly because, based on her internet sleuthing, she had pressed the doctors to diagnose her with acanthosis nigricans, which later turned out to be a self-misdiagnosis.[22] She had written to Mike Jempson about this medical concern, detailed her symptoms and diagnosis, speculated about being removed from the doctor's patient list, and panicked about possible scenarios.[23] These letters are unusual for including personal details about her state of mind and medical conditions. This speaks to her psychological distress. She had begun her complaints by delving into the intricacies of law. Now, she was detailing private health concerns, which was highly irregular and thus ineffective.

Sally forcefully assessed the tabloids: "They tend to target people without means and social influence, who are therefore unlikely to be able to [defend themselves] due to law."[24] She explained that the article reignited her post-traumatic stress disorder, which prohibited her from completing her doctoral thesis.[25] Eastbourne was no longer a safe space for her to explore her gender identity and the implications it had for her vocation. "The experience shook me to such a degree that I found that I could no longer work on my thesis, for which I had been able to produce more drafts of good quality in the three months which preceded the appearance of the story," Sally lamented. "Challenging the story through the Press Complaints Commission gobbled up a whole year of my life, and proved fruitless."[26] Sally had resolved to prioritize the reputation of the Catholic Church over her season for discernment. Tabloid reporters, unconcerned with her physical or emotional well-being, placed undue pressure on Sally to declare a definitive gender identity. There was no room for ambiguity, multiplicity, or gentle contemplation.

Gould responded to Sally's complaint and contested her right to privacy: "I do not think that a person's sex can be regarded as their 'private life' as clearly a person's sex—unless they are a total recluse—is visible to the world at large without 'enquiry of intrusion.' Therefore, anyone who knew Father Gross and subsequently met Sally Gross would realise that the former Catholic priest was now living as a woman."[27] Gould's statement demonstrates the assumption that a person's sex is self-evident and unwittingly acknowledges that this classification is integral to public life. It inadvertently admits that medicine, the church, and the state manage sex and gender. Society's intolerance for non-cis and nonbinary persons motivates the public's interest in the article. Mike Jempson agreed with Sally's position: "We can never know who is inter-sexual or trans-sexual just by looking at them."[28] Her adherence to paperwork and procedures offered no haven.

Discourse

Determining a person's sex simply by looking is not always straightforward, even for medical practitioners. Advancements in technology and medicine have complicated this matter further. Ongoing debates about the validity of Olympic athletes, such as South African Caster Semenya, are a case in point.[29] Alice Dreger's *Hermaphrodites and the Medical Invention of Sex* traces shifts in definitions of sex difference from gonadal to chromosomal distinctions to gender traits and even sexual orientation. Dreger writes:

> In medical practice sex seemed to slip and slide all over the body; in scientific and medical theory sex came to be limited successfully to tiny bits of tissue. Indeed, this classification system developed in direct response to the exigencies of hermaphroditism and especially in response to the pervasive interest among medical and scientific men in keeping social sex borders clear, distinct, and "naturally" justified.... Experts had to keep changing their definitions to stay ahead of the possibility of living "true" hermaphrodites.[30]

Philosopher Michel Foucault traces the historical shift in medicine when the body became an object for mapping.[31] As mentioned, Sally's intersexuality escaped the discursive discipline that produces two types of bodies—male and female. Foucault's *The Birth of the Clinic* historicizes shifts in medical history wherein doctors observed patients superficially to later pursue the "secret depth of the body"—making the invisible visible.[32] The "medical gaze," as he calls it, seeks sovereignty. Its power lies in the mastery of truth presumed to be self-evident in "nature."[33] The act of observing and speaking, according to Foucault, is the process of producing *being* through discourse.[34]

What this means for Sally is that her intersexuality did not exist within the church or state until a medical professional entrusted with the power to understand declared her so. Had she not subjected herself to these "dreadful" medical exams, her condition would not exist in their eyes, thereby invalidating her complaints against the tabloid. Sally's intersexuality was illegible to civil law apart from the authoritative gaze and diagnosis of medical doctors. Moreover, her diagnosis masks the actual ongoing processes within the body that produce sex throughout one's lifetime. When considered alongside Foucault's interrogation of "fixity" within the practice of medicine, the pressure to demarcate Sally's flesh as either male, female, trans, or intersex is itself a dubious social production.[35]

Intersex scholar Morgan Holmes understands intersexuality as a socially produced concept written upon bodies. She writes about the violent process of discourse shaping literal and social bodies:

> Physical violence, if we understand the surgical removal of healthy tissue from a child who cannot be consulted as merely one of the means

employed in this process of control and intervention, functions as part and parcel of medical *discourse* rather than as an isolated surgical *act*. Indeed, the (f)acts of medicine discussed in this book, from diagnostic categorization to surgical intervention, may all be interpreted as *inscriptions* onto bodies of particular forms of meaning that create as much as they discover. The material and symbolic management of intersexuality is therefore part of a larger field of cultural discourse and cultural demands.[36]

Too often, medicine is presumed to observe and describe phenomena objectively. Holmes and Foucault demonstrate that medical practitioners, to which I would add religious and civil authorities, form and ascribe value to bodies through discourse. Intersexuality is not a biological fact extant a priori. It is a category written upon bodies such that they become disenfranchised.

Holmes argues: "The biomedical approach may claim to provide a neutral, merely descriptive view of intersexuality, but the classification of difference as disease is not, in fact, a neutral activity; it is an ideologically loaded choice, because sex and gender norms function in the service of larger political demands," and "intersex is an actively produced category that has captured the abject fascination of medical practitioners since their rise as professionals in the nineteenth century."[37] Intersex scholar David Rubin nuances this point by countering "the popular misconception that gender's cultural construction is either a purely discursive or sociological process. Gender is literally inscribed into the flesh of situated bodies."[38] Drawing upon Anne Fausto-Sterling, Rubin explains the process of bureaucratic inscription: "[Sexual difference] is a material-semiotic practice, one that human institutions—western biomedicine and its globalizing cultural circuits of influence, in particular—inscribe onto bodies."[39]

For Holmes, the devotion to managing sex and gender can be attributed to power: "*Control* is an accurate description of the goals of the social and cultural systems of thought, of the linguistic constructions of subjects and identities, and of the actual physical interventions used to fashion both sex and gender. That this control is neither purely abstract nor metaphorical is important: it is often a physical and material imposition enforced through violent means."[40] While sex, sexuality, and gender are often presumed to be self-evident features to which individuals are privy, Holmes's analysis underscores the social and political processes that regulate individual bodies in service to collective ideologies, such as capitalism.

In the introduction to the memoirs of Adélaïde Herculine Barbin, Foucault describes the eighteenth-century medical insistence on uncovering the so-called true sex among intersex people: "He had, as it were, to strip the body of its anatomical deceptions and discover the one true sex behind organs that might have put on the forms of the opposite sex."[41] Ambiguity, Foucault explains, is presumed to be criminal. Underlying the imperative to demarcate bodies as either male or female is the assumption that sex difference reveals the essence of an individual. As with Foucault's broader corpus, he argues against psychoanalysis, which he associates with the notion that one's sex harbors the true self.[42] About Barbin's memoirs, Foucault writes, "And what she evokes in her past is the happy limbo of a non-identity, which was paradoxically protected by the life of those closed, narrow, and intimate societies where one has the strange happiness, which is at the same time obligatory and forbidden, of being acquainted with only one sex."[43] He continues, "The intense monosexuality of religious and school life fosters the tender pleasures that sexual non-identity discovers and provokes when it goes astray in the midst of all those bodies that are similar to one another."[44]

Lest we mistake this limbo for a pleasant state, David Rubin clarifies, "*Limbo/les/limbes* has a theological connotation (especially in the French): etymologically, 'limbo' means a state wherein one is at the edge of hell but locked out of paradise."[45] Perhaps the concept of purgatory accurately describes a state of liminality between heaven and hell. The refusal to participate in the production of identity wherein intersex persons are coerced into revealing their bodies to medical professionals endowed with the discursive power to define bodies is, according to Foucault, freedom. During these early years of navigating her intersexuality, Sally submitted to this process, wherein she proclaimed her "true sex" to be female within the church and state as authored by medicine.[46]

Many intersex persons today have also been rejected by religious communities, misunderstood by legal definitions, misdiagnosed by the medical community, impoverished, and left without robust social support networks. Sally's emotional nadir underscores the norms and practices that reduced her to a tender state. Georgian Davis describes having been told that she had underdeveloped ovaries that needed to be removed due to a high risk of cancer. Her doctors actually removed her undescended testes.[47] Hil Malatino criticizes "the repeated characterization of the medical practitioners able to green-light gender assignment technologies as saviors," as though they are "capable of bestowing life to people in dire existential circumstances, often shaped by grappling with suicide, poverty, social disenfranchisement, and significant quotidian violence."[48] Malatino argues that this and other tropes characterize a loss of faith in the capacities of medicine to aid rather than harm intersex persons. While Sally was not subject to gender assignment surgery, she did mistrust medical professionals, in part because they assigned her male at birth.

Identity Documents

Because she lacked references from her time in the order, employment remained elusive for Sally. She contemplated returning to her homeland. The ANC had been unbanned, which enabled her to restore her South African citizenship.[49] She discovered, however, that employment case law in South Africa entitled employers to dismiss her without notice or severance and without any possibility of redress simply due to her gender. Sally began the process of having her passport renewed. Not only was it about to expire, but it also described her as male and listed her former name.[50] This would have created problems for several reasons, not least that all her other documentation marked her as female. Below, I detail the paperwork that Sally submitted, not only to demonstrate her thorough case but also as another example of how she worked with bureaucratic systems as a method of self-preservation. She used the very systems that dehumanized and disenfranchised her to procure what she wanted.

The South African Department of Home Affairs determined that they could not issue Sally identity documents under any gender description. Sally interpreted this to mean that she could not get confirmation she had been born and thus had ceased to exist as a legal person. Legal scholar Julie Greenberg details the importance of one's legal sex as it relates to marriage, serving in the military, identity documents, public bathroom use, and housing: "These documents are used for a variety of purposes including security clearances, proof of identity in financial transactions, and proof of citizenship when crossing borders or applying for a job. Carrying documents that do not match the apparent sex of the holder can lead to embarrassment, denial of benefits, and other more severe consequences, such as detainment and incarceration."[51] Greenberg cites a 1967 US case in which "Dennis was neither a man nor a woman but was a combination of both. In other words, the court determined that Dennis, as a nonman/nonwoman, did not have the legal right to marry at all."[52] As mentioned earlier, to attain legal recognition of her sex, Sally submitted to two medical examinations, which she described as respectful but unpleasant.

The Board of Management of Home Affairs referred Sally to the Department of Health for advice. It was informally suggested that the matter could be resolved were she to have genital "disambiguation" surgery—either vaginoplasty or phalloplasty.[53] Her brow lifted, and her eyes widened in disbelief. She considered it an immoral suggestion for her to undergo dangerous and unnecessary surgery as a condition for having a valid legal identity. Sally drew a line in the sand. She would take legal action if this recommendation were put to her formally.[54] It was another instance of her intersexuality being misinterpreted as her being transgender. She was born intersex, not definitively male, and now presented as female. By contemporary definitions, that might be considered trans, but at the time, transitioning was often presumed to entail surgical intervention, without which she was not able to leverage laws about trans people to protect herself.

Preemptively, Sally wrote a précis for a barrister highlighting which sections of South Africa's Constitution and Bill of Rights pertained to her situation, who connected Sally with a prominent human rights lawyer for aid. Among the files on Gross's computer hard drive was a presentation for a Human Rights Law Conference titled "Intersex and the Law in Post-Apartheid South Africa: Executive Summary."[55] "After assessing her situation in light of the South African Constitution and Bill of Rights, Gross found that there was a case to be made and that a prominent human rights lawyer was likely to be interested in taking it up," Coan reports. "This possibility eventually helped concentrate official minds."[56] Next, Sally appealed to a government minister to plead her case and threaten further legal action. Sally gathered testimonies of her intersexuality to build her case. Intersex activist Mani Mitchell confirmed her intersexuality, as did renowned Oxford professors Sebastian Brock and Helen Brock.[57] In *Intersexuality and the Law: Why Sex Matters*, Greenberg details convergences and departures in legislating intersex and trans persons. She historicizes such requirements "that people with an intersex condition undergo gender transition, based on a similar requirement for transsexuals, even though gender transition for people with an intersex condition would be inappropriate in many circumstances. It was only after intersex advocates critiqued the new rules that appropriate changes were made."[58]

The process of rectifying her passport led to yet another problem. Sally had never been issued a birth certificate. Although she could not be sure, she wondered if her ambiguous genitalia played a role in this oversight.[59] Sally flew to Israel to visit her parents and to learn more about the details of her birth. Had her parents and the medical team been aware of any physical abnormality? Had there been intentional deception or a lack of information? Her mother waved her hand in the air, as if to push the questions aside, and her father changed the subject. No matter how intense Sally's curiosity, she relented. "I found that difficult," she stated, "but felt, given their age and health, it was not prudent to push the matter. But whatever happened, I am profoundly grateful I was spared surgery and was brought up in a way which left me pretty unneurotic about my body, all things considered, and that, I believe, is quite an extraordinary achievement. And the one thing which I certainly never had any reason to doubt was my parents' love."[60] Their eyes filled with warmth and their small gestures, a pat on the hand or a tender remark, reminded Sally that their love outweighed her desire for clarity.

Ultimately, she succeeded in obtaining a South African passport under the name Sally, issued on April 25, 1999, and again on February 11, 2008. "Receipt of the letter stating that I was a [South African] citizen," she wrote, "Taking possession of my South African passport and Identity Document were deliriously joyous occasions."[61] She had her bachelor of arts diploma in philosophy and theology and master of arts from Oxford University reissued in her name on June 19, 1995. A letter from Oxford University dated May 28, 2008, was addressed to "Ms Gross."[62] The South African Department of Health ordered Sally's birth register classification to be updated on the grounds that the original had been erroneous. For the first time, Sally held documentation that stated she was born female.[63] As momentous as she found the occasion, it was soured by all it took to obtain these documents. She felt that her legal personhood had long been denied.[64] Each piece of paperwork was hard-won. They afforded Sally some power to combat institutions, which tend to, at best, ignore and, at worst, harm intersex persons. Hers was a constant battle to survive spiritually, physically, and socially.

6. Bodies of Land

The U.S.-Mexican border es una herida abierta where the Third World grates against the first and bleeds. And before a scab forms it hemorrhages again, the lifeblood of two worlds merging to form a third country—a border culture. —GLORIA ANZALDÚA, *Borderlands*

And if you defile the land, it will vomit you out as it vomited out the nations that were before you. —LEVITICUS 18:28

What do individual human bodies have to do with bodies of land, social bodies, or political bodies? Care for the land, or lack thereof, has consequences. Carving up territories harms bodies and relations. Our relationships with places inform how we understand ourselves and others. Sally's body politics granted her access to some privileges, but those were contingent because her body did not align with institutional structures. Her particular body shaped her relationship to specific places at significant historical moments. This chapter meditates on how those around her read Sally, how her privileges were granted then revoked, and how her access to mobility shifted as she pursued good relations with the land.

The concepts I am working with here are abstract. The results are opaque for some because they are rooted in Indigenous epistemologies and scholarly theories. The struggle to understand oneself as obligated to cultivate good relations with the land points to the mechanisms driving problem bodies. That is why embracing the challenge of thinking, feeling, and relating differently with the land is worthwhile.

Supposed problem bodies bear the scars inflicted by regulating bodies. There is an intimate connection between individuals, governments, and the land. We form an ecology. Scars point to histories of harm both personal and political. Jewish studies scholar Julia Watts Belser analyzes the meaning of Rabbi Tsadok's body in Bavli Gittin (a part of Jewish legal canon) to argue that the political and cultural significance of a scarred Jewish body signifies "the cultural logic of imperial victory, emphasizing the subversive power of disabled Jewish flesh."[1] Although written about a distinct time and place, her analysis is helpful for our reception of Sally. Instead of imagining the human body as a sovereign individual separate from nature, Belser understands interconnections with the land, which "itself becomes a repository for the materiality of rabbinic memory" and through which she reads "the cultural grammar of conquest."[2] Belser argues that while "subjugated bodies bear the material costs of opposition to the imperial project, these very bodies can also become potent sites of resistance, sites through which communities can critique Roman power and dominance—and also articulate the subversive potency of the unruly, dissident body that refuses to perform as desired beneath the imperial regime."[3]

Our individual bodies attest to the social and political bodies we inhabit. They tell stories of colonization. Sally's unruly body was injured, and her self-described disabled body bore the scars of social and political imperialism like Apartheid—these are cultural grammars of conquest. Settler colonial bodies have historically exploited Indigenous bodies—living and nonliving, human and nonhuman. Within this framework, people are deemed problematic if recalcitrant. So long as they serve the interests of governing bodies, which are most often driven by hunger for capital, Indigenous persons and nonpersons have a legible place within political bodies—hence the insidious term "noble savage." A land and people are moralized depending on how much they submit to settler colonizers.[4]

By taking nonhuman bodies more seriously, we might appreciate Sally's nonbinary body. Anthropologist Elizabeth Povinelli's scholarship has transformed my imagination. She writes that Tjipel is a creek that was once a woman.[5] Her statement perplexes the Western mind. Does she romanticize animism? No. Povinelli explains that Indigenous Australians ask Tjipel about her directionality (the course along which she was moving), her connections (to bodies of land), and perhaps more importantly, how and why she responded to different people and human actions—either giving or withholding fish. What matters is that Tjipel changes the arrangement of her existence either toward humanity or withdrawing her resources away from it. If her resources are exploited, the creek Tjipel will remain in a different form. She might dry up, but she will not be extinguished. Povinelli's critique of neoliberal economics illuminates Indigenous Australian innovative maneuvers against the settler state. Throughout her book, she unsettles colonial categories, epistemology, and ontology. Her insights are helpful if we are to be changed by Sally's story.

Like most subjects, Sally vacillated between privileged and disenfranchised status within various nation-states depending upon whether her body served or disrupted institutional bodies. Regardless of her awareness or intentions, her body was read and written upon as threatening or accommodating. Presenting in a male role granted S. access to exclusive spaces from which she would later be barred in a female role. When classified as white, she benefited from systemic racism. However, her Jewish identity rendered her affiliation with whiteness tenuous. Like bodies of land reshaped by bodies of water, her body was not a fixed essence. At a significant personal loss, Sally dedicated her life to advocating for the marginalized, whomever they may be, from one context to the next. We might read her subjugation as a potent site of resistance to powers that seek to regulate race and gender. Like the creek Tjipel, the arrangement of her existence changed, either toward or away from collective bodies, depending upon their rapport. Rather than submitting to institutions that regulate individuals into a homogenous and docile collective, our aim is to nurture biological diversity and good relations.

Sally waded into these choppy waters. Regardless of her position of privilege or precarity, she consistently advocated for justice. Despite being told that she was a rightful heir to the Holy Land in Israel or desirable property in South Africa, Sally recognized the costs for Palestinians and "Coloured" South Africans. Her work within government organizations and agitation as an activist was aimed at disrupting harmful relations between human bodies and bodies of land. It is significant that upon her return to South Africa as an adult, Sally's work entailed returning "Coloured" South Africans to their land in District Six, which I detail later. Although many Westerners are unfamiliar with reflecting on their relationship with bodies of land as significant or something other than self-serving, I believe Sally's rapport with the land is significant and takes on distinct forms depending on her context. Zionism and Apartheid are but two examples of the stakes for her. This chapter examines her complex relations with land as social and political.

Though infamous, South Africa is not alone in its management of bodies, human and nonhuman. Sally's visits to Israel reveal controversial claims to land rooted in appeals to religious heritage. Her trip to Brooklyn, New York, would bring to the surface both Black Americans and Orthodox Jews understanding themselves as rightful heirs to the biblical promise that God made to Moses when he liberated the Hebrews from slavery under Pharaoh. Whom did *God* choose to inhabit lands of milk and honey? Secular collective bodies also enter the fray—redlining privileges whiteness and wealth with access to valued neighborhoods.[6] Beneficiaries of redlining in the United States need not fear pipelines uprooting their communities' long-nurtured relationships to land.[7] Some bodies are presumed to possess the earth as property, while people are either exploitable resources or, worse, pests to be driven out. The children of the latter are especially vulnerable to disciplinary education and assimilation through adoption.[8] Like us all, Sally was shaped by the land from which she came and by those to which she traveled. Their histories and politics shaped her, but not to the extent that she would quietly accommodate injustice.[9]

Linksfield Ridge

S. was born in 1953 in Wynberg, a suburb of Cape Town nestled beside coastal mountains on the southern tip of Africa. The hills of myrtle and oak trees provide shelter against harsh weather. Dutch settlers forced out the Khoikhoi people native to this region. British settlers brought additional competition for the bucolic land. By 1795, the British had gained control of the Dutch settlement and developed it into a town. Gradually, schools, churches, and a military base crowded the countryside. Wynberg became a convenient midpoint for commercial activity between Table Bay and False Bay where travelers restocked supplies before continuing to Europe or India.

A few years after her birth, the Gross family moved to the Johannesburg suburb of Linksfield, where their flat sat below a north-facing slope. Venomous creatures, including scorpions, puff adders, and cobras, lived on the ridge. Dense trees and shrubs blanketed the northern slope, whereas aloes and protea flowers spilled down the south side. "The ridge was also inhabited by a black hermit, a man who doubtless took refuge there from the endless pass-raids, humiliations and risks to life and limb which Apartheid forces upon its victims," S. later recalled in a sermon.[10] Pass laws monitored and restricted the movement of Black people in South Africa, and under Apartheid, people of color were forcibly removed from their homes and ghettoized.[11] She remembered, "My friends and I would sometimes play on the ridge, and we would occasionally glimpse the hermit in his white robes. As a child I imagined that he believed that the end of the world was coming, and that he was wild-eyed and deluded."[12]

Though she could not make sense of it as a child, the injustices the Black hermit suffered would stay with S. for decades to come. "I daresay the police eventually screwed up enough courage to brave the snakes and scorpions in order to imprison him for living in a 'white group area,'" she went on, "and that he ended up spending time working on a farm-prison and was eventually 'resettled' in one of the starvation-ridden dumping grounds the government of South Africa calls 'the black homelands.'"[13] As an adult, Sally would work for South Africa's Land Claims Commission to redress these injustices that had perplexed her as a child.

When her brother Ray returned to South Africa for the first time in thirty-seven years to take care of Sally's deceased body, he was flooded with memories of how space had been racially regulated. He walked streets once familiar, now in a state of what he called postcolonial decay. As Ray passed cricket and rugby grounds, he thought about a Black child who sold peanuts out front. Once, the police spoke harshly with the boy and kicked him around. Ray defended him. Without regard for histories of rapport between people groups and places, the government carved up the land into residences for white, so-called Coloured, or Black people. Indigenous persons were displaced. The most desirable plots were accessible only to whites, which, you may recall, Jews were only provisionally categorized as.

It was not unusual for police officers to assault or harass Black people during Apartheid. Entering a residential neighborhood, Ray recalled seeing an old African man drape his jacket on a veranda and sit on some steps with a cold drink in hand. A police wagon screeched to a stop in front of the man and demanded to see his pass. When he stood up to reach for his jacket, the police stopped him. They arrested him. Apartheid had ended decades prior to Ray's return, but so much felt exactly as Ray remembered it.[14] The land and space remembered the racialized and gendered management of bodies. Scars and traces were pointing to ongoing harm.

Redistribution

Following South Africa's first democratic election in 1994, violence escalated around the country—especially homicide on farms. As unemployment soared, the deprivation of material needs led to alcohol and drug dependency. Crime reports indicated that victims were predominantly white Afrikaners and implied that the attacks were politically motivated. Some believed that renegade armed guerrillas were behind the murders.[15] They interpreted these events as retaliation for decades of exploitation and abuse under the Apartheid regime. Others more overtly accused the ANC of producing a spike in violent crime. Repeated dislocation bred revolutionary violence targeted at farms in the Western Cape.[16]

The transition to democracy did not quiet attacks, partly because many families still awaited land restoration. The Apartheid government had dislocated designated Black and "Coloured" people from their land. Desirable locations were legally accessible only to designated white people. The move to democracy brought these histories of violence to the fore. Would there be land restitution and reparations? White, Afrikaans-speaking farmers claimed to be frequent victims of grievous bodily harm, sexual assault, and homicide. Although South Africa's new progressive policy promised to redress matters, it offered a minor reprieve from centuries of exploitation.

In 1998, Pan Africanist Congress (PAC) president Stanley Mogoba reportedly stated that if land reparations were not issued, people experiencing poverty would grab land unsystematically.[17] President Nelson Mandela's Rural Protection Plan reportedly mitigated violent crime against farmers.[18] Unfortunately, sensationalized news reports exacerbated racial tensions and political instability. Journalist Rian Malan, for example, represented Afrikaners as a persecuted minority suffering ethnic cleansing.[19] The South African Police Service website's crime report stated, "It is also clear that the ongoing attacks have created [and are] still creating perceptions regarding a conspiracy to drive farmers from their land through a campaign of violence and intimidation verging on terrorism."[20] Land Affairs and Agriculture minister Derek Hanekom said criminality, not politics, was the primary motivation behind the attacks. Free State PAC chairman Mofihli Likotsi pointed to the murders of Black and Indian farmers.[21] This was the political climate to which Sally returned in the late 1990s.

After being pushed out of priesthood in England, Sally went to work for the South African government, researching the politics of land. She was assigned to investigate whether these were retributive crimes connected to the country's broader history of racial injustice. Sally found that attacks, as well as evictions and harassment of Black rural inhabitants and farm workers, were significantly underrepresented. The issue of land reform, which is inextricable from evictions, also had been neglected. In addition, most of the evidence, Sally explains, points overwhelmingly to robbery as the primary motive—not politics. To rectify gaps and inconsistencies in previous reports, Sally conducted case studies aimed at interrogating the unacknowledged background of rural violence in relation to the attacks.[22]

Accounts of Sally's time working in the South African Land Claims Commission vary. According to six sources, Sally never worked quietly. Donning bright green-and-orange kaftans, she would bellow into the phone: "It is *Ms.* Gross, not Mister. I am a woman, not a man!"[23] Claimants displaced by Apartheid would arrive at the office to meet with her and have a fright. White colleagues spoke affectionately of her, especially concerning Sally's quirks. A few described her with the idiom "She could talk the hind legs off a donkey."[24] During long meetings, Sally would pull out a two-liter bottle of soda and make her way through bottomless snacks. Sally worked to reunite people with their land, but her ample body in a female presentation distracted and offended some.

It did not help that if someone irritated her, Sally would whip out of her office, walking cane in hand, and thwack it on a table to emphasize her shouting.[25] The rest of the office would roar with laughter as Sally ambled after someone down the corridor. They had all learned to move aside when she was cross because her logic was that if they got in the way of her cane, it was their fault. Amazingly, her colleague Michael Worsnip explained, no one brought charges against her for barreling out of her office wielding her cane.[26]

The Land Claims Commission office employees came from diverse backgrounds, cultures, first languages, and ages that might have shaped their varied responses to Sally. Her colleague David Smit explained that Sally's crisp English accent and high level of education stood out among the mostly Afrikaans- and Xhosa-speaking coworkers. If she found an error, rather than simply flagging it, Sally would write pages commenting on the methodology and arguing about necessary changes. Her coworkers were overwhelmed by her lengthy instructions. David describes having to boil her concerns down into bullet points to assist colleagues in understanding how to be in compliance.

Many of the Black and Coloured coworkers who were significantly younger than Sally genuinely feared her. Regardless of racial labels, those I interviewed who were similar in age to Sally or older were emboldened to stand up to her outbursts. David Smit and Benjamin Mars are people of color, and Daniel Malan Jacobs and Michael Worsnip are white men; all described the imperative to establish firm boundaries with Sally and push back when she cursed or shouted at them.[27] According to David, "She would start to swear at me, and I would say this is not going to work. She chased a lot of people out of the office. We agreed on boundaries, and it worked.... I said you're not going to swear at me, intimidate me, or shout at me anymore."[28]

Younger coworkers (and, I speculate, women) also might have avoided interacting with Sally due to feeling intimidated by her. I include this because it is relevant within the political climate of an office dedicated to restoring land rights to Coloured people whom Apartheid forcibly moved. Benjamin Mars's family was a victim of the Forced Removals Group Areas Act, for example. His work in the office is inseparable from his embodied life experiences, in which his grandfather, father, aunts, and uncles were among the 153 households in District Six affected. It might explain why most coworkers maintained a frosty relationship with Sally, to borrow David's description.[29] Sally seems to have been oblivious to her privilege as white, educated, and older than some colleagues. David also pointed out that Sally was an outspoken atheist at the time and that religious coworkers might have feared the unknown rather than asking her what that meant for her.

It is worth pausing here to clarify that many religious people identify as atheists. The assumption that one believes in God is particular to specific groups, often Protestant Christians, and certainly is not a requirement for most people born into a religious culture. The definition of God is itself highly contested and nuanced among religious folks. Disagreement over what distinguishes a holy person from a deity or monotheism from the doctrine of the Trinity, for example, accounts for the great variety of schools of thought within religions. For example, the difference between calling a Hindu statue an idol or an icon has immense ramifications. How we imagine religious traditions is often filtered through worldviews and languages that, in an attempt to categorize and make sense of difference, too often assimilate features to familiar concepts and therefore misrepresent them through terms like *God, gods, prophet, guru, master, angel, saint, idol, charlatan, demon, witch, monster,* and so on. Also, you will see below that a different Christian coworker perceived Sally to be very spiritual because she meditated over her lunch breaks and enjoyed theological discussions. Sally remained immersed in religious communities and practices throughout her life, which I interpret as thoroughly embedded within religiosity. Often, this did not entail theism, which she was correct to point out is not central to Buddhism. As religious studies scholar Sarah Imhoff persuasively argues, "seemingly unorthodox approaches to religion can go hand in hand with a single, strong religious identity—and ultimately that these combinations and recombinations aren't all that unusual."[30]

Benjamin Mars praised Sally's intellectual contributions to the commission. He observed that while some were thrown by the dissonance in her deep voice and bright kaftans, she remained confident and won most people over with her unique competency layered by empathy. David Smit confirmed that sometimes people would privately express to him, as a manager, their unease with Sally. They wondered how Michael Worsnip could feel comfortable being alone with her. Michael was in a relationship with someone else, and his relationship with Sally was professional. According to his memory, even "macho Xhosa blokes" in the office, who were unsettled by his being gay, appeared to have no issue with Sally.[31] Conversely, David described some of the discrimination Sally suffered when a claimant became frustrated that, despite her deep phone voice, she was a woman. Sally challenged the claimant to visit the office and see for himself.[32] He was shocked by her appearance and demanded answers from David: "You are sending this *thing* to me; I am not sure if it is a man or a woman."[33]

For many, Sally was difficult to accept and understand. Benjamin remembers Sally being socially isolated and leading a lonesome, insular life. Whenever colleagues were discussing their weekend or holiday plans, Sally spoke of reading a good book in the company of her cat.[34] The intensity of the work took a heavy toll on Sally's health. David described a shift in contracts and said that by the time Sally left their office, she did not qualify for a pension.[35] She was angry, but David stood firm that the commissioner could not break the rules for her no matter how unfair she thought them.[36] David tells me that after her father died, Sally asked for the standard five days for bereavement, but because these coincided with two days of a Jewish holiday, she requested a total of seven days off. He thought this preposterous and laughed: "You've been abusing me for years; you're an atheist and want a Jewish holiday, and you are not speaking to your father but want bereavement time off. No."[37] While her abrasive conduct with colleagues was unacceptable, she was also on the receiving end of unsympathetic words. Daniel Malan Jacobs paints a picture in which Sally regularly closed her door during lunch breaks to practice Buddhist meditation and was deeply concerned about her father's well-being.[38]

Benjamin recalled with warm affection his lunch breaks with Sally, where they would discuss family, religion, and gender. From Benjamin's perspective, Sally saw him as a fundamentalist Christian, so the two would have heated discussions about salvation, justification, and life after death. Though they held oppositional perspectives, he remembers their relationship as one of mutual respect. Benjamin also pointed to her relationship with Daniel, a traditional Calvinist Afrikaner, who could profoundly relate with Sally despite his markedly different background and political commitments. She could discuss Islam, Buddhism, Hinduism, Judaism, Catholicism, and Protestantism with ease; she had an inquiring mind and enjoyed the journey of exploration rather than making truth claims, according to Benjamin.

When Sally took a position at the Regional Land Claims Commission, she stepped into the complex workings of restoration.[39] In a sense, her work sought to right relations with the land. There are three components to land reform in South Africa—redistribution, tenure reform, and restitution. Apartheid stripped designated nonwhite people of their land and property under the Group Areas Act enacted in 1950. By the 1970s, more than sixty thousand inhabitants of Cape Town were forcibly removed from what is known as District Six.[40] South Africa's 1996 Constitution gave people and communities who had been dispossessed of their land (after June 19, 1913, when the Natives Land Act passed 87 percent of land to white South Africans as a result of racially discriminatory laws or practices) the right to restitution of that property or to fair compensation. They only had until December 1998 to lodge their claim for restoration with the Land Claims Commission. The Land Claims Court would hear disputes arising from the Restitution of Land Rights Act 22 of 1994 and the Land Reform (Labor Tenants) Act 3 of 1996.

At the Regional Land Claims Commission, Sally managed some of the largest outsourced projects, including the Cape Metro and the District Six Tenants validation projects.[41] She also became the research coordinator for the Protea Village Community Claim. According to Sally, her report was crucial to the judgment of the Land Claims Court, which favored the claimants despite challenges from locals. Until then, her colleagues were frequently appointed short-term contracts and thus did not have pensions or many legal safeguards against exploitation. Once it was determined that permanent positions were being treated as short-term contracts, the arrangement was deemed improper. Their contracts were converted to standard public service positions. Although this established pensions, it also dropped salaries by approximately 30 percent.[42]

Sally's responsibilities multiplied as her income declined. She described the economic effects in an email to friends.[43] Daniel Malan Jacobs confirmed such changes, which he witnessed in his twenty-one years working for the Land Claims Commission. He explained that the workload became insufferable, partly due to bureaucratic inefficiencies that measured performance according to flat numbers of completed claims regardless of whether it was simple or complex, whether it took one day or three months to complete.[44]

When Sally became a research and policy advisor, she worked under Jennifer Williams—the same person who later discovered Sally's corpse.[45] When the two first met, Sally walked directly up to Jennifer and said in her low voice: *Hello, you are going to be my boss.* Jennifer admits that she assumed Sally was a man in drag. Sally swiftly disabused Jennifer of her misconception concerning her gender, and the two became fast friends. Jennifer later served as an original board member of Sally's nongovernmental organization, Intersex South Africa. Jennifer encouraged Sally to offer her insight into complex cases. This freedom resulted in Sally's developing software-based systems that became standard instruments within the commission nationally. Sally created templates for evaluating settlement claims, deliverables from service providers, business plans, and so on. David Smit, who served as the director of operational management for the Land Claims Commission, presented a printout of the Monetary Values of a Claim (MVOC) Escalation Calculator to me, boasting that the office still uses the program Sally developed. The program assists in calculating the value of the land from which people were dispossessed in light of inflation.[46] Her work aimed to reunite people with land.

Sally drafted policy documents, correspondence for the Chief Commission, responses to ministerial inquiries, and submissions for the Parliamentary Portfolio Committee. She was frequently assigned to complex claims due to her reputation for diligent work and high intelligence. Jennifer tells me that Sally was called to testify in a court case. Someone from the Queen's Council cross-examined Sally, and she proved unflappable. Sally offered a clear and persuasive explanation for each question, favoring the dispossessed party. Eventually, the junior counsel tugged his superior's coat and implored him to sit down. Sally's testimony was weakening their case.[47] Michael Worsnip, however, had a less laudatory version of events in which he described Sally's nonbinary (my word) appearance to be an unwelcome distraction in the courtroom.[48]

Several participants I interviewed observed Sally's mobility deterioration, especially during her final two years at the Land Claims Commission in 2009–10. "The work, which was intense, took a heavy toll on my health," she explained. "Over the years, my mobility deteriorated inexorably to the point where I was unable to walk or stand for long enough to use public transport."[49] Initially, she was able to walk at a brisk pace, but over time, she toddled slowly with the aid of a cane. Multiple sources stated that

Ronald Buthelezi drove Sally around regularly.[50] As Benjamin remembers it, there was an ongoing joke about him driving Miss Sally—a reference to the film *Driving Miss Daisy*.[51] Likewise, Eugene van Rooyen taxied Sally about Cape Town.

Her disability was another sticking point for David, who remembered her claiming that a vehicle was too high for her to climb into. Despite the inconvenience, he sent for a van. Sally explained that she could not fit in the van seats. Exasperated, David asserted: "I'm sick and tired of your nonsense. Are you going to stand there all day?"[52] David found Sally to be extremely difficult. From his perspective, she wanted disability services but never produced the necessary paperwork from a doctor. He recalls her wanting to be lifted onto a plane and getting angry when that was not organized, so she had to hobble on.[53] The extent of Sally's needs in relation to David's reluctance to provide accommodations is difficult to adjudicate. However, between her experiences with the Catholic Church and her South African government job, she might have learned some hard lessons in bureaucracy that prepared her for starting a nongovernmental organization.[54] David expressed his awareness that she felt mistreated and underappreciated, especially by the new hires in their department. Hardly a blameless figure, Sally was both abused and abusive within this work environment. This misery in the office and in rectifying state wrongs, Daniel speculated, fueled Sally to start up the Intersex Society of South Africa.[55] Establishing good relations with the land entailed transforming public policy.

Body Aches

Like many ANC activists after the transition to democracy, Sally was disappointed to see what unfolded. Activists did not support all the initiatives and policies that the ANC put in place, and many felt that those in leadership positions failed to curb corruption within the party. It was not the dream they had been striving to actualize. According to Benjamin, Sally did thorough, pioneering work at the Land Claims Commission, "lots of groundbreaking, spade work that we still use today. She took pride in her work and was willing to share her findings."[56] David explained that the ANC members who took credit and were given leadership positions were not the activists working on the ground for change. Many people felt betrayed, he explained. Those late to join the cause jumped on the bandwagon and claimed the benefits. In his estimation, Sally had made sacrifices and thought she merited appointment to a higher position.[57]

It is apparent that Sally was struggling with feeling out of place on all sides—from her biological, spiritual, and activist families. By chance, the office learned that one of their coworkers was, in fact, Sally's biological cousin. Coworkers were unaware of this because he did not acknowledge her as such, except years into her work there, and only to make disdainful remarks about her shift to female presentation.[58] Ray attributes the cousin's scorn to his Jewish beliefs. Ostracization stoked Sally's longing to see her father Jack, in Israel, more often, though she could not afford it.

As with most people with whom she conversed until her death, Sally expressed to her coworkers the pain of having been cut off from the Catholic Church. It seemed that at every turn, her immense contributions and labor did not outweigh the anxiety people experienced about her body—she was not distinctly male or female, and this troubled family, religious folks, and progressive government employees. Daniel speculates that the emotional toll of her isolation exacerbated Sally's temper: "A big part of her bad relations was because she was physically ill from stress at work and with family; she was physically worn out."[59] Benjamin also speculated that Sally's mood swings may have resulted from hormone therapy.[60]

Along with others, David recalls Sally not being adept at managing money: "[Food] delivery was here every day. She was using a meter taxi to and from work; it was a lot of money. Why don't you use dial-a-ride?"[61] Benjamin similarly observed a dissonance between Sally's self-proclaimed frugality and consistent expenditure on food. She did not dress elaborately or crave expensive items, but day to day she did not appear to be mindful of restricting her cash flow.[62] Daniel also noticed the frequency with which Sally purchased prepared food, followed by requests for funds to support her. I wonder if Sally experienced their disapproval as ableist and fatphobic, though those terms might be anachronistic.[63]

It seems likely that she splurged on taxis and food delivery because of her physical limitations. Sally was never able to drive due to near blindness in one eye and her increased struggle to walk. Toward the end of her life, she emailed Daniel: "It would indeed be good to meet up for coffee. I do need to warn you, though, that my mobility is significantly more limited than before—I cannot manage more than a few meters without risk. For some time, even small physical efforts such as walking a few meters have triggered attacks of angina."[64] Necessary tasks like getting to and from work and feeding herself were a great burden. Perhaps to avoid asking colleagues to drive her more than they already did, she opted to pay for these services, but then she had to face the judgmental glances.

A former member of the Afrikaner Broederbond, a secret all-male Afrikaner Calvinist group committed to advancing their own interests that peaked during Apartheid, Daniel Malan Jacobs explained that the reason he was able to befriend Sally—a Communist, ANC activist, and Jewish atheist—was in large part due to her being a sad figure. Certainly, she was intelligent and endlessly fascinating. She enriched his life as a colleague and friend. But the main substance of their relationship, he stressed, was his compassion for her sadness. He explained, "I have never had contact with anyone else in my life that needed compassion as much as Sally."[65] Daniel conceded that she could be very rude and that the commission did not always treat her fairly, but, in her totality, she was a good person.

There were times when Sally attributed her combative qualities to her culture. Were a passerby to witness Sally speaking with brother Ray and father Jack at the breakfast table, they might think the family was quarreling, but that was just their way, she once explained to Daniel. Dissatisfied with this explanation, he pressed Sally to conduct herself with more restraint. One clash stood out to Daniel. As their argument heated, he suddenly caught a glimpse of deep sadness in her eyes and stopped himself. With purposeful eye contact, he reassured her, "I love you."[66] He sensed that he had to turn the conversation around. Although there were many occasions in which he felt she was out of order, ultimately, Daniel learned from Sally a lesson in common humanity regardless of religion or background. Their friendship surpassed political and religious boundaries, and together, they formed a bond that concretely confirmed for Daniel that people can love one another amid profound disagreement.

The friendship went both ways, of course. Unlike most of their colleagues, Daniel did not seek out his position at the Land Claims Commission. Daniel's father was a minister in the Dutch Reformed Church, his sister married a farmer, and his name, Malan, hails from Daniel François Malan, the prime minister of South Africa from 1948 to 1954, early Apartheid years. In a way, he and his family were the enemy against which the Land Claims Commission was working. His namesake did not go unnoticed among claimants and colleagues. He had been invited to work there due to his research skills, having been trained as an historian and archivist—not because of a political commitment to post-apartheid land restitution. No one mistreated him at work, Daniel assured me. But it seems he and Sally formed a sort of outsider friendship. He candidly admitted that, at first, Sally appeared male to him. With time, that faded. Daniel began to see her female qualities as coherent with rather than contrasting her body. He learned a great deal from her about intersexuality.

Daniel explained that he supported Sally's intersex activist pursuits because she looked profoundly worn down at the Land Claims Commission. He recalled concerning results from her blood tests, which revealed life-threatening medical conditions. Daniel said he felt their manager, David, was insensitive to Sally's health concerns. To make his point, Daniel told a story about a colleague who was diagnosed with schizophrenia. Upon returning to the office just days after being in a psychiatric ward, the employee was instructed to complete her work without accommodation.[67] From Daniel's perspective, Sally was put in some similarly impossible positions and ultimately became a scapegoat. He feared that the job would be the death of her and thus encouraged her risky move to found Intersex South Africa (ISSA). Daniel forwarded an email from Beverly Jansen dated January 7, 2011, in which she announced that she and others, including Sally, would not renew their contracts at the end of March. Several employees seemed ready to transition jobs as Sally became more invested in establishing a South African branch for intersex activism.

In retrospect, the Black hermit who once perplexed S. as a child might have informed her work at South Africa's Land Claims Commission to redress the injustices of pass raids and the Group Areas Act. Additionally, her time in the West Bank and her Palestinian friends discussed in part III likely shaped her perspective on this knotty return to land. Personal experience ignited her passion for activism. When Sally went to apply for medical aid, which the government was seeking to make obligatory at the time, her intersexuality exposed the limitations of the process. She identified the loopholes in law regarding intersex persons and sought to rectify them. Sally generously attributed these shortcomings to ignorance rather than ill will. It was a time of optimism for her. South Africa was making radical political changes that fueled her trust in bureaucratic systems to be redirected such that they would advance social justice. It was not within her to advocate merely for herself. Sally wanted to make impactful changes to government policies internally.

Joerstad's and Povinelli's books assist us in seeing Sally's government work as an effort to restore right relations between problem bodies and bodies of land through bodies of paperwork. Initially, she worked within the law. Later, Sally would agitate to change laws. Whether living or nonliving, human or nonhuman nature, Sally's labor contributed diversity to literal and political ecologies. Bodies and persons exist within relations. To focus on a single issue or identity marker was nonsensical to Sally. Patriarchy and racism are tied to religiosity and governmentality. Governing bodies problematize individual bodies that challenge order, even when that order is unjust. Unlike anarchists, who seek to dismantle governmentality in favor of self-rule, Sally worked within religious and political structures. The results were mixed. Sally accomplished landmark breakthroughs in policy changes but also experienced the limitations of working within these parameters.

If institutional bodies—religious, medical, legal, and national—are the actual problems, not individuals, then what is the best strategy for positive change? Are diverse ecologies of reciprocal relationships nurtured within or against regulating bodies? For Sally, no single tactic was most effective or ethical. She engaged in a multipronged approach, both within and against collective bodies, with the aim to improve the well-being of all. Part III delves into her breakthroughs and limitations as an activist. Sally boldly confronted governing bodies with their inconsistencies and injustices. She labored to change policies and laws for the benefit of all people. But there were also times that she grew weary from this work, and ultimately, her premature death might suggest a need to break current systems to allow for fundamental transformation in how we form communal bodies.

III

AGITATING BODIES

What you are told you need to do to progress further in a system reproduces that system. —SARA AHMED, *Complaint!*

It is important not to be content to let failed revolutions be merely finite moments. Instead we should consider them to be the blueprints to a better world that queer utopian aesthetics supply. —JOSÉ ESTEBAN MUÑOZ, *Cruising Utopia*

Activists agitate for change. How is instigation to be understood? Like an allergy, activists have the potential to be dismissed as an overreaction of the immune system to a harmless substance; they are hypersensitive hysterics who need to be quieted with antihistamines in the form of regulatory political bodies. Alternatively, I suggest that activists be understood as antibodies. Antibodies are proteins produced as a part of the body's immune response to infection. They help eliminate disease-causing microbes from the body through blocking or destruction. Importantly, antibodies remember in a highly specific manner. When the body encounters that microbe again, immune cells residing in the body as memory cells respond quickly and can stop an infection from taking hold. Antibodies are a lens through which activists can be best understood as agitating bodies that block, destroy, and remember societal harms in highly specific ways.

The antibody analogy has implications for communal and individual bodies. Recent studies in trauma illuminate the nonverbal and noncognitive traces of trauma that shape the body and its responses. Psychiatry professor Bessel van der Kolk demonstrates how these changes compromise someone's capacity for pleasure, engagement, self-control, and trust.[1] While his research looks at individual bodies and strategies for healing, it is worth considering how social bodies might also account for histories of pain and work toward healing.

Like an antibody, a Holocaust survivor remembers in a highly specific way that is quick to identify and actively resist anti-semitism. Bodies unfamiliar with anti-semitism need longer to learn about the infection. The survivor's body remembers as an individual who is always also part of a collective. For this reason, a threat need not be personal or intentional to cause alarm. When a people group has been targeted by bigotry, which is always inherently illogical, they learn to be alerted to whiffs and hints of this pattern from a long distance because their lives depend upon it. The stakes for forgetting are high. Medical anthropologist Didier Fassin argues that political amnesia in contemporary societies produces indifference toward social injustices. In his book *When Bodies Remember: Experiences and Politics of AIDS in South Africa*, he shows that colonization and segregation persist in scientific discourse and public policies around HIV/AIDS in South Africa to engender socioeconomic and health disparities. While subtle to those outside a group, the danger is obvious and immediate to survivors.

Sally was an agitator who called attention to prior grievances to prevent exacerbating injury. She served as an antibody when she readily identified what ailed society—sexism, greed, racism, and ableism to name a few—and sprang into action. Sally's body remembers the trauma of anti-semitism, both personal and communal dimensions, in a highly specific way. From this knowledge she extrapolates to diagnose all manner of injustice. Hers is a finely honed skill to detect discrimination from long distances. Instead of us adjudicating whether agitation is reasonable, Sally's story suggests that we would do better to listen, empathize, and collaborate. We need not dismiss fervor as an allergy, an overreaction to harmless substances. To fixate on the agitating body rather than what it points to is to miss the purpose of the message.

Part III focuses on the benefits and limitations of Sally's transnational activism. Her awakening to the need for agitation began in Israel in the 1970s. What she learned there she took back to South Africa during a time of immense social unrest. Sally's activism resulted in the need for political asylum. Once enlightened to social injustice and the need for activist agitation, Sally set on a restless journey in pursuit of social justice. Country to country, religion to religion, and from one activist community to another, there was no ideal—only glimmers of conditional belonging. Sally glided across diverse religious and activist communities, never committing to a single issue but rather understanding all versions of injustice as unacceptable. The costs for her commitment to social justice were immense. She suffered harassment, loneliness, and poverty. While she did not accomplish her dream of fully belonging to a diverse ecology, through her life and death, she calls us to continue and expand her work such that we attend to good relations with one another, living and nonliving, human and nonhuman.

7. Transnational Activism

Israel 1970s

From 1972 to 1973, S. studied at the University of Haifa. There, she made Palestinian Israeli friends and got to know refugees from various South American juntas. Yesh (a left-wing coalition of radicalized students primarily hailing from Latin America), members of the left-wing kibbutzim, and the Arab Students' Committee controlled the Student Union. S. became involved with Yesh and was the registrar for a project to set up a Free University. She notes that the Labor coalition of the revisionists, then called Gahal, orchestrated the overthrow of Yesh. Likewise, the Free University project was thwarted by rumors of ties to a Syrian spy ring.[1] Within this context, S. became aware of the ongoing expropriation of the land belonging to Arab villages within the Green Line, the 1949 armistice line. Many of her Palestinian friends were members of the Communist Youth League or the Communist Party itself. At the time, the latter was called the New Communist List, or Rakach in Hebrew. It was predominantly Arab and pro-Soviet, unlike the Communist Party of Israel, Maki, which was predominantly Jewish and increasingly anti-Soviet after the 1967 war.

The student body personalized frictions among political bodies; these relationships opened S.'s eyes to a new narrative. Palestinians were no longer abstractions. Their mistreatment shocked her. When she learned about the restriction orders that Palestinian students were subject to, she could not help but note their similarities to ban orders in Apartheid South Africa. On a visit to Kiryat Arba, a large West Bank settlement overlooking Hebron, S. viewed the inhabitants as zealous Zionist settlers laying claim to what they understood to be the historical land of Israel:

> With the fortress-like buildings of the settlement towering in the background, a fervent woman from Kiryat Arba told us with glowing eyes about their wonderful plan to surround and to strangle the Palestinian city of Hebron, which we could see from our vantage-point above it. This sounded uncomfortably like the oppressiveness of the Apartheid regime.... Like it or not, I was in effect a settler in what I thought of as a colonial-settler state.[2]

From her education and friendships, S. began to see connections. To carve the land into territories is a contested settler colonial activity. It has severe consequences for individual persons, who are regulated accordingly. If we are shaped by the structures we build, there is even more reason to attend to them carefully.

Initially optimistic about the democratic socialist country, S. found herself confronted by a radicalism that she could not push out of her mind. Consequently, she became involved in anti-Zionist politics, which grew to encompass activism in South Africa and Botswana:

> I went to Israel because I wanted to get away from the wickedness of apartheid. Something which dawned on me in Israel was that there was an embryonic apartheid in Israel as well....
>
> I made many Palestinian friends and Jewish friends who had come as refugees from various military juntas in South America. I was involved in radical groups, but I decided to go back to South Africa specifically to see if I could involve myself in the struggle against apartheid. Rather than be in Israel where I felt like a settler, I'd rather be in the country where I was born, struggling against apartheid.[3]

There was no promised land free from discrimination. S. observed continuity among separatist strategies for regulating individuals. Instead of seeing social injustice as something outside herself, a containable evil, S. recognized her culpability and responsibility to her people and place of origin.

With time, S. also came to appreciate the gendered dimensions of her political concerns:

As a young adult, involvement with comrades active in women's movements in Israel and Palestine as well as in the context of our own struggle for liberation in South Africa, and study of the issue, led me to realise that the oppression of women in our land would not end with formal defeat of apartheid, and there would be a need in post-apartheid South Africa to struggle long and hard to bring about the transformation which would translate the regulative non-sexist ideal into a lived reality.[4]

Single-issue activism no longer made sense. Advocacy for racial justice requires attention to gender, land, and faith. Her physical body would later aid S. in uncovering a knot of various inequalities that structure our environment and relationships.

Southern Africa 1970s

In 1974, S. registered at the University of Cape Town to study law, which she believed would enable her to serve the National Union of South African Students (NUSAS) Wages Commission.[5] In her first year at university, S. deepened her understanding of gender studies. In a 1993 letter to Father Timothy Radcliffe, she would later reflect:

> It dawned upon me that there is a significant difference between sex and gender, and that gender roles are social constructions. This led me to think that my gender dysphoria was primarily the product of a pathologically disordered society, which delineated gender roles too narrowly, and not primarily a personal disorder. One's sex, by contrast, was chromosomal and physiological.
>
> This enabled me to see myself as a male, sexually, and alleviated the sense of miasma associated with my gender dysphoria. It led me to seek to accept myself as I was, at one level, though at another level it led me to deal with the dysphoria by "gritting my teeth and bearing it," in the hope that the sense of loss and the grief would vanish. . . .
>
> My *modus vivendi*, for all that, was still an attempt at stoic indifference to the pain and the hope that I would grow used to it in time. This was still the state of play, to a large extent, when I entered the Order: I had convinced myself that the gender dysphoria was an apparent problem but not a real one.[6]

Eventually, S. understood that her gender identity might have a political edge, suggesting it could be a source of pride rather than shame. Her life as a whole demonstrates the political charge of intersex and trans bodies, and at this point, she was only beginning to connect those dots gingerly. For the time being, she put her head down and pressed on in a male role. Perhaps if gender dysphoria was a socially constructed problem, then she could control it.

By the mid-1970s, the Black Consciousness Movement (BCM) was well established in South Africa, largely due to anti-apartheid activists Steve Biko and Rick Turner. Young people organized protests in the late nineteenth and early twentieth centuries, which laid the foundation for the later generations who formed the ANC Youth League in 1944. Some members, such as Hilda Bernstein, later joined the Communist Party of South Africa. In 1975, the government required the Department of Education to teach half of school subjects in Afrikaans. Most Black South Africans were already learning in their second or third language, English. For those who viewed Afrikaans as the language of their oppressors, this legislation was especially cruel. The South African Student Organization gained traction on campuses nationwide, and protests increased. The state cracked down on the anti-apartheid movement under the pretense of what became known as the Internal Security Act (1976)—it was a revision of the 1950 Suppression of Communism Act.

Within this political climate of social unrest, S. recognized that there was no neutral position. Wedged between the pressure for Jews to toe the Apartheid line and the blatant mistreatment of persons of color, she prioritized her thirst for justice over fear of retaliatory discrimination. According to Daniel Magaziner, the Christian faith in the 1970s South African context went from complicity with colonization and dispossession to liberation.[7] Thus, in her last three years of university, S. became increasingly outspoken about her moral objections to Apartheid and socialist sympathies. From the Holocaust, she recognized discrimination as an evil. Because apartheid's architects supported the Nazis throughout World War II, she was leery of their policy. She began reading banned literature about the liberation struggle.

In her penultimate school year, S. and a friend typed and reproduced a publication called "Eyes Left." She described it as a samizdat of sorts, in which she would argue in favor of socialism paired with reluctant Zionism. At the same time, her comrade advocated for non-Zionist internationalism and capitalism. Later that year, S. read Albert Luthuli's autobiography, *Let My People Go*, whose appendix included the ANC's core statement of principles and the Freedom Charter.[8] S. typed out the Freedom Charter and pinned it to the notice board at the back of her classroom. The book and the charter inspired S. and others to form an anti-apartheid group. In her last year of school, she established a clandestine group focused on exploring the possibility of political sabotage.[9]

Some members of the anti-apartheid group were drafted into the army and stationed at Youngsfield Military Base in Cape Town. They provided S. with the camp layout with the intent that she would share it with the ANC. In retrospect, S. recognized this effort as naive.[10] Although Luthuli's firsthand account of the Defiance Campaign Against Unjust Laws (1952), the first mass challenge to Apartheid, had galvanized the youth, it would take time for them to sort out how they would contribute to the struggle against Apartheid. The campaign would become the largest nonviolent resistance effort in South Africa, but it was more moderate than some of the activities that S. and her anti-apartheid group enacted.

The Soweto Uprising in 1976 was a watershed moment in South African politics. That June, Black schoolchildren held daily marches in the center of Cape Town. Police met them with extreme force. Nevertheless, the children assembled daily. Father Peter-John Pearson, who would later become a Catholic chaplain at the University of the Western Cape, was S.'s university friend. The two came to Christianity at the same time. Together, they went to the city center—the Grande Parade—to participate in the protests. Thousands of children in school uniforms gathered. Opposite the church, adjacent to town hall, masses of police in camouflage riot gear stood ready. Armed with batons, tear gas, and automatic rifles, the police began surrounding the children. An officer bellowed into his bullhorn: *This is an illegal gathering! You have two minutes to disperse!*

The children replied by singing the hymn "The Lord Is My Shepherd," based on Psalm 23. A few verses in, police fired their rifles and launched tear gas canisters. Chaos ensued. S. witnessed schoolchildren being beaten and shot. Sean Viljoen, a friend of Pearson, caught sight of Pearson and S. At grave risk to his life, he rushed into the human maelstrom and guided them to a borrowed car.[11] The children were not so fortunate. Many were injured, incarcerated, or killed. In later years as a priest, S. would interrupt her sermon on loving one's neighbor as oneself to share this story. It proved to be a powerful illustration of what it might mean to be a neighbor to someone on the road from Jerusalem to Jericho.[12]

In response to the violence, S. advocated for radical armed resistance. She explained, "The Soweto Uprising brought me to face a dilemma: should I get on my knees and pray for Christian fellowship, or should I try to find a duplicator to try to put out seditious pamphlets? I prayed long and hard about it, and the answer that seemed to come was get a duplicator and get involved and start a group."[13] She joined several movements. The students' Jewish Association at the University of Cape Town used their school newspaper,

Strike!, to critique indifference and tacit endorsement of Apartheid. Some members were also involved in the NUSAS Wages Commission, which is credited with reigniting a democratic trade union movement.

S. drafted a program that included cooperation with the ANC and an armed struggle clause.[14] It was a bold move in a context where communism was illegal. She organized two groups to disseminate the material and encouraged members to establish their own groups insulated from one another. If they were unaware of one another's activities, it would afford each group some protection while adding momentum to the struggle. The meetings often occurred in a heavily forested mountainside and ascribed to strict security protocols. If anyone did not arrive within five minutes of the prearranged time, the meeting was canceled on the spot.[15] These were acts of bravery within the Cold War period. Agitators for justice were threatened, harmed, and fled for asylum.

Botswana 1977

In retrospect, S. realized she might have been in over her head. Handwritten copies of the draft program went missing from where she had hidden them under her bed. Prior to this, S. was aware that she was under surveillance.[16] Her comrades encouraged S. to leave the country and seek asylum, as many other radicals had: "The dynamics of this led to a situation where I almost certainly was going to be detained at any time. I was quite clearly in target sights. . . . My comrades instructed me to get the hell out."[17] Her parents, who were not active in the struggle against Apartheid, relocated to Israel. With one final exam to pass to obtain her degree at the University of Cape Town, S. fled to Botswana, where a number of activists sought asylum. The university refused a request from the United Nations High Commissioner for Refugees to allow her to complete the exam outside the country.

Drawing on a metaphor from the Hebrew Bible, S. referred to this as her period of exile. Initially, the ANC placed her in a house in Botswana owned by someone linked with the movement. A next-door neighbor and fellow exile with whom S. enjoyed chatting was a member of the Society of Young Africa (SOYA)—an intellectual movement aimed at mobilizing students and young workers in the struggle against Apartheid. During these lonesome days, she turned to writing for solace. She explored South Africa's political dynamics in a series of analyses that she later considered some of her best work. All that material, she regrets, was lost.

S. was then moved to an ANC residence in Bontleng, where she provided political instruction. It was there that she became aware of the breadth of movement-related publications, such as the Strategy and Tactics document produced at the Morogoro Conference.[18] She recalls having held to a one-stage theory of struggle rather than a two-stage one. The latter approach calls for the implementation of socialism prior to communism. The more radical position, which S. preferred, was for South Africans to sever ties to colonial metropoles.[19] But she kept to herself because she sensed it to be a minority position. Again, S. turned to her notebooks, where she could express herself freely despite feeling cut off from the community. It was a time marked by deep depression for her.

Eventually, S. found work teaching English in Mochudi. There, she lived in a sparse hut without a lock or electricity. A sleeping bag placed atop a foam sheet served as her bed. From there, she maintained contact with two exiles active with SOYA in Gaborone but found herself disillusioned with the intellectualism of the political culture. For S., it needed more action. She wrote about the reason for her leaving Mochudi:

> One evening I returned to my hut, lighting my way with a battery-powered torch. Getting onto my sleeping bag, and intending to strike a match to light the candle on a brick beside my head, I became sharply aware of an acrid odour and noted that my sleeping-bag was damp, and realised that someone had evidently poured petrol into my sleeping-bag. Had I lit a match, I would probably have been killed, though most of the petrol had probably evaporated by then. The following day, I got someone to corroborate that the bag did smell of petrol.[20]

Botswana had failed to provide a safe harbor. Exacerbated by isolation and depression, this event precipitated a psychological plummet that S. does not detail. Certainly, she was shaken by the notion that an attempt might have been made on her life.

Israel 1977

When Jack learned of S.'s situation in Botswana, he felt the need to convince her to come to Israel, where the Gross family had relocated.[21] He misled her by suggesting that her mother was dying of cancer. S. concedes that Jack had done so in her best interest. Although she entered Israel on a short-term visa, Botswana barred her return. Apartheid authorities pursued her extradition from Israel. When her visa expired, she was technically in Israel illegally. According to S., the Israeli government was closely aligned with the Apartheid regime; allegedly, the two shared uranium and a nuclear arsenal.[22] This political relationship thwarted her attempt to gain refugee status in Israel. The safety of her physical body hung in the balance between national bodies.

When S. met with a clerk at Israel's Ministry of the Interior, she stole glances at the thick file he leafed through in front of her. She saw police stationery dating back to her days as a University of Cape Town student. "You were very naughty," the clerk scolded.[23] She surmised that the South African security branch had shared information with its Israeli counterparts. In addition, she observed a letter on the South African Zionist Federation stationery advising the Ministry of the Interior not to grant her Israeli citizenship. S. interpreted this to mean that the South African Special Branch wished her to be returned to Apartheid South Africa. Legal counsel advised her to apply for Israeli citizenship, but she later wondered if she was technically already a citizen by virtue of her father. Ultimately, she was granted citizenship, perhaps because her deportation would violate the 1951 United Nations Convention on Refugees. In 1979, S. was drafted into the military.[24]

S. described her time in the Israeli military as unpleasant. She completed basic training, but she claims that comrades in the anti-Zionist left instructed S. to extricate herself immediately. She had been given a job loading and unloading trucks, even though she had been assigned to the medical corps.[25] Due to her high blood pressure, this assignment felt punitive, so she resolved to get herself released from military service duty. Meanwhile, unbeknown to S., her brother Ray sought out a social worker about his home troubles. He did not want to live at home, though he was still in high school. The social worker recognized that Ray had developed skills of manipulation and deception that were potentially useful for Israeli security services. To do that work, he was explicitly forbidden to discuss it with his sister. "They were very aware of Sally; therefore, we had limited interactions," he said.[26]

Getting out of military service began with a visit to the hospital for high blood pressure. Once there, S. requested to see a psychiatrist. She made her case. Doctors gave her injections and instructed her to rest for three days. When she returned to base, her commander complained that they allowed S. to go to the hospital for a medical check, not to rest. When they put her back to work, she passed out on the job and fell off a ramp. She recalled thinking, "If I don't do something I am going to die. It was a question of preservation."[27] A psychiatrist validated S.'s concerns and made changes to her profile such that she would be under supervision. This protected S. from mistreatment and enraged her base commander and deputy commander.

Eventually, a doctor examined the data on her blood pressure and determined that she was unfit to serve. S. feigned disappointment. A year later, she provided evidence of high blood pressure and photographs of a retina abnormality, and with that, she was made exempt. Within three months, she secured release on the grounds of poor health. "Then I lost a lot of weight and my blood pressure normalized," she explained dryly.[28] When she felt physically threatened, she would leverage bureaucratic policy to facilitate her relocation. Due to her principled temperament, she took delight in using rules to protect herself from harm.

S.'s journey to Israel promised a reconnection with family, but as a converted Catholic combined with anti-Zionism, she was at odds with both blood and national relations. After her medical discharge, she felt unable to endure the physical and psychological toll of working at a bank in Israel. Isolated and deflated, S. resolved to move again. "Over time," she explained, "I also forged a connection with the Dominicans at the Ecole Biblique in East Jerusalem, who put me in touch with the British Dominicans to whom I applied to enter the Order in Britain as a novice. I moved to the UK towards the end of 1981, joining the Dominican Priory in Oxford as a novice, studying there, becoming a priest in the Order, and later teaching there."[29] She seems to have hoped that clerical bonds would prove to be more substantial than those of her biological family, nation-states, or activist communities.

England 1980s

During the 1980s in Oxford, clergy and laity were protesting nuclear war and Apartheid. Some joked that a protest was not valid unless a friar was present. One friar would be designated to avoid arrest and bail the others out. When I first came across the photographs documenting these events, I thought them a bizarre reenactment of Jesus's arrest and trial.[30] Father Timothy Radcliffe described the actual arrests of his brethren.[31] He explained that there was much theological debate at the time over the Christian obligation to obey the laws of the land.

S. maintained a clandestine membership in the ANC, but this undercover quality of the relationship dissatisfied her. From S.'s perspective, her contribution to the movement in open structures was far more significant: "I was chairperson of the Oxford Anti-Apartheid Group for a time.... I was instrumental in the establishment of an ANC religious desk in London.

George Johannes, at the Office, often asked me to give talks to groups all over the country on behalf of the movement."[32]

Police surveilled the Blackfriars community. Timothy casually disclosed that the priory phones were frequently tapped before demonstrations. Once, he went out for a walk, and a police car crept alongside him at a close distance. Timothy darted down a narrow road that could not accommodate the car. Another time, S. alerted Timothy that police officers were parked in front of the priory. Timothy positioned himself where he was visible to the officers from a window and pulled out a camera. It did not have film—he smiled while telling me this—but when he aimed it at the officers and pretended to snap photographs, the car peeled off.[33]

On a different occasion, S. informed Timothy that some police officers were lurking about the priory entrance. Timothy crept to the front door, paused, and flung it open. There, two police officers who were crouched over blushed with embarrassment. They had been peeking through the letter box flap. Timothy invited them inside. Initially, the two unconvincingly claimed to have been looking after the brethren's safety. Over a cup of tea, however, they explained their curiosity about the religious group's participation in protests. Timothy laughed warmly. "It was," he said, "a chaotic, fascinating, rich time."[34] S. believed she had found her home and chosen family among Blackfriars. With her they seemed to appreciate the study of religion, care for one another's well-being, and agitate with activists.

Diana Tickell was a fellow activist and friend of S.'s who led the antiapartheid group who met in a room below the Blackfriars' library. At the time, Diana was housing Teboho "Tsietsi" Mashinini, the exiled South African activist responsible for initiating the pivotal Soweto Uprising.[35] The three bonded over meals with Diana's large family, sharing their passion for social justice. Diana was eighty-four years old when we met and reminisced about the energy and engagement that once gripped the Oxford community. Meetings had no fewer than twenty attendees, she explained. They stayed apprised of South African politics and aided the ANC whenever possible. S. proved to be a helpful informant and connection. In addition, she had contacts with a good number of South Africans in exile.

At one point, a pleasant young man joined one of their meetings. Although altogether affable, he struck S. as untrustworthy. After some investigation, S. reported to Diana that the man had in fact been a spy. Diana teased S., "What interest would a spy have in the Oxford anti-apartheid group apart from *you* being here?"[36] After the treason trials, in which ANC members were imprisoned, Diana was active in the International Defence and Aid Fund.

John Collins created the fund in 1956 to pay legal fees and support families of activists, such as Nelson Mandela, who were accused of treason for protesting Apartheid. Diana was one such person who would send money to families of incarcerated Black South Africans. "It was all rather cloak and dagger," she reported.[37] Agitating networks stretched across oceans and contents to maintain momentum and strength.

Binational 1990s

After the government's ban on the African National Congress was lifted in 1990, Dominicans living in South Africa invited S. to visit. This was a dangerous proposition due to domestic terrorism; it was not unheard of for activist priests to be assassinated. Moreover, the South African Embassy resisted S.'s return, precipitating months of struggle.[38] When she defected in 1977, she lost her South African citizenship, though by 1991, it was restored. Once her citizenship was restored, she began a routine: as mentioned before, half of the year she would work on her thesis at the Cambridge House in England, and the other half she would teach at St. Joseph's Theological Institute, a Catholic seminary in Cedara, South Africa.

Once the back-and-forth became permanent, S. joined a local ANC branch. Activists there hoped that the immense political unrest heralded a democratic future. S.'s British brethren expressed to me their doubts about S.'s life-threatening activism. They suspected her of exaggeration, perhaps even histrionics. It has been difficult to determine whether her life was in direct danger, but she certainly kept company with anti-apartheid extremists willing to engage in armed resistance.

S. gasped upon receiving a manila envelope that contained Afrikaner Weerstandsbeweging (Afrikaner Resistance Movement) material and a membership form containing her personal details.[39] Comrades Cedric Mayson and Sipho Pityana received similar packages. Forged documents alleging to bear the signature of Lawson Naidoo, who was serving as the Council for the Advancement of the South African Constitution (CASAC) RPC executive secretary, were disseminated. These, S. explained, were likely the work of South Africa's Civil Cooperation Bureau (CCB), a government-sponsored death squad during the Apartheid era, who stole membership details from the ANC office. S. felt that the envelopes were a threat and that the next might contain explosives.[40] While her brethren in the UK might not have grasped the threat fully, within the South African context her concern was not unfounded.

As I learned more about the radical activist company that S. kept in South Africa and the attempts made on their lives, I began to understand the reasons for her concern. In speaking with Father Michael Worsnip and later Andre Zaaiman, I recognized my understanding of anti-apartheid activism as naive. Celebrated revolutionaries tend to be moderates. Nelson Mandela, Desmond Tutu, Martin Luther King Jr., and Mahatma Gandhi are figures retrospectively crafted for public consumption. They practice restraint and advocate for nonviolent protest. More radical groups such as the Black Panthers and Antifa anarchists are denounced publicly for their use of force, and their accomplishments are attributed to moderate figureheads. Their contributions are as crucial as they are unrecognized. After listening to Worsnip's and Zaaiman's experiences and learning more about their activism, I realized that S. had moved among radical political circles.

The city of Cedara sits between Lesotho and the coastal city of Durban. Southeast is Pietermaritzburg, founded in 1838 by Voortrekkers following the defeat of the Zulu king Dingane's army in the Battle of Blood River. Cedara is where Mahatma Gandhi was forced off a train when a white man objected to him riding in a first-class carriage. During Apartheid, nearly the entire Indian population was forced into the suburb of Northdale and the Zulus to Edendale township. The city became a killing field as anti-apartheid activism heated up. Mandela was arrested in Cedara in 1962, an event that today is remembered with fifty steel columns forming a sculpture of his face. There, S. met Father Michael Worsnip, who would become instrumental in her permanent return to South Africa.

The stakes for anti-apartheid activism were high. Worsnip (I use his last name to avoid confusion with Father Michael Lapsley) describes the horror of seeing Father Michael Lapsley in hospital after he survived a letter bomb:

> It was an awful sight. His face was charred and blackened. His beard had melted into his skin. His face was swollen to twice its normal size. In fact the only way that I could recognize him was by a single gold filling which he has in his teeth. Both of his hands were taken off. He needed to hold his stumps up all the time because anything touching them caused him the most extraordinary pain. His lips were swollen and bleeding. His one eye was damaged completely by the explosion, and he could see nothing at all out of the other one. We had to shout to make him hear, but it seems as though he could hear just a little. He was in a terrible state. His sister Helen who was with him told us about how he would wake up at night screaming, re-living the bomb.[41]

Years later, after offering his testimony at the Truth and Reconciliation Commission, Worsnip expressed his desire for the person responsible to make themselves known. Doctor Alex Boraine explained that determining specifically who typed the letter bomb, who sealed it, mailed it, and so on might not be possible. He asked Worsnip and Lapsley if they would agree to the persons responsible being offered amnesty in exchange for their public confession. Father Lapsley replied that he would prefer a trial but that under the threat of civil war, he was willing to accept amnesty, citing Desmond Tutu's teachings on Christian confession and forgiveness. Tutu admitted to finding Father Lapsley obstreperous, but despite their ideological conflicts, he stated:

> I give thanks to God for you, [Father] Michael [Lapsley], and I also give thanks for the experience through which you went, because you can talk about crucifixion and resurrection because it is real, it is in your body. You should see when he celebrates the Eucharist, I have sometimes stood next to him and I got a little worried whether he was not going to overturn the Chalice or something, and there is an incredible kind of hush in almost every service that I have been with you, because people somehow feel that they are in touch with goodness, in an awful situation somehow they are aware that they are in touch with light in darkness, that they are in touch with life in death, and somehow they know goodness is going to triumph over evil.[42]

Before serving as an Anglican priest, Worsnip sought asylum in Lesotho, where he first experienced life integrated with Black people. He described the profound effect of participating in radical political circles. "It was Black ANC members and the people of Lesotho who gave us [white people] back the humanity that Apartheid had robbed us of," he reflected. "Jacob Zuma held underground meetings in our back bedroom. Tito Mboweni learnt to drive in our Volkswagen Beetle. Ngoako Ramatlhodi ironed his shirts in our living room."[43] He would later explain, "It was a house of protest, it was a house of debate where people met in real terms and could discuss and disagree and that sort of thing, but it was a house essentially of peace. It was sometimes a house of prayer."[44] Worsnip had traveled to Britain on behalf of the ANC to deliver messages to journalists at the BBC about how the South African government's death squads were kidnapping young children and torturing them to death. Recklessly, journalist Suzanne Voss published Worsnip's name in one such article. Consequently, he was deported from Lesotho by the military government for speaking against the abductions and executions of South African refugees.⁴⁵ He turned to the quieter cover of working in the priesthood at the Federal Theological Seminary in Pietermaritzburg.

During our interview, Worsnip candidly explained that Sally had the capacity to be unbearably rude, she took umbrage at bizarre things, and occasionally, her physical presentation, unfortunately, overshadowed the claims cases. She struggled to discern when it was appropriate to engage in sensitive topics. In conversations, he frequently found himself plunged into a maelstrom of intersex medical ethics and obscure theological references. He often felt overwhelmed by Sally's intense outpouring of expertise, which he described as a Niagara Falls of information: "She filled every corner of the room and had 15 references for each thought, which made one feel stupid. Not that she intended that; she just always had something to add to the conversation."⁴⁶ Sally could not be shushed, he explained. Worsnip warmed to her considerably but always with firm boundaries in place. He would not invite her over for Sunday lunch because he felt she was a black hole to his energy. The two occasionally met for tea, and Worsnip only once visited her Cape Town flat. He never agreed to give her rides nor responded to her subtle requests. The two would hug and kiss one another on the cheek when they met, but Worsnip would not allow Sally to get too close emotionally.

Unlike other underground church activists organizing against Apartheid, S. was loud-spoken. Worsnip told me that he encountered S. in the market with some regularity. He cringed whenever he caught sight of her bounding down the road. Her voice thundered a torrent of reflections on Thomas Aquinas, Frantz Fanon, and Karl Marx. She would rattle off Hebrew, Koine Greek, and Aramaic passages. Worsnip would blush as onlookers gawked. Unfazed, S. bounced from one side of Worsnip to the other as he attempted to peel away. It was not that he disagreed with S.'s politics or lacked affection for her: She was just too loud, too overt, and thus far too recognizable for safety.

Worsnip had good reason for concern. More than 1,600 people were killed in South Africa within the first six months of 1990. Pietermaritzburg was at the epicenter of the violence, becoming known as the "Valley of Death."⁴⁷ In 1990, priest Victor Vivian Sipho Africander was murdered while taking his niece's six-year-old daughter to school in Pietermaritzburg. The child survived the shooting physically unharmed, but Africander suffered fatal wounds to the head and chest. Africander had been known for burying dead persons regardless of their political or religious affiliation, a bold action at the time.⁴⁸ Shaken after the killing of Afrikander, Archbishop Tutu declared that Anglican priests were not to join political parties. Worsnip snapped back, "You might think you're the prince of the church, but you're not the prince of me."[49]

The underground church was guided less by the globally revered Tutu and more by Father Albert Nolan. Nolan hosted regular meetings to strategize, to which S. was invited only once. The group felt that her bizarre appearance, perhaps a reference to her long orange hair, made her easily identifiable and, therefore, dangerous to associate with—an accurate assessment. Later, Worsnip divorced his wife and partnered with a man. The church sighed with relief and bid him farewell, he told me. Although S. felt isolated at the time, she could not have known that her friendship with Worsnip would span decades and that he would be pivotal to her reentry into South Africa.[50] Their agitator kinship endured the test of time.

Global Intersex Network 1990s

In 1997, after flying across the Atlantic Ocean, Sally folded herself into a small car, and her friend drove for two days before they arrived at the second international intersex retreat. They snaked up North Carolina's mountains in awe of brilliant fall leaves. The modest cabin sat on a campground retreat center in Asheville. In the evenings, everyone settled around an open fire to share stories about their extraordinary journeys as intersex persons. Upon the group's first venture down the slope to the camp mess hall, they were met with hostile gazes. Consequently, they resolved to self-cater. Everyone formed into cooking groups and took turns serving. Sally only remembered seven people in attendance, four of whom were from the United States. There, intersex persons built a community through which many found companionship and healing. Part of what the group explored was what it takes to survive in a world that defines humans as either male or female—never ambiguous.

It was only the second of such retreats and almost did not happen due to a dispute among the intersex participants. More than one framed it compassionately: hurt people hurt. What they meant by this is that people who have experienced trauma can lash out. It is noteworthy, however, that this was shared with me never in an air of judgment but rather in a tone of sadness. Sally and Mani Mitchell had traveled internationally for the event, so with that in mind, Max Beck resolved to move forward with the retreat. The first retreat had been impactful, so participants were eager to reunite.

Mani, executive director of Intersex Trust Aotearoa, New Zealand, met Sally at the 1997 international retreat in Asheville.[51] Mani and Sally were older than most participants and were born in the same year. Both had been assigned male at birth and only began exploring their intersexuality in their early forties. The similarities uniquely bonded them. Mani was reclassified as female as a toddler and was subject to exploratory surgery.

Mani is currently a practicing psychotherapist counselor and intersex activist in New Zealand. Their sartorial style celebrates whimsy.[52] A narrow, white beard dangles from Mani's chin. Patches of teal blue illuminate their hair. They don black leather biker gloves, hats, and vests. According to Sally, the reason that she and Mani were assigned male at birth, despite ambiguous genitalia, was to avoid denying them the advantages society affords men. Sally wrote about their similar histories:

> Back in 1953 it was decided to classify me as male. At that time there were certain advantages in law which accrued to those classified as male. Mani was also born intersexed and classified initially as male, though it was decided two or three years later to reclassify hir as female. They tell me that a textbook used in New Zealand at the time advised that infants born with ambiguous genitalia should be classified as male if at all possible in order not to deny them "the prerogatives of maleness."[53]

At the retreat, the two became fast friends.

Retreat participants were invited to discuss their unique physical attributes and to show them to one another. The latter is particularly powerful because it might be the first time they had done so on their own terms. Stories might include painful memories of surgical procedures enacted to conform their bodies to one of the binary sexes. "Sally had never shared her body with anybody before," Mani explained.[54] Beyond probing doctors, she had kept to herself. It says a great deal about the group that she felt safe showing them her body. In Mani's assessment, Sally's genitals were extremely ambiguous—neither stereotypically male nor female. Later, when Sally would pursue legal documentation to change her sex designation from male to female, she would get a letter of reference from Mani attesting to her atypical anatomy.[55]

Sally made a strong impression on everyone present at the retreat, as they on her. "It was there," she writes, "that I decided to seek to set up an Intersex Society of South Africa if and when I would be able to go back home."[56] Although she was spared "disambiguation" surgery, Sally learned that many infants are subject to clitoral recessions at birth. Without the informed consent of the patient, and sometimes even the parents, such interventions are unethical. Sally began educating the public on the prevalence of children born outside definitively male or female classification. She exposed the arbitrary standards by which persons are deemed abnormal. Because these medical interventions typically were not necessary to sustain life or health, she reasoned that they could wait until children were of age to self-elect intervention. Sally took a hard line: "The surgery isn't really about the child's health, but about protecting society from the child's unacceptable body. Imposing intersex surgery is genital mutilation."[57]

Increasingly, Sally agreed to public appearances and interviews. The *Mail and Guardian* newspaper agreed to do a piece on intersexuality. She met with medical professionals about androgen insensitivity, and Cheryl Chase (also known as Bo Laurent) advised that Sally announce Intersex South Africa as an organization to attract comrades.[58] Cheryl's testimony about the harmful secrecy surrounding intersexuality had a strong effect on Sally: "[Chase] grew up with a sense that something had been shamefully wrong with her body when she was born, something which had required repeated bouts of surgery on her genitals, but she had no real idea what it was. As a young adult, she had to battle long and hard (as do many intersexed activists) to get sight of her medical records and to learn the truth about the nature of her own body."[59]

Although Sally was not subjected to such surgery due to her delayed diagnosis, presumably, she resonated with Cheryl's alleged fear that sacraments performed under the assumption of maleness might be ineffective. For Cheryl, "learning that she was intersexed and that she was originally baptized as a boy precipitated her into breakdown. She emerged from this determined to end the stigmatisation, shame, secrecy and isolation which affects intersexed people, and founded the Intersex Society of North America (ISNA)."[60] Sally commended Cheryl's activism: "Through ISNA, a number of adults who had been subjected to genital surgery as infants and children by virtue of the standard protocol of practice sought to tell professionals and the public at large that their experience suggested that the imposition of genital surgery quite simply did not work."[61] Conversely, a prominent lesbian activist declined to come out as intersex along with Sally, which indicates the measure of stigma Sally was up against.[62] For this reason, many activists have remarked upon Sally's bravery for being openly intersex.

Perhaps Sally felt that she had finally found her people—those neither male nor female. For them, she was willing to brave fetishizing inquiries. Sally offered her body to the public. She confronted society with its inability to grapple with indeterminacy amid humanity. Sally met with doctors and reporters alike.[63] On March 22, 2002, Lisa Chait interviewed Sally about intersexuality for Cape Talk Radio. An acquaintance phoned Sally to tell her about a rebroadcast of the interview over Easter weekend and that it was her favorite broadcast, second only to John Maytham interviewing Nelson Mandela.[64] Despite hurtful questions, Sally was committed to introducing the public to intersexuality.

8. Community Building in South Africa

Sally grasped the imperative of community. Communal bodies sustain individuals. Agitating bodies especially need an authentic community to keep from burnout. Sally understood that injustice took many forms, so activism should not be limited to any single issue. Like her intersex body, social bodies have interconnected, inextricable elements. To care for one requires care for the whole. We cannot thrive apart from society or our environment. Harm ripples throughout our relationships, as does care. Flourishing ecologies require diverse interdependence.

Closed communities were inhospitable to Sally's complexity. The pain of that rejection inspired her to forge new communities. With activist comrades, she built communal bodies that included local and global intersex folks. She found fellowship with Jewish people against Zionism. Sally eagerly collaborated with members of the LGBTQ+ activist community even when her efforts were not reciprocated. Perhaps romanced by idealism, she was disappointed about the limitations of her efforts. Others likely did not respond in kind due to a dire sense of competition for resources.

The life of an agitator can be lonely and harsh. Instead of assimilating to religious or social bodies, Sally sought to make them more inclusive and supportive. Her work was marked by successes and failures, the latter not for lack of effort but because the work is always bigger than any individual or group. Our need for others, human and nonhuman, need not discourage agitating efforts. If anything, it demonstrates the importance of such efforts. No one can go it alone.

Founding of Intersex South Africa

As the 2011 founder and director of Intersex South Africa (ISSA), Sally informed the public about contested classifications of sex and gender with a multipronged approach. In addition to detailing medical distinctions, such as androgen insensitivity and congenital adrenogenital hyperplasia, Sally also described cultural and religious positions on intersexuality. She sought to educate the general public about intersexuality by appearing on television and in newspapers. Sally collaborated with medical practitioners on developing new standards of care, and she appealed to human rights rhetoric and worked to have intersexuality added to laws dealing with sex discrimination.[1] Sally framed intersexuality as a societal problem rather than a medical illness, similar to the way that crip theorists and disability rights activists describe a social-political model of disability. She never divorced her activism from race or religion. Sensitive to all forms of injustice rather than prioritizing one issue over another, Sally readily partnered with activists in various venues for the common good.[2] While comrades admired Sally for her accomplishments, she struggled interpersonally and expressed feeling intensely lonely.

Deborah Ewing and Justine van Rooyen were funded by the AIDS Foundation to oversee NGOS researching attitudes toward trans and intersex persons, including ISSA. They interacted with Sally at conferences and workshops. Deborah first met Sally in England at an activist march in the 1980s, after which they lunched together. Deborah was a journalist at the time, and the two bonded over their interest in South African politics. In the mid-1990s, during the transition from Apartheid to democracy, Deborah reported on the elections. She received an email from Sally explaining that she had returned to South Africa and worked for the Land Claims Commission. This was followed by a phone call in which Sally shared the details of her transition. Although Sally did not fully embrace a female identity, she explained to Deborah that presenting as female was marginally more comfortable. They rekindled their friendship, which would later turn into an activist collaboration.[3]

Activist Estian Smit introduced Sally to Liesl Theron, who currently lives in Mexico City and works at the Good Hope Metropolitan Community Church doing a Saturday workshop on gender identity. Liesl is credited with cofounding Gender Dynamix, the first registered African-based public benefit organization focused on trans rights. She explains that she had acted as a public face to protect her trans partner, Lex Kirsten. Lex was transitioning at the time, so this seemed the best strategy for ensuring his safety while establishing Gender Dynamix in South Africa. Liesl acted as its first director from 2005 to 2014, after which she stepped down because it looked safe enough for a trans person to fill that role.[4] Liesl and Sally had mutual friends and often shared meals.

Regarding their activism for gender rights in South Africa, Liesl recalled Sally's matchless work ethic. By all accounts, Sally was highly intelligent and resourceful. She used her gifts and strengths to serve others. In an interview, Liesl described how whenever Sally suffered an injustice, she would commit herself to making institutional change rather than remedying matters on a merely personal level. These included but were not limited to fatphobia and ableism. Sally sought to improve conditions for all persons. Liesl also chuckled at memories of Sally bringing levity to meetings. She recalled that Sally could joke and pull silly faces to the delight of her comrades, all while hammering out complex, technical documents.[5] She characterizes Sally's contributions as silent, selfless work. Despite Sally's unquestioned value to NGOs, she was not adequately compensated. In addition to low wages, Sally, like many activists, struggled to acquire health-care benefits.[6]

Sally had returned to South Africa to participate in its rebuilding post-apartheid, but she could not shake her disappointment. The struggle for liberation from Apartheid, according to Sally, is like the seamless garment of Jesus. By this, she meant that liberation is for all. It does not begin or end with combating racism or sexism; it must pursue the liberation of all persons.[7] She wrote, "The past three years have convinced me that, while NGO involvement is helpful, it is not sufficient. Government needs to act as a catalyst."[8] While David Rubin is critical of human rights rhetoric approaches to intersex, they praise Sally's refined activism: "As Gross implicitly acknowledges, intersectionality and postcolonial critique can be enhanced by considering the place of intersex in contestations over what counts as intelligible human life within and beyond the South African context. Intersex has never been an issue extricable from processes of racial/sexual formation.... Here I find myself in agreement with Gross that a human rights perspective can still provide useful resources for re-situating intersex as *one of many* issues at stake in debates about differently situated bodies subject to doubt."[9] In the uncut footage of an interview in Grant Lahood's 2012 documentary *Intersexion*, Sally expressed her long-term goals to work within the government to advance intersex rights: "I want to motivate for a position in government where I can push the issue and help to foster conditions which will then get people who are intersex a greater voice, greater visibility and help to bring about an accelerated change in perceptions and attitude."[10]

Jewish Community

On December 7, 2001, Ronnie Kasrils and Max Ozinsky published a newspaper article on the Israel-Palestine conflict titled "Declaration of Conscience." Ronnie compiled 220 signatories from South Africans of Jewish descent to renounce Israel's occupation of Palestinian territory. He explains: "Israel's measures to oppress the Palestinian struggle are an intolerable abuse of human rights, so we raise our voices as Jews and cry out—'Not in my name,' as we join with all those in the world demanding justice for Palestinians and peace and security for all in the Holy Land—Christians, Jews, Muslims, and non-believers."[11] According to Jon Jeter of *The Washington Post*, the article triggered intense debate among Jewish South Africans. Some deemed Kasrils and Ozinsky traitors, and others praised them as heroes: "Cyril Harris, chief rabbi of the Union of Orthodox Synagogues in South Africa, said comparisons between apartheid and Israel are misguided. . . . Israel's state-sanctioned assassinations, he said, target known terrorists, while the apartheid government killed anyone considered a threat to its rule, regardless of whether they were involved in violence."[12]

Ronnie, an anti-apartheid activist, founded Not in My Name as a solidarity group for Jewish South Africans against occupation in Israel. At their gatherings Bradley Bordiss formed a friendship with Sally and other leftist Jewish South Africans.[13] Bradley explained that he had converted to Judaism in his early twenties because, as an adopted person, he resonated with a people group seeking belonging. The first time Bradley laid eyes on Sally was to give her a lift to one of Ronnie's meetings.[14] Her appearance surprised him because he thought he had spoken with a man on the phone when planning the pickup. Immediately, the two bonded over intellectual curiosities. They shared boisterous laughter, witty banter, and progressive political commitments. A deep friendship formed that would last until her death.

On a Sunday morning near the end of October 2018, I waited for Bradley at St. Michael and All Angels Church in Observatory, Cape Town. The stone building, which is more than one hundred years old, suited the Catholic-Anglican High Mass. Bradley and his two children joined me in a pew just after the service began. We sang and bowed for over an hour prior to uttering a word to one another. Bradley is a self-described dandy. His straw hat, bow tie, and tan suit bore the signatures of a US Southern gentleman. The coffee hour following the Mass was lively due to a few children celebrating their First Communion. Bradley made his way about the dining hall, holding court with various parishioners. After introducing me to a few friends, he drove his children and me to their home for lunch.

Bradley had hosted Sally's memorial in his home after she passed away. The first house we walked through serves as his office. A magnificent collection of rare leather-bound books dressed an entire wall—a passion shared with Sally. We then walked across a garden. I imagine famed English gardener Monty Don would approve of it. In the family home, Bradley guided me directly to another display of books and art. A nook of the house formed a library replete with liquor in crystal decanters, a quill pen flanked by inkwells, cigars, and incense. A staircase folded through the center, creating tranquil symmetry. Eager to share his collection, Bradley shifted some chairs to make way for us to sit cross-legged on the floor beneath the staircase to peruse his books. As we discussed our interests, his wife and children retreated to various corners of the home. Eventually, we made our way back to the sunroom where he had hosted Sally's memorial.

When Bradley fell in love with his now wife Odile, a Black Catholic woman from the Democratic Republic of the Congo, Sally was the logical officiant for their wedding. Sally embodied their Catholic Jewish commitments. Leafing through their wedding albums and loose photographs, we searched for a photo of Sally. When I inquired about a large photo of Odile embracing an older woman, Bradley nonchalantly explained that she was an unsheltered passerby they invited to join the festivities. Odile emerged from the family room with the photos of Sally officiating her marriage to Bradley. When their son Yannick was born, a Jewish doctor circumcised him, and the family returned to their home, where Sally performed a Jewish naming ceremony. Sally invoked feminine pronouns for God and carefully included Odile as much as Bradley. After reciting the duties of Jews, she added: *and to protest injustice*. Their son Yannick slept throughout the ceremony until the final amen. Someone teased that being from a Catholic Jewish family, Yannick might one day exclaim, "Oy vey Maria." Everyone chuckled.[15]

With fondness, Bradley recalled the Shabbat and seder meals over which Sally would preside. They were a group of "detribalized Jews," as he put it.[16] When Sally read from the Talmud and Haggadah, Bradley explained, she would reinterpret their meaning and change some of the language to make it more inclusive. Triumphal passages about Israel's election she would reframe to advocate for universal justice and liberation for all oppressed peoples.[17] Work colleague and friend Jennifer Williams recalled Sally even changing the traditional foods for a seder to contextualize the cultural meaning.[18]

It was at these seders and at Not in My Name that Sally reconnected with Andre Zaaiman. The two knew each other through the ANC meeting in Dakar. Although a Karoo farm-born Christian Afrikaner who would have benefited from Apartheid policy, Andre chose to join the ANC underground and went into exile in 1986. Like Michael Worsnip, Andre exposed undercover death squads. Andre is another example of the more extreme activists. He was willing to work undercover and risk his life in the struggle against Apartheid. He lived and worked in West Africa for over a decade and was a former senior official at the Institute for Democratic Alternatives in South Africa (IDASA).

Andre appreciated that Sally was not apologetic about being intersex and that her presence required others to cope with that ambiguity. He recalled people being uncertain whether to greet Sally with a handshake or kiss on the cheek because she did not appear to be distinctly male or female. One time, when the two went out for Chinese food, Andre remembered the waiter did not know how to address Sally and asked him for her order. Although he is not particularly religious, Andre found Sally's expertise helpful for his activism in the Middle East. He remembers her being informative about all religions. When her health declined and finances were sapped, he was one of the close friends to whom she would reach out.[19]

Medical Community

When South African "Patricia" was pregnant, doctors informed her that she was having a little boy, but out came a girl.[20] Endocrinological testing revealed her daughter to be intersex. Allegedly, medical practitioners refused to connect Patricia with other intersex persons, families, or support groups. Instead, they focused on her child and recommended that her daughter's testes be removed by age four so that there would be little to no conversation about intersexuality with the child. Although one might excuse this as dated behavior, just a few years ago, Patricia attended a lecture on intersexuality wherein the surgeon advised the audience to seek surgical intervention early. Patricia connected with Sally through a UK intersex support group website.[21] Timid, she did not include identifying information, just a post office box number.

After connecting with Sally, Patricia explained that Sally confronted her: She needed to admit that her daughter was intersex. It took time for

Patricia to embrace this diagnosis because, externally, her child appeared to be female. Reflecting on their conversations, Patricia described Sally as healing and supportive. Their relationship prompted Patricia to create a community among South Africans affected by intersex conditions. She offered her contact information for doctors to share with their intersex patients. Regrettably, although patients and their families reached out to Patricia, she found that many white families were unwilling to meet with families of color. She speculated that the cultural divide meant that they had less in common.

Like Patricia, intersex scholar Morgan Holmes reports that there is a painful absence of community for intersex persons and their families.[22] Holmes finds that the intersex community exists mainly online and in email discussion groups on websites. She explains, "Intersexuals represented or representing themselves in these forums come from geographically dispersed and distinct locations, from many religious and spiritual belief systems, from disparate educational backgrounds, and from many different language backgrounds and ethnicities. . . . However, intersexed people meet each other only rarely in person."[23] In *More Than Belief: A Materialist Theory of Religion*, Manuel A. Vásquez identifies the simultaneous mobility and containment of transnational biopolitics in contemporary digital communities. "Although networks are deterritorializing—deeply implicated in globalization's time-space compression and distanciation—they are always territorialized and prone to hierarchization," he explains.[24] Cyberspace has not democratized the community, and intersex groups are no exception.

Sociologist Georgiann Davis points out the difficulty of finding virtual support groups and the prerequisite of resources—access to the internet and money to travel to conferences.[25] She argues that parents of intersex children need more than medical information; they should be connected with support groups wherein they can learn about the experiences of intersex persons and their families. "When parents have access to information that originates in the intersex community rather than in the medical profession," Davis writes, "they are able to exercise what Rose and Novas (2005) call informational biocitizenship, which empowers them to make autonomous decisions about the bodies of the children for whom they are responsible—decisions that more often respect the autonomy of those children."[26] Although Rubin criticizes Davis's commitment to neoliberal notions of individualism, few intersex scholars or persons disagree that there is an ongoing need for support groups.

One of the great benefits of Sally having connected her to an intersex community, Patricia explained, was learning the function of keeping her daughter's gonads. Because her daughter's hormones are produced in the gonads, she would not have developed breasts had they been removed as the doctors prescribed. Patricia expressed how difficult it had been to educate her daughter's doctors on intersexuality. That was something she appreciated about Sally: "She knew far more about the physiology of intersexuality than doctors."[27] In the future, Patricia hopes to organize a conference in South Africa with medical practitioners worldwide. "The intersex community needs support, especially in our society. We all feel isolated like we're the only ones," she lamented.[28]

Patricia explained to me that she never hid from her daughter that she is intersex but wonders how many of their family members know this truth. Her daughter has always been aware that she is infertile and that some girls have X and Y chromosomes; her androgen insensitivity means that she does not have the receptors to recognize testosterone. Friends and family simply assumed that the doctor had made a mistake in saying Patricia was going to have a baby boy. When her daughter was about ten years old, Patricia's in-laws brought up this myth. Patricia explained the truth. They asked, "Oh, is she a boy then?" Patricia clarified, and her in-laws fully embraced her intersex granddaughter. She expressed frustration with racist doctors who assume that poor Black communities would not understand intersexuality. Empowering parents to make informed decisions that prioritize the intersex child's consent would entail improving education and communication among medical practitioners. Ellen Feder reports that one family support group was so helpful that parents of intersex children began to question the need for medical intervention, a testament to collective organizing. She explains, "Ruby herself suspected that it was the questions parents were beginning to raise that prompted doctors to withdraw their authorization of the support group and to take measures to ensure that it no longer met."[29] Despite her success in mentoring and assisting Patricia in forming a community among intersex persons and families, Sally struggled to settle into a sense of belonging, even among activists. Isolation was Sally's constant companion.

Uneasy Activist Community

Activist Sharon Cox specializes in sexuality and spirituality at Triangle Project, an activist organization in South Africa. Sharon invited Sally to speak with helpline counselors about intersexuality. "Unlike others," Sharon explained, "Sally was unafraid to use herself as a learning tool. She put herself out there as being intersex and shared her journey. Everyone learned so much from her. One could ask her questions without fear. Since then, I've adopted her style because it opens people to asking questions that they otherwise might not."[30] Sharon admired Sally's patience and measured speech in the face of hurtful questions. Unlike most activists, Sharon specified, Sally's reach had been global. She described how Sally inspired bravery and informed pioneer intersex activists around the globe. Sally's focus was always structural change beyond any individual. As someone who is also unafraid of confronting religious injustice, Sharon admired Sally's ability to critique religion. She pointed out that Sally came from relative privilege as a white person in South Africa. Remarkably, Sally advanced justice for all, not one particular group.

According to Sharon, activists often die too soon due to the emotional impact on one's physical and spiritual being. She asked rhetorically, reflecting on Sally's passing, how many activists have we let down? To be clear, she was not advocating for more self-care so much as community care.[31] Teams of people are needed to provide consistent meals and transportation. Sharon asserted, "We failed Sally. She couldn't get out or see to herself. . . . I'm not sure how many people were physically there for her, beyond [Facebook] Messenger. Nothing takes that place."[32] Sharon stressed the multitude of injuries that collided within Sally's body, speculating that the pain must be unbearable. Moreover, she was speaking from personal experience. Sharon and her partner are both currently facing life-threatening ailments. They have lost comrades to illness. Activist emotional labor is intense, and the individuals who do this work often lack financial security and caregivers. Sharon imagined the difficulties Sally faced as she became immobile—what it must have been like to wait for someone to deliver food or transport her to a doctor's appointment. "Many of us activists depend upon one another as family. Where does that leave us if we emphasize self-care?"[33]

Journalist Charlene Smith communicated with Sally mainly on Facebook and by email, though sometimes by phone, about strategies for effective activism. Although focused on different issues, Charlene and Sally were dismayed by how medical professionals treated them. According to Charlene, they learned to cope with their pain by focusing their energy on changing laws and informing the public. "We both needed to raise consciousness about issues that people don't like to talk about," Charlene explained. "No one wants to be the one to talk about rape."[34] The friends also appreciated interreligious activism, which allowed each to critique injustice without jettisoning all religions.

There were marked differences in how Sally approached her activism compared to Charlene, who currently lives comfortably as a journalist in the United States. Although several NGOs and political parties approached Charlene, she refused their funding because she believed she would be more powerful on her own. She did not want to serve anyone else's agenda. Conversely, Sally became embroiled in power plays and fell victim to some opportunistic activists. Charlene is not the only participant to suggest that Sally suffered mistreatment at the hands of fellow activists. Several participants I interviewed implied that funds were not properly allocated, and Sally frequently went unacknowledged and without payment for her labor. Many benefited from Sally's efforts and acknowledged her contributions posthumously, but Charlene wondered, "Wouldn't it have been nice if they did that when she was alive?"[35]

Fingers point in various directions. The main thrust of it is that Sally felt too emotionally bound up with fellow activists to confront them safely. She earnestly desired to advance social justice and trusted that others did as well. Conversely, Charlene recalls the post-liberation moment in which she felt exhilarating freedom to assert herself: "I gave everybody hell and got away with it. People applauded me. There were no personal consequences. Today I might be sued."[36] From what Charlene could tell, Sally was manipulated by various actors within a maelstrom of marginalized groups competing for funding and significance. Sally found herself in perilous financial straits and without community, whereas Charlene kept to herself. "Hers is not the first story of a person doing the right thing and ending up penniless. Her problem," Charlene summed up, "was that she was honest and an idealist."[37]

In November, just months before Sally passed away, she phoned Liesl Theron of Gender Dynamix. Liesl often traveled the Northern Hemisphere during South Africa's hot summer months. Before leaving for these stints, Liesl made sure to share a meal with family. She and Sally fancied themselves gourmands and enjoyed exploring new restaurants together. Sally called Liesl to say that they would need to go out for dinner before Liesl's trip if Liesl wanted to see her again. The implication was, according to Liesl, that Sally knew she was near death. It would be a farewell dinner.

Jacaranda blossoms carpeted the roads in purple and scented the walk to Sally's modest home in Observatory, Cape Town. Liesl rang the bell, but it would take Sally some time to locate her purse with a long chain, upon which she had hooked the key to the exterior security gate. Liesl patiently looked at the overcrowded garden.[38] Once inside, the two made their way down a long passage of wood floors. They passed what might have been designed as a dining or living room on the right but that Sally had transformed into her study. Atop Sally's desk sat an oversized computer monitor. Books in English, Greek, Hebrew, Latin, and other languages lined nearly every surface throughout the apartment, spilling into the kitchen. The only surface Liesl recalls having been clear of books were two La-Z-Boy recliners and a television set in another room. The fur shed by Sally's two beloved cats coated everything—the sound of classical music occupied all else.

Liesl speculates that Sally might have felt lonely because she always spoke at such a high intellectual level, laden with jargon. Few companions could keep up with her head and heart. Thoroughly charming, Sally longed for deep and lasting friendships with persons who could engage her diverse commitments. Her wit made her approachable and warm. Although Sally explained her medical conditions to Liesl after having researched them in medical journals, Liesl could not recall her technical diagnosis.[39] The two laughed with one another over steaks at a Hastings restaurant that November night. It was a surreal experience, Liesl recalls, knowing she was having a final meal with her friend. Due to a lack of health benefits and finances, Sally had pursued every avenue for assistance. All her networks came up empty. Fellow activists were struggling to make ends meet themselves. The NGO industrial complex, as Liesl calls it, places the burden on employees to practice self-care rather than providing sufficient accommodations. The harsh accountability for using all funds renders employees sick and overworked, according to Liesl. Some desperately took to social media and GoFundMe to raise funds for Sally.[40]

As with several of Sally's other confidants, Liesl recalls that Sally expressed great fear that she would die without dignity. Although Liesl regrets having been preoccupied with preparations for her travel, she is not alone. Many, in retrospect, wish they had asked about Sally's end-of-life wishes. Making such inquiries can feel intrusive, if not outright offensive. It is not unusual for people to avoid such topics with a loved one. It speaks more to the great affection people had for Sally than to any shortcomings of one individual. Sally had done the math. She shared the breakdown of her bank statements, monthly expenses, and medical expenses with Liesl and others. In her estimation, she had three to four months to live, which proved accurate. Liesl stressed, "Activists do *not* have to die without dignity."[41]

Professor Helen Brock wrote about Sally's religiosity to Jennifer Williams: "Personally, I have known Sally as a Quaker and a [B]uddhist and found her to be knowledgeable on religion, Judaism, Christianity, and even Islam. What touched me was that Sally remained a 'pastor' whatever the context, she showed an ability to counsel and give advice that showed more than an intellectual understanding of people's needs."[42] Sally had long practiced Buddhist meditation and then, after leaving Catholicism, joined a Quaker community. According to Intersex International Australia President Morgan Carpenter, Sally found a new religious community in her activism: "In a sense, the intersex community became her congregation, where she continued to live out her vocation, and where she was surrounded by people she loved right to the end."[43]

As with her experience in religious communities, Sally struggled to find her place among the very networks she created. Activism promised a new chosen family and support system, but one that Sally felt an urgency to produce precisely because she continued to feel out of place. Activists, progressive Jews, and intersex communities all spoke to an aspect of herself, but none seemed to embrace wholeness fully. In a sense she had found her people, but Sally paid a price for her commitment to agitating. Sally labored to pull unlikely groups of people together. It seemed clear to her that the only way forward was through collective efforts, but how does one unify agitators committed to competing issues? It is a trick of institutional power to pit marginalized groups against one another. Perhaps because it seemed evident to her that all flourishing is mutual, Sally could not ascribe to single-issue activism or compete against agitators.[44] Her friendships with comrades were at once profound and also alienated. In retrospect, activists express their debt to Sally. But, interpersonally, their affection for her personality wavered in no small part because of her idealism. No one can fulfill her lofty aspirations.

9. Costs of Activism

If we're serious about addressing the production of burnout, fatigue, exhaustion, debility, and disability within trans lives and communities, we cannot afford to internalize and operationalize a concept of care as debt. —HIL MALATINO, *Trans Care*

Harassment

After Easter in 2002, Sally found a small blue envelope in her mailbox. After tearing it open, she unfolded the paper. Absent was a date or signature. As she remembers it, the letter was sent by a group of people disquieted about her intersexuality, who likely learned about her through *The Felicia Show* on television:

> It claimed that a doctor or [*sic*] had been consulted about the issue of intersexuality, and that it was common knowledge that intersexed people who had not been subjected to early surgery were associated with particularly bad criminality and perversion.
> I think that it associated intersexed people with the abuse and rape of children, and gestured at a then-current and widely publicized spate of incidents of child-abuse in this regard.

The letter took the view that people like me were less than human, were a danger to public safety and were to be put down (I think that the phrase "put down" was used in the letter) in the interests of public safety like wild or rabid animals on the loose. Lethal injections were mentioned, if I remember correctly.[1]

The contents so deeply revolted Sally that she destroyed the letter. It was another attack on her sense of personhood. She wondered how anyone might suggest that she would abuse a child merely because of her anatomy.

By May, Sally learned that a significantly similar letter had been delivered to her employer, Lauren Waring. Waring reports receiving a phone call from the secretary to the commissioner that April. Commissioner Shamiella Vallie had received a letter with hate speech focused on Sally: "The letter characterized Ms Gross as a dangerous animal and an abomination that should have been put down at birth. It went on to say that the writer(s) insisted that the Commission immediately terminate the services of Ms Gross, as there were deserving citizens who required her job, home and livelihood. The gist of the letter was that Ms Gross and all those associated with her were depraved."[2]

Then came the harassing phone calls. Sally describes, "I returned from work to find a voicemail message on my Telkom line. The message consisted of an indistinct track of music and what seemed to be deep breathing. This shook me." Three days later, she found another harassing letter, which she reported to the police. One officer, Sally reports, refused to investigate her harassers because her intersexuality put him off. When she asked her employer if he still had a copy of the letter sent to him, he regretted having thrown it away.[3] According to her employer's recollection, the letter referred to her as human vermin that cannot be tolerated in a civilized society. He informed the regional head immediately, who requested that he not discuss the matter with Sally.[4]

Sally pushed back. She would not be intimidated or retreat into the shadows of society. In an open letter to her harassers, Sally declares, "You characterise me as a danger to public morals, welfare and safety by reason for the fact that I am born intersexed, connecting what I am from birth with criminality and depravity of the worst kinds. You say that, like a dangerous animal on the loose, I must be put down in the interests of public welfare and safety, perhaps by lethal injections."[5] For her, the unsigned letters reflected cowardice: "What I can gather from your actions, however, is **what** you are: a coward. . . . Those born like me are neither freaks nor monsters, and that natural diversity and difference is to be celebrated rather than being suppressed. Appreciation and celebration of diversity is fundamental to the ethos of our post-apartheid South Africa, and the fact that it is something in which I and all who value the defeat of Apartheid take great pride."[6] Sally rejected the notion that her harassers reflect public opinion in casting intersexuality as a freakish monstrosity. All intersex people, Sally asserted, are a part of natural diversity that merits celebration in post-apartheid South Africa. Despite the harassment, Sally explained, she would continue working to destigmatize intersexuality.

Loneliness

Only the second time Justine van Rooyen saw her, Sally's eyes filled with tears, and she asked: *What's the point?*[7] At the time, Justine was a young research assistant who did not know how to respond. She asked her activist mentor, Deborah Ewing, whom she described as an endlessly compassionate soul, to step in. Deborah always knew how to assuage Sally's pain. Another time, Justine recalled, Sally struggled with stairs at a conference lacking accessibility. Due to her physical ailments, Sally required an elevator. She made her discontent known, and, according to Justine, everyone ignored Sally. Deborah remembers Sally agreeing to be carried, which she experienced as a painful and undignified entry.[8] Disgruntled by the inconvenience of Sally's request for accessibility accommodation, other activists directed their attention to work.

Deborah felt immense sympathy for Sally, acutely exposed due to her voice, size, and limited mobility.[9] Collaborators and even strangers assumed they had a right to know what her genitals looked like, whether she had had surgery, and if she took hormones. But once they had the opportunity to get to know Sally, Deborah observed, they would literally sit at her feet to learn from her. Sally was able to expand people's minds by asking freeing questions. Their meetings gave South Africans an opportunity to confront the prejudices that Apartheid imposed. Deborah felt that her world expanded by collaborating with people from various backgrounds on similar political concerns. People gravitated toward Sally, she explained, because she made people feel safe.

When Sally offered a session on intersexuality from a faith-based perspective, so many people signed up that they had to move the talk into the hotel lounge. Hotel staff and guests even stopped to listen in. Sally surveyed resources from Christian, Jewish, Islamic, Buddhist, and Hindu traditions about intersexuality. She went over the scheduled time by thirty minutes, and the film crew, who had planned to get snippets from each room, refused to stop filming her. At the Land Claims Commission, Sally had attentively listened to people's stories of being displaced from their homes and did everything she could to have their land returned to them. Now, she worked tirelessly to advance gender-based rights for LGBTQI+ persons globally. Many admired her, but only a few extended their friendship to her.

Over time, Justine developed an earnest friendship with Sally. As she learned Sally's story, she realized the extent to which society is built on a gender binary. She admired Sally for refusing the categories offered: "She was odd as a woman with her deep voice. People assumed she was trans, but she wasn't. We still think in a dichotomous way, even if we don't want to, because that is how the world is organized. If [society] validated different identities, her experience could have been different."[10] Sally's impact on Justine was so profound that Justine went on to write about intersexuality for her global health master's thesis in Ireland.[11] She explained that it would have been far easier for Sally to hide her intersex status to blend in. People still do not understand what intersex is, Justine explained, which made it harder on Sally and deepened her depression.

Sally was struggling to survive, whereas the lesbian and gay communities were more successful at securing funding. While working on her master's thesis, Justine remembers missing many Skype calls from Sally. She appreciated Sally but was swamped with her studies and could not keep up with Sally's need for connection. She wondered who Sally's primary confidant was. Many activists found emotional and psychological support outside of their work community. Justine would later dedicate her master's thesis to Sally, which she completed in the year of Sally's death. She admired that Sally dared to reach out from the depths of her despair: "She just wanted to be accepted and understood. Her eyes were searching: Do you *get* me?"[12] As Sally's activism gained traction, she became a well-known public figure. Activists working in a variety of subfields were indebted to her for the legal advancements she had made. But as Justine's story intimates, many activists struggled interpersonally with Sally.

A revered activist on the one hand, Sally was still an outlier of sorts when it came to social and emotional relationships. One venue through which she attempted to forge friendships was with a local Go club in Observatory.[13] Andrew Davies has been hosting the club's monthly meetings in a quaint house turned restaurant and bar for decades. The club meets in a cozy room to the left of the main entrance, where drawings of flowers compose a gallery wall interspersed with hanging plants.

The game Go was invented in China centuries ago. One player uses white beads, the other black. Approximately five games are played in this club at any time, and an odd player might sit out from time to time. A few members are highly ranked. Architect and Go enthusiast Lloyd Rubidge explained to me that he estimates Sally was somewhere in the average range. The more serious players use a clock and record their results online. Rubidge drove Sally to their meetings. She preferred an adjacent room with more comfortable seating, where players would take turns joining her. Rubidge explained that although Sally was one of the weaker players, she enjoyed the social and intellectual stimulation, and he enjoyed learning about Marxism over meals with Sally. By way of thanks for all the lifts he provided, she once bought him a Go book, which surprised and delighted Rubidge.[14]

Hyjin Kim is a nonbinary NGO advocacy officer who was learning Go from Rubidge when I visited the club. Kim confided that Sally was not an easy person to get to know in depth. She was awkward, and, they explained, many people gossiped about her.[15] Kim expressed that people were put off by Sally talking too much. In Kim's estimation, how Sally handled situations among fellow activists made her unpopular. They expressed frustration with Sally for not taking advice and being too passive: "It gets vicious [in activism]. She was a kind, sweet person. [Intersex South Africa] was defrauded because she trusted that people would do the right thing."[16] For Kim, the fallout after global donors ceased funding South African activist groups is still pronounced. "To this day," they went on, "we don't talk to certain people."[17] Candidly, they reflected, "[Sally] was very kind in a very unkind world. I wasn't always kind to her because I found her to be difficult. As much as I disagree with how she ran ISSA, she single-handedly started it. No one spoke about intersex issues before her. The start of the intersex movement in South Africa was Sally Gross."[18]

Kim's account illuminates the challenges within activist communities. On the one hand, everyone is working collectively to build a more just society. On the other, capitalism pits various causes and people against one another to compete for funding. Sally's idealism made her useful to others but did not ensure friendship in kind. Advocating for intersex persons proved lonely, even as she made strides. She improved political policies but not her personal sense of belonging.

Financial Precarity

By 2007, Sally was in significant debt. When her mother, Mildred, passed away, Sally flew to Israel twice.[19] Due to the severity of her financial state, Sally reflected upon the possibility of having to sell her books to stay afloat: "Having to sell my books is like having to amputate bits of my body—and for what? ... When everything which constitutes the fabric of my life has gone, life on the street—which is nasty, brutish and short in South Africa, particularly since there will not be much tolerance for someone who is intersexed or disabled, and where I can expect my life to be taken even for a few cents—awaits."[20] The anticipation of turning fifty-four years old led Sally to believe that her chances of finding employment elsewhere were low, but early retirement would preclude a pension.[21] A disabled, intersex, aged person, she found herself precarious without savings, social security, or a family safety net.[22] "It has been noted that public servants in my age-band take sick-leave more often than younger people, and measures have been put in place to eliminate this putative abuse of sick-leave." She explained the systemic injustice at hand. "The situation is apparently being managed by making it costly for those who are ill or disabled to take leave by reason of illness."[23]

It was risky to leave the Regional Land Claims Commission and found Intersex South Africa. While employed at the Regional Land Claims Commission, she couldn't get to or from work. Sally reflected in one of her letters that she sensed she did not have many more years of health. She made the difficult decision to leave the commission for early retirement in 2011 at great personal sacrifice because it negated any entitlement to a pension. The financial and subsequent health effects of this decision would be immense, but by starting ISSA, she could prioritize educating medical practitioners and intersex families.[24] The AIDS Foundation of South Africa and Atlantic Philanthropies were the two major sources of funding that equipped Sally to found Intersex South Africa. Based on Sally's impressive record of amending bills that disenfranchise intersex persons, the AIDS Foundation of South Africa promised four years of funding for Intersex South Africa.[25] The Netherlands Culture and Health Program had also promised Intersex South Africa four years of funding. However, they withdrew all funding from the AIDS Foundation of South Africa, which threw ISSA into a financial crisis. Sally resolved to abstain from taking a salary so that she would be able to afford her employees' salaries.

How is an activist to survive financial precarity? South African activists frequently must travel, which proved especially financially and physically burdensome for Sally. She wrote to her friend Bernice: "It seems fairly clear in any scenario that I am dying.... I can go knowing that I will have left both South Africa and the world a kinder place for people who are intersex like myself, as a direct consequence of years of personal activism.... Were I to drift off in the night in my own bed, it would be a blessing.... What are needed are support-structures which go far beyond the capacities of individuals."[26] In an email to Frances Flatman and Father Martin Flatman, Sally explained:

> I lack familial and social safety-nets. My brother in Boston has far more pressing concerns than my survival right now, something he has made clear to me, and I am a physical monster, a gentile and a tax-collector, an apostate, an opponent of the Israeli regime of occupation in the West Bank and hence a vicious anti-Semite, a former opponent of apartheid in South Africa—some of my relatives remember the "good old days" with nostalgia—and an embarrassment unworthy of life, for the relatives whom I knew when I was growing up, all of who[m] seem to have landed up on the West Coast of the US and in Canada. I am a pariah as far as they are concerned, and am wanted out of sight and out of mind.[27]

I squirmed in my seat as Ray Schmidt-Gross got to this section of the book draft, which I had flagged "ask Ray for his response." He was kind enough to comb through the manuscript line by line and correct any misrepresentation. To my surprise, he confirmed Sally's statement. It was true that their extended family did not embrace Sally as Christian or intersex. Although she and Ray, and certainly Ray's wife Sharon, differed on their politics, namely regarding the state of Israel, Sally felt the freedom to openly express her views with Ray and Sharon without fear of rejection. Despite that, they were not always able to financially support Sally.[28] Sharon and Ray also described to me the financial stress they were under at that time. After reading the book draft, Ray felt the weight of Sally's tragic end: "Could I have done more? Maybe I should have taken out a loan for 10 or 20k to get her through a bit longer. That would have been a big conversation with Sharon. [But] I'm her *brother*."[29]

Sister-in-law Sharon thought it was irresponsible of Sally to have left her stable government job to start the NGO Intersex South Africa. It irked her that Sally was not more proactive about caring for herself. "It was more important to her to help people than to take care of herself," Sharon vented.[30] Scrolling through Sally's Facebook wall, Sharon noted all the causes that

Sally got behind—refugees, autism, whales. "She talked about everything but not herself. Sally never complained about her childhood. You didn't know anything about her, just bits and pieces. . . . I feel bad that I never knew who she was when she was alive. You can have somebody next to you and you don't really see them. That's sad."[31] To be clear, there were many attempts that church, state, friends, comrades, and family made to keep Sally afloat. The crowdfunding and personal gifts speak to how much Sally meant to the various networks in her life. However, these piecemeal offerings were neither sufficient nor sustainable.

Provocatively, Sally asked: How can a tree possibly flourish once its roots have been destroyed?[32] Without a biological family with the means to support her financially, Sally struggled to make ends meet as an activist. Her comrades have survived by means that were incompatible with Sally's temperament. Many still feel the sting of the struggle to exist in a culture that burdens them to practice self-care rather than establishing policies that enable citizens to serve as activists for social justice. Sally reached out to all her contacts in various sectors—the church, government, activists, friends, family, etc.—but ultimately, in my opinion, she died of poverty.[33] Without funds, she struggled to maintain adequate housing, food, and health care. Absent being independently wealthy, most people require a community to see them through emotional, spiritual, and physical hardship. Sally's principled disposition alienated her from these social networks, and she had no government aid to fall back on for support.

Compromised Health

Sally reflected, "My body is like a car which bears the marks of heavy and productive use."[34] Sally's efforts to confront injustice took a toll on her physical condition, and her body was transformed through resisting Apartheid. Julia Watts Belser maintains, "[Disability] is not an unusual case, but a pervasive experience of subjugated bodies. Disability is central to the corporeal architecture of domination."[35]

Due to anemia, Sally received blood transfusions and iron infusions. This improved her health a bit, but a marrow biopsy revealed that her iron reserves were exhausted. Her hematologist was perplexed. She did not have signs of bleeding. Doctors instructed her to avoid physical exertion. They also discovered that her cardiac blood vessels were calcified, which was causing angina. A gastroenterologist gave her a capsule endoscopy. Sally swallowed a capsule the size of a large vitamin with an LED light and a miniature camera that transmits tens of thousands of photos while passing through the digestive tract. From this, they learned that the villi in her small intestine, which absorb iron and other nutrients, were flattened and destroyed. Doctors diagnosed Sally with autoimmune villous atrophy. Apparently, an autoimmune reaction can damage villi.[36] According to Sally, there were only eleven known cases at the time and no cure. The cost of her prescribed medications was beyond Sally's means. "What this medical situation means," Sally wrote to Ronnie Kasrils, "and something I can certainly feel, is that I am dying."[37]

On November 14, 2011, Sally emailed Professors Sebastian and Helen Brock about her bleak circumstances. Her sense of impending death and the detail with which she described her medical conditions intimate that recipients of Sally's emails might have experienced empathy fatigue. This might explain why some friends were shocked to learn of her death, even though she had been predicting it for some time. Discerning between false alarms and her actual end proved murky for some. For Sally, her health and finances were not salvageable. She did not exhibit illusions of rescue or permanent recovery. Instead, she made a modest plea for palliative care. But more than any physical discomfort, she suffered the pangs of loneliness: "Something which has been particularly difficult is seeing the apparently intractable crisis coming for a long time, having to face it alone and in physical isolation, and not being able to find a way of 'managing' and mitigating the situation."[38] While brave about confronting death itself, Sally cringed at the prospect of suffering alone.

The Brocks were consistently generous and sympathetic. Sebastian wired large sums of money to Sally, upon which she became entirely dependent for her survival until the day she died. She emailed the Brocks again on January 19, 2014, with further descriptions of her health, explaining that she had her expenses covered until February 14, eerily close to the day that she is estimated to have died. "In an ideal world, there should be some kind of socialised safety-net. There is none here. . . . I wanted to explain why this is, to say farewell and to thank you for your friendship and your great kindness to me over the years," she wrote.[39] Upon receiving her email, the Brocks immediately sent £800 to Sally.[40] Timothy Radcliffe arranged with the order to send money for Sally's iron supplements. He reflected, "She had so much to give—her experience in politics, religious knowledge. If only it could have worked for her to remain in the Order and flourish. We could not receive her gifts at that time."[41]

In the months and weeks leading up to Sally's passing, she sounded the alarm. Her financial and physical states were dire. She had been living off donations from friends in South Africa and the United Kingdom for over a year, but these were depleted. In a letter addressed to her fellow activists, she requested help for herself and a plea to make systemic changes for their sake:

> I am neither the first nor the last activist to be in these straits and believe that this needs to involve approaches to international institutions, states and international donors and will require the setting up of a support-system. Our issue—intersex—is being taken up both at the level of states and at the international level, and I believe that safety-nets can be put in place for activists though it will require much lobbying, time and patience.[42]

These words would haunt their recipients. In many of my interviews, activists bemoan not having done something to allow Sally to die with dignity. They heard her requests for assistance but, for manifold reasons, did not act. Personally, I am not convinced that activist groups who exert most of their energy advocating for others should be held primarily responsible for how things unfolded. However, I must acknowledge the activists and scholars who disagree with me.[43] Some believe that their activist community's responsibility is to one another even while they struggle for institutional change.

Some comrades came to Sally's aid. On November 8, 2013, Gabrielle Le Roux sent out an email to Sally's friends: "Anyone who knows Sally, knows how stoic and private she is, and how hard it is for her to ask for help. . . . It is her dream that she will be able to recover enough to put some more energy into her project of recording her memoirs—her life is an extraordinary, and important story by any measure—but at present her stressful circumstances and failing health prevent this."[44] The email included a two-page document written by Sally in which she explains her commitment to intersex activism as born of personal experience but driven by a thirst for systemic justice:

> I promised myself that I would do whatever I could to ensure that no other intersex person would be treated by ecclesiastical authorities in the way I was treated. . . . What informed it was a sense that the way in which my situation was handled was systemic rather than personal, and that a failure of courage on the part of just a handful of decision-makers, who were at an utter loss to know how to handle the issue, drove it.[45]

Mani Mitchell—the activist Sally befriended at Max Beck's intersex retreat in Asheville in 1997—was also among the friends she alerted. Though living on different continents, they stayed in touch by Skype and caught up in person at international intersex events.⁴⁶ Upon learning how severe things had become, Mani made appeals throughout the intersex community and initiated a fundraising project for Sally. Amid this trying time, Mani remembers Sally's laugh. She could speak frankly about death and still embrace a belly laugh. They discussed life after death, thinking critically and learning together. "Her faith was still growing and consolidating to the end. It was as nonbinary as her embodiment," Mani recalled.⁴⁷

Sally shared her banking account details with Mani, who then reached out to fellow activists for support. On the website GoFundMe, Mani wrote, "I have known Sally for over 15 years and consider h/er [*sic*] a friend, mentor, inspirational human of the highest order—fellow intersex activist. Sally needs our help. She writes to us below in her own words."⁴⁸ Sally addressed a plea to her fellow activists and friends. In it, she explains her struggles with anemia and angina. Exacerbating matters, Sally explained, she was unable to work. Even when working, Sally abstained from taking a salary to pay employees of ISSA. In no uncertain terms, she asserts, "I am currently unable to replenish my stock of medication which is crucial to my survival. . . . What I seek is to be able to die in a bed (ideally my own) with the possibility of some palliative care and with such dignity and comfort as is possible."⁴⁹

Dignity

As someone who was routinely dehumanized and denigrated, Sally's last request was to die with dignity. It was not that she sought to be rescued from illness, poverty, or death. Rather, hers was a modest appeal for funds and support for her to pass away in bed. The humility she had to muster before publicizing her financial status and medical history did not come easily. She signed it off with, "It embarrasses me to make these requests."⁵⁰ These words reflect how dire circumstances had become for Sally. Mani reports that one payment did go through to Sally, so she died knowing that a few people were organizing funding for her.⁵¹

In the GoFundMe version of her letter, Sally stated, "For the longer term, we need to think about seeking to get a support-system in place for intersex activists who find themselves in similar circumstances, and this will require more than the private resources of members of our intersex activist community and investment of energy, time and patience."⁵² Perhaps she addressed this need specifically to activists. However, I am inclined to wonder if, rather than pressuring an already-depleted group, this call to care for activists might more rightly be an indictment of society. If the NGO industrial complex and capitalism more broadly lend themselves to Sally's dire circumstances, perhaps it is up to us to offer community support that includes but is not limited to financial contributions.[53]

Sally's ten-page, single-spaced letter to Ronnie Kasrils detailed her life story, activism, and declining health. It opens with the mention of a phone call the day prior in which Ronnie requested a letter with her relevant background. The purpose of her letter was to justify Sally's request for financial support: "What worries me, though," Sally wrote, "is the conjunction of the health challenges and the exhaustion of my financial resources." "What I fear, though," she disclosed, "is that the means for basic requisites of survival—shelter, a bed, basic food and clothing and medical care and medications—will be exhausted before my body has packed up. Given my severely limited mobility, there is no way I could survive, and that is a type of death I do fear. I would like to die in a bed, with basic care [*sic*] shelter and food."[54] Despite their relationship formed among "detribalized Jews," as Bradley Bordiss put it, Kasrils did not come to Sally's aid.

Sally acknowledged in the letter that she was no more worthy of employment than anyone else. She recognized that there are many impoverished people worldwide, and she has no greater right to life. Her wish, she shared, was for a world in which intersexuality would not be stigmatized. The birth of healthy intersex infants should occasion celebration. No surgery needs to be imposed unless the infant's physical survival requires it. A best guess of gender might be offered temporarily for rearing. She wanted secular and religious institutions to embrace intersex persons.[55] Sally would later reflect upon the difficulty intersexuality posed:

> There is no room for ambiguity or for liminality, which are perceived as deeply threatening because they do not fit into society's neat preconceived categories. When I was thought to fit the binary, I had a recognised identity and status. I was deemed to be a competent priest and preacher, and an able teacher, someone who had a powerful voice. When it became increasingly clear that what I am challenges the dichotomy, it is almost as if I was seen as threatening the very order of creation. I was no longer seen as a legitimate inhabitant of a shared social and moral world.[56]

She grieved the loss of dignity and privileges she once enjoyed when believed to be male. The incomprehensibility of intersexuality cut to the core of what it means to be human for Sally: "In the first place, not fitting into the binary, I was not really human and my existence threatened the set of categories which were deemed to be constitutive of humanity and of the ordering of human life."[57] The problem, as she understood it, was not her body; it was the limited imagination of social and moral bodies. As Sally experienced them, the effects of this were the loss of rights: "As someone who was beyond the pale, an outcast and outlaw, I had absolutely no rights and was denied information about steps taken in relation to my situation."[58] Her exclusion from religious and political communities translated into social death.[59]

Pamela Sykes explained that Sally kept her relationships compartmentalized and, as such, only asked certain people for specific kinds of assistance. She speculates that Sally did not want anyone to know the grim severity of what she was facing and that she was not coping. Her deteriorating health was exacerbated by her inability to cook for herself. Increasingly, she had to have food delivered, which also contributed to the mound of rubbish accumulation. Sally was increasingly isolated because she had trouble getting out and could not invite people to socialize in her home when it was in such a state. It took courage for her to ask Sykes for help removing the mounds of trash accumulated in her home due to her immobility.

Beyond the disarray of her living quarters, Sykes recalls Sally's religious items, such as candles, oils, and Buddhist bells.[60] Ultimately, her heart, according to Sykes, was in the monastery. She imagined the difficulty Sally must have faced upon leaving Blackfriars without the life skills most people develop between their thirties and forties: "She left the world, took her vows, and the Catholic Church pushed her back into the world unprepared. They might have been clueless, but it was still cruel."[61]

Over time, Sally became increasingly dependent upon the virtual community and communicated primarily through Facebook Messenger, email, and Skype. It is a not uncommon experience for intersex persons and persons with disabilities to seek one another out. An inhospitable environment confines certain bodies to cyber relationships, which, while vibrant, also reinforces society's rejection and abandonment. In one of their last conversations, Sykes remembers Sally saying that the one thing she envied was that Sykes had children. She would have loved to have had a family. Although Sally did not desire a reproductive sexual companion, she valued the companionship that a family affords. Sally had suffered repeated dislocation throughout her life. Societies that organize living space around heterosexual reproduction isolate and abandon partnerless, childless, asexual persons like Sally. For Sally, religion once promised refuge from this structure.

Within capitalist societies, there tends to be an assumption that family members are financially responsible for one another, so some interviewees have asked why Sally's brother Ray did not come to her rescue. Some were under the impression that he was a successful businessperson with the means to do so. Therefore, it struck them as cruel that he did not aid her. However, Ray was facing his own financial troubles. When he and his first wife separated, he worked multiple jobs despite a back injury. The emotional pain of divorce weighed heavily on him, but Ray remained motivated to support his two young children. His herniated discs were further injured after a car accident, which rendered him bedridden. Ray lost his job. At the time, the government unemployment agency in Israel was on strike. He remembers not having water or electricity. He relied on friends for an occasional meal and drank water from outdoor hoses. Reading a draft of this book brought him to tears. He empathized with Sally—he, too, lived through bouts of poverty. It pained him that he could not offer Sally more financial resources.[62]

Theorist Michel Foucault explains society's interest in placing the burden of care upon the families of impoverished, sick people. He writes, "The sick man is no doubt incapable of working, but if he is placed in a hospital he becomes a double burden for society: the assistance that he is given relates only to himself, and his family is, in turn, left exposed to poverty and disease. . . . The care spontaneously given by family and friends will cost nobody anything; and the financial assistance given to the sick man will be to the advantage of the family."[63] Foucault argues that the professionalization of medicine serves state power and not impoverished individuals: "Poverty is an economic fact for which assistance must be given while it exists; disease is an individual accident that the family must respond to by ensuring that the victim has the necessary care. The hospital is an anachronistic solution that does not respond to the real needs of the poor and that stigmatizes the sick in a state of penury."[64] Due to Sally's impoverished state and ailing health, one might have the impulse to blame her brother Ray for not caring for her needs. However, Foucault's insight suggests that she fell victim to the professionalization of medicine, in which her body was considered a problem.

Looking through various versions of Mildred's and Jack's wills, I was struck that earlier versions named one another as primary beneficiaries and their children as secondary beneficiaries; in contrast, after Mildred died, Jack's later versions named only Sally.[65] Jack did not have much to his name, but even a small bit would have been useful to Sally due to her lack of income. Jack had not appointed an executor for his will, which made the funds inaccessible.[66] Sally would have had to fly to Israel and hire an attorney to represent her, which would have cost more than was in the bank.[67] Exacerbating matters, the assisted care facility where Mildred and Jack had lived in their later years, funded by the South African Zionist Federation, claimed the parents signed loans for large sums. Though they approached Sally and Ray to collect on these, Ray found that no legal paperwork obliged them to make such payments.[68]

Underlying Sally's description of having lost her biological and spiritual families is the presumption that these communities are responsible for vulnerable populations. There is an expectation that between these communities and the state, persons with disabilities and folks who serve society will theoretically not slip through the cracks. Sally reached out to the Catholic Church and requested reparations. When they refused, she asked whether a priest might perform her last rites. According to Jennifer Williams, they also denied her this.[69] Sally writes:

> Christian faith was, in a real sense, my *modus vivendi* with myself, and it was smothered. The Order was my family, my home and the indispensable locus of my vocation and my sole provision for illness and old-age. As matters have stood for a good few years, I have no family in any conventional sense. My natural family rejects me, on the whole, because I am intersex and because I was Christian. While I know many people, I am unable to visit others because of my increasing limited mobility, and am not visited.[70]

Sally's demise was premature, which speaks to the urgency at hand. Community is essential for one's faith and well-being. Without a religious community or family connections, Sally struggled to create an activist community. The difficulty she had with establishing emotional intimacy among comrades disheartened her. She was dehumanized in life and deprived of dignity in death. Her dreadful death suggests a need to break current systems to allow for structural transformation to how we form communal bodies. Part IV returns to the cycle described at the beginning of this book: body problems, problem bodies, agitating bodies, and bodiliness. It speaks to Sally's motivation. What could be worth such sacrifice? What breaks are we willing to endure? What sutures can we offer? We need clearings from institutional bodies to nurture diverse ecologies. Resonance awaits.

IV

BODILINESS

Indigeneity is also often distinguished by relationships to the more-than-human worlds. These relationships exist in, between, and across bodies, lands, waters, and world. Rooted in specific languages, histories, and traditional teachings, these relationships situate human beings in networks of responsibilities to human and more than-human-beings. These relationships are ancestral and emerging, situated in particular territories and among particular peoples. —ABEL R. GOMEZ, "Indigeneity"

There's an obvious intersection in terms of really looking deeply at what it means to fight for sovereignty of land and body. I'm excited to look at how we think about our bodies as environments, and really expand this idea that environment is not just something that is external to our actual physical bodies—it is all of our political, physical, spiritual, and emotional environments. —LAURA JIMENEZ, KIERRA JOHNSON, AND CARA PAGE, "Beyond the Trees"

What might Sally have meant when she coined the term *bodiliness*? She could have used the word *embodied* or something more familiar, but she did not. Instead, she chose this strange word *bodiliness* to point to something unique. Bodiliness has to do with the relationships we share through our bodies. Sally reached for the term *bodiliness* to distinguish it from philosophical dualism and Gnosticism, with their propensities to subordinate the concerns of the flesh. She rejected the idealization of the mind or soul over the body and challenged the regulation of bodies. Intersex bodies, she specified, undermine assumptions about sex and gender. She described her experience of bodiliness as an awkward and painful realization that gender stereotypes and racial oppression result from the unjust regulation of bodies. Additionally, Sally preached bodiliness as a vehicle through which Christ crucified makes God known to humanity and by which humanity will be glorified:

> We are not essentially immaterial ghosts in machines of flesh, we are living human bodies, so to speak, and the future God has stored up for us is one which involves and glorifies the whole of us, spirit and body. We encounter God in our flesh, the flesh which God takes on in Christ, the flesh which is raised and glorified at Easter. Some of us (I certainly speak for myself) might sometimes wish that some of this "too solid flesh might melt"; but to reject one's bodiliness *tout court*, to reject the glorification by God's grace of this very flesh, is to reject God's grace to us in Christ, who came to redeem all flesh and not just immaterial spirits.[1]

Eric Plemons describes the importance of discursive productions of the body as well as the very concrete, day-to-day stakes: "The stakes are high for those whose lives depend not on thinking about trans- bodies but surviving in them."[2] To his insight, I have presented here the indispensable contribution that religion supplies to the making and remaking of bodies.

Bodiliness is a shorthand for the cycle I described at the beginning of this book. The setting for bodiliness is a clearing. The events that take place include breaks and sutures. The aim is resonance. Breaks sometimes happen upon us; other times, we leverage them against problem bodies. Breaks allow sutures, or the pulling together of what regulating bodies have torn apart. It is a restructuring. These events, breaks, and sutures are aimed at resonance—where difference enriches belonging. There is suffering and joy in bodiliness. Through our bodiliness, we laugh, cry, and dance as Toni Morrison's Baby Suggs character instructed. Bodiliness grounds us in a particular place and time while also connecting us to other possibilities. This is at once spiritual and material. Bodiliness points to the resonance we experience when our interdependence rings with the intimacy of belonging.

Scholars Yolanda Covington-Ward and Jeanette S. Jouili explain, "'The experience of being embodied is never a private affair but is always already mediated by our continual interactions with other human and nonhuman bodies.' This insight has allowed for a more capacious understanding of how human bodies, nonhuman material bodies, and nonmaterial entities (e.g., spirits, divinities, and deities) interact with each other, which is crucial for the study of religion."[3] We miss her bodiliness when we consider Sally a private individual, independent from human and nonhuman bodies, material and spiritual. For Sally, bodiliness was a bothersome gift.

In what follows, I say more about the setting, events, and aims that accompany bodiliness. Sally held onto this strange term because it points to how bodies are unruly; they refuse to ascribe to one thing. It was at once plain and mysterious. With her, our bodiliness reminds us of our mortality; we are creatures in need of others, human and nonhuman. While not an entirely pleasant or certain journey, we might seek out the bodiliness that Sally reluctantly loved.

10. Clearings

The Clearing—a wide-open place cut deep in the woods nobody knew for what at the end of the path known only to deer and whoever cleared the land in the first place.
—TONI MORRISON, *Beloved*

Listening in wild places, we are audience to conversations in a language not our own. I think that it was a longing to comprehend this language I hear in the woods that led me to science, to learn over the years to speak fluent botany. A tongue that should not, by the way, be mistaken for the language of plants. —ROBIN WALL KIMMERER, *Braiding Sweetgrass*

A clearing in a forest contains little to no trees or bushes. In banking, a clearing is the settlement of differences. A clearing in the sky emerges from between drifting clouds. What I find intriguing about clearings, as opposed to cleansings, is the restructuring and reordering of elements that need not destroy or expunge. In fact, a clearing does not exist in the absence of crowding. A clearing might entail breaks and sutures, but it is not exclusively a destructive process. To clear is to make room, to make space. It is also a constructive effort.

Clearings create space for bodies to flourish within diverse ecologies. Land clearing provides greater stability for local species.[1] It allows remaining plants to have improved access to sunlight, water, and nutrients. Clearings also limit the spread of fire and airborne viruses that infect nearby vegetation. Overclearing has harmful effects on the environment, suggesting that it is a delicate balance to strike. Creating and maintaining clearings is labor. To agitate and initiate breaks is dangerous and exhausting. To do it well we cannot do this work alone. Collaborating with one another and our environment, we experience diverse belonging to ecologies. We are confronted with the reality that humanity is not the center of communal bodies but rather a piece of a broader ecology.

Hebrew Bible scholar Mari Joerstad persuasively argues that ancient scripture writers viewed nonanimal nature as alive and active. She uses the provocative term "persons" in reference to nonanimal nature to challenge modern Western notions of personhood. In so doing, Joerstad aims to inform contemporary applications of biblical interpretation to environmental action with a more accurate understanding of "personalistic nature texts."[2] What I appreciate most about Joerstad's analysis is her embrace of limitations. Despite her scholarly training to translate ancient texts, she foregrounds her inability to access the worldviews of biblical writers and nature itself. This frustration, she explains, "can be a means to greater openness to views of nature that differ from our own. The difficulty of getting to know unfamiliar views of nature sits within Christian and Jewish traditions—it appears on the scene before religions of the book encounter other religions and worldviews—and that difficulty reminds us to be humble when considering the 'rightness' of traditions that conflict with our experiences of the world."[3]

What Joerstad proposes here is remarkable. Despite carefully attending to scholarship on these biblical texts and adroitly explaining their uses and weaknesses, she avoids the temptation to assert herself as knowing rightly. Each time Joerstad comes up against worldviews foreign to her, she responds with humility and curiosity. Joerstad's posture comprises the invaluable substance and form of her book. It is not a definitive interpretation but rather devoted attention to an unknowable text and environment. Certainly, there are more and less accurate interpretations of the Hebrew Bible, which she parses. And yet, her main message to readers is a vision of humanity not at the center of the universe but as part of dynamic ecologies that have their own relations to God. She concludes that humanity should play a more courteous role within a broader ecology.

What if we engaged with Sally similarly? Instead of attempting to categorize her flesh, read or write upon it, what if we acknowledged our incapacity to fully know this person, not in a defeatist manner but rather as an act of tenderness? When we bump up against human beings of different worldviews and embodied experiences, it is an opportunity to expand and reorient our perspective while also accepting the inherent inaccessibility of these. "Frustrations," as Joerstad puts it, offer potential breaks that make room for clearings where not only can we experience the fullness of our bodies and emotions as beloved but also revel in our relations with the trees, which might have their own relations to one another and God.[4]

How can clearings serve intersex bodies specifically and social bodies broadly? As the gardener toils continually, so also persons committed to social justice enter an ongoing relationship that is never static or complete. Good relations are nurtured. With pastor Baby Suggs, we might experience ourselves as beloved—our overworked bodies that governing bodies have deemed a problem are loved. After exhausting her work within intuitions, Sally forged clearings through breaks followed by sutures. She hoped to make space for intersex persons to experience resonance within community and to feel beloved.

Sabbath

A religious Sabbath is a clearing. There are economic, agricultural, and spiritual elements to observing the Sabbath and its culmination—Jubilee. By decentering humanity within creation, Sabbath facilitates cyclical decolonization, liberation, and justice.

Reflecting on her time of rigorous study at Gateshead yeshiva, S. described the sweetness of Sabbath rest:

> As a fourteen-year-old student in Rabbinical College, studies left time for no more than about four hours' of sleep a night and sleep was therefore at a premium. There were no vacations, so there were few opportunities to catch up on sleep. One of the greatest pleasures of the Sabbath, and a real life-saver for all the students, was the chance to sleep for two or three hours between the end of lunch and the beginning of the Sabbath afternoon prayers.[5]

A temporary clearing, the Sabbath harbors weary bodies. It is time and space for acknowledging the limitations of embodied experience and reveling in dependence upon God and community. The Sabbath initiates a break, an interruption of labor to tend to bodies as gifts from God. Abraham Joshua Heschel describes the purpose of the Sabbath: "Man is not a beast of burden, and the Sabbath is not for the purpose of enhancing the efficiency of his work.... Labor is a craft, but perfect rest is an art. It is the result of an accord of body, mind and imagination."[6] Within holy time and space, S. tried to find a place for herself to exist.

The Sabbath is not merely for humans to abstain from work. God rested on the Sabbath. Scriptures instruct the land to have a Sabbath rest every seven years.[7] While crops ought not to be sown or harvested, any naturally occurring produce food should be available to farmers and those experiencing poverty. Moreover, debts accrued to produce poverty are to be canceled at the end of every seventh year. After seven cycles of sabbatical years, the fiftieth year was deemed a Jubilee. These laws were created to protect people and the land from exploitation. It is to acknowledge God as the Creator of all creation. We do not own one another, land, plants, or animals. These are gifts to be shared. The Sabbath is the setting for justice and liberation. It requires setting aside time and opening space for the sacred. Honoring the Sabbath is a sign of the covenant between God and creation.

The Sabbath offers a clearing for us to break from regulating problem bodies. Jason Crawford writes, "Our modern forms of labor, as Heschel imagines them, tend toward servitude, toward the exercise of violence both against the earth and against our own bodies and communities."[8] In clearings we come together in new ways. There is something holy about stopping to enjoy our bodies, individual and collective. God takes pleasure in all of creation. We too are called to pause regularly to delight in nonutilitarian appreciation. Pastor Suggs invites us to laugh, weep, and dance with a twisted hip.

Should we not heed this call to praise God, Jesus says that rocks will cry out.[9] Biblical scholar Sandy D. Rogers warns readers of the consequences for failure to maintain good relations with animals and land: "If the people do not join God in the creative activity of Sabbath, not only for the poor or even for the animals but for the very earth itself, the Holiness code portrays a God that will step in and provide for the land without humans.... If humans neglect the creation care that allows the earth to maintain its right relationship with its creator too long, it may be that God will relieve humanity of its stewardship so the earth can lie desolate and make up its Sabbaths."[10]

11. Breaks

Decolonizing intersex, then, also entails fostering an emphatically unnatural tolerance for pain at once individual and collective, which also paradoxically unfolds as a holistic capacity for epistemological disobedience and an ethical willingness to be undone and remade by our relationships with others. —DAVID RUBIN, "Provincializing Intersex"

"Break" can have negative connotations but need not be reduced to a destructive process. Breaks can be painful. The breaking of bones, alliances, and commitments hurts. Like clearings, breaks can also refer to making space for rest. We break-fast, join someone for a tea break, or go on a restroom break. These breaks attend to the body, its needs and limitations. They bring us together in clearings. We know that land needs breaks from farming. Thriving ecosystems cycle in and out of breaks.

Breaks facilitate innovation. In his analysis of improvisatory jazz, theorist Fred Moten argues, "We might look at the temporal-spatial discontinuity as a generative break, one wherein action becomes possible, one in which it is our duty to linger in the name of ensemble and its performance. That break allows, indeed it demands, a fundamental reorientation that we might call novelty, that always exists at the heart of tragedy and elegy."[1] The absence of sound is a prelude to resonance. Interruption is needed for governing bodies to stop problematizing individual bodies. Prior to resonance, there are breaks.

Sally experienced both painful breaks and generative ones. When Christian groups would break from Jews, she was pained. How could Jesus, a Jew, be extricated from Judaism? The breaking of genders, separation of maleness from femaleness, threatened to split her intersex self in two. Apartheid imposed fissures between racialized groups and the land. When the Catholic Church broke from her, Sally mourned once again.

We will see Sally confronted by breaks as governing bodies attempt to sever one part of herself from another. Disturbed by perhaps unintentional yet still harmful supersessionism within Christianity, she was equally appalled by Jews who expressed racist ideas about Black people. Breaks and tears to communal bodies can be lethal. Sally responds by breaking with discrimination rather than from particular groups. Unlike a purging movement, hers was aimed at collective good. She will then pull pieces of herself and various communities together, forming something dynamic and diverse. Sally later tended to these injuries like a skilled surgeon, suturing damaged flesh.

From these breaks, Sally discovered reorientations and worked to bring together what was broken apart. She made connections and recognized relations that others did not. For Sally, to be Christian was to be Jewish. She was intersex and whole. Sally was not beholden to any citizenship or collective that mistreated a people group. Her activism empowered Sally to initiate breaks rather than only suffer breaks. With others, she broke from injustice. She broke away from dehumanizing institutions and systems. It was an artful relationship, marked by improvisation not unlike Moten's jazz ensemble. Through agitating, Sally and her comrades made space to allow for reorientations that, with some suturing, would facilitate resonance.

Schisms

For S., the worst experiences of her time in the Dominican Order were attributable not to a difference in political standing but to anti-semitic microaggressions. Later in life, she surmised that this was the reason for her delayed acceptance into the order. "Some of them didn't like Jews. That was an explicit element, I gather, in the earlier vote. What was put to me by someone 'as a cultural thing.' One remark which was reported to me by some of the senior brethren was that there was an attempt to push me out of the group on prejudice. [Shrugging, she gestured to herself and whispered] Jewish. That's what that was about ultimately."[2] In an interview, Father

Malcolm McMahon recalled seeing S. praying in Hebrew while wearing a prayer shawl.³ She openly incorporated Jewish traditions into her life as a Catholic priest. S. claims to have heard brethren grumbling at her use of rabbinical material in her sermons, especially one that she based on *Nostra Aetate*—the Declaration on the Relation of the Church with Non-Christian Religions of the Second Vatican Council promulgated in 1965 by Pope Paul VI:

> One of [the brethren] once complained to me that it was scandalous that there were "Jewish goings-on" in the refectory, to which I was able to reply in perfectly good conscience at the time that he should be more concerned at the almost perennial real presence of a Jewish body in the church's tabernacle. The hatred probably diminished when facilitation of the Seder was taken over by someone not descended from deicides the clique which did not like Jews and things Jewish were also antipathetic to Vatican II and particularly to the Vatican II document *Nostra Aetate*, with its official rejection of the accusation that Jews are deicides.⁴

S. appreciated the interconnected histories of various traditions. The idea that Judaism ought to be excised from Christianity was incomprehensible and violent.

According to Father Timothy Radcliffe, there were many Jewish converts to Catholicism at the time, and, if anything, it would have been a valued aspect of S.'s heritage. He also stated that interest in Buddhism was a part of the climate in Oxford.⁵ S. was among these curious Catholics. She discovered a Theravada Buddhist group and started practicing meditation in the early 1970s. She explained that she was a deist and a Christian but that meditation was an important daily practice. S. worked to understand it in context, "not picking and mixing [religion], but understanding it on its own terms. Knowing how a Theravada Buddhist who was not theistic saw it from the inside."⁶ This statement aligns with the content of her lectures and sermons, which attempt to inform students that Buddhism is not a deistic religion. For a time, S. enjoyed the friendship of Mogg Morgan, who published occult books and ran the Golden Dawn Occult Society monthly meetings. The two exchanged books and brought one another to tears of laughter.⁷

Although associated with Christianity, baptism is not exclusive to that tradition.⁸ S. preached that, more than absolution, baptism initiates a new creation for Jews and gentiles. This rite that manifested Jewish exclusivism, S. explained, is now open to all people in Christ. Through baptism, Christians are joined to the righteous body of the Messiah. It is a ritual that some Christians consider to be a hallmark of their tradition, but S. pointed to its origins in Judaism:

> Not many people realise that baptism—immersion in living water, whether in a ritual bath or a river—is a common Jewish practice. Many pious Jews baptise themselves in a ritual bath at least once a week.... My feeling is that the baptism of converts, too, is a baptism of purification, a rite which marks the convert as a member of a community which sees itself as marked out from others, in part, by virtue of its consecration to God in purity.[9]

Note that some take umbrage at S.'s characterization here, particularly her use of the word baptism rather than ritual bath. She later preached a similar sermon on baptism. Whether in a ritual bath or a natural body of water, immersion in living water is a common Jewish practice. Orthodox Jewish women are "baptized" shortly before marriage, S. explained. Some pious Jews take weekly ritual baths. For women, it represents incorporation into the covenant of Israel; for men, it follows circumcision and completes incorporation into the Jewish community. In other words, baptism initiates integration into Jewish common life. She closed her sermon with a prayer that listeners might receive the grace to see this fulfillment in every person.

After she was pushed out of the church, Sally fretted that her baptism might no longer be valid. No one in the church seems to have suggested this. Her rigid adherence to doctrinal consistency led Sally to this interpretation. If she was laicized based on never having been truly ordained as a priest, because she was intersex and therefore incapable of ever having been a priest, it is consistent for her to wonder whether her baptism was also invalid—both were sacraments performed when it was thought Sally was male. From the Catholic Church's perspective, her gender is significant for ordination but not baptism. But for Sally, who wanted to be accepted as is by church and state, it was not so clear. In 1995, Sally wrote to Father Timothy Radcliffe concerning her baptism: "It has been said and argued for some time now that I never was Christian, that I could not have been baptized validly, that my so-called 'conversion experience' was a mere nothing or a cunning piece of dissimulation.... My Christian commitment meant everything to me and it is not a mere nothing which can blithely be dismissed."[10] Timothy reassured her that her baptism was valid.[11] Sally's identity and sense of self were anchored within her interreligious commitments. The pain of breaks imposed upon her soul galvanized Sally to forge something otherwise.

Crown Heights

In 1988, S. walked down Oxford's Cowley Road, and a Chabad house caught her eye.[12] Chabad houses are typically located in large cities or near college campuses and are intended to inspire Orthodox observance and Lubavitch beliefs among secular and non-Orthodox Jews. Hoping to spark an interesting conversation, S. introduced herself to Rabbi Gershon Overlander as a Dominican priest and Jew. Initially, he was taken aback.[13] She assured the rabbi that she had no missionary intentions and merely desired to study Lubavitch Hasidic literature in the company of devout Jews. A friendship formed, and soon S. was returning to Chabad for the Sabbath and Jewish festivals.

A few days before the Sukkot festival, S. met with Rabbi Overlander. He discussed his plans to travel to Brooklyn, New York, for the festival's final days. She was aware that the eight-day event comprised the festival proper, and the holy days in between were Chol Hamoed. Sukkot is followed by a pair of back-to-back festivals, Shemini Atzeret and Simchat Torah—the latter being a festival of rejoicing over the Torah. Many Hasidic Jews travel for these holidays, and a guest at Oxford's Chabad house had given Rabbi Overlander a standby travel voucher to the United States. Rabbi Overlander's wife, however, was near the end of her fourth pregnancy and had fallen ill.[14] He proposed that S. use his travel voucher and stay with his contacts in Crown Heights.

After obtaining permission from her superior, S. rushed to acquire a passport and travel visa. This was before S. became a naturalized UK citizen, and she was concerned that as a member of the African National Congress, she might make herself vulnerable to prosecution if she traveled on an old Israeli or South African passport. She wrote about the process:

> I had a covering letter from [Rabbi] Gershon and another from [Father] Paul, which confused the clerk at the embassy. "Might I ask a question, sir? Maybe it is my own ignorance, but you are a Dominican priest, which means that you are a Catholic, right?" I told her that she was correct. "And you are going to New York to see the Rebbe of Lubavitch, who is a Jewish Rabbi, right?" Again, I confirmed what she said. "So why is a Catholic priest going to see a Jewish Rabbi in New York?" I told her that the Catholic Church is interested in ecumenical dialogue, and that this was a rare and precious opportunity for such dialogue.[15]

The clerk granted S. the visa.

Luggage in hand and messenger bag on her hip, S. eagerly deplaned in New York. The Shemini Atzeret festival and the final day of Sukkot were about to begin. She hopped into a taxi and provided Rabbi Berel Futerfas's address.[16] Consulting a Brooklyn map, the driver made his way to the center of the Lubavitch Hasidic community in Crown Heights. He dropped S. off forty-five minutes before the festival began. Rabbi Futerfas offered S. some food and explained she would be staying with Shimshon Stock—a well-respected man and a bit of a character.[17]

As is customary in some Jewish communities, a warning siren sounded eighteen minutes before the festival. S. swelled with excitement. Soon, there would be singing and dancing in the street as in Jerusalem before the destruction of Herod's temple. Rabbi Futerfas and S. walked briskly down Kingston Avenue, the main shopping area in the Lubavitch Hasidic community, which was decorated with banners reading *Simchat Beit Hasho-evah*.[18] They arrived at Shimshon's house ten minutes before the festival was due to begin. They were met by a stout man in his early sixties. In addition to philanthropic work in the community, Shimshon was a sought-after matchmaker. His wife Martha offered a warm greeting, as did their son Benjy.[19] Benjy showed S. to her room in the basement, where she splashed water on her face and changed her shirt. Together, they attended a synagogue across the road for afternoon and evening prayers.

S.'s time in Crown Heights was bittersweet. On the one hand, she relished reconnecting with her Jewish identity and a Jewish community. On the other, dyadic gender roles and the cultural presumption of heterosexual reproduction came up against S.'s asexuality and gender ambiguity. Additionally, S. was troubled that this community was not more overtly opposed to racism. Shimshon and S. would conflict over matters of theology, racial justice, gender, and sexuality. The forty-page account of her time in Brooklyn from which this chapter is drawn demonstrates her ongoing self-avowal of Jewish identity and continual difficulty in finding a community hospitable to her multiplicity—be it religious, biological, or political.

As S. and Shimshon walked together, a large house connected to a synagogue came into view. Locals call it seven seventy because the address of the building is 770 Eastern Parkway. It had been purchased for the previous rebbe when he moved from Europe to Brooklyn in the early twentieth century. At the time of S.'s visit, Rebbe Menachem Mendel Schneerson lived in part of the home, using the rest for offices, study, and prayer.[20] Within the synagogue, two women's balconies had windows that allowed the women to see over to the men's main section. Shimshon guided S. through the crowds of men dressed in black hats, trousers, and coats. Men stood on milk crates atop benches and precarious planks. S. peered through the door, catching glimpses of undulating black fabric. Frustrated by the crowd, Shimshon took hold of S.'s elbow and pulled her out. They attempted the back entrance of the synagogue, which was congested but manageable. Rabbi Futerfas and one of his sons assisted S. in entering the main section of the synagogue.

S. paused in awe. She recalled seeing people along the walls, standing on any ledge available. Those fortunate enough to be at the front of the synagogue were afforded a view of the rebbe. A few people had brought stepladders upon which perched half a dozen men. Others used homemade periscopes of wood, cardboard, or metal. At various times, the rebbe encouraged singing. S. caught sight of him turning to face the throng and mark time with his hand. The crowd sang more vigorously and faster until the rebbe would turn his back. Then, silence and prayer. As the ritual came to an end, Shimshon grabbed S. They needed to position themselves next to a door at the back of the synagogue if they were to encounter the rebbe.

As the rebbe left the synagogue, the tangle of people previously immovable somehow formed a passage. During his exit, the crowd sang "Vesamachta Bechagecha," increasing in intensity when the rebbe came near.[21] It took effort to avoid being pushed out of place. S. planted her feet, eager to take in the melody and sights. She heard English, Yiddish, Israeli Hebrew, and French. As bodies pressed in on hers, she felt she could not bear it anymore, and then the rebbe passed. She describes the encounter with ambivalence:

> He glanced at me, and turned for a moment and looked again: not really something that surprised me, because I was wearing a grey and red windbreaker and a bright-blue shirt, and though my hair is now quite short, it is longer than the standard Hasidic length and I am still clean-shaven. I must have stood out in the sea of black-clad, bearded figures. The double-glance that the Rebbe gave me did become the subject of an instant myth in the making, for Rabbi Safrin remarked [he] was impressed by it.[22]

Jews outside of the movement sometimes criticize Lubavitch Hasidic for their high regard for the rebbe. "Hasidim are distinguished," Henry Goldschmidt writes, "in large part, by their devotion to their Rebbes—a devotion considered idolatrous by some non-Hasidic Jews—and by their efforts to infuse the observance of religious law with an enthusiastic spirituality grounded in esoteric mystical thought."²³ Some believed their rebbe to be the Messiah.²⁴ S. seems to have not been aware of this and reflected, "[Tali's] remark also suggested that the Rebbe is like the High Priest, who used to intercede on behalf of all the people. I do not know whether Tali intended to suggest this, but it is part of the ambience of the place."²⁵

Despite her reservations, later into her stay in Crown Heights, S. defended her hosts' reverence for the rebbe. Two visitors criticized their sister and sister-in-law for worshiping the rebbe, and S. reflected, "They were viewing the community and its practices purely from the outside, and it was bound to seem exotic and offensive to reason from this perspective. One had to look at the community from the inside, to some extent, and to ask [about the] function devotion to the Rebbe and the customs and beliefs of the community fulfilled." She writes, "The Rebbe's devotion to his followers, and his followers' devotion to him were really two sides of the same coin. . . . He did this for love of his followers, and such love calls forth love in return." And yet, privately, she confessed: "To tell you the truth, I was also worried by the extent to which the people I met idolised the Rebbe. It did seem to me that an appreciation of the context might make it easier to understand."²⁶ This speaks to her temperament. She longed to promote receptivity amid religious bodies.

The lengths to which Lubavitch Hasidim was prepared to go to catch sight of the rebbe at prayer continued to amaze S. That evening, the synagogue began to fill with people. S. stood on a bench with a backrest, even as some men stood atop the backrest itself. A few men objected to her presence, claiming she was in a spot designated for elderly people. S. was pushed into the flood of bodies. Elbows came down on her head, which twisted to its limit. Her face pressed into the backs of men taller than herself. At the start of each *hakapha*, or circling of the reader's platform, the pressure would ease as the men shuffled toward the center of the synagogue where the rebbe danced. Then they would return, and S. wondered if she would pass out.

She looked up and noticed that metal girders stretching from floor to ceiling supported the roof of the synagogue. Some had metal rings welded onto them about twelve feet off the ground. Later, S. would learn that these were intended to secure spotlights and video equipment. She noticed a young man standing on a table who managed to wedge a plank into two of the rings. He then tightly locked a chain around the girder's top section for added support. During the service, the platform began to splinter. He clung to the chain, and eventually, the platform broke entirely. It struck S. that he was risking life and limb for a chance to see the rebbe.

As people began to drink alcohol, their dancing became increasingly hectic. Rabbi Safrin and S. paused to rest on the sidelines. Someone playfully tugged Rabbi Safrin's beard, indicating that they should rejoin the fun. Although scandalized by the gesture, Rabbi Safrin behaved with forbearance. As Shimshon and S. made their way to the back of the synagogue, someone poured a plastic tumbler of cola over Shimshon's shirt, and S. felt a hand yank the neck of her shirt. She could not determine if it was hostile or a drunken invitation to dance. Upon reflection, S. came to appreciate the importance of dancing before the Torah:

> Rabbi Safrin turned to me and asked me whether I realised that it was a *mitzvah*, a commandment of God, that Jewish men should dance in this way on *Simchat Torah*, and that it was a duty which was equal in importance to the solemn fasting of the Day of Atonement, *Yom Kippur*. The "Ten Days of Repentance," the period from the Jewish New Year, *Rosh Hashanah*, which had been celebrated only a fortnight before, to *Yom Kippur*, had been followed by *Sukkot*, the festival of Tabernacles or Booths. . . . It was not even meant as a time to rejoice over the Torah: that was too contemplative. *Simchat Torah* means making the Torah rejoice by dancing before it.[27]

Benjy invited S. to the synagogue at 770 for a *farbrengen*, or a gathering of the rebbe's followers. He guided S. inside to stand on the edge of the back of a long pew. S. stood sideways, pushing against an adjacent wall for support. The row of men swayed such that S. wondered if they would eventually drop to the floor one by one like dominos. To S.'s surprise, the synagogue's interior had been transformed since the morning service. The rebbe and several leaders sat at a long table. She could not hear him very well but was discouraged from moving. At the rebbe's prompting, the crowd began to sing and jump. S. marveled that no one fell from their modest perches throughout the four-hour service. She was awestruck by this religious embrace of the body. The call to act rather than reflect may have been a refreshing counterpoint to the overly intellectual forms of activism that troubled her. Reverence for the body—to dance before the Torah for the Torah to rejoice—relates to the theme of her doctoral thesis.

After evening prayers on the second day, there was a reflection with refreshments, to which *der gantze oilam* (Yiddish for "the whole wide world") was invited. Reconnecting with her Jewish identity and community was delightful but not free from the nagging question of gender. "It should be noted," S. wrote, "that this world was too narrow to contain women. There were no women in the synagogue itself, though it was possible to catch glimpses of some women in an adjacent room.... Both Shimshon and I were given a chance to dance with a Torah-scroll. Shimshon opened the ark at the beginning of the ceremony so that the Torah-scrolls could be taken out, and I was asked to lead the recitation of one of the verses."[28] Had she been aware of her intersexuality at that time, S. likely would not have participated in male-exclusive traditions.

The next morning, Tuesday, October 4, Shimshon was late to prayer in the synagogue, which reminded him of a story from his youth: "[Shimshon] said that when his attention would falter in synagogue, his late father would shout at him and beat him, and would order him to go upstairs to the women's section where his mother was. Shimshon used to protest that he was past the age of *Bar Mitzva*, the age of responsibility, and that it was not right of his father to humiliate him in this way."[29] Such an example points out that the organization of gendered bodies in sacred space communicates power relations.[30]

Later, on a walk to exchange pounds into dollars, S. observed the sharp divide that Kingston Avenue cut through Crown Heights. On the south side of Eastern Parkway, she browsed bookshops stocked with Lubavitch Hasidic literature. Tailors advertised suits and caftans; wig shops catered to Orthodox Jewish women who cut their hair as a sign of modesty after marrying. Signs fixed to the front of bagel shops informed customers that the bagels and pita were made of dough that qualified as cake or a biscuit rather than bread. This meant that one only needed to say a short grace after the snack rather than a much longer one that included hand washing for bread. Down the avenue, S. noticed a shift to predominantly Black businesses. Evangelical and Pentecostal churches appeared. Shops sold pork and lobster. She enjoyed the brilliant colors and modern music juxtaposed against a Lubavitch aesthetic.

S. recalled thinking it would not be tactful to mention being a Catholic priest to Shimshon. Instead, she informed him she was a lecturer in ethics at Blackfriars and a doctoral student at Oxford University. Additionally, S. discussed being born in South Africa and a member of the African National Congress. While her association with Christianity was successfully sidestepped, S.'s commitment to equity for Black people seemed to touch an unanticipated sore spot. S. came to learn that some residents of Crown Heights perceived their Black neighbors to be anti-semitic and violent. As S. remembers it, Shimshon stated:

American Jews marched for the blacks, and where did it get them? The blacks turned against them. In Crown Heights the blacks were anti-semitic. They beat up, robbed and murdered Jewish men and raped Jewish women. That was what blacks were like. People came to Crown Heights with liberal attitudes, but seeing what was happening around them soon put paid to this misguided liberalism. Even likable blacks were anti-semitic when you scratched beneath the surface. Why was it that Jews campaigned for everyone except for themselves? Let the gentiles kill one another: a few million less gentiles in the world, a few million less anti-semites in the world. But why should the Jews put their lives on the line for gentiles? Would gentiles lift a finger for Jews? Did the Pope lift a finger when millions of Jews were gassed by the Nazis? Let the gentiles kill one another, and let Jews look after their own people.[31]

Although this account rings with racism, anthropologist Henry Goldschmidt argues that tensions between Black and Jewish residents should not be confused with racially charged distrust rooted in phenotypes; it might more accurately be attributed to a theological concept of the godly soul—that all gentiles are fundamentally anti-semitic.[32]

Goldschmidt contends that there is a significant distinction between racism and Jewish election. His anthropological research in Crown Heights underscores conflicts among "people of the book" who claim the story of Exodus for themselves. In that biblical story, Moses leads the Hebrews from slavery under Egypt's pharaohs. It is an iconic story of God electing a specific group of people, facilitating their liberation, and ensuring their subsequent entitlement to a promised land. In addition to grounding Zionism, this biblical passage has also been used to endorse the liberation of enslaved Black people in the US context and Black people in South Africa's Apartheid. Goldschmidt and others report that both Black and Orthodox Jewish residents in Crown Heights claim this story as their own.

In an email to a colleague, S. would later write about the complexity of people of color as well as white supremacists understanding themselves to be elected by God: "Fundamentally, observant Jews are enjoined to let this imagery shape their very lives, and contemporary history becomes an anamnesis—a recapitulation of the Passover and the Exodus. With its enormous emancipatory appeal, this imagery made its way into Christianity, and came to South Africa, where it appealed to forces of liberation and oppression alike."[33] She continued:

The same imagery, ironically, was also appropriated by Afrikaner nationalist discourse, and pressed into service in the interests of apartheid. This account cast the British government and its colonial officials as the wicked Pharaoh, while the Great Trek into the interior, away from land under British control, represented the journey to the Promised Land. According to this narrative, Afrikaner nationalists cast themselves as God's chosen people, chosen to rule over South Africa. In terms of this imagery, the country's majority was the equivalent of the Canaanites and other nations that dwelt in the land of Canaan before they were driven out by the Israelites, at God's command. Thus, the Exodus imagery has been a double-edged, too: it has served forces of oppression and forces of liberation alike.[34]

I include this lengthy quotation to flag the contested claims to the election (the idea that God chooses a people group), liberation (from whom/what), and providence (access to resources). How is it that the same biblical narrative has been used by Zionists in Israel, Black Americans, and white nationalists in South Africa? Is this story exclusively for ancient Hebrew people?[35] If not, who else is included, and what do we make of conflict among these diverse groups? The gravity of these questions persists today, perhaps most grievously in Gaza.

Tensions among Crown Heights residents rose at the time of S.'s visit, peaked in 1991, and have resurfaced more recently.[36] In 1991, driver Yoself Letish, who was a part of Rabbi Menachem Mendel Schneerson's motorcade, accidentally struck two Guyanese immigrant children, killing seven-year-old Gavin Cato. A Hatzoloh ambulance, staffed and funded by Orthodox Jews, arrived at the scene and immediately took the driver and passengers to a nearby hospital. Meanwhile, a New York Emergency Medical Service ambulance treated Gavin Cato and his cousin Angela at the scene. The disparity in health care did not go unnoticed by Black witnesses. Within hours, crowds were enraged. Lemrick Nelson, a Black teenager, joined a crowd punching and kicking Orthodox Jew Yankel Rosenbaum, whom he fatally stabbed four times in the back and torso. Due to an untreated wound, Rosenbaum later died of internal bleeding and a punctured lung.

Both the Black and Jewish communities made sense of Cato's and Rosenbaum's untimely deaths within their larger cultural histories—not as isolated incidents.[37] Some Jewish residents interpreted the death of Yankel Rosenbaum as a pogrom—an anti-semitic massacre—while some Black residents understood the death of Gavin Cato to be racially motivated. The complexity of defining race and religion muddies the conflict between Black and Orthodox residents in Crown Heights. Both parties have histories of being discriminated against. It is difficult to articulate whether their conflicts with one another were rooted in racism or religious discrimination because inherent to contextualizing conflict is the need to reconsider the very categories of race and religion. Goldschmidt's account of the events suggests to me structural problems among police and health-care professionals that were misplaced upon Black and Jewish communities. Inequity of social services bred distrust and resentment.

Although S.'s visit occurred shortly before Cato's and Rosenbaum's deaths, she certainly entered a scene in which tension was mounting within Crown Heights. Remembering debates with her father, S. was sympathetic to Shimshon's position. She knew her objections to his comment would need to be made delicately. The friendships she forged with Palestinians while studying in Israel and her radical activism alongside the ANC in South Africa during Apartheid made her reluctant to favor Jews over Muslims or Christians, Israelis over Palestinians or Black Americans. Instead, S. understood these groups as allies: "I said that in South Africa there had been cases of black people who sacrificed their lives for the sake of Jewish comrades so that it was not a one-way commitment; and that the struggle in South Africa was not a racist struggle in the first place, and should not be viewed in 'race against race' terms."[38] S. writes that Shimshon offered barbed comments about Jesse Jackson's anti-semitism and launched into

> his diatribe, which could probably have been heard a block away, by saying that he was like "Meirke Kahana" (a Brooklyn-bred Rabbi who founded the Jewish Defense League, emigrated to Israel, and founded the fascist party called *Kach*, which campaigns for the forced removal of Palestinians from Israel and the occupied territories). At that point in time, *Kach* had not been barred from the Israeli elections and was expected to secure up to six seats in the Knesset. It was later barred from the elections because of the virulence of its racism.[39]

S. responded provocatively, "If Kahana were ever to come to power, God forbid, there would be extermination-camps with gas-chambers for Palestinians."[40] To this, "Shimshon then shouted that Jews would never be guilty of genocide. They might kick them out, but they would not kill them en masse. Unlike gentiles, Jewish people had good hearts. He added that the Lubavitcher Rebbe agreed with these sentiments, though he did not actually hate gentiles in the way that Shimshon did."[41] Goldschmidt's argument that religious discrimination is often misinterpreted as racism is displayed in the distinction that S. alleges Shimshon made next:

> Shimshon added that, despite the fact that he hated black people in general, and hated Christians even more, he had some black people who were his friends. His next-door-neighbour, was black, and was normally a wonderful person. But her latent anti-semitism emerged whenever his grand-children dared to play on her lawn. And Jews were abused even by black traffic-wardens. One black traffic-warden had told him that Hitler should have gassed all of the Jews. A member of the community had come to the aid of a woman who had been attacked by a black man who had ripped her gold chain off her neck. He had chased the perpetrator of the assault, and recovered the chain from him. The robber had laid a charge against him for assault, and the Jewish man was being charged by the police.

"They were all anti-semites," S. remembers Shimshon explaining, "and people like me ought to struggle for Jews and not for them."[42] Following the emotionally charged exchange, S. learned about the historical context from which Shimshon spoke. Many of his relatives had been killed by the Nazis, and his uncle, who had gone to Poland after the war to see whether any relatives had survived, was murdered by anti-semitic Poles. Living through that period had been traumatic and had made him suspicious of gentiles.[43] To Goldschmidt's point about racism being confused with religious distinctions, S. conceded, "Crown Heights Hasidic racism is more a matter of Jewish antipathy towards gentiles than Jewish antipathy towards '*schwartzes*,' though black gentiles do seem to come in for especially noxious abuse."[44] (Note that "schwartzes" is considered a racial slur by many Jewish people.)

Discrimination in the United States is frequently reduced to visual differentiations, such as skin color.[45] The Lubavitch community's distrust of their Black Christian neighbors, it seems, is mistaken for racism. Today, scholars continue to wrestle with the difficulty of delineating racial and religious discrimination because they are mobile and contextual concepts.[46] It is challenging to grapple with the painful histories of tension among Crown Heights neighbors while refusing to attribute blame or victimhood to one group or another. As my colleague Marvin Wickware noted, systemic racism plays a role in religious discrimination.[47] It matters that the gentiles in Crown Heights are Black. A particular history accompanies Black Americans and sets the context for interactions. Economic and power relations are additional contested factors that complicate questions of race and religion.

S. met a couple there who shared a great interest in languages. Their conversation would return to the thorny question of community among Black and Jewish neighbors in Crown Heights. The husband used to frequent a synagogue in Tripoli, Libya, which had housed Torah scrolls from Babylon. These were destroyed when Muammar Gaddafi came to power. Quite suddenly, the wife wondered aloud why the Ku Klux Klan had not killed the "*schwartzes*."[48] Stunned, S. reproached her. Their disagreement escalated: "I was shocked by this wicked statement and upbraided her for it. She replied that they were filthy, slimy animals, they were not human, and that anyone who lived in Crown Heights knew that her wish was justified. She said she came from California and lived in an affluent area. Some blacks had lived there, and they were really like white people, but that blacks in New York were sub-human."[49]

S. attempted to underline the hypocrisy of the woman: "I pointed out the fact that such things had been said in justification of the attempt to exterminate the Jewish people, and that Jews of all people ought not to fall into the same pattern." According to S., her approach was ineffective:

> She refused to take the point, and said that the Nazi persecution of the Jews was wrong because Jews were human beings, but that these New York *schwartzes* were not. She worked in the Jewish Community Relations Office, and knew what these greasy and filthy vermin got up to. A friend of hers had been raped by one of them, and it was all very well to look at a situation from the outside and to preach. She had also been shocked by the attitudes of the Jewish people in Crown Heights when she first left California, but she soon discovered that these attitudes were fully justified.[50]

Instead of finding solace in her host, S. writes, "Shimshon turned to me with a look of triumph and said: 'You see? I told you so!' He said that this was living proof that his attitude was not exceptional, and that it was perfectly reasonable." Clarifying the position of her audience, "Shimshon then turned to the woman, who was looking at me indignantly, and said that I was fighting for the *schwartzes*, that I was a member of the African National Congress which was an organisation in South Africa. A stunned silence followed, and both husband and wife expressed surprise, dismay and disgust."[51] Undaunted, S. continued:

> I went on the offensive again, and said that I felt no need to apologise, and that I was opposed to racism of any and all kinds. I said that I

had no objection to revulsion at the acts of a minority in a community which engaged in crime, and that there were some crimes which were particularly obnoxious.... It seemed to me that the genocidal views that the wife expressed were a *chillul hashem*, blasphemy, and that those who rejected God's handiwork in the way that she did risked rejection by God.[52]

Her point here more accurately describes the position of many Jewish people—that racism and genocide are blasphemous. The few people whom S. quoted in this account represent neither everyone in that particular community in Crown Heights nor Jewish people in general. The point is that she was dismayed by discrimination of any kind, which made her pursuit of community conflicted.

According to S., Shimshon's wife Martha attempted to ease the tension by redirecting their attention to cultural and class differences: "She said that it was probably more a question of social class and training than of race and that South Africans she had met had said that South African *schwartzes* were different. The South Africans she had met had been nursed as children by black women who had loved them and been loved in turn, and these *schwartzes* were unlike the local *schwartzes*."[53] S. relented: "For my part, I was too angry and upset to say any more." S. writes about her dissatisfaction, "I found the argument profoundly depressing, and was made no happier by Shimshon's cheery declaration that it had really amused listening to that woman complain about the *schwartzes* and then shocking them with the fact that they had been seeking sympathy from someone who was fighting for the *schwartzes*. We were not amused."[54]

Previously, S. had struggled to understand how South African Jews, having only contingently been classified white under Apartheid, endorsed racism as a survival strategy. She had not been familiar with the uniquely racist form of slavery in the US context—how it shaped Black American identities and why there might be tension between Black and Jewish communities in Crown Heights. Conflicted, S. enjoyed the hospitality and warmth throughout the Lubavitch community but could not stomach its terms of inclusion because she could not reconcile discriminatory attitudes toward gentiles with Jewish histories of suffering.

The Crown Heights Lubavitch community's integration of religious study with attention to the body expanded S.'s understanding of embodiment. With them, S. was able to discuss her passions—racial justice, sexuality, and religion—although a sense of belonging to a lived community eluded her.

She appreciated the ritual aspects of the Lubavitch Hasidic community but could not come to terms with male/female or Jew/gentile distinctions. She was granted access to male-only spaces, from which she would have likely been barred if she and others were aware of her intersexuality. While she relished the opportunity to participate in Lubavitch traditions, S. rejected negative attitudes toward Black neighbors irrespective of their being rooted in Jew/gentile distinctions. As a Jewish and religious activist who had seen the consequences of xenophobia, S. spoke boldly against prejudice. Her heated debates did not offend her Crown Heights hosts to the extent that they wanted her to leave. In fact, they urged her to stay and even marry.

Despite the abundant hospitality and invitation to relocate to Crown Heights, S. had not felt entirely at home there either. Her Jewishness might not be fully embraced at Blackfriars, but at least her brethren were committed to a shared vision of antiracism. The complexity of her religious identity made many communities alluring but none entirely fitting. She was able to foreground aspects of her religiosity in diverse contexts—a Shabbat meal, Buddhist meditation, Easter Mass—but never the entirety of her commitments in any one space. Perhaps this is why she felt alone, even within communities.

Each collective of persons mandates a boundary to demarcate outsiders, with which S. could not make peace. There was not a space for S. to unapologetically present her whole self, which signaled to her broader systems of injustice. It was an ongoing challenge to find an antiracist, interreligious, gender nonbinary community that could cope with her bodily complexity without compromising her religious ideals or social justice. The experience of these breaks prompted her to introduce sutures to rearrange and incorporate a more diverse body before deep resonance could permeate.

In a 2007 letter, Sally renounced her commitments to "Abrahamic faiths," citing the scriptural endorsement of genocide:

> In religious terms, given the continuing violence and shedding of innocent blood which it and its derivatives have engendered over the millennia on the basis of spurious religiously-derived identities, I reject the covenant of Abraham with its propensity for the licensing of the extermination of certain other nations, and for the brutal oppression, death and destruction that identities deriving from the nation continues indiscriminately to visit upon people under Israeli occupation and, when it is deemed convenient, upon the innocent people of Lebanon as well.[55]

Secular studies scholars point out that rather than a break from religion, secularism has historically been a reaction to religion, thereby requiring religion to exist. In addition to its ties to modernity, secularism has often reinforced whiteness, Eurocentrism, and patriarchy.[56] Moreover, secularism also exists within religious traditions. This is why what Sally described here is not a break with religion, as some might presume, but rather about how she found any form of Apartheid abhorrent. Access to privilege—be that due to her whiteness, assigned maleness, or divine election—did not entice her. Sally is remarkable not because of the unavoidable challenges she faced but in large part because of the easily avoidable hardships she suffered to advance social justice.

Sally's complex identity meant not that she was clearly an outsider or oppressed person in all circumstances, but rather that she grappled with the very dynamic of community itself, which pushes some out to embrace others. That mechanism troubled her. She did not set out to make her way in. Instead, Sally pressed at the boundaries to fracture them. She could not stomach Zionism, Apartheid, white supremacy, patriarchy, or claims to God's favor. Whatever the form, and regardless of whether she was positioned to benefit or suffer injury from it, Sally said no. And she did not say no quietly or privately. Sally challenged identity markers for the haves and the have-nots in her everyday gestures and public actions. But not without cost. Creative suture work sometimes necessitates initiating breaks, however counterintuitive that might be to those familiar with the trauma of having breaks imposed upon them.

12. Sutures

It is still being stitched and hemmed. In the meantime, this vision insistently calls on us to see the universe as our body, the earth as our body, the variety of human groups as our body. This body is in evolution, in creative ecstasy, in the midst of destructive and regenerative labor, of death and resurrection. Everything is our body, our trinitarian body: it is a continual tension and communion of multiplicity and unity, all within the ecstatic and mysterious adventure of life. —IVONE GEBARA, *Longing for Running Water*

I explore tensions between the body in books and the body on the table. It is ethnography that provides a meeting place between the two, insisting that it is in the situated practices of living bodies, like ideas, acquire potential and meet their limits. Cutting, sawing, and suturing are examples of potential and limit, both for me and for the patient whose deeply intimate transformation I witnessed. —ERIC PLEMONS, *The Look of a Woman*

The term *suture* can be used as a noun or a verb. In surgery, sutures fasten together the edges of a wound. A seam is formed through sewing together parts. Zoologists identify sutures as junctions between shell chambers. These create buoyance in conch shells and serve as movable joints in crustaceans. Botanists recognize sutures as the point of dehiscence (splitting open or bursting) in seed pods. In geology, it refers to junctions where crustal plates have collided, forming mountains. Craniofacial sutures are less stiff than the bones they join, and their flexibility is key to the mechanical role they play in cushioning the stress of trauma. The scars and ridges that form from sutured elements attest to a history and future possibility of division. These elements have been drawn together. They collaborate, like the valves of a mollusk, but can also be burst apart like seed pods. Pulling, crashing, meeting. Sutures are made, happen, and simply exist.

As an agitator and activist, S. worked to initiate breaks from injustice and exploitation and also to suture together what those forces—religious bodies, medical bodies, political bodies, and so on—had wrongly torn apart. In so doing, she and her comrades created religious buoyance, facilitated political movement, and strengthened social flexibility such that our ecologies would become more resilient to trauma. Sutures are essential to movements. Without them, we become rigid and brittle, vulnerable to destructive breaks. For ecologies to thrive, they require sutures to avoid harmful breaks and to make good use of generative breaks leading to resonance. This chapter examines Sally's sermons and interreligious commitments. Through her interreligious suture work, she identified problematic regulating bodies and also encouraged flourishing diverse ecosystems.

Mixed-Up House

Galvanized by her visit to Crown Heights, S. returned to her new home in England, the Blackfriars' Cambridge House. Unlike monks who live apart from society, friars there lived with laypeople, including women, from 1980 to 1999. Some brethren joked that the blending of clergy and laity, male and female, in the Cambridge House merited the appellation "the mixed-up community." That might have been controversial outside of the order, but within the order, even the conservative members regarded it a suitable arrangement. Together, clergy and laity shared in the rhythms of the Divine Office and common meals. The day began with Office Readings, then Morning Prayer (Lauds); next Daytime Prayer; then Evening Prayer (Vespers); and Night Prayer (Compline).

The Cambridge priory was built upon the wildlife corridor.[1] In 1938, friar Hugh Dominic and his sister Leonore received the Italian-style house from their mother, Enrichetta Bullough, widow of Professor Edward Bullough. The siblings were the priory's first members, and they studied Hebrew and Aramaic at university. Decades later, in 1955, the friars purchased an

English cottage next door; its brick foundation, white walls, brown trim, and thatched roof contrasted with the Italian villa. By the 1960s, an architect was hired to integrate the two houses. Interestingly, he opted for a minimalist aesthetic that amplifies rather than masks the dissonance between the parts. The architecture of the building visually represented an integrated, diverse community, a fitting parallel for S.'s future exploration of intersexuality and transnational interreligious commitments.

When a visitor walks through the front door, they see oversized sliding glass doors with light wood trim that frames a spacious garden. To the right is the Italian home, to the left, the English cottage. One glimpses a parlor through the first door on the right where the famed Blackfriars' translation of Thomas Aquinas's *Summa Theologica* is housed, along with other books. Beyond that is a kitchen, sectioned off with a stained-glass window that bears Aquinas's coat of arms, which leads to a winding stairwell lined with an iron filigree banister. Deeper into the villa, in what may have once been the garage, is the clerical chapel. The walls and floor are mostly bare. Wood chairs with high backs are joined together, the armrests creating a small barrier between sitters. Two chandeliers hang from the ceiling. An apse houses a modest altar, small rug, white tablecloth, the sacrament, holy water, two candles, and a stone-carved silhouette of Jesus on the cross. A stately common room lies down the hall. Wood ceilings, floors, windowpanes, and bookshelves invite visitors to find a seat upon damask burgundy armchairs at a long wood table or atop a luxurious rug before a fireplace.

Perhaps the building itself, with its integrated architecture a reflection of the community within, sparked S.'s hope that there was a place for her to hold together Jewishness with Christianity, maleness and femaleness, citizenship and activism. Built environments not only offer clues to people of the past; they also leave their impression on us. They are made but also shape us. Our reactions to disharmony in the "mixed-up" house are worthy of reflection. Did this building initiate a clearing for S. where she could imagine room for her abundance of knowledge, flesh, and emotional needs?

Jewish-Christian Sermons

Sermons themselves are more than texts; they are embodied, communal performances. It is relevant that S. performed her sermons from a fat, disabled, intersex, Jewish body. As one would acknowledge that a trans man has a different history of social formation compared to a cisgender man, so too must we keep in mind that S. was not a cradle Catholic trying to incorporate other religious traditions into her sermons. She was born Jewish, and she reported having suffered anti-semitic microaggressions within the order. When she preached as a Catholic priest, it was not as an authoritarian figure assimilating various traditions. Hers was a voice always marked by difference. Literally, she had a different accent from most of her listeners. Additionally, she occupied a position of power tempered by reminders of precarity. She was only conditionally white, assigned male, and a convert to Catholicism.

As S. began to recognize intersections between her gender, religion, and politics, she turned to Catholicism. Despite her love for the Torah, S. could not accept a staunch anti-Palestinian position nor endure pressure to partner and procreate in an Orthodox Jewish context. She also had misgivings about mainstream Judaism in South Africa. Notably, her turn to Christianity was wedded to Judaism:

> The Judaism of the mainstream community in South Africa was something about which I was extremely diffident, to put it mildly, given the accommodations the community made with Apartheid and its marginalisation of people engaged in struggle for fundamental change. . . .
>
> In a curious way, [Catholicism] also gave me a back-way in to Jewish tradition and values without the racism and parochialism and free from the taint of tacit condonation of Apartheid.[2]

S. had observed South African Catholics who were involved in the struggle against Apartheid and began learning about Buddhist meditation, which she enjoyed practicing. She described seeing the potential for an integrated life in the crucified Christ and was emboldened to take a stand for personal and social justice: "I had become overwhelmed by the power of the crucified Christ as an icon of oppression and suffering of all kinds—of my own people over two millennia and more, and during the Holocaust; of the Palestinian people; of the majority of South Africans under Apartheid; and my private sense, which I dared not articulate or explore in dangerous environments, that something bearing on sex and gender was significantly different about me."[3] S. describes being fascinated by "the human and Jewish figure of Jesus"—a telling description that hints at the antisemitic whitewashing of Jesus.[4] "[In] Christ Jesus," she wrote, "there was neither Jew nor Greek, neither male nor female—in which all of these dividing binaries were transcended—spoke to my condition with overwhelming power."[5] She began taking religious instruction within a Christian context. Priests like Albert Nolan, who was deeply committed to the struggle for change, were willing to put themselves in harm's way for the cause. When S. became active in the University Catholic

Society, she did so while maintaining her Jewish identity and for the purpose of radicalizing people. She explains, "I found Jesus as it were. I became Roman Catholic."[6]

S. was baptized in St. Michael's Catholic Church in Rondebosch, South Africa, in 1976. Disillusionment with forms of institutional Judaism that tacitly endorsed Apartheid informed her decision. It seemed to her that Catholic clergy more overtly challenged racial injustice. Still, she may have understood Catholicism as a complement to, rather than a supplement for, being Jewish:

> Awareness of anti-semitism made me sensitive to the horror of Apartheid in South Africa, where I lived; and a period of study in Israel had made me aware of the tragedy of the Palestinian people in the Holy Land....
>
> It dawned on me that it was through this death and resurrection that Jesus could be seen to be the righteous Messiah of my people, the anointed one of God, the Christ, who brings God's hope to God's people.[7]

She described having found within the crucifix an image that could hold together her religious devotion, political activism, and asexuality. Her soul, mind, and body need not be at odds with one another; in the cross, S. saw them function in concert:

> The image of the cross seemed to be an icon of all manner of confusion and suffering. The Holocaust was there, the horror of apartheid was there, and my own personal confusion and pain—which I could never publicly admit—was there as well. And in the resurrection was a symbol that this was transcended. And in the back of my mind, there would have been an awareness that in Christianity there are strands of tradition in which celibacy is valued and turned to positive use.[8]

It was an essential suturing of worlds and commitments. Where others constructed social, religious, and political barriers, S. leaned into fissures that eventually caused breaks. From these openings, she could do the creative work of pulling together and fastening what was presumed incompatible.

Some characterize S.'s baptism as an intellectual and political event rather than a personal conversion. While testimonies of personal experiences might dominate conversion narratives, it is not unprecedented or necessarily disingenuous for S. to have become intellectually involved in the Catholic Church due to its political engagement. She was a person who enjoyed the mores of traditional religions but never at the expense of advancing social justice for all persons. To be clear, it was not the case that there were no anti-apartheid Jews in South Africa. Social justice is often the central, overriding concern of many Jewish communities. The immense pressure on Jewish South Africans to be complicit in Apartheid put them in a precarious social position. Her baptism suggests a conscientious turn to this religious institution because it was privileged to resist Apartheid actively, but hers was not a move away from Judaism. Certainly, S.'s baptism was controversial within her immediate and extended family for reasons described earlier—many were Zionist and devoted to Jewish nationalism. Even among secular Jews, her connection to Catholicism could be perceived as aligning oneself with the very group that has persecuted Jews for centuries. For her, Catholicism enriched rather than attenuated her Jewish identity.

In 1987, S. wrote an article for the *Los Angeles Times* describing the integration of faith and activism: "As a South African, as a Jew steeped in the tragic history of my people, as a Christian and a priest of the Dominican Order of Preachers, committed to the active propagation of the Christian gospel of justice and love, my Christian faith and the struggle against apartheid and for justice in South Africa are inseparable."[9] The Holocaust taught her to combat racism in Apartheid South Africa, and she called all people of faith to anti-apartheid activism.[10] Sally preached about the beauty of diversity.[11]

To be a person of faith was to be a person for social justice. She longed for the sort of diversity that did not erase differences or consider identity to be singular. Sally embodied unity in diversity and made space for others to join her. In a 1992 article, she wrote, "I believe that we remain Jewish in Christ, and that Christ calls us to strengthen, to nurture and to cherish our Jewish identity within his body, the Church. . . . There have long been Christians who believe that Jews are called to *abandon* their Jewish identity when they are baptised into Christ, and who see the persistence of Jewish identity among baptised Christians as an affront to our Lord."[12] It was another example of Sally living in the overlapping spaces, which others sought to rend. Her ministry helped people embrace their multiple identities.

When S. began preaching, she dedicated her attention to the relationship between Jews and gentiles two millennia ago to make the case that the church cannot be whole and cannot be Catholic unless it rediscovers its links with the Judaism. Heady sermons might be an acquired taste, but they were certainly S.'s style. Remarkably, she walked a line that affirmed Jewish special election while also promoting diversity within universalism.

Although interreligious efforts risk masking differences and surrendering doctrinal commitments to prioritize unity, S. did neither. In a brilliant maneuver, S. held traditions to their own distinct doctrinal commitments within her call to social justice for all. She criticized all forms of social injustice, whether those be committed by Jews, Christians, Muslims, or atheists. It stands to reason that S.'s embodied experience as an intersex, Jewish, Christian, technophile Communist informed her complex biblical analysis.

At times, S. sensed her status precarious, and I wonder if she felt the need to defend her existence within the order from the pulpit. S. fled her birthplace, seeking asylum in Botswana, then Israel. She left when she thought her life or well-being was in danger. Homesteading at Blackfriars might have been a pragmatic strategy for keeping a roof over her head. S. admired Jesus as a fellow Jew, but she did not express faith in Jesus as God in the way that Protestant Evangelicals understand it. Friends and family who described her commitment to the Catholic Church as intellectual might have been alluding to this distinction. It is possible that S. justified her place as a Jew in a Catholic clerical role and could inhabit that space with integrity, not because she claimed Jesus the same way that some Christians do—as Lord and savior—but rather because she appreciated him as one of many compelling rabbis. Without the context of her physical body and social history, her sermons might be misinterpreted as assimilating various traditions to Christianity. My reading is that she was defending her position as a Jew within a Catholic space to survive physically.

Seemingly effortlessly, S. preached about the Jewish heritage of traditions often presumed to be specific to Christianity. For example, she grounded any mention of Easter in Passover—the ancient Jewish holiday with which Easter is associated. Something as hackneyed as Jesus being called living bread in Communion, S. revitalized through contextualization. She reminded listeners that bread would be at the forefront of Jewish people's minds during Passover because observant Jews eat unleavened bread during the festival. Themes of liberation and life are symbolized in the bread, and by linking these to his body, she explains, Jesus takes on affliction for our redemption.[13] For S., to participate in the Eucharist and receive Communion at Easter was to recognize Jesus's body as a Passover incarnate. The structural logic of her sermons simultaneously informed and grounded listeners because she adroitly made the familiar unfamiliar and vice versa. Her contemporaries might have considered Judaism to be foreign, even oppositional, to Christianity. But the ease with which S. overlays the two traditions elucidates a historical, inextricable relationship.

The centrality of biblical texts as sacred within Christian traditions has resulted in immense significance being placed on their interpretation. Some priests turn to rabbis for insight, though many others would never contemplate such an act because they consider Jewish and "pagan" interpretations heretical.[14] Remarkably, S. read, interpreted, and preached in a Catholic Church by continually returning to rabbinical insights for mutual enrichment. Years later, she would write to Father Timothy Radcliffe that being pushed out of the church injured her Jewish commitments, just as acting as a priest had deepened her Judaism.[15] The interdependency of the two traditions that was visceral for S. remains opaque to many practitioners today.

Another tactic S. used was exposing distinctly Jewish traditions and making them relevant to all people. The Sabbath, S. explained to her audience, is an observance that some understand to be particular to Judaism which celebrates God's election of and covenant with the Hebrew people. She distinguished this from Christian observance of having church services on Sunday.[16] In S.'s reading, the Sabbath is for all of creation: "Sabbath-observance recognises God's goodness to all humankind in creation at large, and his goodness in creating not just the Jewish people but humankind as a **whole**."[17] Her method was to begin with the particularity of Sabbath for Jews and then to apply that universally. She explained that the Sabbath reorients time by foreshadowing eternal joy to come. This is the telos, or end, which God intends for humanity.

S. deemed any Christian dissociation from Judaism illogical and pernicious by suggesting to audiences that Jesus fulfilled the Jewish prophecy. For example, she explained the relevance of the Jewish Feast of Tabernacles for understanding Palm Sunday.[18] Redirecting a biblical passage typically interpreted to maintain salvation exclusively in Christ as open to all persons, S. similarly preached about rabbinical traditions in her sermon on the Holy Spirit, or Paraclete, who is sent as a counselor after Jesus ascends into heaven.[19] By weaving her understanding of Judaism into her reading of Christian texts, S. implied that the Paraclete is not for Christians in particular and certainly is not a possession for imperialists to wield. She warned listeners that the Holy Spirit can be friendly or hostile depending upon human fulfillment or transgression of God's commandments. In both sermons, S. argued against a passive posture of faith. One does not receive salvation from Jesus or the Holy Spirit, she labored to clarify. Rather, these two persons of the Trinity offer humanity back to us such that we can love one another justly.[20]

Insightfully, S. argued, "The first, most painful and most tragic schism in the Church itself was the break with the Jewish people."[21] Rather than casting the Jews as obstinate, as some Christian theologians and priests regrettably do, S. guided parishioners through seeing Jesus Christ as healing the gentiles of their "deafness" to God. Somewhat attuned to disability, she also underscored people with disabilities in the New Testament who recognized Jesus as Christ.[22] Her emphasis on healing, which sometimes rings of ableism, would shift over time. When preaching on Peter being the rock upon which the church is built, S. resisted supersessionist triumphalism.[23] Instead, she described a hallowed muddling in which a community seeks friendship with God and inspiration from the Holy Spirit.[24] The body of Christ shared at the Eucharist, she reminded listeners, is Jewish, and the conscious rejection of Christ's Jewishness is a rejection of his shared body.[25] She preached that the church cannot be whole and cannot be Catholic unless it remembers its roots in Jewish people, faith, and practices. God's Word, the Torah, became flesh in Christ.[26]

S.'s efforts were as much about promoting unity within the Christian tradition as advancing interreligious collaboration. On the Feast of Peter and Paul in 1991, S. examined the two apostles to make an argument in favor of ecumenism—collaborative efforts to promote unity among various Christian denominations. Peter, she explains, focused on Jewish-gentile relations: "[Peter] opened the Church to gentiles as gentiles and made a mission to the gentiles possible."[27] Peter did not require gentiles to convert to Judaism first, which was a highly contested stance at the time. S. described the relationship of the two faiths as both collaborative yet distinct.[28] To contemporary readers who think about Judaism and Christianity as distinct traditions, it may come as a surprise to learn that these apostles permitted Jews to remain Jews in Christ and gentiles to remain gentiles in Christ. Thus, she informed her audience about the Jewish-Christian origins of the church. In her preaching, S. enriched otherwise naive notions of Christian identity and church history by illuminating their interdependence with Jewish persons and traditions. She preached that unity among Christian denominations rests upon Jewish-Christian relations, and therefore, Catholicity—meaning a universal church—is not possible without Judaism and Jewish people.

S. used scriptures and doctrines internal to Christianity to challenge antisemitism within the church. She reminded her predominantly Christian audience of their humble standing in relationship to God and salvation. The turn to graft gentiles into God's promise was circular; it was intended to save Israel. This suggests that Jews remain the origin and end of God's plan. In preaching about Paul, she uses the phrases Jewish Christians and Jewish Christianity to emphasize their inseparability: "[Paul] certainly did not teach that **Jewish** Christians should give up their identity, let alone their practices, though the Christian tradition subsequently misinterpreted him; Paul himself went to the Temple when he was in Jerusalem. Paul would surely not have welcomed the demise of the Jewish Christianity from which he derived his own authority to spread the gospel of Christ among the gentiles."[29]

S.'s analysis also offers insight into her self-understanding—how she considered her ministry as a Jewish Catholic priest—and, more broadly, how she thought about contemporary interreligious relations. She speculated that the Jewish-Christian church withered away in no small measure due to the exclusion of Jewish Christians from the synagogue in 90 AD. "In any case," she preached, "it is clear from Paul's declaration of love for the Jewish people that he could never have approved of the anti-Judaism which has sought support from his letters to the churches of his time."[30] S. closed her August 1990 sermon with a firm reminder to Catholic listeners to make space for Jewish Christians because their messiah is Jewish.[31]

S. also reminded audiences of the ongoing dangers of anti-semitism. On the fiftieth anniversary of the Wannsee Conference, S. preached a sermon at Cambridge, attributing the Holocaust to a fundamental misunderstanding of Jesus. She informed listeners that in the 1942 conference, public servants discussed a solution to the so-called "European Jewish question." They decided to eliminate eleven million Jews in Europe. Next, she described Nazi techniques for massacring Jews in graphic detail. Should anyone mistake these for the actions of a few powerful people, S. reminded listeners of the indispensable contributions that administrators, engineers, craftspeople, and companies made. Not lightly did she claim that Jews and gentiles are united. She told the story of Zvi Michalowski, a sixteen-year-old who escaped Nazi execution by knocking on the doors of Christians, saying, "I am your Lord, Jesus Christ; I came down from the cross."[32]

S. explained the alignment she saw between persecuted Jews in the twentieth century and Jesus.[33] Attempts to exterminate European Jews are rooted in the erasure of Jesus's Jewishness. According to S.'s logic, Christians cannot cling to Jesus while simultaneously recoiling from Jews. Rather, Christians are called to see their God in all human suffering and thus intervene before that suffering turns to death. The ease with which S. preached interreligious sermons is profound, and we must acknowledge that her insights are still innovative interventions for the twenty-first century.

To clarify the Jewish election, S. preached on a biblical text familiar to many Christians that includes a parable of laborers in a vineyard who worked different hours but were paid the same amount. Again, S. informs her predominantly Christian audience that, "in the prophetic literature of the Old Testament, and particularly in first and second Isaiah, the people of God are portrayed as God's vineyard. The vineyard is where God is served."[34] There are three places in Matthew's gospel that use the image of the vineyard. S. reminds us that they each point to the grace of God, prompting election.[35] As with most religious insights, S.'s suggestion that divine election can be enjoyed only when it is for all people is easier thought than lived. Her consistent commitment to all people, rather than any particular people group, offended most. The very notion of election implies insiders and outsiders, elect and non-elect. Likely informed by friendships formed in her youth in Israel, S. interpreted the scriptures to proclaim God's grace for all people, including Jews, Christians, Muslims, and atheists.

Most of S.'s sermons centered on Jewish-Christian relations, but she also integrated theological connections among Muslims, Jews, and Christians into her preaching. The tenth-century Jewish thinker Moses Maimonides, she explained, has influenced Christian scholasticism in general and Thomas Aquinas in particular. The ninth of his Thirteen Principles of Faith declares that the Torah is God's law given to Israel and will not be replaced. "In writing this," S. speculated, "Maimonides had in mind Muslim claims about the Qur'an—he lived in a Muslim country—and what he took to be Christian claims about the New Testament. As far as Christians were concerned, he was probably thinking of the claim that the New Testament, as God's new covenant, supersedes the old covenant represented by the Hebrew scriptures and that the New Testament breaks with these scriptures."[36] She explained various accounts of Jesus being questioned in scripture—sometimes as hostile attempts to trap him and other times as genuine attempts to square his teaching with Jewish tradition. Jesus responded that the greatest commandment is to love God and one's neighbor as oneself.[37]

Although the language of "new" and "old" testaments suggests that the former replaces the latter, S. asserted, "The new covenant in Christ does not supersede the Torah. It reaffirms it and renews it, bringing the covenantal commitment to perfection and seeking to make the nature of that commitment clear in Christ. . . . Fidelity to Christ is, in essence, fidelity to the Torah; and real fidelity to the Torah is, implicitly, fidelity to Christ."[38] As noted above, S. acknowledged that some rabbis limit their understanding of the command to love one's neighbor as exclusive to fellow Jews. According to S., Jesus opens this to all people:

> *Theravâda* Buddhism claims to be *"ehipassiko dhammo,"* a "come and see [for yourself]" teaching. Christian witness should also be *"ehipassiko dhammo"* in an important sense. An important part of Christian witness in general, and Dominican witness in particular, is the invitation to **"come and see."** ... This brings us to the term *'edah*, the congregation, assembly or community of the people of God. It is a **community of witness,** and witness is not primarily the action of the individual but rather of the community.[39]

Her Dominican family, S. explained, was an *'edah*, a community of witness, albeit in a somewhat narrower sense: "The communality of the Order displays in microcosm the corporate character of the body of Christ as a whole, and its structures and observances testify to the vitality of that body. In and of itself, it constitutes a witness in an increasingly individualistic world."[40]

S. did not hesitate to criticize any group she perceived to have committed an injustice. She opened one of her sermons by summarizing a Hebrew newspaper article written by a Paris-based Iranian-born journalist. The article reported on the death by stoning of a young married Iranian woman at the hands of men of her village, just after the country's Islamic revolution: "What appalled me most about the events described in the article was the striking lack of compassion displayed by the elders, including the village Mullah and the father of the woman accused of adultery."[41] S. then drew on her knowledge of rabbinical literature to interpret the scripture reading for that day: "Our Lord's writing finger is an image of judgment, and he suggests thereby that their uncompassionate judgment upon the woman has brought God's judgment upon themselves: as they judge, so will **they** be judged."[42] To be inclusive, then, was not to reserve judgment.

For S., ministry required recognizing that every people group commits sins and that God mercifully calls all people to turn from sin. S. was not silent in the face of injustice. She stood beside persons condemned by unjust institutions and encouraged them to pursue righteousness. Interreligious work is sometimes criticized for failing to appreciate differences among traditions and ascribing to flat liberalism. S.'s sermons display her careful attention to complex interrelationships and held a line against all forms of disenfranchisement and injustice.

Despite her progressive politics, S. maintained doctrinaire commitments that might surprise some readers, including her belief in a bodily resurrection. The topic occupied much of her time and became the subject of her doctoral thesis. In a sermon she expressed her dismay at contemporary people uninformed about resurrection.⁴³ Scholars who theorize the study of religion have similarly pointed out that European thinkers exhibited a colonial system of categorization in which the lower-order belief is labeled superstition, higher up are so-called major religions (Judaism, Islam, and Christianity), and at the pinnacle of civilization is atheism. To maintain credibility in an increasingly secular society, European Christians, S. explained, construed Jesus's resurrection as a spiritual rather than literal event. She does not, however, succumb to the pressure to adhere to an evolutionary narrative that learned persons are beyond doctrinal commitments. On the biblical witness S. preached: "In an appearance-passage in Luke, our Lord asks the disciples to handle his hands and feet, telling them that 'a spirit has not flesh and bones as you see that I have.' These accounts of post-Resurrection appearances go out of their way to affirm the physicality of our risen Lord and to pre-empt spiritualising interpretations."⁴⁴

Given her commitment to justice, it should be no surprise that S. also criticized the Blackfriars and the Catholic Church at large for its imperialism and exploitative power. In her sermon on the second Sunday after Advent in 1988, S. shared her childhood memory about the Black hermit who took refuge from Apartheid pass raids along the Linksfield ridge near her Johannesburg home. As noted earlier, she had wondered as a child if the man had abandoned his people during the struggle against Apartheid. Now a Catholic priest, S. understood him differently. She likened him to John the Baptist and Moses—two biblical figures who did not see the fruits of their labor within their lifetime.

She urged her brethren to step into a similar role as the Black hermit she had observed in her youth: "We are called to be fearless in confronting people who seek a monopoly over the body of Christ."⁴⁵ In retrospect, we might assess S. similarly. She was faithful to God and religious communities. She did not, however, enter into the promised land—if that is defined as a just society. Like Moses, S. glimpsed the promised land from afar and pointed others toward it. In a later sermon, she clarified her meaning: hope is not to be confused with triumphalism. Strikingly, she stated the kingdom of God will entail the withering away of the Catholic Church, although she was careful to distinguish this from attempts to abolish the church. As an institution, the church's means must suit its end—love.⁴⁶ Her message boldly challenged her Dominican brethren.

Although her sermons might have unnerved some, S.'s interreligious expertise and nonbinary body made her uniquely valuable to the Catholic priesthood. In 1993, S. had the esteemed privilege of delivering a sermon in

Westminster Abbey. She preached on 1 Corinthians 1:23 ("We preach Christ crucified, a stumbling-block to Jews and folly to Gentiles"), explaining,

> The crucifixion stands in stark contrast to this philosophical detachment from bodiliness and its demands. It is the epitome of bodiliness at its most overwhelming and urgent—all-encompassing, brute physical pain so great that it leaves little place for the thought of anything else.... At least two elements, then, would seem to have entered into the excoriation in Paul's time of preaching centered on the cross of Christ: the hallowing of this-worldly success of a certain kind, and diffidence about bodies. These were what made the preaching of Christ crucified seem scandalous and foolish; and they are alive and indeed thriving today.[47]

Her analysis of the cross and physical bodies is thoroughly personal. Not only did she bring in her Jewish expertise, but she also connected her theology directly to her political experience as an intersex person: "The centrality of the cross also demands that we see Christ in our bodiliness, flawed though it is; that we embrace our bodiliness, awkward and painful though it often is, with honesty, dignity and courage."[48]

The challenge, as S. described it, was to recognize Christ in one's own body. When the church and state deem your body a problem, S. dared her audience to see what God sees—a good and new creation. Understandably, one grows weary of proclaiming the Gospel in solitude. The Christian life, as S. understood and experienced it, is only sustainable within a community. All persons require others for their survival. The fantasy of autonomous individualism is maintained by privileged persons who, ironically, stand on the backs of others. Many at the bottom of the social and economic ladder know full well that survival is not an independent accomplishment. It requires people to work together.

In February 1990, S. preached a celebratory sermon after Nelson Mandela was released from prison and the African National Congress unbanned. She opened with a brief history of Mandela's political action and subsequent imprisonment on Robben Island. Despite hard labor and indefinite incarceration, Mandela and his comrades made disciples of fellow prisoners, who joined the struggle for a free and democratic South Africa. "Mandela University," as some called it, produced many influential figures in South African politics. S. explained that Mandela represented something precious to people around the globe that is quintessentially Christian—a deep faith exemplified in fidelity to his comrades, a vision for a more just society, and commitment to the struggle to bring it to fruition. "The humane vision, a non-racial, united and democratic South Africa in which **all** South Africans have a place, a vision which has informed all aspects of the struggle, is a marvelous paradigm of love." She asserted, "Thus in the struggle of Mandela and his comrades we see the major Christian virtues displayed."[49] It inspired S. that Mandela's political action drew courage from his people in the struggle. "He has never sought to go it alone," she stressed. What S. admired most in the ANC was the close-knit community she herself would be denied. She preached, "We belong together, and are called to find our fulfillment together, in cooperation with one another and dependent upon one another, disciplined sharers of the same life."[50]

Thirteen years later, just after Mandela's death, S. would share that sermon transcript with Father Timothy Radcliffe. In the accompanying email, she expressed nostalgia for the hope and joy she felt when Mandela was released.[51] Timothy replied, "Thanks for that lovely sermon. You really are a preacher!! And my condolences for the loss of a great man."[52] Implicit in S. having resurfaced this sermon was her grief over the loss of the sort of community she so admired in Mandela and the ANC. She had joined the order largely because S. appreciated that these Dominicans were active in progressive politics. At Blackfriars, faith and social justice worked hand in hand. But S. never experienced a release. Her story was marked by struggle against discrimination and feelings of isolation.

S. challenged Christians to resist anti-semitism with fervor, not unlike the way she admonished Jews to love gentiles. She preached, "The first Christians were Jewish, and early Jewish-Christians doubtless continued to be observant Jews on the whole, keeping the Sabbath and attending local synagogues. The book of Acts reports that Gamaliel, a prominent Pharisaic teacher before the destruction of the Temple in 70 AD, said of Jewish Christians that they should be tolerated on the grounds that their community would be certain to fail if it were simply of men, but that it would succeed if it were of God."[53] S. then provided context for the biblical story of Jesus healing a blind man. Although Jesus was Jewish, the stakes for embracing Jesus in years after his death entailed being pushed out of Jewish community. Eerily, S.'s analysis of this story offers insight into her disquieting experience of pressure to choose between Christianity and Judaism. She preached about the back-and-forth discrimination between the two traditions.[54]

"Over one thousand six hundred years," she said, "Jews were subjected to increasing civil restrictions, put into ghettoes, slaughtered, and expelled from a host of Christian countries." Even in the present day, S. asserted, discrimination persisted.[55] Opposing all modes of religious discrimination continued to spark controversy, but S. persisted. Two months later she offered an inclusive reading of the Second Vatican Council, which met from 1962 to 1965.[56] Three years later, she would return to the Council's *Declaration on Relations with Non-Christian Religions* to preach that this Christ who has the power to redeem without limit is Jewish. In so doing, S. maintained the particularity of Israel's special election, while also proclaiming that God grafts Christians into that covenant. She asserted, "Our universality in fact **depends** upon the particularity of Israel and of that first call to preach only to Israel. . . . The visibility of our own presence here is the effect of the light of gospels which breaks the bounds, making Israel, in Christ, not just a consecrated nation but also a light to all the nations."[57]

Her theology makes room for her own existence as a Jewish person serving in a Catholic clergy role, but also for all people. She worked for a more just society, which was simultaneously self-interested and others-focused. S. often linked her spiritual insights to social activism. For her, the love of God spurs people to love their neighbors justly.[58] Justice is at the center of the commandment to love, she preached.[59] The holy scriptures and Catholic Mass inspired S.'s resistance to unjust political structures like Apartheid. She was a compelling storyteller who communicated the very real stakes to listeners.

Buddhism

S. informally attempted interfaith work. According to the Douai Abbey archives, S. frequently offered the Eucharistic Prayer, a high point of Mass. In addition to preaching sermons and playing the role of Christ in a passion play, S. also hosted a Passover seder at the Cambridge House. Members of the Cambridge community and congregation attended. Jimpa, a Tibetan Geshe of the Gelugpa sect and translator for the Dalai Lama, joined the brethren for dinner. S. was no stranger to Buddhism, as evident in her lectures and sermons. She honored each tradition as distinct yet interdependent.

Sally wrote to a *Rinpoche*, a Tibetan word meaning "precious one" that is typically used as a title for a teacher, that after decades of practicing Theravadin methods, her physical constraints had made meditation impossible.[60] She mentioned two dreams and an experience. When she was five years old, Sally explained, her parents were leaving for the evening and arranged a sitter. Even though the sitter did not arrive, her parents put her to bed and went out. It was the first time she had been left alone in the flat at night. Jack and Mildred left the passage light on with her bedroom door ajar as a measure of comfort. She was understandably anxious and struggled to embrace sleep. At this time she recalls seeing a luminous blue figure standing in the doorway looking at her. It was a beautiful woman with a protective presence wearing blue robes. This soothed her to sleep.

Around thirteen years of age, she recalls having had a vivid dream that began in a forest fire. A newspaper headline announced an apocalyptic disaster. A panicked woodsman fled from the forest. She sensed that an alien spacecraft had landed, but there was nothing to fear. The alien had a shaved head and humanoid figure. He was wise and compassionate as they shared a warm exchange. Sally understood herself to be one of the being's two disciples—the other a shadowy figure around her age. The Master, as Sally then called the alien, entered a space vehicle to leave the earthly dimension after promising to return. She wondered what she should do to initiate the Master's return. The letter ends abruptly. In its opening, Sally expressed a lifelong sense that the dreams expressed something fundamental about her life.[61]

Sally had been meditating since the early 1970s. She praised Buddhist meditation practices and practiced mindful breathing daily from her recliner. According to friend Jennifer Williams, Sally reported having once achieved pure bliss.[62] One of her most profound experiences was a weeklong Buddhist meditation retreat when she was in the order: "For a while, the mind was free of hindrances. Its inherent luminosity emerged, and time seemed to stop in an extraordinary epiphany of bliss and sheer grace."[63] Sally appreciated Buddha's teaching on Dhamma, especially in the Pali canon of Buddhism. Through it all, she asserts, she was Jewish. She thought Buddhism might be better classified as a philosophy of life rather than a religion.[64] Her affinity for Buddhism was compatible with being Catholic and Jewish at the same time.

As a student in her Catholic order, S. incorporated Buddhist concepts into her essays, joined a Buddhist meditation group, and served as the secretary of a University Buddhist Society. In her essay titled "Hume's Theory of Personal Identity," dated November 1984, she wrote, "One major difference between Hume's account and the *Abhidhamma's* account rests in the fact that the compiler of the *Patthāna* seems to use conditional relations as ontological entities where Hume does not."[65] The same year she wrote a paper titled "In What Sense Did Kant Think That Empirical Knowledge Requires Synthesis?" In it she points to Buddhism: "I suppose one could set up a position diametrically opposed to this, perhaps along the lines of some variants of the Buddhist *Vinjñānavāda* doctrine, to the effect that what appears to us to be real is in fact just a construction of the mind."[66]

In a 2012 interview, Sally summarized her interreligious atheist standing: "Early into the novitiate I had discovered a Buddhist meditation group and I started practicing a lot of Theravada Buddhist meditation from an early age. I still do; it is a daily feature of my life. If I were to put a label on myself, I'm a member of the Religious Society of Friends [Quakers], I am an atheist, and I suppose a label that fits is a Theravada Buddhist. I do the practice."[67] A Buddhist friend connected Sally with an acupuncturist-cum-rabbi who informed Sally that the Zohar distinguishes between *derekh*, the well-trodden path of conventional communal and religious life, and *netiv*, uncharted courses. Identifying with the latter, Sally wrote, "Rejection by my Order and the Roman Curia still hurts, and I still miss religious life."[68] This prompted Sally to reach out to the priest who she thought to be harsh and duplicitous with her—Father Malcolm McMahon. She was pleased to receive a prompt and honest reply; he still felt that what she'd done was wrong and that he had acted in the order's and the church's best interests.[69] Father Timothy Radcliffe responded warmly to her next letter debriefing this exchange.

In addition to referencing Buddhism in her sermons, S. also lectured on Buddhism in her philosophy of religion course and referenced Buddhist concepts in her doctoral thesis. In an opaque lecture, she explained religious experience by comparing Christian and Buddhist traditions. *Samatha* is a practice of concentration that claims religious experience somewhat similar to theists. The experience of *jh~na*, she explained, is a high level of calm sometimes translated as "absorption." A naive theist, as S. put it, could easily misinterpret this as an experience of God. Often the event of *jh~na* is preceded by an experience of light or an object of religious devotion, accompanied by blissful rapture of joy and awe. This *nimitta*, as it is called in Pali, according to S., is considered a concomitant of refined, calm concentration. Meditators ignorant of the theory of meditation are puzzled when *nimitta* appears. Because some Christian contemplative practices are similar to *samatha*, one might mistake *nimitta* for an experience of God. The attainment of *jh~na* is associated with the acquisition of saintly qualities. Although the symptoms coincide perfectly, S. asserted that Buddhism and theism differ strikingly.[70] In her doctoral thesis on bodily resurrection, S. illuminated Christian concepts compared to Buddhist ones.[71] "As the Pali canon of Theravada Buddhism states," S. writes, "**sabbe sankhârâ aniccâ**, 'all compound objects are subject to decay.'"[72]

Understanding Christian theology, for S., entailed deeper knowledge of Buddhist thought.[73] S. gained insight into her inquiry through interreligious dialogue. She incorporated her expertise in Buddhism to demonstrate for her students why appeals to experiences of God's presence do not necessarily suggest that God exists. Her engagement with Buddhism deepened over the years, but it is noteworthy that her interest and understanding of the tradition took root decades prior. Hers was a slow process of suturing together what she had received in fragments. At this time, she was only beginning to explore what that might mean in relation to gender and politics.

Scars

Scars sometimes attest to injury, but in what follows, I consider scars formed by Sally's efforts to initiate breaks and sutures. The gnarled flesh that forms attests to life continuing; scars do not form on the dead. They are the result of wound healing. Scars can embody beautiful histories of intervention. They testify not only to the unique resurrected body of Jesus but also symbolically to Sally's efforts to pull together religious traditions wrongly rent apart. What does flesh healed by sutures look like?[74]

One of the first signs of Sally's spiritual renewal came in May 1996 when she presided over a Passover seder for her Orthodox-affiliated Jewish friends in Oxford the same weekend she attended a Quaker meeting Easter morning. Professors Sebastian and Helen Brock had invited her to cat- and house-sit for them after spending Easter together.[75] Sally first met Sebastian as a student in his Syriac course at Oxford. He is widely regarded as the foremost academic in the study of this ancient language. Helen is a renowned scholar in her own right, specializing in the archaeology of ancient Greece.

When I arrived at their home, just a stone's throw from Oxford, Sebastian greeted me with a warm smile, and Helen instructed me on how to navigate the piles of papers, books, and boxes crowding the passage. "If you need the toilet," she explained, "you should go now because it is upstairs." I assured her that I was fine and marveled at the agility of the octogenarians as we wound downstairs to an office. We sat on one side of a wooden table, the other side occupied with papers and books. The Brocks described hosting dinner parties in which Sally was excellent company. Sally hosted them for dinner at Blackfriars, and the three chatted for hours about her book collection and expertise on obscure topics. Sally had the ability to stoke the Brocks into roars of laughter with her sound effects and stories.

When Sally phoned the Brocks about visiting and informed them that she would be presenting as female, Helen surprised herself with her immediate reply: "Well, join the club!" As Helen opened the door to Sally, she felt at ease with her friend. Sally was the same kind, intelligent person, simply in different clothes. Sebastian felt similarly. Everything they loved about Sally was still there. She described her run-ins with the tabloids and asked if she could hide at their place for a few weeks. Helen suggested ways that Sally could disguise herself so that she would not be as easily recognized by the photo the journalist Qualtrough had published. At our meeting, Helen fetched her diary and a guestbook to confirm the dates that Sally had stayed with them from 1996 to 1997, sometimes just for a night, other times for three weeks. I was impressed with her record keeping and curiously asked where Sally slept.[76] Helen and Sebastian chuckled and explained that one of their studies once had an accessible bed for her.

As Sally presided over the 1996 Passover seder, the celebration was punctured by the excitement of a total eclipse. In the middle of the narrative, guests trooped outside to observe it in what turned out to be an exceptionally clear sky. The next day, Sally shared an Easter meal with Sebastian and Helen, then attended the local Quaker meeting. A public Eucharist was offered, and Sally was made welcome. She agonized over whether taking the Communion or refusing it would be worse. Settling on the latter, she received the elements for the first time since September 1994.[77] Even recalling the moment stirred her emotions:

> There is a Zulu saying: "*Umzima lomthwalo*," the burden is heavy; and I felt the heaviness of the rejection, the exclusion and of the calculated psychological torture to which I have been subjected since 1993. I went back to my seat trying desperately to hold back the tears, sat down, and screwed my eyes tightly shut in order to keep the tears at bay. It did not work: they forced their way through my closed eyelids, and I sat there quietly heaving with tears. There was so much hurt in the tears, but the experience was a good and cathartic one. It brought home the extent to which I have missed the comfort of the sacraments, and the intensity of it all came as a surprise.[78]

It came as a shock to her how profound this reintegration experience had gripped her.

A few years earlier, in 1992, S. had taken an opportunity to participate in anti-apartheid activism as a Catholic priest. Armed men associated with the Inkatha Freedom Party (IFP), a rival to the African National Congress, had attacked Boipatong township, resulting in the deaths of forty-five people. The ANC accused the police of cooperating with the IFP to orchestrate this attack and ceased negotiations within the Convention for a Democratic

South Africa (CODESA).⁷⁹ The student representative body at St. Joseph's Theological College decided to protest the perceived government involvement in the Boipatong Massacre. S. planned to hold a service followed by a march through Howick, in which members of the surrounding communities would be invited to participate.⁸⁰

Local authorities initially granted permission for the march and route, but that was withdrawn at the eleventh hour. There was not enough time to inform people in the surrounding communities, so the students decided to proceed with the service and reevaluate the situation. "In the course of the service," she recalled, "in a church packed with people from the surrounding townships, we heard helicopters overhead. I asked a student to look outside, and he returned ashen-faced, saying that there were hordes of police and that the senior officer had said that they would take action should we march."⁸¹ After the Eucharist and before the end of the service, S. informed the congregation of the situation. The group lacked consensus, so, with the congregation's consent, S. gathered a small group of community leaders to speak with the senior officer about where matters stood:

> What I wanted to pre-empt was a situation in which either the police would burst into the church or in which a section of the congregation would act unilaterally.... There had been a conspicuous march and the actions and statements of the police initially made it seem that confrontation, and quite possibly deaths, would be inevitable. In the end, we managed to do what we had set out to do, without violent confrontation or risk to anyone's lives against steep odds.

S. was thrilled to have facilitated a peaceful protest.⁸²

S. experienced the various modes of sutures in her Jewish Catholic body. The built environment of the Cambridge House, as well as its inhabitants—ordained and lay, male and female—concretized possibilities of assemblage within Christ's body.⁸³ Holiness and activist agitation could collaborate. At times, she felt she was sewing flesh together that had been injuriously or therapeutically divided. Other times, bodies seemed to bash into one another, leaving scars. There were also moments of synergism, where parts functioned as a whole. Ongoing exchanges between individual bodies being treated as a problem and her identifying systemic injustice within social, political, and religious bodies are marked by wounds. S.'s body materialized the suturing together of flesh presumed incompatible. Where some saw a need for excision, she would graft. She refused to prioritize one injustice over another. For S., racism and anti-semitism were inextricable from sexism and xenophobia. Interreligious suture work honored her particular body and social justice for all. Both processes of breaking and suturing entail suffering of a different kind with divergent aims. Sally sought to resist regulating communities and to pursue diverse ecologies of good relations via interreligious suturing. Resonance came through religiosity.

13. Resonance

If you see people as they are, it's hard not to be fond of them. —FATHER TIMOTHY RADCLIFFE

Resonance is full-bodied sound. It occurs when one object vibrates at the same frequency as a second object, forcing it into motion. To "resound" is to make a loud sound together. In the absence of resonance, the sound of vibrations is not loud enough to discern. In chemistry, resonance describes the bonding of molecules or ions by contributing structures. Delocalized electrons are otherwise inexpressible in a single structure. It enables us to describe the otherwise indescribable. In sociology, resonance theory refers to the social conditions conducive or obstructive to harmonious relationships. Political repression, for example, inhibits resonance. Ecological crises limit possibilities for resonance, as does alienation.

Resonance is not to be confused with homogeneity or harmony. Scholar Hartmut Rosa explains, "Resonance certainly is not just consonance or harmony; quite the opposite, it *requires difference* and sometimes *opposition* and *contradiction* to enable a real encounter. Thus, in a completely harmonious or consonant world, there would be no resonance at all, for we would be incapable of discerning the voice of an 'other.'"[1] Sara Ahmed writes, about the queer temporality of resonance, "race can be heard *as* resonance, something one can hear, a sound that connects things up, a disturbance in the rhythm of things.... When we follow the sound, we are dislodged ... [and] dislodging can be a promise.... We can bring things to life, create new life."[2] Resonance connects dots across time and space to unveil unjust patterns. It relies upon difference rather than domestication. According to resonance theory, resonance is both the good life and the difficult path to its pursuit. Homogeneity is not the aim. Resonance requires difference.[3] How do activists instigate and agitate for resonance?

Sally's body remembered and resonated with the classical music her mother played at the piano and with the memory of when her father returned to the flat after quitting a job because a colleague was not paid living wages. She was in tune with them biologically, religiously, and socially. While she was well-spoken and educated, emotional responses swelled up inside of her too quickly for the mind or mouth to rein in. Bodily intonation exceeds logic and reason. Like an antibody, Sally held highly specific memories of threats to her body and would spring into action whenever they resurfaced.

Bodiliness is a shorthand for the cycle I described at the beginning of this book. The setting for bodiliness is a clearing. The events that take place include breaks and sutures. The aim is resonance. Sally became a problem to collective bodies when she braved identifying injustice and initiated breaks from them. Like Morrison's character Baby Suggs, Sally calls us to gather in clearings to laugh, dance, and weep. She wants us to love our bodies and emotions over the violence inflicted upon them. There, bodies are religiously re-membered. The space in a clearing invites resonant movement and embodied sound. Sally's term *bodiliness* points to the resonance we experience when our interdependence rings with the intimacy of belonging. Resonance is the flourishing of all bodies in responsible relationship.

While examining Sally's interreligious work as activism, consider: How might resonance look in the present, and how do bodily remembering and agitation change us?

Sally found her way to the Quaker Peace Centre in Observatory, Cape Town, where she eventually served on the executive board.[4] According to Quaker friend Jen Stern, their meetings are not programmed.[5] They are mostly silent meetings followed by a short time set aside for announcements and tea. Someone might stand up for thirty seconds or a minute to share their thoughts. Only once did Sally rise. She spoke in Aramaic, which Stern remembers as melodic. Of course, most of the Quakers present could not understand the meaning of Sally's words. But her deep voice moved Stern.

She felt a sense of praise.[6] According to Stern, Sally was another oddball in a group of oddballs. Stern was fascinated by Sally and did not sense any untoward sentiments aimed at her. She expressed regret for not inquiring as to why Sally stopped attending meetings. The Quaker community is currently accommodating an elderly person by holding meetings in her home, which makes her think they could have done more for Sally.

Stern believes Sally was caught between desperately wanting to find a place to be comfortable and serving other people by making the world a better place. She explained that Sally was pressured to conform to heteronormativity—to marry and have children—which is why the Catholic Church had been a place where she was able to be her asexual self. Stern stressed that Sally could have been a wealthy, educated white South African man, which would have been the easy path. Instead, Sally cared for others and served society as an activist. But Sally carried the scars of rejection by the Catholic Church that made her slow to connect with her Quaker community. After this traumatic experience, she never found a spiritual home. At one time, Stern proposed to write Sally's biography for her. Although it never came to fruition, Stern did write a blog post with an obituary.[7] Sally has described her universalistic Quaker beliefs and how the deterioration of her mobility prohibited her from participating in Sunday morning meetings.

In a documentary interview, Sally mentioned having worked as a co-clerk for the Quaker house in Eastbourne, where she instructed a course called "Male and Female God Created Them," in which she showed the film *Hermaphrodites Speak*. Much of the video had been filmed at the first Intersex Society of North America (ISNA) retreat in Sonoma, California. Sally described one person's response to the video: "I got a note from this person. It read a verse from Isaiah: forgive me for I have impure lips, I am of impure tongue. People were crying after seeing that video. I had not realized that it had that power. It shook the people who were there to a degree I had not imagined. It was so powerful. It brought things home so powerfully, the horror of treating us as monsters, the horror of the imposition of surgery, and that we are human."[8]

To reporter Stephen Coan, Sally would later reflect, "At some level I think I'll always see myself as a priest and a religious. I hanker for religious life, and I hanker for the ministry."[9] Though her faith began strong in Eastbourne, it could not survive without Christian communion. Her faith withered and died.[10] It was unsustainable without caritas—Christian love.[11] But she was able to redirect her ministry: intersex activism became her new vocation.

Legacy

Initially optimistic about South Africa's progressive post-apartheid constitution, Sally eventually realized that the legal definition of discrimination based on sex omitted intersexuality. She writes,

> The Equality Clause in our Constitution rules discrimination on a number of listed grounds, including sex, gender and sexual orientation, unfair unless and until proved fair. The term "sex" was not defined in statute. It could therefore have been argued that the dictionary definition of "sex" governed its application as well.
>
> In addition, as I realised, there is a closed lexical loop in English and most modern languages in terms of which "human being" and "(natural) person" are defined as having a sex in the binary sense noted above. It was thus open to anyone to argue that the intersexed, being neither exclusively male or exclusively female, were neither human beings nor natural persons.[12]

Intersexuality fell under discrimination on analogical grounds rather than under the 2003 Equality Clause. On analogical grounds, intersex discrimination is deemed fair until proven unfair, which places the burden of proof on the victim of discrimination. She interpreted this to mean that intersex persons did not fit the legal definition of a person or human being, stripping them of the locus standi necessary to challenge discrimination in person or through representation. In an email to friends, she explained the troubling consequences for herself and other intersex persons:

> Neither the Bill as it stands nor the administrative criterion being considered engage with the fact that many people who are intersexed are born with ambiguous external genitalia.
>
> A consequence is likely to be a legislative and administrative *imprimatur* for the imposition of non-consensual genital surgery on intersexed infants and children, something which continues to be standard practice in this country although its theoretical basis was undermined comprehensively by a paper published in the United States in 1997.
>
> For me, it looks as if I could be confronted by a formal demand that I submit to genital surgery as a condition for having an identity, and my identity document may well be withdrawn. I will not submit to any such surgery.

> In the event that my identity document is withdrawn, there will be a number of consequences, the least of which will be that I will be disenfranchised.... Withdrawal of one's identity document renders one a non-person in effect.[13]

While watching a then-popular South African television program, *The Felicia Show*, Sally learned that the Alteration of Sex Description Bill would enable trans people to register in their sex.[14] In 2003, Sally worked to alert the South African government that although the bill intended to allow trans people to have their birth registers altered in accordance with their sex, it problematically necessitated definitively male or female genitalia—congenital or constructed. Sally interpreted the terms to impose disambiguation surgery on intersex infants and adults in exchange for their identity documents to be valid. Throughout Sally's life, she refused to submit to such surgery. She feared that were this bill to pass, her identity documents might be withdrawn, rendering her disenfranchised. As a public servant, she relied on these documents to receive her income. They are also needed to access bank accounts and health services. In short, Sally understood it to render intersex persons legally nonpersons. Sally resolved to work with the Lesbian and Gay Equality Project to submit comment to the Parliamentary Portfolio Committee concerning the bill.

Sally immediately went to work on drafting and submitting her concerns. Estian Smit, a trans man who also proposed amendments to the bill, contacted Sally. Together, Sally and Estian successfully lobbied for amendments to the bill in 2003.[15] Many trans activists are indebted to Sally for what she accomplished, yet she still found it difficult to get traction around intersex activism. Several participants I interviewed offered their perspectives on the possible mistreatment of Sally in activist circles and even the misallocation of funds to which she was entitled. Distilling the facts from conflicting perspectives might be futile in this instance because Sally was reticent to lay blame on any of these activists.[16]

Through her ANC connections, Sally met lawyer Fatima Chohan-Khota, who informed her that while an amendment to the Equality Clause might prove fruitless, the Promotion of Equality and Prevention of Unfair Discrimination Act (PEPUDA) governs the interpretations of the Equality Clause and might offer the opportunity for an effective strategy. Sally wrote:

> Arguing that someone was not human, was not a natural person in law, and lacked the locus standi—the legal standing—to challenge

anything in law or to be represented in the mounting of any challenge in law, because the individual was intersexed, was fair [in] law as it stood at the time until the one suffering the discrimination proved it to be unfair.

Unfortunately, the argument about legal standing made it possible to block legal challenges to this discrimination. The consequence, technically, though it was surely unintended and reflected ignorance concerning intersex, was that the intersexed could be denied any and all rights including the rights to dignity and to life itself, and that any challenges to such discrimination could be blocked.

In practice, had this come up before the Constitutional Court at that time, the court would probably have bent over backwards to try to craft a remedy for the intersexed; but it would have taken ages and might not have succeeded. . . .

What turned out to be the simplest way to remedy the situation in law was to target the Promotion of Equality and Prevention of Unfair Discrimination Act (PEPUDA), which determined the judicial interpretation of the Equality Clause. Two simple and self-evident definitions for PEPUDA achieved this. One states that sex includes intersex, in effect bringing intersex within the scope of sex as a listed ground. The other one defined intersex as congenital sexual differentiation which is not typical, to whatever degree.[17]

Sally drafted the definitions, which Chohan-Khota presented formally. Then, the Justice Portfolio Committee instructed the Department of Justice to evaluate the proposal and report back. As with many bureaucratic machines, the months slipped away with little progress. Sally's headstrong fortitude kept the initiative alive. She had the good fortune of being introduced to Jody Kollapen, the South African Human Rights Commission chairperson, who then connected Sally to Judith Cohen. Sally persuaded Cohen that the law did not sufficiently protect intersex persons.

Sally successfully drafted amendments to the Alteration of Sex Description Bill and the PEPUDA, which were lobbied into South African law. She persuaded the South African Human Rights Commission to recognize intersexuality as a human rights issue, which yielded a SAHRC workshop on the problematic imposition of genital surgery on intersex infants and children.[18] Through the NGO Engender, Sally created Intersex South Africa to inform the public—especially educators, medical professionals, and religious leaders—about intersex persons. She wrote on her curriculum vitae that her submission and oral presentations led to the passage of the bill into law with her amendments concerning intersex persons.[19]

"The drafting of the definitions inserted into PEPUDA took around fifteen minutes," Sally explained; however,

> lobbying them into law took several years. The amendment was signed into law in January 2006. The effect of the amendment in formal legal terms was to close the unintended loophole described above. As matters now stand, South African law recognises that intersexed people exist and protects us from prejudicial discrimination because we are intersexed. Since the amendment brings intersex within the scope of a listed ground in the Equality Clause, in technical terms it renders any legislation which discriminates against the intersexed in effect, be this intended or not, formally invalid.[20]

At present, intersex persons fall under the definition of human beings in South African law and are protected from discrimination.

The National Dialogue on the Protection and Promotion of the Human Rights of Intersex People 2018 meeting report opens with a foreword honoring Sally's work:

> Sally, who worked tirelessly to ensure visibility and redress of the ongoing human rights violations of intersex people in South Africa, secured the first known mention, globally, of intersex national law through the inclusion of "intersex" within the definition of "sex" in the *Promotion of Equality and Prevention of Unfair Discrimination Act*, which governs the judicial interpretation of the *Equality Clause*. She subsequently helped to draft legislation on the *Alteration of Sex Descriptors and Sex Status Act 49* of 2003, which allows intersex citizens to change their sex descriptors on their identification documents.[21]

In her work-related documents, Sally expressed her personal pride in these two accomplishments.[22] In a 2007 email to friends, Sally explained the far-reaching effects of her work: "This closes a dangerous loophole in the law which technically made it possible to deny rights, including the rights to dignity and the right to life, and indeed the right to challenge any such discrimination through the South African legal system, to intersexed people on the sole ground of intersexuality. More than anything else, the elimination of this loophole in South African law was something I wanted to see within my lifetime."[23] In addition to numerous other achievements, Sally also mentioned this in her application to the commission on gender identity, for which Judith

Cohen wrote her a reference letter.[24] Drafts of Sally's work on PEPUDA—including comments, a presentation, and a Home Affairs response letter—are on her computer hard drive under the folder ISSA. Files also included her work on constitutional revisions, meeting minutes, drafts on amendments to the Gender Equality Bill, reports, National Health Insurance Policy white paper documents, submissions to Parliament on National Health Insurance white paper in terms of the Health Act 2003 and the Constitution of 1996, and a National Interim Strategy for addressing violence against lesbian, gay, bisexual, and intersex persons.

Intersex activist Mani Mitchell and Sally last saw one another at the 2011 International Intersex forum in Brussels.[25] There, twenty-four activists representing seventeen intersex organizations gathered to make a public statement on intersexuality:

1. To put an end to mutilating and "normalizing" practices such as genital surgeries, psychological and other medical treatments, including infanticide and selective abortion (on the grounds of intersex) in some parts of the world.
2. To ensure that the personal, free, prior, and fully informed consent of the intersex individual is a compulsory requirement in all medical practices and protocols.
3. Creating and facilitating supportive, safe and celebratory environments for intersex people, their families and surroundings.[26]

Mani recalls Sally pressing the point of infanticide, which other participants shied away from: "She was fierce and determined it be included in the statement."[27] The intense meetings were not without levity. Sally was fun to be around despite not feeling well. The group visited cathedrals and restaurants with abandon. Mani secured a wheelchair for Sally.[28] Pushing Sally's wheelchair over the old-town cobblestone made for a bumpy ride. When the wheelchair would get stuck, more and more intersex friends came to Mani's aid. Their collective pushing ebbed and flowed between roars of laughter, which Sally initiated.

Reflecting upon Sally's journey, Mani shared the perspective that although Sally requested feminine pronouns, she was actually nonbinary.[29] Intersexuality was so foreign a concept to Sally's doctors and religious order that when she first learned of her unique physical characteristics, she was advised to choose between male or female presentation. Learning to do makeup and dress as a woman did less violence than living as a man. Ultimately, Sally just wanted to exist as a person: "I am Sally. I am human."[30] There were not legal protections for nonbinary people when Sally planned her return to South Africa. She needed some semblance of safe passage, and so, in Mani's estimation, she ascribed to the binary and changed her legal documentation to female. It was pragmatic. The documents were for the government, not for Sally.[31]

The demand to ascribe to male or female, cisgender or transgender, as opposed to the rich complexity of her intersexuality, interreligious, and international embodied reality, continued to press upon Sally. To survive, she was compelled to foreground one facet of her being at a time, depending upon the context. While many people can relate to her craving to belong, few respond as Sally did. Most people conform in exchange for acceptance. Sally threw herself deep into rigid religious and state institutions to make systemic change.

Her commitment to moral and ethical good meant that she was not merely seeking to make space, or a clearing, for herself in the world; rather, Sally set out to remake the world such that it would have the capacity to embrace us all in our beautiful, bodily diversity. Her very existence as an unapologetic confluence of categories was itself politically charged. Moreover, she never dissuaded persons of faith from adhering to their religious commitments or communities. She also did not demand that anyone raise a banner proclaiming a distinct gender identity. Sally met people where they were. Her sense was that the world needed to change, not that any individual physical body was a problem. Whether presiding over a Passover meal or rewriting South African policy, Sally was clearing space for us all, even though she was harmed in the process.

Portraits

Amid packing up their flat, Gabrielle Le Roux made room in their schedule to phone me for the first of multiple interviews. It was late at night for Gabrielle, and they had not made as much progress sorting their things as they would have liked. As with everyone who met Sally, Gabrielle praised Sally's intellect: "She was the most erudite person. She had radical politics, having joined the South African Communist Party during apartheid. For her, politics and spirituality were linked and central."[32] Sally's strong presence and impressive intellect were singular. Although Sally could be aloof and reserved at times, Gabrielle explained that once you got to know her, you would realize she was warm. But Sally did not suffer fools. Gabrielle explained that she could be argumentative due to her strong ethics, which would sometimes get people's backs up, but during it all, Sally was the kindest person because she always prioritized the most vulnerable. This was a generous assessment to which often only close friends are privy.

Before becoming an artist, Gabrielle ran the Women's Media Watch from 1995 to 2000. The project entailed interviewing a diverse group of South African women on the heels of the first democratic election. They did focus groups with Muslim women, sex workers, women with disabilities, and those in stages of homelessness. They learned that the media misrepresented women. Participants suffering from domestic violence explained that they were emboldened to leave abusive relationships only when they heard a firsthand account from someone who successfully left. Consequently, Gabrielle met with journalists and editors to challenge them to redress their sensationalist articles by relying instead on first-person narratives. Gabrielle also held workshops to train journalists and editors in more ethical reporting. Ultimately, Gabrielle resigned from their position because their health collapsed under the strain of burnout. Their experience prompted a career shift to art. Gabrielle is best known for hand-drawn portraits created in collaboration with trans and intersex persons globally. Gabrielle invites those sitting for portraits to write personal statements directly onto the paintings. Through this process, Gabrielle fell in love with portraiture. After years of holding a shoulder to the wheel as an activist, Gabrielle realized that art had a political use.

Gabrielle used "herm" pronouns for Sally.[33] They explained that although Sally suffered immense discrimination for presenting as female, especially as a Catholic priest, she was far from a binary person. Remember that this was before they/them became common gender-neutral pronouns. "I was advised to live as female," Sally explained, "and did what this required. My body doesn't fit either standard checkbox, but society demanded that I tick one of them."[34] A decade later, and a couple of years before her death, Sally reiterated in a documentary, *Intersexion*, that she had been advised to live in a female role.[35] Reflecting upon this insight, Gabrielle explained that Sally paid a heavy price for something she did not fully embrace. She was not entirely committed to living as a woman, but society pressured her to choose. According to Gabrielle, Sally was an intersex, celibate clergyperson. But there was no place for a clergyperson who could not be designated one sex or another. Gabrielle underscored the irony of God creating Sally this way.

In 2002, they met at a conference in Pretoria, where Sally gave a presentation and Gabrielle showed a series on "Proudly African and Transgender." Gabrielle learned about intersexuality from Sally. They intended to co-create a six-portrait series to represent different stages of Sally's life.[36] During the collaboration, Sally was suffering from multiple health problems. She shared stories of being harassed in the street and called a monster. Her body was under constant scrutiny by strangers. Usually, it was her weight against which people brazenly discriminated. Gabrielle admired that Sally remained true to herself despite these verbal assaults.[37] When the two discovered a mutual passion for swimming, they began devising a plan to sew one of Sally's kaftans into a jumper so she could return to the pool.

Gabrielle smiled fondly at the memory of Sally between sips of tea. We sat in their new Johannesburg flat—a trove of antiques and inherited furniture. Sketches plastered the walls, a paintbrush forgotten on a side table. Vases of fresh, orange roses livened the room. With the windows open, birds and schoolchildren could be overheard as diaphanous curtains billowed in the breeze. Gabrielle donned a hat over their short hair, under which blue eyes peered. Colorful shoelaces popped against neutral clothing. Their presence recreated what Sally must have trusted during their portrait sessions: a tender soul who advanced social justice charcoal stroke by charcoal stroke.

Typically, Gabrielle selects political subjects to whom they seek to pay tribute. Portraiture has historically been exclusive to elite classes. Gabrielle explained the importance of immortalizing activists. When they collaborate on a portrait, Gabrielle asks their subject to meditate on their political work so that they can capture something of a commitment to justice and an inward journey through a gaze: "It is a wordless place I go to if someone has the capacity to go with me. I ask them to find stillness and we journey together. We have a shared intent, co-creating. The work is meant to go out without us. It is not art for art's sake; it is an intervention. It is very intense!"[38] This is combined with storytelling because, after completing the pastel drawing, Gabrielle invites subjects to write directly onto the portrait. For Gabrielle, portraiture is a performative space. The artist and subject carefully choreograph what signifiers to include. Sally lived so many lives in one, Gabrielle explained, that the two decided on a series of portraits to represent distinct chapters of Sally's life visually.

In the first portrait Sally wrote, "I am what I am" in Hebrew. This references the book of Exodus in the Hebrew Bible. The story is about God having instructed Moses to set the Hebrew people free from enslavement under Pharaoh. Moses asked what authority he could claim; in whose name could he assert that he was acting? The response he heard from God was, "Say this to the people of Israel, 'I AM has sent me to you. . . . This is my name forever, and thus I am to be remembered throughout all generations.'"[39] This is especially interesting when we remember that Sally was continually pressured to give an account for herself. To categorize oneself has significant religious and political consequences depending on whether one is male, female, cisgender, trans, queer, or straight. And yet, society continues to struggle with how to regulate intersex persons. As Sally experienced, there is pressure on intersex persons to get surgery to conform to male or female categories because the ambiguity of intersexuality challenges the social order of church and state.

When Sally writes, "I am what I am," she draws herself into the sacred religious text of her heritage. She reminds us that the Hebrew people might have demanded a proper name from Moses but that God refuses human categories. The story suggests that God simply affirms existence, and that is enough. The verse is ambiguous in Hebrew, so the phrase is open to be interpreted in the future tense: "I will be." In the uncut footage of Sally in Grant Lahood's 2012 documentary *Intersexion*, Sally explains this first in Hebrew and then English, "I am what I am. I am what I would be. That is something that I have found so many times that I need to assert. . . . I [sometimes] get pushy about it and insist that I am intersex and classified as female. I want to be addressed appropriately. I am what I am. I am not ashamed of it."[40] Today, we might interpret this as a refusal of identity politics. The simple claim to being is quite radical and unnerving. By invoking that she is what she is, Sally confronts her viewers with being uncategorizable. She exists even though her body exceeds the imaginations of those around her. Church and state might understand people as male or female, yet she is. Sally and other intersex people are. Gabrielle informed me that "Anicca" is the Pali word for impermanence, and "Anatta" means "no-self." These are two of three characteristics of all things including humanity.[41] Previously, in an email to intersex friends about the social quality of identity, Sally had written, "In a very real sense, one belongs to others because one is dependent on others for self-knowledge and because one's personal narrative is inextricably linked with the narratives of those around me. . . . There is, however, another option: to recognise that the taxonomy is not able to cope with rare difficult cases and to be willing to modify the taxonomy so that it accords better with the way the world actually is."[42] It reflects her complex gender identity analysis as embedded within a community but resistant to binary categorization.

Upon Gabrielle's second portrait, Sally wrote, "I am an unmutilated, whole intersex person."[43] What might she be signaling here? In a society that personifies objects with gendered pronouns, there can be an assumption that gender-neutral terms are dehumanizing. That is, if we define what it means to be human as either male or female, there is no room for intersex persons. To assert that she is a person and intersex, then, is significant. Why "unmutilated" and "whole"? Although we cannot be certain, Sally appears to be referencing her refusal to seek surgery to attain wholeness. She does not need to conform to male or female categories to become fully human. Instead, she is free to reject surgical interventions without compromising her complete personhood. And yet, Sally was ritually circumcised as an infant in accordance with Jewish custom. Some consider circumcision to be normalized genital mutilation. Why it seemed important to her to assert that she has not been mutilated and her body remains whole might indicate a residual trace of her Catholic natural theology, which she understood to object to sex reassignment surgery. Insisting that she was medically intersex by nature and not changing her body in the way that transgender people were imagined to—medically, which, of course, is not necessary—Sally appears to have been threading a theological needle such that she could resist rebuke from the Catholic Church.

Initially diagnosed as trans, Sally experimented with Fran's suggestion that she ascribe to a female role. While Sally later identified as intersex rather than trans, the distinction is perhaps less clear today. Sally was not cisgender in the sense that she was assigned male at birth and later did not identify as such. Although it was important to her that surgical modification be avoided, I suspect that, for theological reasons, the alterations that she made to her presentation and demands for changes to her name and pronouns align with contemporary notions of transitioning.[44] Inside the *o* in the word *whole*, Sally drew the sacred om symbol, which is a revered sound used in meditation that centers on oneness.[45] Some practitioners believe that om is the sound from which everything emerged. It is a vibration that connects individuals to the universe. The resonance found in shared acoustics via mediation is embodied and transcendent. Sally used rainbow colors to draw the symbol, which might reference a diversity of gender and sexuality.

Unfortunately, Gabrielle does not recall Sally's plans for the remaining four portraits. They only vaguely recall that for the third portrait, Sally planned to wear a scarlet habit with a hood to comment on her experience as a Catholic priest. In a tribute to Sally for *The Feminist Wire*, Gabrielle wrote, "One of her dreams was that she would share her experience with the church in a way that would make them change their policy on intersex people. To this end she recently wrote to the new Pope as she hoped that, with a more humane world view than his predecessors, he might make some significant changes when he heard about the devastating impact on her of their prejudice."[46] According to Gabrielle, Sally continually searched the scriptures of

FIGURE 13.1 *I Am That I Am*. Portrait of Sally Gross by the artist Gabrielle Le Roux. Courtesy of Gabrielle Le Roux.

FIGURE 13.2 *I Am an Unmutilated Whole Intersex Person*. Portrait of Sally Gross by the artist Gabrielle Le Roux. Courtesy of Gabrielle Le Roux.

various traditions for places that acknowledge the sacredness of life beyond dualisms and binaries. In Gabrielle's reading, Sally had a beautiful love for her body. Despite being body-shamed by others, she took comfort in her form.[47]

It is unclear to me which pronouns Sally desired in her final days. Because she worked so hard to secure government documents with the name Sally and female pronouns, I have used those here. It seems that Sally consistently challenged either/or frameworks, whether those be national citizenship, religious commitments, or gender categories. She was always both/and: a transnational citizen, interreligious, and intersex.

Remember

Should I die in my bed tonight, be I remembered for it or not, my life and endeavors will have laid the legislative foundations in our law for the significant enhancement of the rights and prospects of people who are intersexed. Knowing this, when I go gently into that good night I can go proudly. —SALLY GROSS

Sally felt that Father Malcolm McMahon was the most malicious actor in the Catholic Church who had pushed for her to be stripped of priestly duties and rendered financially precarious. Twenty-five years later, speaking from the wisdom that comes with experience, Malcolm reflected that he would counsel Sally differently today. He stated, "Sally was a person given to us by God, who didn't fit any of our categories. That was a failing on our part. We failed to understand the complex person who was given to us.... We are becoming better in our culture about not categorizing people. It was a failure on my part and on the part of the Order that we didn't know what to do with someone who didn't fit our boxes."[48]

Sally's intersexuality did not align with a male vision of priesthood. Her interreligious and transnational commitments confused binary categories. It was not her body that was the problem as much as the institutions for which she was illegible. To share in the authority of Christ is not to disenfranchise other people groups; it is to be joined with despised persons. Like the disciples who lived and served God alongside Jesus struggled to see him as their messiah, so also did Malcolm need time to recognize Sally's body and talents as God-given. This is not to excuse Malcolm's actions or the mistreatment of Sally. It is worth observing, however, that people have the capacity for growth and change.

There are things that have long been considered wrong within the church, Malcolm explained, but we now understand the psychological factor, and we know not to blame the person. He believes that Sally was having a crisis of conscience, and he should have encouraged her not to have transitioned so quickly but rather to have focused all her energy on completing her dissertation thesis. Malcolm spoke about a man who flew to Brazil to transition to a woman. To afford surgery and hormones, the man did sex work. Recognizing the intense desperation that prompted risky sex work persuaded Malcolm that gender dysphoria was not rubbish. He admitted that he might have been unkind at times but that he remembers Sally with great warmth.

During our conversation, Malcolm affirmed women's ministry in the church, insinuating that Sally should have had a place. About male priesthood, he reflected: "There is a theological issue around making things holy, which is odd because women make the world holy through bearing children. It's something we [as a church] need to work on—understanding male and female relationships beyond complementarianism. Patriarchy is the obstacle."[49] His comment is not to be taken lightly. The core obstacle to Sally being able to serve as a priest was that her body was not definitively male. At the time, the question of whether women could be priests thundered throughout public discourse. In March 1997, Sally added a footnote to her letter discussing the issue of priests having to be male:

> It is no coincidence that God the Son chose to be incarnate as a man, because nothing about the incarnation is coincidental, and it is therefore essential to Christ that Christ be male. . . .
>
> It was essential to the incarnation that God the son was incarnate as a Jew. . . .
>
> If you want the iconic argument against the ordination of women, you cannot evade the iconic argument against the ordination of gentiles [or, at least, the uncircumcised].[50]

Here, Sally points out the logical limitations of gentiles who limit the priesthood to men based on Jesus's anatomy. She points out these logical fallacies in a way that would allow women to be ordained.

In a sermon about the apostle Thomas, Sally expressed compassion for those who struggle to perceive spiritual qualities. She speculates that most of Jesus's disciples likely thought him an inspired prophet and messianic figure but not necessarily God incarnate. Thomas encounters the risen Lord, she preached, an infinitely greater mystery. Sally argued that present-day Christians are not called to naive faith; rather, the persistence of the church is evidence of Jesus's divinity: "In this encounter we, like Thomas, are called to the recognition that God's presence among us in Christ is a mystery of love which neither our senses nor intellects can plumb. This recognition—that the presence of God among us in the person of Christ's humanity and the presence of Christ among us in our own life as his body, the Church—is the greatest mystery of all, one which confounds senses and human intellect."[51] Sally's body confronted the church with the mystery of God's presence. It took time for brethren like Malcolm to recognize her as such.

The following week, Sally returned to this theme of misrecognition in her sermon titled "Road to Emmaus," in which she explains that Jesus uses the scriptures to help his disciples recognize him: "Jesus reveals himself to be the definitive and perfect form, the summation, of the Hebrew scripture as a whole. Christ, God's Word incarnate, also the revelation of God's Word in scripture incarnate. The disciples, encountering our risen Lord and following him, encounter and follow the *Torah*, the sacred scriptures of the Jewish people. Rejection of the canon of Hebrew scripture which Christ cherishes, explains and indeed embodies, is rejection of Christ himself."[52] Mary Magdalene also mistook the risen Jesus for a gardener. "It is also significant," S. preached in a later sermon, "that it is a woman who remains to face the emptiness [of the tomb], that the risen Christ does not reveal himself first of all to a male apostle or to some other man remembered by later tradition as a central leader, but rather to a person consigned to the margins of the society of the time by virtue of her gender."[53] Previously, I have argued that people misrecognize trans and intersex persons whose baptismal identity is that of co-heirs with Jesus.[54] Many times over, the disciples failed to see Jesus as God, and priests did not recognize Sally as one of them once she took a female role. It is an unfortunate burden of prophetic voices to suffer misrecognition.

In Flannery O'Connor's short story "A Temple of the Holy Ghost," we read of the need for divine intervention to help us rightly recognize one another. A child knelt in church between her mother and a nun. Suddenly, she was interrupted, "her ugly thoughts stopped and she began to realize that she was in the presence of God."[55] It was an extraordinary shift in space, time, and body: "Her mind began to get quiet and then empty but when the priest raised the monstrance with the Host shining ivory-colored in the center of it, she was thinking of the tent at the fair that had a freak in it. The freak was saying, 'I don't dispute hit [sic]. This is the way [God] wanted me to be.'"[56] Earlier in the story, this child learned from her second cousins that the so-called freak "was a man and woman both. It pulled its dress up and showed us."[57] As the child looked to the monstrance, a vessel in which the consecrated wafers are carried and displayed, she saw God in the wafer and in the intersex figure.

Replaying the declaration that God made the intersex person's body in alignment with God's desire, the child had laid in bed and reimagined the fair tent as another kind—the tent of a Protestant revival, rhythmed by call-and-response:

"Raise yourself up. A temple of the Holy Ghost. You! You are God's temple, don't you know? Don't you know? God's Spirit has a dwelling in you, don't you know?"
"Amen. Amen."
"If anybody desecrates the temple of God, God will bring him to ruin and if you laugh, He may strike you thisaway [sic]. A temple of God is a holy thing. Amen. Amen."
"I am a temple of the Holy Ghost."
"Amen."[58]

Although the child in this story did not meet the intersex person, she contemplated the declaration that their body exists as God intends. Before, during, and after Mass, the child's imagination expanded beyond categories of male and female, Catholic and Protestant, sinner and sanctified. On the drive home from church, the child observed, "The sun was a huge red ball like an elevated Host drenched in blood."[59] Sun, wafer, and freak. God was within each.

Prior to God's intervention, the child had judged others ugly and unintelligent. It was not a quick or easy transformation of her perspective. When told that all people are temples of the Holy Ghost and that God could also strike her "dumb and blind," the child reasserted her superiority. Conversely, when the presence of God during religious ritual brought an intersex person to mind as being a temple of the Holy Ghost, the child came to internalize this truth. Through her encounter with God, the child came to see that the testifying intersex body, Christ, and natural environment are temples of the Holy Ghost.

Like O'Connor's child, we need not to have met Sally to be changed. At "freak shows," in hospitals, and in even contemporary athletics, intersex people have been gawked at.[60] Such performances have been theorized as potential political tools for renegotiating social narratives.[61] This child, however, only heard about the intersex person and, with God's help, saw the connection across bodies. O'Connor's intersex character draws upon the provocative label of "freak" to threaten onlookers that God might strike them the same way, shifting the power dynamic by appeals to the divine. It is an explicitly religious phenomenon.

The monstrance shares a Latin root with the word *monster*. Both confront us. They teach by revelation. It is an admonition, a frightening warning. Disability scholars rightly point out that we are all only temporarily, if ever, independent or able-bodied. We, too, might come to appreciate our bodies and their relationships differently. What if the body society deems monstrous is an interdependent vessel for showcasing the divine? A monstrous monstrance. Ogling intersex bodies risks losing perspective on our interconnectedness with religious bodies and the natural environment. It is to look at the finger rather than what it points at. The temptation in learning about Sally is to only look at her to learn about intersexuality. As monstrance, however, she informs us about ourselves—we, too, are vessels for God, forming diverse, ecological social bodies.

Instead of counting ourselves among those who criticize and injure prophetic voices, what if we committed to bravely enter clearings to join the chorus of voices, embrace sutured bodies, and participate in resonance so powerful that it recalibrates governing bodies? It is a vocation for weary souls whose bodies have been beaten and scorned. Those who seek to belong while refusing homogeneity agitate for change. Rather than suffer breaks imposed upon our flesh, we can become problems to governing bodies when we name injustice. It is a constructive alternative to accepting the falsehood that our bodies are problems. Sally shows us what happens when sutures follow breaks. Then comes the best part of all: resonance.

Resonance is neither a destination nor an accomplishment but an ongoing communal activity. There in clearings guided by prophetic voices, we laugh, cry, and dance. We create art. In clearings, we tend to one another's wounds, emotional and physical, scarred over and fresh. Disabled flesh contributes meaningfully to the gathering. Sally called it bodiliness. Together, we form a vibrant ecology with the trees, fungi, breeze, and brooks. These persons—bodies of land and water, humans and animals—labor for right relations. Biological diversity strengthens our belonging to one another. We are beloved.

POSTSCRIPT

While this book features Sally and her story, it is also imperative to recognize the ongoing need for intersex awareness and advocacy. Sally expressed that much still needs to be done to educate people about intersexuality. In her 2007 "wish-list" she dreamed of

> a world in which intersex is not stigmatised, whether by governments, statutes, courts, forces of law and order, religious or secular institutions or individuals, where the birth of a healthy infant who happens to be intersexed is not a cause for dismay and can be celebrated, where infants born with healthy intersexed bodies are reared on the basis of a best guess at optimal gender of rearing considering the aetiology and other factors, where no surgery is imposed unless, and purely to the extent, required for the preservation of physical life or health; where an intersexed person can live without problems in the gender which affords him or her the least discomfort, be it male, female or neither, and where it is not a big deal when the judicious best guess at optimal gender of rearing for an intersexed person turns out not to be the most appropriate one in practice.[1]

These remain worthwhile aims for religious leaders, medical professionals, and legislators.

Sally was not without limitations, some of which I assess below to demonstrate that our understanding of religion impacts the effectiveness of intersex activism. After that, I introduce the activists Sally mentored—Hiker Chui, Pol Naidenov, and Nthabiseng Mokoena—for two reasons. First, it is essential to recognize Sally's impact as a first-generation intersex activist who made way for the next generation. Second, attesting to the hardship that Sally faced is simultaneously a call to support present-day intersex activists who continue to face similar challenges. Although it is too late for us to help Sally, we can honor her legacy. Like her, we can be mindful of those marginalized in all societies and seek to provide adequate physical, emotional, and spiritual care. Accordingly, I have included information about intersex activists whose work readers might support. For additional concrete suggestions, see the Healing Justice Toolkit and Healing in Action: A Toolkit for Black Lives Matter Healing Justice and Direct Action.[2]

Limitations

Sally is worthy of high praise for her accomplishments, though she is not without error. She reported having been told by Indigenous women at workshops that intersex infants were either killed or subjected to surgery. While I found limited evidence to support the claim that intersex children are frequent victims of infanticide, Sally might counter that the shortage of evidence is due to a lack of funding to conduct intersex research. That might be true, but it still concerns me that one might interpret her account as denigrating Black African cultures and communities as superstitious and intolerant outliers. Naming this limitation of hers does not disqualify Sally's profound contributions to intersex activism. Failing to point out the importance of religious literacy and racial aspects of alleged intersex infanticide, however, would be irresponsible.

Hopefully, Sally did not intend to suggest that Black Africans were especially prejudiced against intersex infants. She was certainly also critical of white cultures being inhospitable to intersex persons. Sally attributed such bigotry in South Africa to a Christian, colonial inheritance: "These attitudes were brought to Africa together by Western colonialism in most of its forms, not least through the propagation of Western styles of Christianity and concerted efforts to suppress and replace traditional indigenous religious and cultural practices."[3] Moreover, Sally informed her readers that Khoi and San *sangomas*—heirs to egalitarian spiritual healing traditions—assert that intersex persons serve as gatekeepers to higher spiritual powers.[4]

However, Sally often detailed the alleged gruesome acts of Black African midwives against intersex infants despite flimsy evidence:

> Eventually someone involved in the organisation of a workshop in which I participated said that such babies are often "given up." When I asked what this involved, I was told that what my informant meant was that such babies were put in plastic bags or boxes and dumped. In effect, there was pressure to throw them away. . . .

The mothers responded by saying that if the surgery was not done, making the genitals look unambiguous, "they"—people in their communities—would kill their babies. A midwife told me that it was common not to let such babies live.[5]

Sally admitted that most of her sources were hearsay but also cited Victoria John's *Mail and Guardian* article "Gentle Man's Brutal Murder Turns Spotlight on Intolerance," published June 28, 2012. According to Sally, Shaine Griqua of LEGBO (which serves the needs of LGBTQI+ communities in the Northern Cape of South Africa) asserted that traditional midwives regularly delivered infants with ambiguous genitalia, which they then terminated. In some cases, mothers were not informed and instead were told their infants were stillborn. Horrific if true.

Worse, Sally characterizes the alleged violence as rooted in superstition:

Activists had apparently spoken informally to ninety experienced midwives. . . . 88 out of 90 midwives had said that it was their practice over the years to break the necks of such babies while the mother was unaware of what was happening, and to tell the mothers that their babies had been still-born. They justified this by saying that their culture held that such babies were the product of witchcraft and that their families were cursed.[6]

In 2020, bioethicist Kevin Behrens published an argument for five principles to inform ethics guidelines for surgical interventions in intersex children. In it, he responds to a 2018 South African newspaper (*Mail and Guardian*) article titled "Intersex Babies Killed at Birth Because They Are Bad Omens."[7] Behrens claims that there is sufficient evidence to suggest that intersex infanticide does take place in South Africa. He cites Tunchio Teriso's informal study in which traditional midwives and birth attendees interviewed allegedly confess to having killed babies with ambiguous genitalia. The presumed motives for infanticide are witchcraft, curses, and bad omens.

I have not found research to corroborate the alleged problem of infanticide. The National Dialogue on the Protection and Promotion of the Human Rights of Intersex People's 2018 meeting report discusses the need for more research into these statistics, especially in South Africa's Northern Cape. Though, again, the need is for prejudiced reasons: "Some cultures believe that intersex infants are 'bad omens,' a sign of witchcraft, a punishment from God and a curse on the family they are born into. In these instances, it is often understood to be preferable to kill the child, by twisting its neck, than allowing the mother to raise it. Birth parents are often told that their child was stillborn and not to ask further questions."[8] What troubles me is that the justifications offered ring with moral panic—a phenomenon characterized by scapegoating supposedly evil actors in new or marginalized religious groups. Women of color in South Africa who manage childbirth outside of medicalized institutions are presumed uninformed and superstitious. Behrens expresses concern that births "in private homes and out of sight of authorities" enable intersex infanticide.[9] The effect of this smokescreen is to mask documented abuses exacted by secular health-care practitioners and mainstream religious traditions. Instead of grappling with atrocities committed by professionalized doctors, humans prefer to construct a bogeyman. Blame the witch, devil worshippers, foolish religious folks.[10] These impulses fortify problem bodies, the regulating institutions.

Contraception and termination of intersex embryos are medical practices worthy of interrogation. According to Limor Danon, in present-day Israel, reimplantation genetic diagnostic testing is offered to families with histories of intersex conditions in order to prevent the conception of fetuses with a variety of intersex conditions.[11] Danon argues, "The prevention of the conception of embryos with known intersex conditions and the termination of pregnancies in which fetuses have different intersex conditions are significant socio-medical practices that control the future existence of intersex bodies in Israel."[12] Julie Greenberg writes about the risks involved in prenatal interventions aimed at curbing congenital adrenal hyperplasia (CAH): "This practice is problematic because it could cause significant harm to the fetus. Prenatal exposure to dexamethasone has been shown to cause brain changes. . . . In addition, some reports have also indicated potential harm to the pregnant mother."[13] Intersex scholar Morgan Holmes uncovers the link between prenatal interventions and abortion:

> In addition, some research centers are developing gene therapies designed to reverse AIS in the prenatal environment, thereby erasing the potential for AIS to be expressed in the population. But in the absence of therapies that work to the satisfaction of clinicians, *termination* is commonly proposed as the most appropriate method of managing a fetus with an intersex diagnosis (Wertz 2000, 279–83). Thus, a woman's right to choose becomes conflated with a clinician-parent contract to choose a heteronormative, clear sex and gender.[14]

Trusted medical professionals aim to prevent the conception of intersex embryos, which, if conceived, are aborted and, if delivered, are subjected to "normalization" surgery.

And yet, public fear fixates on South African spirituality. The pattern of diverting attention is gendered, racialized, and spiritualized. On November 26, 2017, the African Intersex Movement made a public statement about intersex infanticide, demanding "to put an end to infanticide and killings of intersex people led by traditional and religious beliefs."[15] Iranti, a media advocacy organization for the rights of LGBTQI+ persons in Africa, announced on their website, "On 11 December 2017, Iranti joined activists and members of the intersex community in the first large scale engagement with government on matters of intersex genital mutilation, infanticide, healthcare procedures and standards of living."[16] Whether the disposal of intersex infants is a literal occurrence or something that Sally anticipated as a culminating social attitude remains unclear to me. Regardless, the dearth of evidence is cause for pause. Denigrative misrepresentation of Black African women and spirituality is at stake. Black African midwifery is branded more dangerous than medical protocols of contraception, termination, and coercive surgery.

However well intended, Sally and others' framing of the need to investigate intersex infanticide in South Africa as spiritually motivated is disturbing. In 2013, when Sally raised her concern again, she claims to have been dismissed: "I attempted to bring it to the attention of South Africa's Commission on Gender Equality and its Human Rights Commission, which ducked and dived and found reasons not to investigate the matter. There have been people who have expressed anger at the allegations being made at all, in the first place."[17] Why stoke hysteria about alleged superstition among Indigenous people when there are documented cases of medical practitioners in the Global North aborting intersex fetuses and imposing sex assignment surgery upon infants and children?[18]

Insufficient religious literacy perpetuates harmful stereotypes about religious women of color, which distract from documented harms inflicted by doctors. The following intersex activists whom Sally mentored continue to grapple with combating misinformation, maintaining the importance of religiosity, and advocating for intersex justice.

Hiker Chui

Taiwanese intersex activist Hiker Chui recalled bursting into tears upon learning of Sally's circumstances. S/he had met Sally at the world's first international intersex forum in Brussels in 2011.[19] In a video chat with me,

Hiker recalled feeling excited and nervous. Previously, s/he had only met a handful of intersex persons. As the only intersex activist from Asia and an English language learner, Hiker requested that the discussions be recorded to aid her/him. It was denied based on preserving privacy. Sally sat opposite Hiker and continually reminded participants to speak slowly for her/his benefit. They held eye contact as Sally flashed reassuring smiles. Hiker explained that Sally was the type of person who, upon first meeting, you feel she is *with* you—a lifelong friend.[20]

At the forum, Hiker immediately felt that s/he had found her/his people. S/he wanted to hug everyone and take photos together. The previous year, Hiker initiated the "Free Hugs with Intersex" movement at Taipei Pride.[21] In part, Hiker aimed to overcome the stigma of being intersex. S/he also spoke of the isolation s/he suffered and the subsequent need for human contact. We all need love and to be loved, Hiker explained, so s/he emphasized that with a simple gesture—hugs. It was special, Hiker explained, to have the opportunity to hug so many intersex persons at the forum.

Sally stood out as an inspiration to Hiker. Though only thirteen years her/his senior, Sally was an intersex activist trailblazer. Hiker would turn to Sally for advice and information via Facebook Messenger in the following years. S/he recalls being very new to intersex activism and relying on Sally's knowledge and experience. As a teenager, Hiker discovered not only her/his intersex status but also that s/he had undergone disambiguation surgery as a six-year-old. When doctors discovered a uterus and ovaries in Hiker's abdomen, they resolved to reduce what was then classified as a large clitoris rather than a penis. Sally strategized with Hiker about implementing new policies in Taiwan to prevent such surgeries on intersex infants and children.

Throughout Hiker's life, strangers have asked whether s/he is male or female. S/he hates this question because s/he does not know how to answer it. Inquiring gazes used to make her/him want to stay home. It used to bother Hiker that people did not read her/him as female, but today s/he explains that s/he does not mind how people gender her/him. The process of learning about intersex persons gave her/him great release. However, Hiker is careful to dress in gender-neutral clothing. S/he explained that Taiwan is still a dangerous place for trans persons and that when s/he wears dresses or feminine clothing, s/he is presumed to be a trans woman. This is a risk that s/he is unwilling to take.

Hiker sensed that Sally was a deeply spiritual servant of God who exuded calm, safety, and peace. Hiker shared with me that several of her/his intersex

Christian friends also suffer hurt and rejection at the hands of the church. S/he expressed confusion. How could such a beautiful person and excellent priest as Sally be pushed out of ministry? Her/his words were heavy with empathy. Although not a Christian herself/himself, Hiker imagined the pain intersex persons of faith suffer when forced to leave their church, and wept. Hiker continues to be inspired by Sally: "I want to have the same spirit like her to serve my community. She gave me energy, love, and confidence.... She was brave to cross so many different borders—religion, identity, and country. She was moving all the time. When she became interested in Buddhism it made me feel even closer to her."[22]

When Hiker learned of Sally's advanced illness and economic difficulty, s/he immediately deposited money into Sally's account. Hiker was in Johannesburg at the time—just a short plane flight from Sally in Cape Town. Still, s/he felt powerless to help Sally. Hiker explained that although intersex activists have bonded at annual forums, most of the time they are alone in their respective countries advocating for intersex rights. "Most of us are infertile and [therefore] can't generate children. We are seen as useless and not worthy of investment. Intersex children are abandoned, kicked out of families, or killed."[23] Through sobs, Hiker explained that due to isolation, many intersex people fear dying alone: "We have friends around the world, but we are far from each other. How can we help? We feel alone as we age."[24] In her/his ten years of activism, Hiker continues to work alone in Taiwan: "This is the life of an activist."[25]

Pol Naidenov

Bulgarian intersex and trans activist Pol Naidenov was among those in the international community shocked and grieved by the news of Sally's passing. Pausing to flick tears from their eyes, Pol explained that if they had known Sally would die alone, they would have invited her to live with them. Though they had few interactions with Sally, the first at the international intersex forum in Malta, Pol, like most of the activists I interviewed, was deeply touched by Sally. Pol explained that the fortitude it takes to be an activist sometimes hardens someone to the extent that an activist's identity is reduced to fighting. It can be dehumanizing. Sally, however, consistently stoked hope and faith. When debates escalated, she helped participants shift from arguing to constructive thought, all while smiling. Her comrades are still mourning the loss of her warmth and smile. Pol described, "She was like an island in the ocean where you can stop and feel safe."[26]

Pol explained that the word *pol* in Bulgarian is the same for sex and gender. This complicates legal rulings. Part of Pol's activism has entailed claiming "Pol" as their first name. Pol shared with me that they were castrated as a child. As with many intersex people, Pol is infertile. However, they are the father of two children. When I asked if Pol used gender-neutral pronouns, Pol explained that it is difficult to translate but that they are a non-male man. It is a play on words in Bulgarian. Pol smiled. Pol was raised as a girl, but even their doctors did not claim Pol was a girl so much as the doctors instructed: you are here to be *like* a girl. "It's not an issue for me so much as it is an issue for others who do not accept the idea."[27]

According to Pol, after Sally's death, the intersex international activist community realized the need for services and support for people with disabilities and those who live alone. Pol offered the example of this ongoing need in discussing a friend who is a refugee from Iraq and recently disappeared. They still do not know what happened to this person or where they are.

What stuck out to Pol was Sally's full acceptance for people as they are, without judgment; learning that Sally was once a Catholic priest, Pol was surprised by her unprejudiced disposition. Pol was accustomed to religious people fretting over what God wants from humanity. Sally focused all her energy on helping people accept themselves. Sometimes, this entailed re-reading biblical stories in a new light, but most often, she simply embodied the love of God. Currently, Pol is advocating for adequate trans and intersex health-care services. To the best of their ability, they are maintaining contact with disabled intersex activists. They expressed a great need for psychological and social support systems for intersex activists.

Nthabiseng Mokoena

Fellow South African intersex activist Nthabiseng Mokoena recalled communicating with Sally by Facebook and Skype about her ailing health and inability to afford groceries. Both Nthabiseng's and Sally's intersexuality confounded medical practitioners, religious institutions, and state laws. Their mother allowed great freedom for gender expression in the home. Outside of the home, however, Nthabiseng was instructed to present as female and never to undress in front of others. This was stressed as a safety measure.[28] As a child, Nthabiseng would have to undress in front of doctors and medical students as an exhibit of disordered sexual development.[29] At the age of thirteen, Nthabiseng did not begin to develop breasts. They explained:

I was clearly different. My living nightmare started when friends teased me about my boyish appearance and flat chest. My mother took me to a totally uninformed doctor, who said he had never come across the phenomena, would consult other doctors and we should return in two weeks time. On our return, he said I must have surgery which my mother flatly refused, saying I could make up my own mind when I turned 18 if that was what I really wanted. It was also the first time my mother told my father that I was an intersex child. Even as a baby, he had never seen me undressed or bathed.[30]

Doctors referred to them as "it" and advised immediate surgical intervention. For years, they sought out a doctor versed in intersex health care.[31] One doctor offered a free clitoral reduction on the condition that he could use it as a case history. Nthabiseng flatly refused.[32]

Prior to becoming a Black, queer, intersex activist, Nthabiseng worked as a metrological engineer in a mine. Having been raised as female, Nthabiseng continued to present as a woman, carrying intersexuality as a heavy secret. Mines are typically a male-dominant space riddled with classism, Nthabiseng explained. The miners tend to be Black men, and the managers white men. According to Nthabiseng, the miners were often treated as commodities, and the managers lacked respect for the miners' boundaries or intellect. Race and gender outweighed expertise in engineering. As such, this was a trying time for Nthabiseng.

On television, trans and intersex people appeared to be targets for violence and hate crimes, causing Nthabiseng to feel depressed. They were not enjoying working as a female engineer in the mines. Church served as a second home but was also distressing. At the time, Nthabiseng served as a highly respected and beloved pastor. A young pastor fluent in English and Xhosa was hard to come by, so Nthabiseng was a popular associate pastor at the five-hundred-member congregation. Nthabiseng shared a house with a female friend during this time. The two would kiss and then pray for forgiveness. The message at their church was that same-sex attraction was an abomination. Feeling a need for deliverance and authenticity, Nthabiseng resolved to inform the lead pastor of their intersex status. The pastor discouraged Nthabiseng from telling anyone else. The pressure to be duplicitous was crushing. Wasn't there room for Nthabiseng to come out as intersex and queer at work or in church? Ultimately, Nthabiseng resolved to leave. "I still miss that spiritually charged environment," they expressed wistfully.[33]

Early on, doctors framed Nthabiseng's intersexuality as a disorder in need of medical remedy. Nthabiseng began searching for other intersex persons online and came across Sally. Sally was able to break down the pathologization of intersexuality. Nthabiseng admired Sally for being comfortable with her intersexuality. Despite claiming a female name and pronouns, Sally did not concern herself with ascribing to social prescriptions for "proper" femininity. Nthabiseng was inspired. Perhaps there was a way to love oneself as is. The two communicated online for years. Sally offered language for integrating intersex bodies with spirituality. When Nthabiseng worked for the Transgender Intersex Alliance, Sally offered medical information over and against the doctors who treated these conditions as disordered. Elsewhere, she explained:

> I do not use the recent label "DSD" because, as introduced, the first "D" stands for "disorders" and I deny that intersex is pathological or a disorder. Had the label actually introduced been something like VSD, "variations of sexual development," I would have accepted it. In general, I reject the pathologising optic through which intersex tends to be viewed, and argue that it should be viewed through the optics of respect for human diversity and human rights. In consequence of this, I am suspicious of the framing of intersex as a disability, which suggests to my mind a disorder, a medical condition which needs to be fixed or worked around. That said, I know from lived experience that rejection, ostracism and stigmatisation are disabling. The disability is a social construct, as it were. The one's suffering from a disorder are those doing the rejecting, not those who are intersexed.[34]

If participants at the Transgender Intersex Alliance were intimidated by medical experts who misrepresented or silenced intersex persons, Sally would interject a philosophical and spiritual insight that boosted Nthabiseng's confidence: "She would always call people out on their B.S. and put them in their place. People had massive respect for her because of the broader human rights [Sally advanced]."[35]

There were difficult times, though, living a life of unreciprocated service. Sally shared with Nthabiseng that she had once saved a woman from choking in a restaurant. The following week, when the woman and her husband saw Sally again at the same restaurant, they refused to greet her. Empathetic, Nthabiseng asked, "How do you continue to work when you help others in need and you're not seen as a human [being]?"[36] When Nthabiseng first appeared in a national magazine, they were overwhelmed. "The hate mail was tremendous, and people were more curious about my genitals than the issues I was trying to raise. . . . I did not expect that speaking out would involve isolation and literal threat to my life at times."[37]

When *National Geographic* contacted Nthabiseng about a show titled "The Third Sex," Nthabiseng required that Sally serve as the expert commentator in this two-part documentary; the first covered Sally's experience of being intersex, and the second Nthabiseng's.[38] Activist work brought media visibility, and with that came hate mail. Through it all, Sally served as a dedicated mentor to Nthabiseng. The articles in which Sally would make religious arguments in favor of intersexuality initially shocked Nthabiseng; but with time, Nthabiseng came to understand their scholarly and spiritual validity. Sally advanced instrumental legislation that activists continue to build upon today.

Nthabiseng explained, "People are afraid to use the word *poor* for white people in South Africa. Sally was really poor."[39] According to Nthabiseng, activists collaborated with Sally and used her story to raise funds for their causes without compensating her or acknowledging ISSA. This was especially problematic when ISSA was hanging on by a thread. Although Sally had a large online community, she was ultimately alone in trying to figure out how to survive day-to-day. Activism works in a socialist system, Nthabiseng asserted, not a capitalist one: "Sally gave up everything for a cause. There was no pension fund waiting, no medical aid. . . . You don't think that you will get old or sick and need those things."[40]

Without the warmth of Sally's companionship, intersex activism in South Africa felt insurmountable. Nthabiseng critiqued the "NGO industrial complex" that renders activists financially precarious. They explained that grants are typically given to support projects rather than salaries or institutional costs. Intersex work is often folded into trans or LGBTQI+ advocacy more broadly. As with most NGOs, Intersex South Africa relied on international donors, project grants, and funds divided among LGBTQI+ advocacies. What disquieted Nthabiseng most was that activists like Sally were expected to run NGOs with little or no money. Add to that burden the message that activists are to prioritize self-care.

Like Sally, Nthabiseng collapsed under the burden. Nthabiseng had been raising a younger brother for over seven years and could not afford his school fees. Insufficient wages compounded with traumatic stories of intersex abuses were too much to endure. By December 2014, Nthabiseng resolved to leave intersex activism to focus on human rights advocacy more broadly. Immediately, Nthabiseng was pelted with shaming questions about why they were not continuing Sally's work, to which they incisively replied, "No-one can effectively advocate and lead on an empty stomach or without proper healthcare."[41]

ACKNOWLEDGMENTS

Archivist Linda Chernis at the Gay and Lesbian Memory in Action (GALA) archives has been generous with her time and resources. To all the participants who allowed me to interview them, on and off the record, thank you. Sally's brother Ray Schmidt-Gross and friends Liesl Theron, Gabrielle Le Roux, Michael Worsnip, and Father Timothy Radcliffe entrusted me with their memories of Sally. Father Oliver Keenan, whom I met at a Karl Barth conference at Princeton University, kindly facilitated my introduction to many Blackfriars in England. Grant Lahood graciously shared the uncut footage of his Sally Gross interview from his documentary on intersexuality.

Farah Markelvits, Julie Eisenband, and Brett Biebel offered thoughtful comments and encouragement. Rabbi Linda Bertenthal and Rachel Heath provided indispensable insight into Judaism and interreligious movements. Kevin Funkhouser read several early, messy drafts. Kent Brintnall shared invaluable comments on the organization of Sally's unwieldy story. Casey Golomski and Marvin Wickware encouraged me to be brave and share more of my thoughts. The late Elizabeth Clark offered "tough love" just when I needed it, and Erin Walsh words of support.

A few indefatigable loved ones stuck with me through years of revisions, helping me organize, reorganize, cut, expand, and turn this manuscript every which way. Korah Wiley, Kimberly B. George, Mari Joerstad, Blair Wilner, and Derek Jones were there for me through the toughest times. I cherish your fortitude in providing feedback on the book as we journey through the tides of life. Lucy Burgchardt asked questions to help me determine the structure of the book. She and Jenny Blair were careful, sensitive readers. It is difficult to express how warm and charitable David Rubin has been to me, which they are to all people.

My best friends and dearest family members provided the stuff of life that, while not directly related to the production of this book, certainly gave me the reprieve needed to step away and return many times over, reenergized from laughter and affectionate exchanges. Emiko Higa Corey, Betsie Cialino, Emily Peck, Julia Abel, Grete Howland, Juliet, Camille, and Joaquin, I love you.

Gisela Fosado and Willie Jennings, thank you both for believing in me and this book even before it existed. I appreciate Gisela and Alejandra Mejia for their assistance throughout the peer review and publication process. Bird Williams patiently shepherded the manuscript through the editing and production stages. The unnamed peer reviewers provided comments and questions that had a pronounced impact on improving the final version of the book. Your expertise and pushback were of great value.

Augustana College's New Faculty Research Award 2018–19 financed my trips to South Africa and England. Their Student-Faculty Academic Partnership Grant enabled Annelisa Burns to offer feedback on my manuscript. There are likely more whom I am forgetting to acknowledge. This book is the collective effort of many people who uniquely contributed to its final form. I hope that it sparks conversation and constructively contributes to scholarly and activist efforts.

NOTES

INTRODUCTION

Epigraph: Malatino, *Trans Care*, 26.
1. Du Bois, *Souls of Black Folk*, 1.
2. See Ahmed, "Sexism," *Willful Subjects*, *On Being Included*, and *Complaint!*
3. See Moten, *In the Break*.
4. Morrison, *Beloved*, 87.
5. Morrison, *Beloved*, 44.
6. Morrison, *Beloved*, 44.
7. For an excellent analysis of play as a subversive divine activity, see Douglas, "Black and Blues."
8. N. Fadeke Castor describes ancestral time/space as an interface with the cosmic realm: "With repetition, the gestures of greeting, prostration, and blessing become ingrained in the body and attached to feelings of connection with both Spirit and community. Thus, they hold resonance with prior moments of ritual fellowship that are accessed anew in new ritual moments." "Spiritual Ethnicity," 83.
9. Joerstad, *Hebrew Bible*.
10. See Townes, "To Be Called Beloved"; Townes, *Womanist Ethics*; and Cannon et al., *Womanist Theological Ethics*.
11. Townes, "To Be Called Beloved," 183–202.
12. Townes, "To Be Called Beloved," 183–202.
13. Emilie Townes and Marcella Althaus-Reid make use of political theorists for concrete Christian theology and ethics, namely by underscoring the economic features of sexuality. Townes integrates Native American and African American histories of exploitation, and Althaus-Reid interrogates the profane by examining religious devotion among Latin American sex workers. See Althaus-Reid, *Queer God*.
14. Terms for intersexuality among medical practitioners and activists have included *hermaphrodite* and *Disordered Sex Development*. While those terms can be reclaimed, as *bitch* and *queer* have been among other marginalized groups, I use the term *intersex* throughout because I understand it to be more accurately descriptive and less pathologizing. Gross read publications such as "Hermaphrodites with Attitude," but spoke of herself as intersex. To my knowledge, she exclusively used the term *intersex*.

15. See Ahmed, *On Being Included*.

16. Among the first generation of intersex activists are Cheryl Chase (founder of the Intersex Society of North America), Max Beck, Mani Mitchell, and others. A video of an initial gathering can be viewed at @etreenquestion's 1997 *Hermaphrodites Speak!*, https://www.youtube.com/watch?v=3IkJU0oL2gU. Some of the well-known present-day activists are Pidgeon Pagonis, Hilda Viloria, and Sean Saifa Wall. See Wolff et al., "Creating Intersex Justice."

17. It is noteworthy that a short biography of her work is included on the South African History Online website—"Sally Gross," South African History Online, https://sahistory.org.za/people/sally-gross, accessed June 21, 2019—and that she is recognized in South Africa's Apartheid Museum. In addition to founding Intersex South Africa, Sally drafted amendments to the Alteration of Sex Description and Sex Status Bill (2003) and the Promotion of Equality and Prevention of Unfair Discrimination Act (PEPUDA) in South African law. She persuaded the South African Human Rights Commission to recognize intersexuality as a human rights issue.

18. Gross, sermon transcript, "Bartimaeus," Sunday, October 23, 1988, 8:00 a.m. mass, (Mark 10:46–52), Sermons, GAL 0121, F4.

19. Alice Dreger discusses the value of "narrative ethics" in intersex biographies, meaning that medical ethics should be informed by the substance and nature of patients' stories. See *Hermaphrodites*, 68. Arlene Baratz and Katrina Karkazis similarly argue, "More than anecdotes, these narratives provide a first-person reflection on care and thus represent a type of long-term follow-up that is largely absent in clinical literature." "Cris de Coeur," 129, https://web.p.ebscohost.com/ehost/pdfviewer/pdfviewer?vid=0&sid=aed74055-6fd3-4363-b00a-aa160173fcc7%40redis.

20. Sally tended to be verbose and used overly technical language, so I have condensed and simplified her concepts. Whenever I have reconstructed an event based on her narration or that of a witness, I have used colons and italics to signal that they are not direct quotations. When information only came from one source, I write "according to" to indicate that it is an individual's perspective. Quotation marks flag when I am directly citing a document, interview, or video.

21. Gross stated, "It was the biggest trauma of my life, one that was surely life-threatening and dragged on for a long time." Coan, three-part series.

22. I say *mother* here because Sally was among the first generation of intersex activists and mentored activists across an array of LGBTQI+ issues, which I describe later. The legacy section explains that Sally lobbied for amendments to the Alteration of Sex Description and Sex Status Bill and PEPUDA. She collaborated with the South African Human Rights Commission and the South African NGO Engender. For her work, she has been praised by the National Dialogue and Promotion of the Human Rights of Intersex People (2018) https://hal.science/hal-02897876v1/file/2019-07-22%20-%201.%20The%20emergence%20of%20intersex%20as%20a%20protected%20category%20in%20international%20law.pdf, https://www.fhr.org.za/2020/09/20/national-dialogue-on-the-protection-and-promotion-of-the-human-rights-of-intersex-people/; the UN Office of the High Commissioner in *Human Rights Violations Against Intersex People: A Background Note*, https://www.ohchr.org

/sites/default/files/Documents/Issues/Discrimination/LGBT/BackgroundNoteHumanRightsViolationsagainstIntersexPeople.pdf; and in the University of Pretoria Centre for Human Rights' *Study on The Human Rights Situation of Intersex Person in Africa* (September 2002), https://www.chr.up.ac.za/images/researchunits/sogie/documents/Intersex_Report/Intersex_report_Oct_Sept_2022.pdf. She drafted amendments to the Gender Equality Bill, National Health Insurance white paper documents, and the Health Act (2003) and Constitution (2006).

23. This approach aligns with Gross's account, "Not in God's Image," in which she writes: "Is my Prior Provincial evil? I think not. He is, as I have noted, someone I liked and could still like. It was my hope that, given time, he would gain some pastoral insight into the issues raised by my situation. In the event, I think that he found himself confronted by a situation completely outside his experience with which he was simply not able to cope, and with which he floundered. . . . The Prior Provincial acted in the way the institution required, and I do not doubt that he did so in the belief that it was in the best interests of the people in his care—the members of the English Province, of the Order at large and of the Church at large." Gross, sermon transcript, "Bartimaeus," Sunday, October 23, 1988, 8:00 a.m. mass, (Mark 10:46–52), Sermons, GALO121, F4.

24. Memmi, *Colonizer*, vii.

25. Special thanks to Kent Brintnall for thinking through how to articulate this distinction.

26. Gross, "Draft, Part 1: Theology, Part 2: Philosophy, and Part 4: Identity," GALO121, A5.5.1 Academic Papers. When read alongside her paper presentations to the Women's Theology Group at Oxford, "Towards a Theology of Humankind," Part I and II (March 1982 and January 1983) Personal Documents, Spirituality and Religion, Miscellaneous, it appears that her interest in theological matters might be related to her personal embodied experience. See also A6 for "Gross's essay on philosophy as part of coursework at Oxford University," Philosophy.

27. See Carter, *Anarchy*; and An, *Coloniality*.

PART I. BODY PROBLEMS

Epigraph: Griffiths, "Queer Theory," 41, 44, respectively.

1. Raymond (Ray) Schmidt-Gross requested that I refer to their father as Jack. Ray Schmidt-Gross, interviews, phone, September 20, 2018; phone, October 16, 2018; Boston, June 23, 2019. All the photographs that Gross had in her computer files also list him as Jack, (GALO121, F4). Mildred's birth certificate states that she was born in Cape Town, South Africa, and that both of her parents were born in Russia (GALO121, A5, Personal documents: official personal documents). Jack's birth certificate indicates that he was born in Pietermaritzburg, South Africa, and that his father was born in Russia, his mother in England (GALO121, A5, Personal documents: official personal documents).

2. Gross does not directly claim to have congenital adrenal hyperplasia (CAH), the name for a group of disorders that can affect sex characteristics. However,

her report that her parents were told she was severely dehydrated at birth aligns with the common metabolic issue that infants with CAH experience at birth. "In the 'classic,' salt-losing form, [CAH] results in vomiting and dehydration and, if left untreated, can lead to death," says Ellen Feder, *Making Sense*, 24.

3. Grant Lahood generously gave me access to his uncut footage interviewing Sally Gross for his 2012 documentary *Intersexion*, which is one hour, fifty-one minutes, and fifty-nine seconds of video that I have transcribed. In it, Sally Gross speculated that the mohel might have wanted to spare everyone the embarrassment of acknowledging the ambiguity of her genitalia because that would have problematized his working and their having gathered on the Sabbath. She also speculates that the participants were aware of her atypical genitalia, though they did not speak openly about it, in "Towards a Theology of Humankind Part I," which was presented to the women's group in March 1982 and "A Theology of Humankind II: Transcending Male Gender Roles" in January 1983 (GALO121, A5.5.1.) See also A6 for Gross's essay on philosophy as part of coursework at Oxford University. Some of these details are also included in Coan, three-part series; and Gross, "Chronicle," of which Sally's drafts are in GALO121, C1.2, Academic papers: Sally Gross essays, and various versions with her comments; a document saved as "lorna_intersex sally gross v2b" and titled "Becoming Sally" on her computer hard drive; the documentary "The Third Sex Part 2," GALO121, F2; and the autobiographical elements of her paper "Not in God's Image," GALO121, C4. Gross emailed Petra Bader of *The Sunday Times* to offer corrections to Oliver Roberts's article about her, dated July 14, 2009. Both of her parents are deceased, so I am not able to request their perspective on Gross's claims about her upbringing. However, her brother Ray Schmidt-Gross has confirmed her account upon reading this manuscript.

4. Gross, "Chronicle," GALO121, C1.1, Academic papers; as described in Coan, three-part series; and Lahood, *Intersexion*.

CHAPTER 1. CONTEXT

1. One of his descendants, Daniel Malan Jacobs, would become a coworker and friend of S. Gross.

2. Gross, sermon transcript, "1990-04-15 Easter," Easter Sunday, 9:30 a.m. mass, Blackfriars, April 15, 1990 (John 20:1–9), Sermons, GALO121, F4.

3. Ray Alexander Simons (1914–2004) was born in Latvia and moved to South Africa in 1929. She became the secretary of the South African Communist Party, the general secretary of the Food and Canning Workers Union, a founding member of the Federation of South African Women, and a recipient of the African National Congress's highest honor, the Isithwalandwe Award, in 2004. Hilda Bernstein emigrated to South Africa at eighteen years old and was prominent in the struggle to end apartheid. She was awarded an honorary degree from the University of Natal for her role in establishing democracy in South Africa.

4. Gross, "Jewish Responses," 301.

5. Unpublished version of Gross, "Jewish Responses," file name "After Helen and Sally3," page 10, forwarded to me from Daniel Malan Jacobs January 24, 2020, original email from Sally Gross to Daniel Malan Jacobs November 23, 2013. The excerpts that did not make it into the published version are noteworthy. Perhaps the editors did not agree with Sally Gross's framing because they found the statements to be untrue or editorialized. The published version calls it "acquiescence" and "the accommodationist policy," stating: "While most South African Jews feared (or disliked) the National Party and thought its policies repugnant, the majority approach to their predicament was not to 'rock the boat,'" Sally Gross, "Jewish Responses," 301.

6. Gross, "Jewish Responses," 311.

7. Gross, "Jewish Responses," 309. Gross defines 'non-Jewish Jews:' "This term refers to people of Jewish descent and perhaps upbringing, who have gone beyond the boundaries of Judaism and are, perhaps, unlikely to identify themselves culturally or religiously as Jewish," Gross, "Jewish Responses," 297.

8. For more on this see McClintock, *Imperial Leather*.

9. During my visit to the Schmidt-Gross home in Boston June 21–24, 2019, Ray Schmidt-Gross allowed me to scan photographs and keepsakes, including Mildred's medal dated 1944 and the newspaper article about her achievement. Each of Jack Gross's Israeli military medals and pins were also well preserved.

10. Information for this part is a synthesis of Sally Gross's accounts in documentaries, newspaper articles, book chapters, paper presentations, sermons, lectures, photographs, videos, and conversations, along with her brother Ray Schmidt-Gross's account when I interviewed him September 20, 2018; October 16, 2018; and June 23, 2019.

11. During my visit to his home, Ray Schmidt-Gross allowed me to scan letters to Jack dated 1958 on Western Province Zionist Council letterhead and South African Zionist Federation, S.A. Zionist Youth Council letterhead.

12. Gross, letter addressed to "Ronnie," no date or further information, but contextual clues suggest that it was written to an ANC comrade, Ronnie Kasrils, to solicit financial support near the end of 2013 or beginning of 2014, just before she died. This document was emailed to me by Pam Sykes on October 31, 2018 and saved as "Letter for Ronnie Kasrils."

13. According to Gross's brother Ray, leaving the kibbutz was Jack's biggest mistake. The kibbutz had been a supportive environment where people appreciated Jack. He was well loved there and likely would have made more of himself. Ray Schmidt-Gross, interview, June 23, 2019.

14. Gross, "Towards a Theology of Humankind," Part I and Part II, Blackfriars, by Selwyn Gross while at Blackfriars, Oxford, 1982–1983. Part I, March 1982; Part II ("Transcending male gender roles"), January 1983, GAL0121. See also A6 for Gross's essays on philosophy as part of coursework at Oxford University under A5.5.1, Personal Documents, Spirituality and Religion, Miscellaneous.

15. Ray Schmidt-Gross, interview, June 23, 2019.

16. Ray Schmidt-Gross, interview, phone, September 20, 2018.

17. As an adult Sally Gross was careful to explain that the Zionist movement is not homogenous. She distinguished between cultural, spiritual, and political Zionism. About the latter she also contrasts socialist left-wing and anti-socialist right-wing political Zionism. Unpublished version of Gross, "Jewish Responses," ("After Helen and Sally3," note 29, page 17), forwarded to me from Daniel Malan Jacobs January 24, 2020, original email from Sally Gross to Daniel Malan Jacobs, November 23, 2013. The published version puts it: "While compliance with apartheid was sometimes the hallmark of South African Jews, sentiments were often not homogenous," Sally Gross, "Jewish Responses," 2014, 302.

18. Gross, letter addressed to "Ronnie."

19. Gross, letter addressed to "Ronnie."

20. Among Ray Gross-Schmidt's albums are multiple photographs of S. in her school uniform with the school crest—one with a crest on a white polo shirt and another on a blazer, which S. wore with a hat and tie.

21. Gross, "A Theology of Humankind II," Women's Theology Group, January 1983, GALO121, C, Academic papers.

22. Gross, "letter to [Father] Timothy [Radcliffe] discussing Judaism, her struggles with her identity and details on the advice and counselling she was seeking," February 29, 1993, GALO121, A3, Communication between Sally and the Catholic Church, thirteen single-spaced pages.

23. Lahood, *Intersexion*.

24. Gross, "letter to [Father] Timothy [Radcliffe]," February 29, 1993, bold in original.

25. Marquis Bey adroitly describes the imposition to narrate one's self: "There is so much tinkering and experimentation and figuring things out, so many false starts. To say that one always knew one was 'trapped in the wrong body,' a paltry and insufficient narrative, erases all the hours of sheer toil, the *years of passionate detective work* that are absolutely integral to forging, piece by piece, trans subjectivity. All the *pained questioning, theories formed, ditched, taken up again, before finally somehow through the osmosis of popular culture, they arrive at the answer that they were always trans*. I, we, needn't say that we have known since the origins of our thoughts that we were not what they claim we are." *Cistem Failure*, 17–18.

26. Gross, sermon transcript, "Feast of the Presentation," February 2, 1992 (Malachi 3:1–4; Hebrews 2:14–18; Luke 2:22–40), Sermons, GALO121, F4, bold in original. This refers to the pidyon haben—redemption of the firstborn son. The ceremony is not performed if the firstborn is a girl, born by caesarian section, or preceded by a miscarriage.

27. Gross's paperwork for a passport is complete, signed and stamped May 3, 1967.

28. Among Ray Gross-Schmidt's albums is a photo of S. with her yeshiva classmates. Shared with M. Wolff in Boston, June 2019.

29. Dansky, *Gateshead*, 28. The Gross family also hails from Lithuania.

30. Dansky, *Gateshead*, 101.

31. Gross discusses this in her sermon "1989-07-23, Love—Mary and Martha," sixteenth Sunday of the year, Oxford Blackfriars, 6:15 a.m. mass, July 23, 1989 (Luke

10:38–42), Sermons, GALO121, F4. Orthodox Jewish culture does not typically initiate women into the study of Torah.

32. Gross, letter addressed to "Ronnie."

33. Lahood, *Intersexion*; and Gross, "Chronicle."

34. A fraught contemporary imagining of a woman intentionally masquerading as male in order to attend a yeshiva is presented in Barbra Streisand's film *Yentl*—based on I. B. Singer's 1962 short story "Yentl the Yeshiva Boy" and insightfully analyzed by Garber, "Tale of Two Singers." The circumstances are markedly different from S.'s; Garber's analysis, however, might be helpful for understanding the allure of religious study despite complex gender performances and rigid social imaginaries.

35. Gross, letter addressed to "Ronnie."

36. Gross, "letter to [Father] Timothy [Radcliffe]," February 29, 1993. For more on the male body and Zionism see Weiss, *Chosen Body*.

37. Gross, "Chronicle," 236. She also writes, "Sense from an early age that something bearing on my anatomy and perhaps my gender was awry, but unsure what it was. Sexual orientation: asexual—one of nature's celibates." "Not in God's Image," GALO121, C4.

38. According to Jen Stern, who knew Sally as a Quaker in Cape Town, Sally was one of nature's celibates and had no interest in marriage or reproduction. Stern, "Betwixt and Between," and Stern, interview.

39. Gross, letter to [Father] Timothy [Radcliffe]," February 29, 1993.

40. Gross, "Summary of Commitments, Skills and Experience Accumulated," GALO121, B3, Work related documents.

41. Lahood, *Intersexion*.

42. Lahood, *Intersexion*.

43. Father Martin Flatman, interview, email. I interviewed him and his wife Frances Flatman in Oxford on February 23, 2019.

CHAPTER 2. ADULTHOOD

Epigraph 1: Crosby, *Body Undone*, 19.
Epigraph 2: Beauvoir, *Second Sex*, 68.

1. It is worth noting now Sarah Imhoff's observation of how "drawing on many religious sources—what I think of as *religious recombination*—is far older than ['seekers' in the US 1960s]. [For example, queer Zionist Jessie Sampter's] story also shows us how these seemingly unorthodox approaches to religion can go hand in hand with a single, strong religious identity—and ultimately that these combinations and recombinations aren't all that unusual." Imhoff, *Jessie Sampter*, 28.

2. Gross, letter addressed to "Ronnie," GALO121, F4. She also describes this in part 2 of the National Geographic documentary that features her as an intersex South African, titled *The Third Sex* (Van Huyssteen, Wessel, dir. 2003. Johannesburg: Tin Rage Productions for SABC3).

3. Gross, "Incomplete correspondence/document by Sally Gross [to unknown recipient]," February 11, 1996, GALO121, A3; letter with the same date and a footnote added "March 1997," GALO121, A8, folder 2 of 3.

4. Gross, "letter to [Father] Timothy [Radcliffe] discussing Judaism, her struggles with her identity and details on the advice and counselling she was seeking," February 29, 1993, GALO121, A3.

5. Coan, three-part series. Gross says something similar in "e-mail B," GALO121, A8; in "Not in God's Image," March 2013 GALO121, C4; and again in Lahood, *Intersexion*.

6. Appendix F, GALO121, A8, folder 2 of 3.

7. Gross, "Towards a Theology of Humankind, Part I," March 1982, GALO121, C2 Academic Papers.

8. Gross reflected on this experience in "letter to [Father] Timothy [Radcliffe]," February 29, 1993.

9. Gross, "A Theology of Humankind II: Transcending Male Gender Roles," January 1983, GALO121, C2 Academic Papers.

10. Gross, "Transcending Male Gender Roles." Her brother Ray shared similar stories of physical and emotional abuse.

11. Gross, "Transcending Male Gender Roles."

12. Gross, "Transcending Male Gender Roles."

13. Gross, "Transcending Male Gender Roles."

14. Gross, "letter to [Father] Timothy [Radcliffe]," February 29, 1993.

15. Lahood, *Intersexion*.

16. She describes the first time she requested a "pretty" and "flicky" haircut to try out feminine presentation in "Transcending Male Gender Roles," 4–5. Gross also mentions, "The eccentricity of my appearance has been a way in which I have sought to cope, and it has been successful up to a point," in "letter to [Father] Timothy [Radcliffe]," February 29, 1993.

17. I purposefully use the word *reveal* rather than *discover* here. See Wolff, "Diptych Reading." Gayle Salamon's *Assuming a Body* provides a useful account of trans theory that avoids dualism by drawing upon phenomenologist Maurice Merleau-Ponty. Salamon's book is not theological; philosophers and theologians who engage Merleau-Ponty's work, however, find insightful connections. Gross makes a number of interesting distinctions between breath, spirit, soul, human, divine, mortal, immortal, body, and flesh, as well as their relationship to one another, that she roots in patristic texts.

18. Jules Gill-Peterson analyzes the hypervisibility of trans persons compared to the erasure of intersex persons despite their interwoven histories in *Transgender Child*. See also Brulmyer, "Archival Assemblages."

19. I had already obtained Gross's account of her visit to Crown Heights from multiple sources prior to this, so while it was not new information, I found it interesting that this was the only document of hers at the Douai Abbey and what name it was cataloged under. Note that I do not presume familiarity with Blackfriars and will provide background information about it and S.'s entry into

this religious community in later parts, then detail her trip to Crown Heights in another chapter.

20. "Oxford house members from 1981–1988," photo album, Douai Abbey. Among Gross's photographs were priests and laypeople in a bounce house, eating pizza delivery, at garden parties, and hosting meals in which the friars wore their robes and laypeople tuxedos and formal dresses, GALO121, P4.

21. Richard Conrad, "The Nature and Rules of Blackfriars Community," 1991, Douai Abbey. It is my suspicion that this is what attracted Gross to the community and in turn hurt her faith so profoundly when she was pushed out.

22. Gross, "Incomplete correspondence/document by Sally Gross [to unknown recipient]," February 11, 1996, letter, GALO121, A8, folder 2 of 3.

23. "Oxford house members from 1981–1988," photo album, Douai Abbey. Ellipses in original. The entirety of the caption is quoted.

24. Gross, sermon transcript, "Sermon: Westminster Abbey," February 5, 1995 (1 Corinthians 1:17–2:5), Sermons, GALO121, F4. Fran Springfield mentioned having attended this sermon with a group of trans friends when I interviewed her on February 19, 2019.

25. Sally later mentioned to a brother the possibility of losing weight if she were supported in exploring her gender identity. That was not the outcome, but it indicates that she felt some shame about her body size and spoke openly on the topic.

26. The friars shared these anecdotes with me. It is significant that the bursar granted many of S.'s requests, even though she came to feel slighted.

27. Sally's brethren, activist comrades, family, and friends all noted that she was not financially savvy. Some disapproved of her decisions, and others laughed it off as a personality quirk.

28. Cambridge House Chronicle, Friday, April 1, 1992, box III, Douai Abbey.

29. "[S.] has already departed for a year (Sabbatical?)," Cambridge House Chronicle, July 9, 1993, box III, Douai Abbey. "A newsletter from the provincial announces that Selwyn has been given one year's leave of absence," Cambridge House Chronicle, September 1–7, 1993, box III, Douai Abbey. None of the material in the Cambridge House Chronicle appeared to contradict Gross's account.

30. *Laicized* is a technical term in the Catholic Church that means to withdraw clerical character, control, or status from someone.

31. Gross describes this incident in "letter to [Father] Timothy [Radcliffe] outlining her distress and the break from the church," February 19, 1995, GALO121, A3, Personal documents.

32. Gross describes this incident in "letter to [Father] Timothy [Radcliffe]," February 19, 1995.

33. Gross, email addressed to "friends," Subject: "News from the wilderness," July 15, 2007, GALO121, A3, 10 pages, single-spaced.

34. Gross, email addressed to "friends," Subject: "News from the wilderness."

35. Boyarin, "Freud's Baby," 130. These themes are also explored in Boyarin et al., *Queer Theory*. Alice Dreger describes the inefficacy of facial hair as a sex determiner because "'many Jewesses had quite a large quantity of both beard and mustache.'

Beards and mustaches, like absent uteri, were not unheard of in women." Dreger, *Hermaphrodites*, 22. For an extended analysis of facial hair as it relates to gender, power, and citizenship, see Najmabadi, *Women with Mustaches*.

36. Boyarin, *Socrates*.

37. Holmes, *Intersex*, 37. As defined by Hortense Spillers in *Black, White, and in Color*, pornotroping refers to stripping a people group of personhood and treating them as objects receptive to violence and sexual assault.

38. Townes, *Womanist Ethics*.

39. Gross, "letter to [Father] Timothy [Radcliffe]," February 29, 1993.

40. Gross, letter addressed to "Ronnie."

41. Gross, email "Dear friends," Subject: "From the Finsbury Park Station," August 24, 2003. A number of Sally's friends emailed this document to me, and it is also found on her computer hard drive, to which Ray Schmidt-Gross gave me access, and in the GALA archives, GALO121, F4. See also Gross, "letter to [Father] Timothy [Radcliffe]," February 29, 1993.

42. Gross, "The Geography of Encounter with Mr Qualtrough," December 21, 1996, GALO121, A8, folder 2 of 3, 2 single-spaced pages.

43. Gross, "letter to [Father] Timothy [Radcliffe] outlining her distress and the break from the church, her financial difficulties and her consideration of suicide," February 19, 1995, GALO121, A3, Personal documents.

44. Gross, "letter to [Father] Timothy [Radcliffe] outlining her distress and the break from the church, her financial difficulties and her consideration of suicide," February 19, 1995. Sally writes that she called Father Malcolm McMahon during one of her ideation episodes and claims he callously replied that it will simplify matters. He does not recall this exchange.

45. Gross, "letter to [Father] Timothy [Radcliffe] outlining her distress and the break from the church, her financial difficulties and her consideration of suicide," February 19, 1995.

46. Gross, "Not in God's Image." See Patterson, *Slavery and Social Death*.

47. Gross, "Not in God's Image."

48. "Santhi Soundarajan, another runner, even attempted suicide after she 'failed' a 'gender test' and was stripped of her 2006 Asian games medal. At this point, not having a policy that allows athletes to know privately, in advance, if they have disqualified as women is like asking bobsledders to head down the track without helmets: it's downright dangerous." Dreger, "Sex Typing," 23.

49. Lauren Berlant theorizes "slow death" in *Cruel Optimism*, and Christina Crosby discusses it in *Body Undone*.

50. Puar, "Coda," 152.

51. Gross, application to a position at the Human Rights Commission, GALO121, B3. See also Gross, "Incomplete correspondence/document by Sally Gross [to unknown recipient]," February 11, 1996, and a footnote, added "March 1997," that physical examination has confirmed that her congenital physical sexual differentiation is atypical and makes reconstruction surgery impracticable, GALO121, A8, folder 2 of 3.

52. Some scholars reserve "social death" to describe Black enslavement. I use it here because Sally drew upon Orlando Patterson's term to describe her experience of intersexuality.

53. See Gross, "letter to [Father] Timothy [Radcliffe]," February 29, 1993; and "letter to [Father] Timothy [Radcliffe] outlining her distress and the break from the church, her financial difficulties and her consideration of suicide," February 19, 1995.

54. Williams, interview. The cats were later taken in by a friend but kept returning to Gross's home. According to Williams, a neighbor eventually agreed to care for the cats. There are a number of photographs of her cats in GAL0121, F4, which also feature in the footage of Lahood, *Intersexion*.

55. This detail has been neither confirmed nor denied by others.

56. Ray Schmidt-Gross, interview, June 23, 2019.

57. Ray Schmidt-Gross shared Sally's death certificate with me via email January 27, 2020. It includes her identity number, name as Sally Gross, gender as female, classification of never married, cause of death natural, and date of issue February 21, 2014, signed by the director general of Home Affairs and stamped by the department.

58. For more on Jewish burial customs see Jütte, *Jewish Body*.

59. Ray Schmidt-Gross, interview, phone, October 16, 2018.

60. Ray Schmidt-Gross, interview, October 16, 2018. Gross had a file folder labeled "Dying and letting Go," with websites about how to prepare for death, GAL0121, F4.

61. Sykes, interview.

62. I first publicly presented my research and analysis on this question at the 2019 National Women's Studies Association conference held in San Francisco on a panel with David Rubin and Amanda Lock Swarr. The paper was titled "Sally Gross: Mother of Transnational Intersex Activism Died Alone."

63. Alison Kafer summarizes the medical model, social model, and identity-first positions on disability in *Feminist, Queer, Crip*. Alternatively, and persuasively, she argues for a political-relational model. Kafer is critical of depoliticizing disability. She argues for cripped coalition politics and queer disabled ecologies.

PART II. PROBLEM BODIES

Epigraph: Salamon, *Assuming a Body*, 8.

1. Margaret Price describes the importance of holding space and crip gathering in *Crip Spacetime*, 2024.

3. RELIGIOUS BODIES

1. The GALA archives also contain her "Psychological Horoscope," *Astro Dienst*, GAL0121 A5.4. It appears to be based on her date, time, and place of birth.

2. Lahood, *Intersexion*.

3. Carmelites were known as "Whitefriars" and Franciscans as "Greyfriars."

4. "Our Unique Intellectual Heritage," Blackfriars Hall, https://www.bfriars.ox.ac.uk/discover/our-unique-intellectual-heritage/, accessed April 15, 2021. The Oxford priory was established in 1221 with the intent to be at the center of learning. There Dominican friars live in community, teach seminary courses, and conduct mass. In 1994, after S.'s time there, Blackfriars Hall became one of Oxford University's permanent private halls, and it houses a specialist library in philosophy and religion.

5. Dominican Friars, "Preaching," https://www.english.op.org/preaching/, accessed April 15, 2021.

6. I toured the Oxford house and met with a number of Blackfriars to discuss their daily routines on and off the record February 28, 2019.

7. There are photographs of Martin and Frances Flatman with their children, and later with a grandchild, in Sally Gross's computer file folder "friends," GALO121, F4. The Flatmans also recalled having toured S.'s room in the Oxford priory.

8. Frances Flatman, interview, February 23, 2019; and Martin Flatman, interview, February 23, 2019.

9. Father Martin Flatman shared this information with me November 4, 2018, by email. I then interviewed him and his wife, Frances Flatman, February 23, 2019, and continued to correspond via email, including an interview with their son Samuel.

10. Samuel Flatman, interview, March 10, 2019. Among Gross's sermons there is reference to Samuel's confirmation: "reception into the Church of Sam Flatman," 1988, GALO121, F4.

11. Lahood, *Intersexion*.

12. Gross, "letter to [Father] Timothy [Radcliffe] outlining her erosion of faith," July 26, 1995, GALO121, A3, Personal documents.

13. Lahood, *Intersexion*.

14. The vote results are confirmed by the records in the Blackfriars *Directory of the English Province of the Order of Preachers* at Douai Abbey, which details the location and rank of all community members.

15. Lahood, *Intersexion*.

16. Gross, email addressed to "friends," Subject: "News from the wilderness."

17. Gross, email addressed to "friends," Subject: "News from the wilderness." I consulted the *Directory of the English Province of the Order of Preachers* to identify S. Gross's fellow novitiates. After speaking with persons who knew the two novitiates who entered with Gross, I invited them to be interviewed for this project. One did not respond and the other declined.

18. Stephen Coan also mentions her participation in the ANC meeting in Dakar. Coan, three-part series. Gross also describes this in Lahood, *Intersexion*. An interviewee mentioned their surprise in stumbling across television footage of this event and recognizing Gross.

19. Lahood, *Intersexion*. "I was ordained a day after getting back from Dakar, Senegal where I'd been 1 of 16 representatives of the African National Congress who met with a group of largely Afrikaners, led by the now former president of South Africa Thabo Mbeki. It was a milestone in the movement toward negotiations which

ended apartheid." Lahood, *Intersexion*. Details also from Coan, three-part series. Helen Brock claims to have attended Gross's ordination in an email to Jennifer Williams: "Why I write now is that while tidying up old papers in my study I have come upon the service sheet for [S.'s] ordination to the priesthood at Blackfriars, Oxford. We were present at that service. If there is a sort of Sally archive, perhaps this could go into it." November 15, 2015, forwarded to me by Helen Brock on February 21, 2019.

20. Certificate of naturalisation, British Nationality Act 1981, "Full name *GROSS*[JEWISH NAME] Name at birth if different *GROSS*[NAME GIVEN AT BIRTH]," August 11, 1998, , GAL 0121, A2; Oath of Allegiance, signed S. Gross, September 1, 1998, stamped by the British Consulate to verify the document July 7, 2011, signed Angela Hodgson, British Vice Consul, GALO121, A2.

21. Timothy Radcliffe, "letter from [Father] Timothy [Radcliffe] giving advice on the options," May 4, 1994, GALO121, A3.

22. Gross, "letter to [Father] Timothy [Radcliffe] a follow up on the previous letter, which was written to him officially as the Master of the Order. This letter was written as Timothy's friend also on the dismissal and Sally's personal struggles," November 10, 1994, GALO121, A3.

23. Radcliffe, "letter to Sally responding to her letter and discussing the dismissal," November 11, 1994, GALO121, A3.

24. Radcliffe, "letter from [Father] Timothy [Radcliffe] in response," March 9, 1993, GALO121, A3, emphasis in original. Gross quotes this in her "letter to [Father] Timothy [Radcliffe] thanking him for his letter and giving him an update of conversations she had had with various counsellors and clergy," April 26, 1993, GALO121, A3.

25. Radcliffe, "letter from [Father] Timothy [Radcliffe] in response," March 9, 1993, GALO121, A3. Gross references this letter at least twice: April 26, 1993, and a year later, April 17, 1994. For a different perspective on the scripture see Boyarin, *Radical Jew*.

26. During this time, Sally alleges that Malcolm lifted the ban on her visiting the houses under his jurisdiction. She suspected that her doctoral thesis supervisor, Kathy Wilkes, forced his hand by making a complaint to the Graduate Studies Committee. Kathy Wilkes (1946–2003) is deceased, so I was not able to obtain her version of events. See "Letter to Dr [Paul] Parvis from Richard Hughes (Graduate Studies Officer and Assistant Registrar: University of Oxford)," March 18, 1996, University of Oxford letterhead, GALO121, A8, folder 3 of 3, 76. Among Gross's identity documents is a Bodleian Library card for the University of Oxford, valid until September 30, 2002, GALO121, A7. Gross notes Wilkes's comments on her thesis, 13, GALO121, C5, Academic papers, folder 3 of 3. Gross, "letter to [Father] Timothy [Radcliffe] telling him about her return to Blackfriars and her interest in the Quakers," May 6, 1996, GALO121, A3, folder 1 of 1. She mentions seeing Paul, David Jones, Dennis Geraghty, Alan White, and Herbert McCabe.

27. Father Peter Hunter described this as a painful disagreement to me in an interview on March 13, 2019, and Sally describes it in her March 19, 1997, letter,

GALO121, A8, folder 3 of 3, 59–83. Remember that colons and italics signal that they are not direct quotations.

28. Hunter, interview, March 13, 2019.

29. Lahood, *Intersexion*.

30. "Malcolm saw me as a member of a slightly disparaged minority in the order—heterosexual. He belonged to the same minority. He thought that maybe I was going to say to him that I got a young lady pregnant. I showed him the letter from Timothy. He was totally taken by surprise. It was fairly clear that various apocalyptic scenarios were going through his mind." Lahood, *Intersexion*.

31. Gross, "Incomplete correspondence/document," February 11, 1996, and footnote "March 1997."

32. Gross, "Incomplete correspondence/document," February 11, 1996; and footnote "March 1997."

33. Gross, "letter to [Father] Timothy [Radcliffe] outlining the events and correspondence around her dismissal from the order," August 12, 1994, GALO121, A3.

34. Lahood, *Intersexion*; and Gross, "Not in God's Image," March 2013, GALO121, C4.

35. Gross, "Incomplete correspondence/document," February 11, 1996; and footnote "March 1997."

36. Gross, "letter to [Father] Timothy [Radcliffe]," February 19, 1995, GALO121, A3; and Lahood, *Intersexion*. See also Gross, "Incomplete correspondence/document," February 11, 1996.

37. McMahon, interview, March 5, 2019.

38. Gross, "letter to [Father] Timothy [Radcliffe] dealing with her reaction to the dispensation, Timothy's letter, hostile process of dismissal and recent developments," October 13, 1994, GALO121, A3. She described Malcolm's terms in "Not in God's Image."

39. Coan, three-part series; Gross, email to Petra Bader of *The Sunday Times*, July 14, 2009, on Sally's computer hard drive, to which Ray Schmidt-Gross gave me access. A similar claim can be found in Gross, "letter to Joanna Low," March 29, 1997, GALO121, A8.

40. Gross, letter addressed to "friends," July 15, 2007, 121, A3.1.1.19, bold in original.

41. Gross, letter to "friends," July 15, 2007.

42. Gross, "Not in God's Image."

43. Gross, letter to "friends," July 15, 2007.

44. Gross, letter to "friends," July 15, 2007.

45. Father Richard Conrad, "email from Richard in reply to Sally Gross's group email with subject heading 'News from the wilderness,'" July 16, 2007, GALO121, A7. Sally kept a few photographs of Richard on her computer, Dominicans, GALO121, F4.

46. Gross, letter to "friends," July 15, 2007.

4. MEDICAL BODIES

1. Lahood, *Intersexion*.

2. Lahood, *Intersexion*.

3. Lahood, *Intersexion*.

4. Lahood, *Intersexion*.

5. Gross, "letter to [Father] Timothy [Radcliffe] discussing Judaism, her struggles with her identity and details on the advice and counselling she was seeking," February 29, 1993, GALO121, A3.

6. Gross, "e-mail B," ca. 1997, GALO121, A8.

7. Gross, "letter to [Father] Timothy [Radcliffe] thanking him for his letter and giving him an update of conversations she had had with various counsellors and clergy," April 26, 1993, GALO121, A3.

8. Lahood, *Intersexion*.

9. Gross, "letter to [Father] Timothy [Radcliffe]," February 29, 1993.

10. Gross, "Not in God's Image," GALO121, C4.

11. Gross describes her misdiagnosis similarly in her letter to "Ronnie."

12. Lahood, *Intersexion*.

13. Gross, "Not in God's Image," GALO121, C4.

14. Fran Springfield confirmed this account; interview, February 19, 2019. Norma is deceased, but Fran shared some photographs of herself with Norma. See Gross, "letter to [Father] Timothy [Radcliffe]" February 29, 1993.

15. In addition, Gross mentions, "In February of last year I saw Fran Springfield for the first time, and I wrote to you about that. One of the things which she urged upon me then was a chromosomal scan," in "letter to [Father] Timothy [Radcliffe] outlining her biological status and letting him know that she would not be returning to life at the priory as a man," April 17, 1994, GALO121, A3.

16. Fran Springfield confirmed Sally Gross's account of this time; interview, February 19, 2019.

17. Gross, "letter to [Father] Timothy [Radcliffe]," February 29, 1993.

18. Gross, "letter to [Father] Timothy [Radcliffe]," February 29, 1993, bold in original.

19. Gross, "letter to [Father] Timothy [Radcliffe]," February 29, 1993.

20. Gross, "letter to [Father] Timothy [Radcliffe]," February 29, 1993.

21. Gross, "letter to [Father] Timothy [Radcliffe]," February 29, 1993.

22. Gross, "letter to [Father] Timothy [Radcliffe]," February 29, 1993.

23. Gross, "letter to [Father] Timothy [Radcliffe]," February 29, 1993.

24. Gross, "letter to [Father] Timothy [Radcliffe]," February 29, 1993.

25. Gross, "letter to [Father] Timothy [Radcliffe]," February 29, 1993.

26. Gross, "letter to [Father] Timothy [Radcliffe]," February 29, 1993, bold in original.

27. Gross, "Not in God's Image," GALO121, C4.

28. Gross, "letter to [Father] Timothy [Radcliffe]," February 29, 1993.

29. "I frequently find, particularly when undressing just before going to bed after a long and active day, that I have lactated slightly . . . It suggests that my body produces progesterone anomalously." Gross, "Appendix F: Document produced at the request of my order describing the regime of treatment and physiological anomalies," April 17, 1994, GALO121, A8.

30. Gross, "letter to [Father] Timothy [Radcliffe]," February 29, 1993.

31. Gross, "Not in God's Image."

32. Gossett et al., *Trap Door*.

33. "I spoke to Kathy Wilkes (one of my supervisors) and to Janet Soskice to get some sense of the impact of this turmoil on my thesis and how I should handle it. Kathy unilaterally suggested that I consider taking a couple of years out, albeit after completion of my thesis, perhaps using my skills by working as a volunteer for something like the UNHCR in Africa, and that I use the time to try to work through some of the issues. Janet felt that it was well worth taking a few months out—'three months are nothing in the life of a thesis'—if it would help me to work this out." Gross, "letter to [Father] Timothy [Radcliffe]," February 29, 1993. Janet Soskice did not respond to my invitation to be interviewed.

34. Gross, "letter to [Father] Timothy [Radcliffe]," February 29, 1993.

35. Psalm 23, New American Standard Bible.

36. Gross mentions this in the closing to her February 29, 1993, letter to Father Timothy Radcliffe.

37. Fran Springfield explained that she connected Gross with John and Allison, though she could not recall their surname. Springfield, interview, February 19, 2019. She gave me an approximate address and parish for where I might find Gross's former landlords to invite them to be interviewed. The address was a few blocks off and the church was closed. Since traveling to Eastbourne in search of the couple, I have emailed the church requesting that they share my invitation with John and Allison. After not hearing back for a few months I returned to Gross's letterhead to find their exact address and mailed them a letter of invitation.

38. Lahood, *Intersexion*; also mentioned in Coan, three-part series; Gabrielle Le Roux also mentioned Gross's ambivalence about taking on female presentation. Le Roux, interview, September 4, 2018.

39. Gross, "Incomplete correspondence/document," February 11, 1996; and footnote "March 1997." Gross also uses the simile of being like a fish thrown into water, GALO121, A8.

40. Gross, email addressed to "Dear friends," Subject: "From the Finsbury Park Station," August 24, 2003, GALO121, F4.

41. For the details of this story see John Colapinto's *As Nature Made Him: The Boy Who Was Raised as a Girl* (New York: Harper Perennial, 2006). For an excellent account of Money's impact on intersex persons see Rubin, *Intersex Matters*. Gross mentions the negative impact of John Money's work in Lahood, *Intersexion*.

42. Rubin, *Intersex Matters*, 31. Rubin explains that Money was not a hardline constructionist as detractors suggest: "In an effort to deepen and extend these analyses, I argue not only that intersexuality played a crucial role in the invention of gender as a category in mid-twentieth century biomedical and, subsequently, feminist discourses; and that Money used the concept of gender to cover over and displace the biological instability of the body he discovered through his research on intersex; but also that Money's conception of gender produced new technologies of psychosomatic normalization." *Intersex Matters*, 25.

43. Malatino, *Queer Embodiment*, 163.

44. Feder, *Making Sense*, 38.
45. I saw this award on display in her home when I interviewed Fran, February 19, 2019.
46. Springfield, interview, February 19, 2019.
47. Springfield, interview, February 19, 2019.
48. Reid also reports not having extant medical records on Sally Gross.
49. McMahon, interview, March 5, 2019.
50. McMahon, interview, March 5, 2019.
51. McMahon, interview, March 5, 2019.
52. Radcliffe, "letter from Timothy telling her about a questionnaire that she would be taking. Attached is a copy of the instructions from John Mills to the other superiors in the clergy as to how to deal with the press," March 17, 1994, GAL0121, A8.
53. Gross, "Incomplete correspondence/document," February 11, 1996; and footnote "March 1997."
54. This document is titled "Appendix F: Document produced at the request of my order." Gross writes, "What follows is an edited version of my response to a request, made in the course of my formal interrogation on 24 March 1994 by the person designated by the English Province of my former Order as Instructor in my case, that I write down in a letter the clinical details I had communicated in the course of the formal interrogation."
55. Gross, "Appendix F: Document produced at the request of my order."
56. Gross, "letter to John [Orme]," March 7, 1997, GAL0121, A8, folder 2 of 3.
57. Gross, "Incomplete correspondence/document," February 11, 1996; and footnote "March 1997."
58. "I contacted David van Ooijen, as you suggested, and made contact with the Prior at Huissen in order to arrange an exploratory visit. My main purpose in sending this message is to tell you about the trip to Huissen, which I believe to have been very helpful indeed." Gross, "letter to [Father] Timothy [Radcliffe] discussing the dispensation, her willingness but inability to return to the order and other options open to her," April 24, 1994, GAL0121, A3. A photograph of David van Ooijen is saved in Gross's computer, Dominicans, GAL0121, F4.
59. Gross, "letter to [Father] Timothy [Radcliffe] dealing with her reaction to the dispensation, Timothy's letter, hostile process of dismissal and recent developments," October 13, 1994, GAL0121, A8.
60. McMahon, interview, March 5, 2019; and their shared correspondence.
61. Dreger, "Intersex and Human Rights," 78.
62. For example, see Greenberg, *Intersexuality*.
63. Lahood, *Intersexion*. Sally discusses her activism to undermine "the John Money paradigm" in South Africa in Lahood, *Intersexion*. She references her participation in *The 3rd Sex* documentary (van Huyssteen, *3rd Sex*), in which she and medical professionals were interviewed on the question of surgery on intersex infants and children. Gross also briefly mentions her conversations with mothers from the Eastern Cape who pursue the surgery due to fear that intersexuality puts their child at risk.

64. See also Tamar-Mattis, "Exceptions." "Gross advocates no imposed surgical intervention at all unless clearly required for preservation of life or physical health." Coan, three-part series.

65. Email correspondence between Gross and Diamond in 1997, along with Diamond's publications, are in GALO121, C1.1, Trans and Intersex papers: Milton Diamond articles and emails. The GALA archives hold emails that contain some private information, not discussed here.

66. Gross, January 22, 2008, in her computer hard drive, to which Ray Schmidt-Gross gave me access. In the GALA archive there is also a handwritten note dated May 19, 1997, with Milton Diamond's article, "Self-Testing: A Check on Sexual Identity and Other Levels of Sexuality," signed "Mickey," which is how his emails were also signed, GALO121, C1.1, Trans and Intersex papers: Milton Diamond articles and emails.

67. See Wolff et al., "Creating Intersex Justice."

68. Kessler, "Medical Construction," 25. This was forwarded in an email to Sally, May 13, 1997, GALO121, C1.1, Trans and Intersex papers: Milton Diamond articles and emails.

69. Greenberg, *Intersexuality*, 28.

70. Wolff, "Intimate Life Together."

71. Gross is careful to distinguish between unnecessary cosmetic surgery and life-saving procedures, such as when an infant is unable to urinate. Turner syndrome, for example, can be diagnosed prenatally.

72. This "functions in this tale as a barbed articulation of Roman dominance, a medical intervention that presses imperial power onto Jewish flesh . . . [but] Vaspasian denies Rabbi Tsadok sovereignty over his own body, claiming for Rome the power to rehabilitate Jewish flesh." Belser, *Rabbinic Tales*, 92.

73. Belser, *Rabbinic Tales*, 95.

74. Fausto-Sterling, *Sexing the Body*, 72.

75. Feder discusses the medical distinction between female genital mutilation and surgery in *Making Sense*, 126–28. See also Rubin, "Provincializing Intersex," 238.

76. Greenberg, *Intersexuality*, 99.

77. Rubin, *Intersex Matters*, 108–9.

78. George Annas, "Siamese Twins," 28.

79. Feder, *Making Sense*, 67.

80. Feder, *Making Sense*, 75.

81. Feder, *Making Sense*, 112–13.

82. Feder, *Making Sense*, 117.

83. Feder, *Making Sense*, 117.

84. Reis, "Did Bioethics Matter?," 659.

85. Reis, "Did Bioethics Matter?," 670.

86. Horowicz, "Intersex Children."

87. Limor Meoded Danon reports, "The World Health Organization (WHO) found that irreversible medical procedures, especially genital surgeries, are frequently performed on intersex infants for reasons other than ensuring healthy physical functioning, and determined that they are unjustified," and yet, "despite the

encouraging changes in some countries, in Israel intersex activism has remained limited." "Intersex Activists," 570.

88. Gross, "De-Gendering Unions," 270. Drafts of this work are on Gross's computer hard drive, to which Ray Schmidt-Gross granted me access, and in GALO121 C1.4, C1.4.1, C1.4.2, and C1.4.3.

89. Feder, *Making Sense*, 72–73.

5. BODIES OF PAPERWORK

Epigraph 1: Crosby, *Body, Undone*, 6–7.
Epigraph 2. Salamon, *Life and Death of Latisha King*, 165.

1. Gross's complaint, namely the document titled "Appendix A: How the Story Was Obtained," GALO121, A8, folder 2 of 3.

2. John Mills, "letter from Timothy telling her about a questionnaire that she would be taking. Attached is a copy of the instruction from John Mills to the other superiors in the clergy as to how to deal with the press," March 17, 1994, GALO121, A3. Although the GALA archives list this letter as being from Father Timothy Radcliffe, the signature is illegible and there is no typed name. The letterhead lists St. Dominic's Priory on South Hampton Road in London, whereas his other letters are printed as from Ordo Fratrum Praedicatorum Curia Generalitia, Convento S. Sabina (Aventino) Piazza P. D'Illiria, 1–00153 Roma. I believe the letter was in fact written by John Mills, who was charged with handling the public relations concerning Gross, or a different brother altogether. In addition, it is addressed "Dear S.," whereas Father Radcliffe typically, though not always, addressed his letters "Dear Sally."

3. There were many folders documenting his legacy in the Douai Abbey. Although the letter enclosed with this document states, "Attached is the copy you asked for of the confidential briefing circulated to superiors to help them cope with follow-up enquiries from local press. As you see, our object is to try to protect you as well as to try to protect the Order," it is difficult to read it as prioritizing Gross. September 2, 1996, GALO121, A8. The enclosed documents detail which newspapers and journalists contacted the order and what was reported to them. One *Time* article is quoted, "The one other Catholic priest known to have had a sex change lived in Italy," an assertion mentioned in a handful of interviews I conducted. September 2, 1996, GALO121, A8. As noted above, this was with "letter from Timothy telling her about a questionnaire that she would be taking," March 17, 1994; however, I wonder if this is misattributed.

4. Mills, "Selwyn/Sally Gross: Press Enquiries," August 2, 1996, GALO121, A8; Mills, "Selwyn/Sally Gross: Press Enquiries," August 17, 1996, GALO121, A8.

5. Enclosed with "letter from [Father] Timothy [Radcliffe] telling her about a questionnaire that she would be taking," document dated March 2, 1994, GALO121, A3. As previously noted, I am not convinced that the letter is in fact from Timothy.

6. Qualtrough, "Priest."

7. Gross, "Letter to [Father] Timothy [Radcliffe] telling him about the tabloids tricking her into giving them information which they published, and how she warned the church of possibly [sic] repercussions," August 19, 1996, GALO121, A3, 4 pages single-spaced.

8. Newspaper clippings, correspondence regarding the complaint that Sally laid against *The People* newspaper for publishing Qualtrough's article, "Priest in Sex Swap," and letters from Father John Mills on how the order should manage the situation are located in GALO121, A8, 3 folders. The account presented in this manuscript draws primarily from the contents of Gross's complaint, namely the document titled "The Geography of the Encounter with Mr Qualtrough," GALO121, A8, folder 2 of 3. Father Mills wrote a letter to Gross dated September 2, 1996, which included his documentation of various presses and journalists who made inquiries with the order, GALO121, A8. He notes on the Qualtrough article, "Sally agrees that, although 80% of it is inaccurate, it is not a dreadful piece. But she will complain to the Press Council about the harassment by Qualtrough." Mills also documents inaccuracies in other articles. He missed at least one article while on holiday and documents his communication with Gross throughout the ordeal, including what he said on her voicemail, GALO121, A8. GALA has the correspondence between Gross and the Press Complaints Commission on letterhead, often stamped "received" with the date and identification number. Documents in these files also include letters from her general practitioner verifying her intersex status, her correspondence with the church throughout the ordeal, and her correspondence with intersex activists globally.

9. Gross, "letter to Susan Roberts," of the Press Complaints Commission, July 12, 1997, GALO121, A8, folder 2 of 3, bold in original. Mike Jempson, executive director of PressWise, echoed her statement in his letter to Susan Roberts, July 16, 1997, GALO121, A8, folder 2 of 3.

10. Gross, "Letter to [Father] Timothy [Radcliffe] continuing with events and her feelings of betrayal and distress after the tabloid incident," September 1, 1996, GALO121, A3.

11. Radcliffe, "Letter from [Father] Timothy [Radcliffe] responding to the letters on the tabloid incident," October 31, 1996, GALO121, A3.

12. "Letters to the Press Complaints Commission from Sally Gross, with 'Breaches of specific clauses of the PCC's Code of Practice' attached," August 30, 1996, GALO121, A8.

13. Mike Jempson, "Letter to Sue Roberts (Complaints Director: Press Complaints Commission)," September 5, 1996, GALO121, A8.

14. Gross dated her initial letter to *The People* August 22, 1996, and complaint to the Press Complaint Commission August 30, 1996; the commission stamped it "received" September 4, 1996.

15. "Letter from Dr K. E. Leeson confirming intersex status of Sally Gross," on letterhead, March 4, 1997, GALO121, A3.

16. "Letter from Fran Springfield of the Gender Identity Consultancy Service," Clinical Nurse Specialist, on Gender Identity Consultancy Services letterhead, May 6, 1997, GALO121, A2.

17. Gross, "letter to John Mills," March 7, 1997, 0121, A8.
18. Low, "letter to Sally from Joanna Low," May 8, 1997, GALO121, A8, folder 2 of 3.
19. Roberts, "letter to Mike Jempson," of PressWise, August 6, 1997, GALO121, A8, folder 2 of 3.
20. Gross, "Letter to Len Gould," August 29, 1997, GALO121, A8, folder 2 of 3.
21. Gross, "letter to Mike Jempson," August 14, 1997, GALO121, A8, folder 2 of 3.
22. According to Sally, her doctor's senior colleague conceded that it might be *acanthosis nigricans*, though she noted their annoyance at her self-diagnosis. Six months passed before a dermatologist disabused Sally of the diagnostic error. Presumably, she attributed the misdiagnosis to her intersexuality, because hormonal disorders are one cause of *acanthosis nigricans*. Gross, "letter to Mike Jempson," August 14, 1997.
23. Gross, "letter to Mike Jempson," August 14, 1997.
24. Gross, "letter to Mrs [Sue] Roberts," August 20, 1997, GALO121, A8, folder 2 of 3.
25. Gross, "letter to Mrs [Sue] Roberts," August 20, 1997.
26. Gross, "Not in God's Image."
27. Len Gould, "letter to Joanna Low," March 14, 1997, GALO121, A3.
28. Mike Jempson, "letter to Sue [Roberts]," of the Press Complaints Commission, April 19, 1997, GALO121, A3.
29. "The Miami meeting failed to produce any clear consensus and only seemed to create confusion about what is now considered fair or allowable so far as sports gender divisions go" Dreger, "Sex Typing," 22. "By now it should be clear why, thanks to scientific advances, it is only getting harder to divide males from females for purposes of leveling the gendered playing field." Dreger, "Sex Typing," 23. Dreger points out the un-evenhandedness of anxiety of sex classification in sports: "The public doesn't seem to be paying any attention to medically sanctioned testosterone pumping going on among 'real' men, however; fans and officials appear much more worried about the women's playing field being invaded by pretenders." Dreger, "Sex Typing," 24.
30. Dreger, *Hermaphrodites*, 12–13.
31. Foucault, *Birth of the Clinic*, 135, 165.
32. Foucault, *Birth of the Clinic*, 136.
33. Foucault, *Birth of the Clinic*, 110–15.
34. Foucault, *Birth of the Clinic*, 95.
35. Foucault, *Birth of the Clinic*, 114.
36. Holmes, *Intersex*, 43.
37. Holmes, *Intersex*, 146, 155.
38. Rubin, *Intersex Matters*, 53.
39. Rubin, *Intersex Matters*, 58.
40. Holmes, *Intersex*, 43.
41. Foucault, introduction, viii–ix.
42. Scholars such as Antonio Viego have argued that despite Foucault's critique of psychoanalysis, his theory is compatible with uses of select psychoanalytic scholarship.

43. Foucault, introduction, xiii, xiv.

44. Foucault, introduction, xiv.

45. Rubin, *Intersex Matters*, 62.

46. Although writing from different social locations and countries of origin, Sally and theorist Hortense Spillers each offer a "grammar lesson" to their readers that includes proper names, gender assignment, dehumanization, violence, and the sacred. By virtue of her Blackness for Spillers and her intersexuality for Sally, both escape the capture of the concept of woman. See Spillers's essay "Mama's Baby, Papa's Maybe: An American Grammar Book," in *Black*.

47. Davis, *Contesting Intersex*.

48. Malatino, *Queer Embodiment*, 10.

49. Coan, three-part series. Her documents include paperwork on letterhead from the Republic of South Africa Department of Home Affairs stating that she did not cease to be a South African citizen when she obtained British citizenship, stamped and signed by the director general. The date is difficult to decipher but appears to be October 31, 1991, GALO121, A2.

50. Gross was issued an Israeli passport under the name [redacted] Gross, sex female, on September 8, 1994, with appendixes verifying her registered name, sex, and identity number, GALO121, A8. Her United Kingdom of Great Britain and Northern Ireland passport was issued prior, on October 11, 1993, under the name Sally Gross and sex female, GALO121, A8.

51. Greenberg, *Intersexuality*, 66. In the US context, "a person's legal sex could change as a state line is crossed. In addition, a person's legal sex can vary within a state depending on whether the state is determining the ability to marry, use public restrooms, or carry a driver's license or other official document with a name and sex indicator that match the person's identity." Greenberg, *Intersexuality*, 49.

52. Greenberg, *Intersexuality*, 51.

53. "It was suggested to me informally that it would probably be possible to get around this were I to submit to genital 'disambiguation' surgery—vagioplasty or phalloplasty, it didn't really matter which one—and I made it clear that I would not submit to any such surgery whatever the consequences." Gross, email addressed to "Dear friends," Subject: "From the Finsbury Park Station," Sunday, August 24, 2003, GALO121, F4. The GALA archives include her paperwork for a legal name change, stamped and notarized, July 30, 1993, GALO121, A2. According to legal scholar Julie Greenberg, the requirement that one undergo sex reassignment surgery in exchange for legal documentation reflecting a new name and sex was not uncommon (*Intersexuality*, 69).

54. Gross describes this in Coan, three-part series, and in "Chronicle of an Intersexed Activist's Journey," GALO121, C1.2, Academic papers: Sally Gross essays; also, Gross, letter addressed to "Ronnie," GALO121, F4.

55. Accessed with her brother Ray Schmidt-Gross's permission.

56. Coan, three-part series.

57. "Testimonial from Mani B. Mitchell Executive Director of Intersex Trust Aotearoa New Zealand," December 21, 1997, GALO121, A2; Professors Sebastian and

Helen Brock, on University of Oxford letterhead, January 25, 1998, GALO121, A2. The GALA archives include a receipt for her emergency travel documents, stamped British Consulate, July 22, 2011, signed Angela Hodgson, British Vice Counsel; and an appointment card and prescription written by Dr. Hilton Kaplan, November and December 2012. One notes that Sally could fly, others note her medical status and fifteen medications she was to take while traveling overseas.

58. Greenberg, *Intersexuality*, 109.
59. Coan, three-part series.
60. Coan, three-part series.
61. Gross, letter to Frene Ginwala, February 11, 1998, GALO121, A5.
62. Letter from Oxford University, addressed to "Ms Gross," May 28, 2008, GALO121, A2.
63. Coan, three-part series. Coan reports that Gross was reissued a birth certificate with the name Sally. This is not included in the GALA archives; however, Gross's various passports are in GALO121, A2, Personal documents: declaration of change of name.
64. Gross, "Chronicle"; and Coan, three-part series.

6. BODIES OF LAND

Epigraph: Anzaldúa, *Borderlands*, 25.
1. Belser, *Rabbinic Tales*, xxxiii.
2. Belser, *Rabbinic Tales*, xxii.
3. Belser, *Rabbinic Tales*, xxx.
4. See Schotten's argument in *Queer Terror*.
5. Povinelli, *Geontologies*.
6. Rothstein, *Color of Law*.
7. See Estes, *Our History*.
8. See Burich, *Thomas Indian School*; Henderson and Wakeham, *Reconciling Canada*; Weglin, *Years of Infamy*; Hayashi, *Democratizing the Enemy*; Westermann, *Drunk*; Boum, *Memories*; Hatcher, *Poverty Industry*; Losen and Kim, *School-to-Prison Pipeline*.
9. "To understand the storying of any place, I must also understand the storying of myself. I must follow traces beneath familiar surfaces to where ancestral structures lie." Savoy, *Trace*, 68.
10. Gross, sermon transcript, "John the Baptist," second Sunday of Advent, 6:30 mass, December 4, 1988 (Luke 3:1–6), Sermons, GALO121, F4.
11. See "Pass Laws in South Africa 1800–1994," South African History Online, https://www.sahistory.org.za/article/pass-laws-south-africa-1800-1994, accessed August 3, 2021.
12. Gross, sermon transcript, Second Sunday of Advent.
13. Gross, sermon transcript, Second Sunday of Advent.
14. Ray Schmidt-Gross, interview, June 23, 2019.
15. Nofal, "Apla."

16. See Nicky Falkof, *Warrior State*, and Scott Burnett, *White Belongings*.

17. "PAC: Give Land to the Poor or They'll Grab It," *Natal Witness*, April 6, 1998.

18. "Plan Cuts Number of Farm Attacks," *Pretoria News*, February 11, 1998; Ryan Cresswell, "Dramatic Drop in Attacks on Farms," *Star*, February 11, 1998.

19. Rian Malan, "Reasons for Alarmist Fantasies," May 29, 1998. GALO121 B3 "Includes material relating to Sally Gross work as a researcher on the Rural Peace and Safety Project, associate with the Institute for Healing Memories." (2 folders).

20. www.saps.co.za/8_crimeinfo/398/attacks_on_farms.htm. This quote is in the "Conclusion" of "Attacks on Farms and Smallholdings," http://www.saps.co.za/8_crimeinfo/398/attacks_on_farms.htm 11/03/99 and http://www.saps.co.za/8_crimeinfo/farm/annexf.htm 11/03/99. The first link is titled "Attacks on Farms and Smallholdings" and the title is "Report by the Crime Information Cenre No 2 of 1998." This report is cited as "Attacks on Farms and Smallholdings: Report by the Crime Information Analysis Centre, No.1 of 1999, » email dated August 15, 2000, from SAPS to Human Rights Watch, and JC Strauss, "Attacks on Farms and Smallholdings No.2 of 1998" (Crime Information Analysis Centre, 1998) and "J C Strauss, Attacks on Farms and Smallholdings, No.1 of 1999" (CIAC, 1999), both available at www.saps.org.za; Martin Schönteich and Jonny Steinberg, "Attacks on Farms and Smallholdings: an evaluation of the rural protection plan» (Pretoria, Institute of Security Studies, 2000); and Duxita Mistry and Jabu Dhlamini (March 2001), a study commissioned by SAPS and based on in-depth interviews in prison with forty-eight individuals in five provinces convicted of crimes ranging from robbery to murder against farm owners.; https://muse.jhu.edu/article/37897/pdf and in other publications (Sally Gross accessed and printed March 11, 1999).

21. Staff correspondent, "Farm Killings Deal Blow to Emerging Farmers," *Independent Newspapers*, 1997. Numerous documents informed her investigation into farm attacks. Her handwritten notes on these can be found in GALO121, B3, Work related documents: department of land affairs; B4, Work related documents: farm killing press clippings; B5, Work related documents: rural safety, folders 1–3. The articles are written in both English and Afrikaans.

22. Sally Gross, Progress Report: Rural Peace and Safety Progress Report, October 10, 1998, GALO121, B3; and Summit for Rural Safety and Security Report, November 18, 1998, GALO121, B5, Work related documents: rural safety, folder 3 of 3.

23. One of Gross's favorite orange-and-green kaftans is located in GALO121, G2, Memorabilia: personal belongings. This is an anecdote that nearly everyone from the commission who I interviewed recalled humorously. Benjamin Mars described his difficulty in reconciling the voice that he first heard on the phone with the woman standing before him. Mars, interview. On January 24, 2020, Daniel Malan Jacobs forwarded to me an email of Sally's that she sent on October 7, 2010, subject: "Telephone Etiquette," in which she provides stern instruction for how to answer the phone. He also shared emails on lighter topics, such as the World Cup or jokes that Sally sent.

24. Williams, interview; Eugene van Rooyen, interview.

25. Gross's cane can be found in GALO121, G2, Memorabilia: personal belongings.

26. Worsnip, interview.

27. Based on interviews with Williams, Eugene van Rooyen, Worsnip, Smit, Mars, and Jacobs. Among those I interviewed were managers over Sally and also persons managed by Sally.

28. Smit, interview.

29. Smit, interview.

30. Imhoff, *Jessie Sampter*, 28.

31. Worsnip heard many of these stories secondhand and attempted to connect me with more firsthand witnesses. However, they did not agree to be interviewed. Worsnip, interview.

32. Mars retold a similar story; interview.

33. Smit, interview.

34. Smit, interview; Mars, interview.

35. Mars also mentioned a restructuring of the whole commission; interview.

36. Colleague Beverly Jansen emailed Daniel Malan Jacobs and others on October 1, 2009. Shared with me by Jacobs on January 24, 2020.

37. As described by Smit, interview. Mars and Jacobs remember Sally's relationship with her father differently—that they were close. They both also discussed Sally's pride in her Jewish Eastern European heritage; Mars, interview; Jacobs, interview.

38. Jacobs, interview.

39. Reports are included in the GALA archives. A certificate of appreciation was awarded to Gross on December 10, 2003, "For excellent services rendered and commitment to the landless people of the Western Cape," signed by the Regional Land Claims Commissioner, GALO121, B3, Work related documents: department of land affairs.

40. The district had been established in 1867, after the freeing of enslaved people in 1833, and developed into a cosmopolitan area after World War II.

41. See GAL121, B3, Work related documents: department of land affairs.

42. Gross, letter addressed to "Ronnie."

43. Gross, "friends," July 15, 2007, GALO121, A3.1.1.19, email to Timothy Radcliffe regarding "News from the Wilderness," July 15, 2007.

44. Jacobs, interview.

45. There are a number of photographs of Jennifer Williams in Sally Gross's files. One in particular is in the file folder "friends," GALO121, F4. Gross discusses their relationship in her letter addressed to "Ronnie."

46. The program includes a section for the year of dispossession, the most recent annual average Consumer Price Index (CPI) for the current date, the CPI to base 1995 for the year of dispossession, a formula (109.7/2.2) X R1750, the most recent annual average CPI converted to base 1995, historical undercompensation at the time of dispossession in rands, and undercompensation escalated using the most recent annual average CPI to base 1995.

47. Based on Williams, interview; and Eugene van Rooyen, interview.

48. Worsnip, interview.

49. Gross, letter addressed to "Ronnie."

50. Smit, interview; and Mars, interview.

51. Mars, interview. According to David Smit, Buthelezi also left the commission on bad terms.

52. Smit, interview.

53. "There is nothing I can do for special treatment from SAA (South African Airways). You need a form." Smit, interview. Jacobs expressed his own discomfort with Smit's management style; interview.

54. In 2011 Daniel Malan Jacobs would reach out to Sally for advice about how to get permission from the director general, the most senior official in his department, to do remunerative work outside of office hours in order to pay for medical expenses of a family member. Sally helped Jacobs strategize and polish his request, which was successful. Emails forwarded to me from Jacobs on January 24, 2020. I ran this chapter past Jacobs in March 2020 for approval of how I depicted him and made changes according to his requests.

55. Jacobs, interview. Gross discusses the mounting stress and strain in her letter addressed to "Ronnie."

56. Description of the situation and quotation from Mars, interview.

57. Smit, interview.

58. Mars, interview. Mars recalls Sally lamenting much of her extended family rejecting her in a female role, which her brother Ray Schmidt-Gross has also discussed.

59. Jacobs, interview.

60. Mars, interview.

61. Smit, interview.

62. Mars, interview.

63. For more on ableism and fatphobia see Kafer, *Feminist*; and Strings, *Black Body*.

64. Gross, email to Daniel Jacobs, August 3, 2013, forwarded to me by Jacobs on January 24, 2020.

65. Jacobs, interview. I ran this section past Jacobs and made adjustments out of respect for his privacy and to ensure accuracy.

66. Jacobs, interview.

67. Jacobs was among participants who noted Sally's declining health at the Land Claims Commission, especially in her final years there. Jacobs, interview.

PART III. AGITATING BODIES
Epigraph 1: Ahmed, *Complaint!*, 225.
Epigraph 2: Muñoz, *Cruising Utopia*, 146.
1. van der Kolk, *Body Keeps the Score*.

7. TRANSNATIONAL ACTIVISM
1. Gross, letter addressed to "Ronnie."
2. Gross, "Chronicle." S. speculated that the woman might have been Daniella Weiss, who became a leader in the right-wing ultranationalist Gush Emunim and the Nachala settlement movements. Gross, letter addressed to "Ronnie."

3. Lahood, *Intersexion*.

4. Gross, "Summary of commitments, skills and experience accumulated," GALO121, B3, Work related documents.

5. "Back in South Africa, I studied at the University of Cape Town from 1974, completing majors in English and Comparative African Government and Law." Gross, "Chronicle," 2011. The commission had played a significant role in the renewal of democratic trade unionism. At the time, Gordon Young was forming a group based on the model of the African Resistance Movement (ARM). From S.'s perspective, Young wanted to root their activism in thorough analysis prior to taking sabotage action—an impracticality that ultimately drove her away. Instead, she joined others to work with the ANC.

6. Gross, "letter to [Father] Timothy [Radcliffe]," February 29, 1993.

7. For more on how South Africans developed a unique political philosophy and the link between existential inwardness and the Black quest for liberation through Christianity, see Magaziner, *Law*.

8. Gross writes in her application to the commission on gender equality, "Since adolescence, I have been actively committed to the struggle against apartheid and for a non-racial, non-sexist and democratic South Africa. In 1970, while still in High School, I formed my first clandestine group inspired by reading an illegal copy of Albert Luthuli, *Let My People Go*, and by the Freedom Charter." GALO121, B3, Work related documents. "In school itself I experienced something of a milestone—I founded my first clandestine political group at school." Lahood, *Intersexion*.

9. Gross, letter addressed to "Ronnie."

10. Gross, letter addressed to "Ronnie."

11. Gross, letter addressed to "Ronnie."

12. Gross, sermon transcript, "1989-07-16, Love—the Good Samaritan," fifteenth Sunday of the Year, 9:30 mass, Blackfriars, July 16, 1989 (Luke 10:25–37), Sermons, GALO121, F4. These events are also discussed in Coan, three-part series.

13. Lahood, *Intersexion*.

14. Gross, letter addressed to "Ronnie."

15. Gross, letter addressed to "Ronnie."

16. Lahood, *Intersexion*.

17. Lahood, *Intersexion*.

18. See Nhlanhla Ndebele and Noor Nieftagodien, "The Morogoro Conference, 2014. There is a version online https://www.sahistory.org.za/archive/morogoro-conference-moment-self-reflection-nhlanhla-ndebele-and-noor-nieftagodien.

19. Due to concerns that Western countries would withdraw support for revolution and to anxiety about communism and ties to the USSR, ANC and South Africa Communist Party members settled on the two-stage approach. See "Decisive and Sustained Action to Build a National Democratic Society," including the 2007 preface as adopted by the 53rd National Conference in *Strategy and Tactics of the*

ANC, December 2012. The Colonialism of a Special Type (CST) conference endorsed the ANC, which declared South Africans colonized people who need to sever ties with metropoles. The CPSA (Communist Party of South Africa) was banned in 1950 and then reformed as the South Africa Communist Party (SACP) in 1953. At the 1962 SACP conference, a program called "The South Africa Road to Freedom" developed the theory of Colonialism of a Special Type (CST). Concerning the impracticality that frustrated Gross, see Mosala et al., "National Democratic Revolution."

20. Gross, letter addressed to "Ronnie."

21. During my visit to the Schmidt-Gross home in Boston June 21–24, 2019, Ray Schmidt-Gross allowed me to scan a newspaper article titled "Cape Town Aliya Farewell," *Zionist Record and S. A. Jewish Chronicle*, February 11, 1977, 15. The caption states, "The main hall of the Albow Centre was filled to capacity recently by members of Tnuat Aliyah and the Histadruth Ivrith who had come to bid farewell to a record number of olim pictured above . . . Jack Gross . . . Mildred Gross, Raymond Gross."

22. Lahood, *Intersexion*. See Schofield, "Israel." Chris McGreal reports that there is documentation of an alliance in "Revealed: How Israel Offered to Sell South Africa Nuclear Weapons," *Guardian*, May 24, 2010, https://www.theguardian.com/world/2010/may/23/israel-south-africa-nuclear-weapons.

23. Lahood, *Intersexion*.

24. Gross, letter addressed to "Ronnie."

25. Her father Jack was also assigned to the medical corps.

26. Ray Schmidt-Gross, interview, Boston, June 23, 2019.

27. Lahood, *Intersexion*.

28. Lahood, *Intersexion*.

29. Gross, letter addressed to "Ronnie."

30. "Oxford house members from 1981–1988," photo album, Douai Abbey.

31. Radcliffe, interview.

32. Gross, letter addressed to "Ronnie."

33. Radcliffe, interview.

34. Radcliffe, interview.

35. Mashinini was elected chairperson of the Action Committee, which was later renamed the Soweto Students Representative Council (SSRC), of which he was the first president. A R500 reward was put out for information that led to his arrest. He fled South Africa for Botswana, as S. did, and for a time lived with Diana in the United Kingdom.

36. Tickell, interview.

37. Tickell, interview.

38. Gross, letter addressed to "Ronnie."

39. Abbreviated as AWB, this is a white supremacist, neo-Nazi nationalist political party.

40. Gross, letter addressed to "Ronnie."

41. "Human Rights Violations: TRC transcripts of evidence given by Fr. Michael Lapsley," Institute for Healing of Memories, September 12, 2010, accessed January 2,

2019, https://www.justice.gov.za/trc/hrvtrans/kimber/ct00654.htm, accessed November 13, 2024. Worsnip also wrote a biography *The Story of Father Michael Lapsley: Priest and Partisan, A South African Journey.*

42. "Human Rights Violations."

43. "Michael Worsnip, Member of the ANC for 33 Out of Its 100 Years," *The Witness*, January 11, 2012, (accessed https://witness.co.za/archive/2012/01/11/thirty-three-out-of-one-hundred-20150430, accessed January 2, 2019.

44. "Human Rights Violations."

45. Index on Censorship, https://journals.sagepub.com/doi/pdf/10.1080/03064228608534179, accessed January 2, 2019. For detailed accounts see Jacques Pauw, *Into the Heart of Darkness: Confessions of Apartheid's Assassins* (Johannesburg: Jonathan Ball, 1997).

46. Worsnip, interview.

47. James S. Henry, "Natal's Valley of Death," July 22, 1990, https://www.washingtonpost.com/archive/opinions/1990/07/22/natals-valley-of-death/5404f59c-b236-43c8-91e5-a8286f212ce6/.

48. Mtshali, "Obituary."

49. Worsnip, interview.

50. Worsnip, interview.

51. Among the photographs at GALA are some from this Intersex North America retreat. There is a particularly charming photo of the group—two intersex activists hugging, another sitting, one crouching, one person standing, another lying down on their back, and Sally lying on her side—which she playfully titled "MORE LYN' ABOUT." One of them is Kiira Triea, who boasts having been one of the founders of the intersex rights movement in North America. Among Sally's hard drive materials is also Dreger, "Losing Kiira." Other named individuals, who are well known in intersex communities, include Mani, David, Heiki, Martha Coventry, and Max Beck. Photos show the group in the forest, sharing meals and their stories. There is also a photograph of Mani under Gross's computer file folder "friends," GALO121, F4. Gross refers to Max and Cheryl in her "E-mail A," GALO121, A8, folder 2 of 3. She quotes Max: "Unless we are fortunate enough to grow up in a very enlightened home, we all come away from childhood thinking that there are two (and only two) types of animals on the playground: boys and girls." To this Gross responded with "some reflections on change, categories, and boundaries," GALO121, A8, folder 2 of 3. Their correspondence suggests an ongoing friendship. Gross also discusses this retreat in her "Chronicle." In Lahood, *Intersexion*, Gross explains that she met Mani, David, Max, and Kiira at this retreat. She claims to have never met Cheryl Chase (also known as Bo Laurent) or Heidi in person but that they exchanged emails frequently. These persons she names due to their participation in the film *Hermaphrodites Speak*. According to Gross, learning about Chase and the Intersex Society of North America had the biggest impact on her founding Intersex South Africa.

52. Mitchell's pronouns are they/them, although it appears that at the time of friendship with Sally they used "hir." Mitchell, interview.

53. Gross, "Chronicle."
54. Mitchell, interview, December 28, 2018.
55. Letter of reference from Mani Mitchell, December 21, 1997, GALO121, A24.4.
56. Gross, "Chronicle."
57. Coan, three-part series. Jacobs mentioned Sally being against intersex surgery. Jacobs, interview.
58. Gross describes in Lahood, *Intersexion*, having sought Cheryl's advice upon initiating the article and that Cheryl suggested she announce ISSA. She writes about this in "Chronicle."
59. Gross, "Chronicle."
60. Gross, "Chronicle."
61. Gross, "Chronicle."
62. According to Gross, she initially collaborated with a well-known lesbian activist (who did not respond to an invitation to be interviewed for this book, so I have redacted her name to protect her privacy) who was nervous to continue due to the level of stigmatization of intersexuality. Lahood, *Intersexion*.
63. Lahood, *Intersexion*.
64. Gross, "Harassment and Responses: A Rough Chronology," GALO121, B2, Work related documents: harassment.

8. COMMUNITY BUILDING IN SOUTH AFRICA

1. "Therefore, in the short run it might be more realistic for intersex advocates to persuade legal institutions to apply existing disability and sex discrimination statues to their claims." Greenberg, *Intersexuality*, 129.
2. "Scholars studying social justice movements suggest that progressive movements abandon traditional single-issue identity politics and move toward an antisubordination framework that focuses on structural systems of inequality"; "Enhancing the quality of life for people with an intersex condition requires a multipronged attack." Greenberg, *Intersexuality*, 130, 135.
3. I include information about how Sally met people in one country and reunited in another to indicate that many persons with leftist politics defied nationalist ties and found community among like-minded persons.
4. The Gender Dynamix website includes more information about the organization's history, mission, and work. Gender Dynamix, accessed September 11, 2018, https://www.genderdynamix.org.za/.
5. Liesl Theron emailed a photo of Sally doing this, which I also found on Sally's computer files, GALO121, F4.
6. Theron, interview.
7. Gross's summary of her paper, "Intersex and the Law in Post-Apartheid South Africa," GALO121, C1.2, Academic papers: Sally Gross essays.
8. Gross, "Chronicle."
9. Rubin, *Intersex Matters*, 138.
10. Lahood, *Intersexion*.

11. Kasrils, "Israel-Palestine Conflict."

12. Jon Jeter, "South African Jews Polarized Over Israel," *Washington Post*, December 19, 2001, https://www.washingtonpost.com/archive/politics/2001/12/19/south-african-jews-polarized-over-israel/4494be3a-6075-4c4b-86ff-73967fedb548/.

13. There are a number of photographs of Bradley in Gross's computer files, one in particular in the file folder "friends," GALO121, F4.

14. For more about Ronnie Kasrils, see his autobiography, *Armed and Dangerous: From Undercover Struggle to Freedom* (Jacana Media, 2013); "Ronnie Kasrils," Jewish Virtual Library, 2007, https://www.jewishvirtuallibrary.org/kasrils-ronnie; and "Ronald (Ronnie) Kasrils," South African History Online, https://www.sahistory.org.za/people/ronald-ronnie-kasrils, accessed December 15, 2021.

15. Details provided in an email addressed to Bradley Bordiss, June 18, 2002.

16. Bordiss, interview. Bradley connected me with a number of participants in these seders who declined to be interviewed. There is photographic documentation of these events. He also shared a friend's email describing this particular event with the "Oi wei Maria [*sic*]" comment.

17. An identification badge for the June 29–July 1, 2004, United National African Meeting in support of the inalienable rights of the Palestine people, forum of civil society in support of Middle East peace, was issued to Sally that features her name and photo, GALO121, G2, Memorabilia: personal belongings.

18. Williams, interview. For example, Sally once incorporated wasabi into the meal and explained its meaning.

19. Zaaiman, interview.

20. "Patricia" asked that I use a pseudonym for her because she respects her child's decision by maintaining her privacy. "Patricia," interview.

21. For Gross's documents on the androgen insensitivity syndrome (AIS) support group see GALO121, C1.3, Academic papers: AIS support group. These include letters, fact sheets, pamphlets, and publications from ALIAS, an AIS newsletter. The ALIAS newsletter covers a number of topics ranging from support groups to the latest medical research. It appears that Gross purchased all of the available publications, which can be found in GALO121, C1.3, Academic papers: AIS support group. Materials also include information about meetings in the United Kingdom and the United States with guest speakers, including gynecologists, physiologists, and endocrinologists. Some members make themselves available to the group to help interpret medical jargon, answer health-care questions, and do informal counseling. According to one document, the AIS support group provides information and support to parents of children with androgen insensitivity syndrome (testicular feminization syndrome) and to AIS adults. It claims to have been established in 1988 and formalized in 1993, and to include eighty families in the United Kingdom and thirty in the United States and Canada since 1995. These numbers increase in later publications as the network expanded. The aims of the group include to reduce stigma, to encourage medical support, to connect AIS families, to make AIS information available in verbal and written form, and to improve medical treatment. GALO121, C1.3, Academic papers: AIS support group. Medical researchers

solicit participants in their studies through ALIAS, including Milton Diamond, which might be how he and Sally became acquainted.

22. Holmes, *Intersex*, 44.

23. Holmes, *Intersex*, 121–22. Holmes mentions the first international intersex retreat in 1996; the second, which Sally Gross attended, in 1997; another the same year in England; and one in Chicago in 1998.

24. Vásquez, *More Than Belief*, 311–12.

25. Davis, *Contesting Intersex*, 132.

26. Davis, *Contesting Intersex*, 143.

27. "Patricia," interview.

28. "Patricia," interview.

29. Feder, *Making Sense*, 52.

30. Cox, interview.

31. See Malatino, *Trans Care*.

32. Cox, interview.

33. Cox, interview.

34. Smith, interview. The racialized politics of rage are important to mention here. See Dalia Rodriguez and Afua Boahene, "The Politics of Rage: Empowering Women of Color in the Academy," *Critical Studies* 12, no. 5 (2012) 450–58; David Rubin, "Anger, Aggression, Attitude: Intersex Rage as Biopolitical Protest," *Signs* 46, no. 4 (Summer 2021) 987–1011; and Gabe Torres, "The Politics of Rage," *Yes Magazine*, April 28, 2022, https://www.yesmagazine.org/opinion/2022/04/28/the-politics-of-rage, accessed December 2, 2024.

35. Smith, interview.

36. Smith, interview.

37. Smith, interview.

38. Theron, interview.

39. Theron, interview.

40. Theron, interview.

41. Theron, interview.

42. Jennifer Williams's email reply to Helen Brock, March 10, 2014, forwarded to me by Helen Brock on February 21, 2019.

43. Ozturk, "Sally Gross Remembered."

44. I am thinking here of what Robin Wall Kimmerer describes in *Braiding Sweetgrass: Indigenous Wisdom, Scientific Knowledge, and the Teachings of Plants*. Canada: Milkweed Editions, 2013), 15.

9. COSTS OF ACTIVISM

Epigraph: Malatino, *Trans Care*, 46.

1. Gross, "Chronicle."

2. "Testimonial concerning the harassment of Ms S. Gross by Lauren Waring," November 1, 2002, GAL0121, B2.

3. Gross, "Harassment and responses: a rough chronology," GALO121, B2, Work related documents: harassment.

4. Gross, "Harassment and responses," and "Testimonial concerning harassment, Lauren Waring, 11/11/02." Gross also mentioned some of these events in an email addressed to "Dear friends," Subject: "From the Finsbury Park Station." A number of Sally's friends emailed this document to me, and it is also found on her computer hard drive that Ray Schmidt-Gross shared with me and in GALO121, F4.

5. Gross, "Open Statement to Whoever has been Harassing me," GALO121 B2, Work related documents: harassment.

6. Gross, "Open Statement to Whoever has been Harassing me," bold in original.

7. Justine van Rooyen, interview.

8. Ewing, interview.

9. In Gross's 2007 email she writes, "My mobility has deteriorated disastrously over the past four years in particular, and I am quite severely disabled in this regard." Gross, 10-page, single-spaced letter addressed to "Dear friends," Subject: "News from the wilderness," July 15, 2007, GALO121, A3.1.1.19, Racliffe.

10. Justine van Rooyen, interview.

11. "Justine van Rooyen (South Africa)," Ireland Fellows Program, January 2014, https://www.irishaidfellowships.ie/case-studies/justine-van-rooyen; Justine van Rooyen, "Kader Asmal Alumni," Embassy of Ireland, https://www.dfa.ie/media/missions/southafrica/newsandevents/Kader-Asmal-Alumni-Booklet-Web-Friendly.pdf.

12. Justine van Rooyen, interview.

13. Gross had an American Go Association Membership Card, AGA #18775, GALO121, G2, Memorabilia: personal belongings.

14. Her Go books were donated to the group, and Lloyd noted that they ranged from beginner to obscure. He has been playing for twenty-two years and there was information new to him. Davies, interview. She kept track of her scores and also games that she observed on her computer. GALO121, F4. Gross also saved articles from the American Go E-Journal and the 2010 American Go Yearbook, GALO121, F4. She had information on Go strategy, lessons, games with commentary, a glossary, interactive tutorials, Go4Go collections from 1940–2010, the 2009 Israel Go Championships, and more. GALO121, F4.

15. Hyjin Kim uses they/them pronouns.

16. Kim, interview.

17. Kim, interview.

18. Kim, interview.

19. Based on Ray and Sharon Schmidt-Gross, interviews, Boston, June 21–24, 2019. Sister-in-law Sharon remembers picking Sally up from the Tel Aviv airport because her plane landed close to the time Mildred's funeral service would begin. She'd never met Sally, and Ray had simply instructed her to look for someone who looks like him with a blond wig. Upon arriving at the service, Sharon was surprised that the Gross family accepted Sally with such ease. They presented her in a natural way, Sharon explained, and because of that everyone accepted her as such. Apparently, Jack enjoyed

boasting of Sally's accomplishments. According to Sharon, Sally was Jack's favorite. When Sharon and Ray married, only one aunt and uncle attended the wedding. Jack claimed to have other plans. On a different occasion, Jack bought gifts for Ray's eldest two daughters, from his first marriage, but not his youngest two daughters with Sharon. Sharon loved Ray, their kids, and Sally. Because Jack and the extended Gross family repeatedly slighted her, she preferred not to engage with them. Even in Jack's geriatric care facility, all the residents greeted Sally with genuine affection. It warmed Sharon's heart to see people in their eighties and nineties embracing Sally as female. Over the course of ten days, Sharon enjoyed chatting with Sally. She loved Sally's deep voice and crisp accent. They held very different political views on the state of Israel but never took offense at one another. Each held their ground.

20. Gross, "friends," Subject: "News from the wilderness."

21. See also Gross, letter addressed to "Ronnie." The letter contains no date or further information, but contextual clues suggest that it was written to an ANC comrade, Ronnie Kasrils, to solicit financial support near the end of 2013 or beginning of 2014 just before she died. This document was emailed to me by Pam Sykes on October 31, 2018 and saved as "Letter for Ronnie Kasrils."

22. Previously, in a letter of application, Sally wrote, "I am disabled: my ability to walk is limited, and am practically blind in one eye. . . . I am effectively night-blind, a genetic predisposition. It is for this reason that I do not have a driver's license." May 16, 2007, GALO121, B4, Work related documents.

23. Gross, "friends," Subject: "News from the wilderness."

24. The 2011–13 budget forms are in her computer files, but one expenditure file is locked and the other won't open. GALO121, F4.

25. These include amendments to the Alteration of Sex Description Bill (2003), Gender Equality Bill (2013), Promotion of Equality and Prevention of Unfair Discrimination Act (2000), National Health Insurance White Paper Documents (2015), Health Act (2003), and Constitution (2006).

26. Gross, letter to "Bernice," January 2014, Survival, GALO121, F4. Gross wrote something similar in 2007: "At present, barring a miracle, [things are moving] probably towards a massive overdose of Paracetamol for lack of anything more gentle, despite my qualms about taking my own life. It will probably result in a very unpleasant twenty-four hour period in the first instance, followed by a day or two of apparent recovery when I will be able to tidy some things up for the Commissioner and my colleagues at work, and then a long and unpleasant slide into death. . . . The prospect of all this does not please me at all—I do not wish to die given a viable alternative, and I certainly do not want to die so unpleasantly. It is something about which I have considerable qualms. Were I to suffer a coronary or a cerebral accident in the comfort of my bed simply in the course of nature, and pass away peacefully, I would count it a privilege and a blessing at this point in time. Finding myself in a position to have a life with a reasonable degree of amenity and dignity assured would be an even greater blessing." Gross, "friends," Subject: "News from the wilderness."

27. After I interviewed Father Martin Flatman, he shared an email from Sally dated November 25 [assumed to be 2013].

28. Sally Gross had a number of photographs of her brother's families on her computer, Family, GAL0121, F4. Sharon Schmidt-Gross showed me her correspondence with Sally from this time of uncertainty during my visit to their home June 21–24, 2019. Sharon was confused as to why Sally was worried about losing contact and tried to reassure her. Sally's nieces were eager to hear stories and look at photographs of Sally when I met them, suggesting that despite the distance, the Schmidt-Gross family cared for Sally and was pleased to preserve her memory.

29. Ray Schmidt-Gross, interview, Boston, June 22, 2019.

30. Sharon Schmidt-Gross, interview, June 23, 2019.

31. Sharon Schmidt-Gross, interview, June 23, 2019.

32. Gross, "letter to [Father] Timothy [Radcliffe] outlining the events and correspondence around her dismissal from the order," August 12, 1994, GAL0121, A3.

33. Her official death certificate lists "natural causes." Provided by Ray Schmidt-Gross.

34. Gross, "Chronicle."

35. Belser, *Rabbinic Tales*, 81.

36. Although the GALA archives include Sally Gross's medical information, I have only included the pieces that she shared broadly with friends, family, and coworkers.

37. Gross, letter addressed to "Ronnie."

38. Father Martin Flatman shared an email from Sally dated November 25, 2013.

39. Father Martin Flatman shared an email from Sally dated November 25, 2013.

40. Sebastian and Helen Brock discussed this during their interview. Helen emailed the executor of Sally's estate inquiring about the £800 after Sally's death; dated March 5, 2014, forwarded to me February 21, 2019.

41. Radcliffe, interview.

42. Gross, letter addressed to "fellow-activists," no date or additional information provided. This letter is similar yet not identical to the one Mani Mitchell posted on the GoFundMe site. It can be surmised that this preceded that.

43. Swarr, interview.

44. Daniel Malan Jacobs forwarded this email to me on January 24, 2020, including his back-and-forth with Gabrielle in which he pledges to send Sally money. In an email dated November 12, 2013, Sally thanks Daniel for his response to the appeal and generosity. She mentions her computer having lost two chapters she had written for publication and all the ISSA data.

45. Jacobs forwarded this email to me on January 24, 2020.

46. Mitchell, "In Memory."

47. Mitchell, interview.

48. "Help Sally Gross," GoFundMe, organized by Mani Mitchell, created November 25, 2012, "A Tribute to Sally Gross," *The Feminist Wire*, February 23, 2014, https://www.gofundme.com/6gc520, accessed December 18, 2018, https://thefeministwire.com/2014/02/tribute-sally-gross/ and "Death of Intersex Activist Sally Gross, South Africa," Trans Intersex History Africa, February 14, 2014, https://transintersexhistory.africa/death-of-sally-gross-south-africa/.

49. https://www.gofundme.com/6gc520.

50. https://www.gofundme.com/6gc520.

51. Mitchell, interview. This was corroborated with an email from Sally Gross to Mani dated January 23, 2014. Unfortunately, a large portion of the funds raised went to banking fees, which is why Mani set up a GoFundMe.

52. https://www.gofundme.com/6gc520.

53. Mani explained that Micro International provides for "rainbow elders" but wasn't able to raise funds in time for Sally. Mitchell, interview. Micro Rainbow, https://microrainbow.org/vision-mission/.

54. Gross, letter addressed to "Ronnie."

55. Gross, "friends," Subject: "News from the wilderness."

56. Gross, "Not in God's Image."

57. Gross, "Not in God's Image."

58. Gross, "Not in God's Image."

59. Gross, "Not in God's Image."

60. Some of these Pam Sykes showed me in her home; others are in GALO121, G2, Memorabilia: personal belongings.

61. Sykes, interview.

62. Ray Schmidt-Gross, interview, Boston, June 23, 2019.

63. Foucault, *Birth of the Clinic*, 19.

64. Foucault, *Birth of the Clinic*, 44.

65. Both Mildred's and Jack's February 20, 1980, wills bequeath the whole of their estates in equal shares to their children, GALO121, A5, Personal documents, Official Documents. Jack's February 18, 2004, will states: "I hereby bequeath my entire estate to my daughter SALLY GROSS . . . and in the sad event of her having predeceased me, I bequeath my entire estate to the SOUTH AFRICAN ZIONIST FEDERATION, [ISRAEL] and BETH PROTEA in equal shares." It includes Jack's Israel ID number, signed by Jack and two witnesses. This I scanned with Ray Schmidt-Gross's permission in his Boston home in June 2019.

66. I was able to verify Ray's claim with Jack's will. His February 18, 2004, will states, "No administrator is appointed."

67. This was also when Sally was too ill to travel.

68. Ray Schmidt-Gross provided his email correspondence with Sally on these matters, June 26, 2019.

69. Williams, interview.

70. Daniel Malan Jacobs forwarded this document to me on January 24, 2020, originally attached to an email dated November 8, 2013, from Gabrielle Le Roux.

PART IV. BODILINESS

Epigraphs: Gomez, "Indigeneity"; Page, "Beyond the Trees," 371–72.

1. Gross, "2nd Sunday in Easter, Cambridge, 26.04.1992," Sermons, GALO121, F4.

2. Plemons, *Look of a Woman*, 128. "That middle way is a body performatively materialized into a definite time and place. It is a historical body enacted, one that

bears the traces of the powerful discursive conditions through which it has acquired meaning but one that exists and must live within those conditions. This body is irreducibly social, irreducibly material." Plemons, *Look of a Woman*, 127.

3. Covington-Ward and Jouili, "Introduction," 11.

10. CLEARINGS

Epigraph 1: Morrison, *Beloved*, 102.

Epigraph 2: Kimmerer, *Braiding Sweetgrass*, 48.

1. "After land is clear-cut, everything changes. Sunshine is suddenly abundant. The soil has been broken open by logging equipment, raising its temperature and exposing mineral soil beneath the humus blanket. The clock of ecological succession has been reset, the alarm buzzing loudly." Kimmerer, *Braiding Sweetgrass*, 283.

2. Joerstad, *Hebrew Bible*, 3.

3. Joerstad, *Hebrew Bible*, 110.

4. To be clear, Joerstad criticizes Western assumptions that Indigenous cultures worship nature as God. She demonstrates that gloss as inaccurate. Joerstad writes, "If the Torah is read as an exploration of how we play our human role fully, and well, within a larger community of persons, it can help us reflect on how we relate to the rest of the world, as urgent a question as any. Torah does not solve or answer it for us, but it invites us into the conversation." Joerstad, *Hebrew Bible*, 97. To understand ourselves not as the main character of the Hebrew Bible and to enter into a conversation rather than a declaration has a profound effect on how we redress body problems.

5. Gross, sermon transcript, "The Sabbath," third Sunday in Lent, 6:15 mass, Blackfriars, March 3, 1991 (Exodus 20:1–17; John 2:13–25), Sermons, GALO121, F4.

6. Heschel, *Sabbath*, 14.

7. See Leviticus 25, Exodus 23, Ezekiel 20, and Deuteronomy 15.

8. Crawford, "Sabbath Reading," 204.

9. Luke 19:40.

10. Rogers, "Sabbath as Creation Care," 244.

11. BREAKS

Epigraph: Rubin, "Provincializing Intersex," 118–19.

1. Moten, *In the Break*, 99. "That breakdown is not the negative effect of grammatical insufficiency but the positive trace of a lyrical surplus, counterpart to a certain tonal breakdown." Moten, *In the Break*, 38.

2. Lahood, *Intersexion*.

3. McMahon, interview. Gross's shawl is in GALO121, G2, Memorabilia: personal belongings.

4. Gross, letter addressed to "friends," Subject: "News from the wilderness."

5. Radcliffe, interview.

6. Lahood, *Intersexion*; and discussed in Gross, "Chronicle."

7. Morgan, interview.

8. What is presented here are Sally's views, which of course are contested among Christians, Jews, and scholars of religion. For an excellent historical account of Jewish and Christian contestation of biblical interpretation, see Clark, *Reading Renunciation*, in which she illuminates both early Christians who liberally borrowed interpretative strategies from non-Christian neighbors and those who "aim[ed] to retain the worthiness of the Israelite past to those that either openly denigrate[d] it or at least consign[ed] its usefulness to the dustbin of ancient history." Clark, *Reading Renunciation*, 69.

9. Gross, sermon transcript, "Baptism of the Lord," Cambridge, January 12, 1992, (Luke 3:15–16, 21–22), Sermons, GALO121, F 4. Gross uses the same material a year later in her sermon "Baptism of the Lord," Cambridge, January 10, 1993 (Matthew 3:13–17), Sermons, GALO121, F4.

10. Gross, "letter to [Father] Timothy [Radcliffe] continuing on the erosion of their faith and stating that she was enclosing an outline of her faith in Jesus. This outline is missing," August 28, 1995, GALO121, A3.

11. "The Feast of the Birth of Our Lady, letter from [Father] Timothy [Radcliffe] assuring Sally that those who doubt the validity of her baptism are incorrect," September 8, 1995. GALO121 A3.1.2.8.

12. The entirety of this chapter is paraphrased from Gross's 40-page account of her week in Brooklyn titled, "An Account of a Visit to the Lubavitcher Rebbe Part A and B," which was on her computer hard drive, to which her brother Ray Schmidt-Gross gave me access; in the Blackfriars archival material at Douai Abbey; shared with me via email by multiple interviewees; and also in the GALA archives GALO121, F4. I was able to confirm her departure date of October 2, 1988, by examining the stamps in her Israeli passport, GALO121, A2. As such, her visit preceded the 1991 violence between the Lubavitch Hasidic community and Afro-Caribbean and African American neighbors in Crown Heights. For more on this significant event, see Goldschmidt, *Race and Religion*; Shapiro, *Crown Heights*; Daughtry, *No Monopoly*; Fishkoff, *Rebbe's Army*; and Smith, *Fires*, to name a few. I had the pleasure of speaking directly with Goldschmidt by phone August 23, 2019, to learn more about the historical sociopolitical context. He was helpful in pointing me to a reading list and made comments for corrections to this chapter. My plans to visit Crown Heights and interview current residents was postponed due to COVID-19.

13. I invited Rabbi Overlander to be interviewed. While he responded to my initial email, he did not accept the invitation.

14. Sarah Leah Overlander, wife of Rabbi Gershon Overlander, died at age fifty-three after a two-year battle with cancer. Anna Sheinman, "Rebbetzin of Hendon Chabad House Has Died, Aged 53," *Jewish Chronicle*, January 22, 2013, https://www.thejc.com/news/uk/rebbetzin-of-hendon-chabad-house-has-died-aged-53-1.41099. According to Baruch Dayan Haemes, they had ten children. "Sara Leah Overlander, 53, OBM," *COLlive*, January 19, 2013, https://collive.com/sara-leah-overlander-53-obm/.

15. Gross, "Lubavitcher Rebbe," 2.

16. For more about Rabbi Berel Futerfas's family history, see Dovid Zaklikowski, "Historic Ukrainian Wedding Pairs Soviet Dissidents' Great-Grandchildren," *Chabad.org*, June 5, 2011, https://www.chabad.org/news/article_cdo/aid/1540622/jewish/Historic-Wedding-Pairs-Dissidents-Descendants.htm.

17. According to Rabbi Michoel Seligson, Shimshon Stock was one of the founders of the Gmilas Chesed Fund, Keren Yisroel Arye Leib, in 1972 and one of the first students of the new Lubavitcher yeshiva in Brooklyn. In his article he also discusses the rabbi's wife Martha and son Benjy. Seligson, "Our Heroes: Shimshon and Martha Stock OBM Part 1," Crown Heights Info, February 23, 2013, https://crownheights.info/blogs/374706/our-heroes-shimshon-and-martha-stock-obm-part-1/. Listen to Stock speak about his encounters with the rebbe here: "Shimshon Stock Retells the Beginnings of His Charitable Organization," posted March 9, 2007, by JEM—The Lubavitcher Rebbe, YouTube video, 4 min., 3 sec., https://www.youtube.com/watch?v=bHr6ipu1qvw.

18. Gross originally had Charlton, which Goldschmidt suspects should have been Kingston. He is careful to acknowledge that Crown Heights includes a broader area where the Hasidim live, a note to which Gross appears to have been less attuned.

19. According to an independent Orthodox Jewish news outlet, Benzion Stock and Avrohom Moskovits continue his parents' legacy: https://collive.com/10th-yartzeit-of-shimshon-stock/. The same source praises Rabbi Benjy Stock's response to COVID-19: https://collive.com/the-real-heroes-of-crown-heights/. Tammuz, "The Real 'Heroes' of Crown Heights," *COLlive* July 13, 2020.

20. Henry Goldschmidt suspects that the rebbe actually lived around the corner on President Street or Union Street.

21. This is a song that translates to, "And they shall rejoice in your festivals . . . and you shall be altogether joyful." It has a lively tune, is three stanzas long, and is typically sung during holidays.

22. Gross, "Lubavitcher Rebbe," 9.

23. Goldschmidt, *Race and Religion*, 20–21.

24. Goldschmidt, *Race and Religion*, 110.

25. Gross, "Lubavitcher Rebbe," 10.

26. Gross, "Lubavitcher Rebbe," 17–18.

27. Gross, "Lubavitcher Rebbe," 15.

28. Gross, "Lubavitcher Rebbe," 11–12.

29. Gross, "Lubavitcher Rebbe," 15–16.

30. It pains me to be barred from religious spaces designated for cisgender men only. Perhaps that is part of my delight in Sally: she has gone where I am forbidden from going, even though she was not definitively male. Religious scholarly communities exhibit a sort of masculinity that Daniel Boyarin describes in *Unheroic Conduct*—not the knight in shining armor but the studious religious man. On October 30, 2018, Professor Steven Friedman shared with me a Facebook message and email from Sally Gross in which she writes, "The two books by Daniel Boyarin which I ordered at your suggestion arrived, and I am working through A Radical Jew. The beginning of his prologue to *Unheroic Conduct* is perhaps the most striking

opening of a prologue I have ever read, and one of the few postings on Facebook I have made during the past three or so weeks was the transcription, at the request of a friend, of its first two paragraphs as an incentive to read Boyarin." Original dated March 8, 2011. In Friedman's email to me he wrote, "Besides exchanging views on the sorts of issues politically engaged people tend to discuss, we did have a significant email exchange on her return to a form of Jewish identity (you presumably know that her chapter was on the Jewish intellectual tradition). She passed away before the book was published." Drafts of Gross's chapter as well as the other contributors' work are on Gross's hard drives.

31. Gross, "Lubavitcher Rebbe." Stock has since died and is unable to verify this account. My plans to visit Crown Heights to conduct interviews was thwarted when COVID-19 hit.

32. "Unlike most other Jews, Lubavitchers locate the essence of Jewishness in an inherited soul that sits, uncomfortably, on the boundaries of social scientific categories like 'race' and 'religion. . . .' Lubavitch theology proclaims, and nearly all Lubavitchers believe, that Jews are distinguished from Gentiles by a uniquely Jewish 'godly soul' (in Hebrew, *nefesh elokis*) that is fundamentally different from the 'animal soul' (*nefesh bahamis*) shared by all human beings. The godly soul, they believe, is a fragment, or spark, of the divine itself—of the transcendent and unknowable *Or Ein Sof*, or 'Light of Infinity'—that has entered the material world, clothed in the bodies of Jewish people." Goldschmidt, "Religion, Reductionism," 554-55. This explains the later reference to the pope and Jews having good hearts.

33. Gross, "Jewish Reponses," 295.

34. Gross, "Jewish Reponses," 296.

35. Williams makes this argument in *Sisters*.

36. Grafton Thomas stabbed five of the seventy people at Hasidic Rabbi Chaim L. Rottenberg's Hanukkah party in Monsey, New York, in December 2019. Multiple news sources covered the hate crime, including USA *Today*, *The Washington Post*, NBC, CNN, ABC, and others.

37. For more on this see Goldschmidt, *Race and Religion*, 58.

38. Gross, "Lubavitcher Rebbe," 5.

39. Gross, "Lubavitcher Rebbe," 5.

40. Gross, "Lubavitcher Rebbe," 5.

41. Gross, "Lubavitcher Rebbe," 5.

42. Gross, "Lubavitcher Rebbe," 5-6.

43. Gross, "Lubavitcher Rebbe," 6.

44. Gross, "Lubavitcher Rebbe," 6.

45. See Tuhkanen, *American Optic*; JanMohamed, *Death-Bound-Subject*; and Seshadri-Crook's *Desiring Whiteness*.

46. For more on the challenge of categorizing race and religion, see Masuzawa, *Invention*; David Chidester, *Savage Systems*; Said, *Orientalism*; and Vásquez, *More Than Belief*.

47. Amaryah Armstrong argues, "Because blackness and the figure of the black maternal enables the reproduction of the illegitimate figure against which legitimate

peoplehood finds its meaning, anti-black violence is necessary to the reproduction of chosen peoplehood," "Blackness and the Problem of Belonging: A Political Theology of Race and Reproduction," PhD diss., Vanderbilt University, 2019. https://ir.vanderbilt.edu/items/a41e2dce-c22a-4fae-9a44-64d53594e660.

48. See Michael Twitty, "Kippahed While Black: The Troubling Resurgence of 'Shvartze' and 'Kushi,'" *Forward*, January 31, 2017, https://forward.com/opinion/361625/michael-twitty-black-jewish-relations/.

49. Gross, "Lubavitcher Rebbe," 36.

50. Gross, "Lubavitcher Rebbe," 36.

51. Gross, "Lubavitcher Rebbe," 36.

52. Gross, "Lubavitcher Rebbe," 36.

53. Gross, "Lubavitcher Rebbe," 36–37.

54. Gross, "Lubavitcher Rebbe," 37.

55. Gross, "friends," Subject: "News from the wilderness." Sally is careful to emphasize that claims to the Holy Land are sometimes secular.

56. See An, *Coloniality*; Masuzawa, *Invention*; Mahmood, *Politics*; Chidester, *Empire*; Asad, *Formations*, and Said, *Orientalism*.

12. SUTURES

Epigraph 1: Gebara, *Longing*, 170.
Epigraph 2: Plemons, *Look of a Woman*, 19–20.
Epigraph 3: Imhoff, *Jessie Sampter*, 35, 36–37.
Epigraph 4. Murray, Genna Raae McNeil interview with Pauli Murray, February 13, 1976. Interview G-0044. Southern Oral History Program Collection 4007. Southern Historical Collection, Wilson Library, University of North Carolina at Chapel Hill, https://docsouth.unc.edu/sohp/G-0044/excerpts/excerpt_8642.html#citing also found a transcript here https://www.wunc.org/racc demographics/2021-02-10/pauli-episode-3-transcript.
Epigraph 5. Imhoff, *Jessie Sampter*, 66–67.

1. According to Father Nichols, with whom I reconnected in Cambridge after having met at the Douai Abbey. He graciously toured me about the order's houses on February 28, 2019.

2. Gross, "Chronicle," and on Sally Gross's hard drive material; also Gross, letter addressed to "Ronnie."

3. Gross, "Chronicle."

4. Gross, "Chronicle."

5. Gross, "Chronicle."

6. Lahood, *Intersexion*, uncut footage.

7. Gross, sermon transcript, Easter Day, April 15, 1990, 9:30 a.m. mass, Blackfriars (John 20:1–9), Sermons, GAL0121, F4.

8. Coan, three-part series.

9. S. Gross, "Apartheid Tests the Soul of the Just," *Los Angeles Times*, October 1, 1987, https://www.latimes.com/archives/la-xpm-1987-10-01-me-11279-story.html.

10. Gross, "Apartheid Tests the Soul."

11. Gross, sermon transcript, "Pentecost," Pentecost Sunday, May 19, 1991 (Acts 2:1–13), Sermons, GALO121, F4.

12. S. Gross, "A Stumbling-Block for Jews and Folly for Gentiles," *New Blackfriars*, September 1992, https://doi.org/10.1111/j.1741-2005.1992.tb07261.x.

13. Gross, sermon transcript, "Living Bread," Corpus Christi, 6:15 mass, Blackfriars, June 14, 1990 (John 6:51–58), Sermons, GALO121, F4.

14. "The Fathers employ 'spiritual,' that is, figurative, readings of Scripture for a variety of reasons. In some circumstances figurative interpretations were usefully deployed to counter the 'literal' citation by 'heretics,' Jews and (to a lesser extent) 'pagans' of various Biblical passages to fault Christianity's embrace of Hebrew Scripture. Against these opponents, the Fathers develop figurative readings that permit the retention of the Old Testament—indeed, claim it as a Christian book—yet give appropriately 'spiritualized' interpretations to verses that otherwise might be taken as immoral, impious, meaningless, or 'carnal' (i.e., 'Jewish'). For the church fathers, the allegedly 'literal' reading by 'heretics' and Jews fails to acknowledge the moral or spiritual dimension of *all* Scripture and does so with nefarious intent." Clark, *Reading Renunciation*, 78–79, italics in original. Clark identifies "three approaches to the Hebrew past—embracing it as the Christian present, distancing it as unedifying for contemporary ascetics, or bypassing modes of exegesis. Both those interpreters who 'unify' the times and those who 'divide' them usually employ a quasi-literal and moralizing hermeneutic that relies heavily on intertexual exegesis, although their commentaries aim variously either to vindicate or to critique ancient Israelite (and some early Christian) mores." *Reading Renunciation*, 154.

15. Gross, "Letter to [Father] Timothy [Radcliffe] continuing on the erosion of their faith and stating that she was enclosing an outline of her faith in Jesus. This outline is missing," August 28, 1995 GALO121, A3.

16. Gross, sermon transcript, "Sabbath, rest and work," ninth Sunday of the year, 6 p.m., June 2, 1991 (Deuteronomy 5:12–15; Mark 2:23–2:6), Sermons, GALO121, F4, bold in original.

17. Gross, sermon transcript, "Sabbath, rest and work," bold in original.

18. Gross, sermon transcript, "Palm Sunday," Cambridge, April 12, 1992, Sermons, GALO121, F4.

19. Gross, sermon transcript, "The Paraclete," sixth Sunday of Eastertide, 6:15 mass, Blackfriars, May 20, 1990 (John 14:15–21), Sermons, GALO121, F4.

20. Gross, sermon transcript, "Vine," fifth Sunday of Easter, Cambridge, May 28, 1991 (John 15:1–8), Sermons, GALO121, F4.

21. Gross, sermon transcript, "Feast of Peter and Paul," June 30, 1991 (Acts 12:1–11; 2 Timothy 4:6–8; Matthew 16:13–19), Sermons, GALO121, F4.

22. "A person who is without sight sees the significance of Jesus clearly, perceives that he is the Messiah, and calls out to him." Gross, sermon transcript, "1988-10-23, Bartimaeus," October 23, 1988 (Mark 10:46–62), Sermons, GALO121, F4.

23. Gross preached, "Our Lord's reference to 'the law of Moses and the prophets and the psalms' in today's gospel-reading is obviously connected very closely with the Jewish scheme of the canon of scriptures, and by expounding them he makes it clear that his teaching makes no claim to abolish this canon of Hebrew scripture or to **supersede** it. . . . Rejection of the canon of Hebrew scripture which Christ cherishes, explains and indeed embodies, is rejection of Christ himself." Gross, sermon transcript, "Road to Emmaus," 6 p.m. mass, Cambridge, April 14, 1991 (Luke 24:35–48), Sermons, , F4, bold in original.

24. Gross, sermon transcript, "Peter," twenty-first Sunday of the year, August 23, 1987 (Matthew 16:13–20), Sermons, GALO121, F4.

25. Gross, sermon transcript, "Paul and the Jewish People," 9:30 mass, Blackfriars, August 12, 1990 (Romans 9:1–5), Sermons GALO121, F4.

26. Gross, sermon transcript, "The Commandment of Love," thirtieth Sunday of the year, 6:15 mass, Blackfriars, October 28, 1990 (Matthew 22:34–40), Sermons, GALO121, F4.

27. Gross, sermon transcript, "Feast of Peter and Paul."

28. Gross, sermon transcript, "Feast of Peter and Paul."

29. Gross, sermon transcript, "Paul and the Jewish People," bold in original.

30. Gross, sermon transcript, "Paul and the Jewish People."

31. Gross, sermon transcript, "Paul and the Jewish People."

32. Gross, sermon transcript, "Remembering the Holocaust," third Sunday of the year, Cambridge, January 26, 1992 (Nehemiah 8:2–6, 8–10; 1 Corinthians 12:12–30; Luke 1:1–4, 14–21), Sermons, GALO121, F4.

33. Gross, sermon transcript, "Remembering the Holocaust."

34. Gross, sermon transcript, "Parable of Labourers in Vineyard," twenty-fifth Sunday of the year, 9:30 mass, September 23, 1990 (Matthew 20:1–16), Sermons, GALO121, F4.

35. Gross, sermon transcript, "Parable of Labourers in Vineyard."

36. Gross, sermon transcript, "The Commandment of Love."

37. Gross, sermon transcript, "The Commandment of Love."

38. Gross, sermon transcript, "The Commandment of Love."

39. Gross, sermon transcript, "Witness," Dominican Day, Cambridge, June 22, 1991, Feast of Saints John Fisher and Thomas Moore, Sermons, GALO121, F4, bold in original.

40. Gross, sermon transcript, "Witness."

41. Gross, sermon transcript, "Neither do I condemn you," fifth Sunday of Lent, Framlingham, April 5, 1992 (Isaiah 43:16–21; Philippians 3:8–14; John 8:1–11), Sermons, GALO121, F4.

42. Gross, sermon transcript, "Neither do I condemn you," bold in original.

43. Gross, sermon transcript, "Resurrection of Jesus," second Sunday of Easter, Cambridge, April 26, 1992 (John 20:19–31), Sermons, GALO121, F4.

44. Gross, sermon transcript, "Resurrection of Jesus."

45. Gross, sermon transcript, "1988-04-12, John the Baptist," second Sunday of Advent, 6:30 mass, April 12, 1988 (Luke 3:1–6), Sermons, GALO121, F4.

46. Gross, notes for sermon at 6:15, Sunday Advent IV, 1988, Reception into the Church of Samuel Flatman. Samuel Flatman, interview, about Gross preparing him for reception.

47. Gross, sermon transcript, "Sermon: Westminster Abbey," February 5, 1995 (1 Corinthians 1:17–2:5), Sermons, GALO121, F4. Fran Springfield mentioned having attended this sermon with a group of trans friends. Springfield, interview.

48. Gross, sermon transcript, "Sermon: Westminster Abbey." Gross discusses this gap in more depth in her essay, "Intersex and the Law in Post-Apartheid South Africa," GALO121, C1.2, Academic papers: Sally Gross essays.

49. Gross, sermon transcript, "Mandela Walks Free," to celebrate Nelson Mandela's release, Blackfriars, February 13, 1990 (Isaiah 61; Luke 4), Sermons, GALO121, F4, bold in original.

50. Gross, sermon transcript, "Mandela Walks Free."

51. Gross, email, subject: "RE: Sermon preached on the occasion of Nelson Mandela's release from prison—a memorial to his life and achievements," December 8, 2013; forwarded to me by Timothy Radcliffe on February 28, 2019.

52. Gross, email, subject: "RE: Sermon preached on the occasion of Nelson Mandela's release from prison."

53. Gross, sermon transcript, "John 9 & Split of Church from Synagogue," 6:15 mass, Blackfriars, March 23, 1990 (John 9:1–41), Sermons, GALO121, F4.

54. Gross, sermon transcript, "John 9."

55. Gross, sermon transcript, "John 9."

56. Gross, sermon transcript, "Many Rooms, Way Light & Truth," fifth Sunday of Eastertide, Banbury, May 13, 1990 (John 14:1–12), Sermons, GALO121, F4.

57. Gross, sermon transcript, "Church and Jewish Particularity," eleventh Sunday of the year, Cambridge, June 13, 1993 (Exodus 19:2–6; Matthew 9:36–10:8), Sermons, GALO121, F4, bold in original.

58. Gross, sermon transcript, "Why Jesus Sighed," September 4, 1988 (Isaiah 35:4–7; Mark 7:31–37), Sermons, O121, F4.

59. Gross, sermon transcript, "Unity," seventh Sunday of Easter, 8:15 mass, Cambridge, May 12, 1991 (John 17:11–19), Sermons, GALO121, F4.

60. Gross, letter to "Rinpoche," GALO121, A4, Personal Documents, Notes on spirituality, retreats, meditation and mindfulness. No date or further information is included, only the suggestion that this was an email. The same letter is located in GALO121, F4. The GALA archives include her notes and photographs from Buddhist retreats, in addition to many Buddhist books and videos.

61. Gross, letter to "Rinpoche." In a different letter, likely written earlier, Sally claims to have recurring dreams about being pushed out of the Dominican Order, her time in the order, and even reconciliation with the order.

62. Williams, interview.

63. Gross, "Chronicle."

64. As previously discussed, some scholars of religion consider the category itself to be an imperial invention harmfully imposed or withheld from various people groups as a power play.

65. Gross, "Hume's Theory of Personal Identity," November 1984, GALO121, C2.

66. Gross, "In what sense did Kant think that empirical knowledge requires synthesis?," November 1984, GALO121, C2, which includes a second essay by the same name, although the content is different.

67. Lahood, *Intersexion*.

68. Quoted in Gina Wilson, "Eighth Day of Intersex: Sally Gross," Intersex Human Rights Australia, November 2, 2011, https://ihra.org.au/15234/eighth-day-intersex-sally-gross/.

69. "[Malcolm McMahon] saw me as a friend, but felt he'd acted in the Order's and Church's best interests. What I'd done was courageous, but he believed it wrong." Gross, quoted in Wilson, "Eighth Day of Intersex."

70. Gross, transcript of philosophy of religion lecture eight of thirteen on religious experience, presumably from her time as an instructor at Oxford, O121, F4; and on Gross's computer hard drive, to which her brother Ray Schmidt-Gross granted me access.

71. Gross, "Forms of Resurrection—Belief in Early Patristic Literature," "Draft—Patristics," 16fn35, GALO121, C5, Academic papers.

72. Gross, "The Reconstitutive Resurrection of Glorified Bodies," in "D. Phil. Thesis Draft, Part 3: Identity," 53, GALO121, C5, Academic papers, folder 3 of 3, emphasis in original.

73. Gross, "Reconstruction and Recreation," 2–3fn4, GALO121, C5, Academic papers.

74. "Many people, maybe even most people, do not fit clearly into one of the discrete religious categories to the exclusion of others," Sarah Imhoff, *The Lives of Jessie Sampter*, 66–67.

75. See Gross, "Letter to Timothy telling him about her return to Blackfriars and her interest in the Quakers," May 6, 1996, A8, folder 3 of 3. The dates align with Helen Brock's guestbook, which she allowed me to photograph. Helen Brock, interview. Gross's entry in the guestbook is written in English and Hebrew to the Brocks and their cats dated April 3–17, 1996. "Dear Helen and Sebastian, Words simply fail me. You have been far and away the kindest and best of friends over the past few traumatic years of my life and without your love and friendship I would not have survived. May God's blessings in your lives abound! All my love, Sally." Other entries are dated August 5, 1996; July 16–August 4, 1997; September 14–19, 1997; October 13–14, 1997; December 6, 1997; and December 7–9, 1999.

76. With the Brocks' permission I scanned Helen's records of their interactions with Sally.

77. Gross, "Incomplete correspondence/document to unknown recipient," March 19, 1997, 59–83, GALO121, A8, folder 3 of 3.

78. Gross, "Incomplete correspondence."

79. See also Operation Marion, a domestic military operation by the South African Defense Force during the 1980s.

80. Gross, letter addressed to "Ronnie."

81. Gross, letter addressed to "Ronnie."

82. Gross, letter addressed to "Ronnie."

83. Within the Christian tradition and scriptures, the body of Christ refers to both the individual person Jesus and the collective group of people known as the church.

13. RESONANCE

Epigraph 1: Radcliffe, Timothy. Interview by M. Wolff, Oxford, England, February 28, 2019.

Epigraph 2: Gross, referencing Dylan Thomas's poem "Do not go gentle into that good night," in "Chronicle," GALO121, C1.1, Academic papers, and described in Coan, three-part series. Gross wrote something similar in her 2007 email: "If I die in my bed tonight, I can pass away knowing that I have helped to make South Africa a better place for the intersexed, at least in legal terms, than it was before, and that I have put intersex firmly on the map as a human rights issue as far as the statutory body charged with oversight of human rights in South Africa is concerned." Gross, email addressed to "friends," Subject: "News from the wilderness."

1. Rosa, "Idea of Resonance," 43, italics in original.

2. Ahmed, "Race," 97.

3. In nearly religious terms, Susana Paasonen argues that affective resonance is an experience of rapture: "Whatever grabs, resonates: it demands attention and has the power to move and touch the one interacting with it." *Carnal Resonance*, 178–79. Paasonen explains, "As bodily knowledge, carnal resonance requires viewers to get close enough to the image to be moved by it and to account for its 'controlled and uncontrollable aspects' (MacDougall 2006, 7). Such affectation results from encounters between bodies (whether human or animal, bodies of objects or thought) and connects them." *Carnal Resonance*, 196. "Resonance is descriptive of what disturbs, tickles, or confuses in such materializations—what moves us in a particular way in specific images and technological assemblages." "Race as sedimented history," *Carnal Resonance*, 197. How might Paasonen's analysis relate to thriving ecologies? Trans theorist Harlan Weaver utilizes Paasonen's work to explore the possibilities of multispecies trans*-affective politics by analyzing the show *Pit Bulls and Parolees*: "This grab-switch revealed to me a form of trans species kinship that I can embrace and be moved by in a way that is not identificatory but politically important nonetheless." Weaver, "Tracks of My Tears," 350.

4. In a reference letter, Jeremy Routledge writes that since 2000 Gross served as the director of the Quaker Peace Centre and served on the board "as a member of the Cape Western Monthly Meeting of the Religious Society of Friends (Quakers) where she served as the clerk and as an elder and also a friend." Routledge, letter addressed to Simon Mahlangu, Department of Justice and Constitutional Development, May 26, 2006. Gross mentions her work for the Religious Society of Friends in Coan, three-part series.

5. Stern, interview.

6. Stern retold this event to me during her interview and also wrote about it in an obituary for Sally titled "Betwixt and Between."

7. Stern, "Betwixt and Between."

8. Lahood, *Intersexion*.

9. Coan, three-part series.

10. Gross, "letter to [Father] Timothy [Radcliffe] continuing on the erosion of her faith and stating that she was enclosing an outline of her faith in Jesus. This outline is missing," August 28, 1995, GALO121, A3.

11. Gross, email to friends, Subject: "From the Finsbury Park Station," August 24, 2003, reflecting on her 10 years living in a female role, GALO121, A3.3.1.

12. Gross, "Chronicle."

13. Gross, email to friends, "From the Finsbury Park Station."

14. *Top Level* was renamed *The Felicia Show* in 1995, then *Felicia* in 2000. It was hosted by Felicia Mabuza-Suttle and generally covered social issues in South Africa. Sally was later a guest on her show to inform the public on intersexuality. Other interviewees included Nelson Mandela, Desmond Tutu, Winnie Madikizela-Mandela, and Cherie Blair. Mabuza-Suttle's website is https://www.feliciainc.com/.

15. Gross, "Chronicle." Gross discusses this in "Intersex and the Law in Post-Apartheid South Africa," date unknown, GALO121, C1.2, Academic papers: Sally Gross essays. Gross also describes this accomplishment in Lahood, *Intersexion*. See also Gross, letter addressed to "Ronnie."

16. I refrain from going into detail about romantic entanglements among various activists because it is difficult to verify and not central to understanding Sally. Gross saved work documents and photographs from her time collaborating with Engender, GALO121, F4. Named attendees include Barbara, Indigo, Mandisa, Sharon, Bernedette, Graham, Barbara, Blessing, Wahieda, and Hussein. She also discusses her collaboration with Engender in "Chronicle," 236. Various participants whom I interviewed also verified Gross's work there.

17. Gross, "Intersex and the Law."

18. In a job application, Gross explains, "Much of my personal activism has focused upon abuse, due to physical ambiguity, of intersexed infants and children. Since 2004, I have worked on this with the Human Right[s] Commission (SAHRC), and persuaded the SAHRC to examine the imposition of surgery on intersexed infants." GALO121, B3, Work related documents: department of land affairs. Gross describes the workshop in "Chronicle," 236, and in Coan, three-part series. She also discusses this in her email addressed to "friends," Subject: "News from the wilderness."

19. Gross, curriculum vitae in application for post of deputy director in the Regional Land Claims Commission, May 16, 2007, GALO121, B3, Work related documents.

20. Gross, "Intersex and the Law."

21. *National Intersex Meeting Report 2018*, which took place December 11, 2017. The first page of the introduction claims, "Indeed any doubts that South African law would not see the provisions of the Constitution as intersex inclusive were

put to rest when Gross submitted amendments to the *Judicial Matters Amendment Act* which saw the *Promotion of Equality Act* and *Prevention of Unfair Discrimination Act* 4 of 2000 amended at Section 1 to state the following: 16. Section 1 of the Promotion of Equality and Prevention of Unfair Discrimination Act, 2000, is hereby amended—(a) by the insertion in subsection (1) after the definition of "HIV/AIDS status" of the following definition: "'intersex' means a congenital sexual differentiation which is atypical, to whatever degree"; and (b) by the insertion in subsection (1) after the definition of "sector" of the following definition: "'sex' includes intersex." GALO121, G1, Memorabilia: memorial documents.

22. Gross, GALO121, B3, Work related documents: department of land affairs. She also discusses this in Lahood, *Intersexion*.

23. Gross, email to "friends," July 15, 2007, GALO121, A3. She also mentions her accomplishments in her chapter "Chronicle."

24. "Letter from Judith Cohen nominating Sally Gross for appointment as a Commissioner to the Commission on Gender Equality," June 15, 2006. Cohen agreed to be interviewed, but we had multiple failed attempts to meet.

25. There are many photos of everyone present at meetings and out to dinner in her computer files, O121, F4. Named participants include Sally, Mani, Hiker, Bill, Gina, Vreer, Dell, Ditte, Jim, Baklawa, Imy, Holly, Dan, Bill, Ruth, Holly, Mauro, Patricia, Tanya, and others, 2011-09-09, GALO121, F4. There are also travel itinerary documents (lodging and transportation information and receipts) that appear to be from this trip in, A10.

26. https://oiieurope.org/wp-content/uploads/2015/05/CRPD_2015_Statement_OIIEurope.pdf, accessed December 29, 2018.

27. Mitchell, interview.

28. There are many photographs from this event, including a group shot of twenty-six people of whom I recognize Sally, Hiker, and Mani, September 2011, GALO121, F4. Mani Mitchell also emailed me many photos from this event.

29. Mitchell, interview.

30. Lahood, *Intersexion*.

31. Mitchell, interview.

32. Le Roux, interview, September 4, 2018.

33. Note that I have not found evidence of Sally using "herm" for herself.

34. Coan, three-part series.

35. "In a sense, presenting as female did less violence to me than it did presenting as male. But the truth is, I'm a person. I'm me." Lahood, *Intersexion*.

36. Le Roux, interview, November 5, 2018. There are photographs of Gabrielle Le Roux sketching, as well as photographs of the sketches at various stages in Sally's computer file folders: 2013-02-13 and Me Myself GALO121, F4.

37. Le Roux, interview, November 5, 2018.

38. Le Roux, interview, November 5, 2018.

39. Exodus 3:13–15.

40. Lahood, *Intersexion*.

41. Le Roux, email to M. Wolff, June 20, 2024.

42. Gross, "E-mail B," October 19, 1996, GALO121, A8, folder 2 of 3.
43. I purchased a couple of prints from Gabrielle Le Roux after interviewing them and have since been analyzing these collaborative portraits of Sally.
44. The complexity of these categories is theorized by Bey in *Cistem Failure*.
45. It appears to be what is described in her computer files as "Guruyoga with SixA-s," GALO121, F4.
46. Le Roux, "Tribute."
47. Le Roux, interview, November 5, 2018.
48. McMahon, interview.
49. McMahon, interview.
50. Gross, "Incomplete correspondence/document," February 11, 1996; and footnote "March 1997." brackets in original. Physical examination has confirmed that her congenital physical sexual differentiation is atypical and makes reconstruction surgery impracticable.
51. Gross, sermon transcript, "Thomas Doubting," second Sunday of Easter, 6 p.m. mass, Blackfriars, April 7, 1991 (John 20:19–31), Sermons, GALO121, F4.
52. Gross, sermon transcript, "Road to Emmaus," 6:00 p.m. mass, Cambridge, April 14, 1991 (Luke 24:35–48), Sermons, GALO121, F4.
53. Gross, sermon transcript, "Easter, leaving community," Easter Sunday, Blackfriars, Cambridge, April 11, 1993, Sermons, GALO121, F4.
54. Wolff, "Diptych Reading," 3.
55. O'Connor, "Temple of the Holy Ghost," 101.
56. O'Connor, "Temple of the Holy Ghost," 101. "Hit" in original.
57. O'Connor, "Temple of the Holy Ghost," 98.
58. O'Connor, "Temple of the Holy Ghost," 99.
59. O'Connor, "Temple of the Holy Ghost," 102.
60. Cameron Awkward-Rich persuasively demonstrates how freak shows can be a space of constrained agency for disabled, trans, and intersex people: "I argue that, rather than only impending or confining trans life, thought, and creativity, forms of maladjustment have also been central to their development." *Terrible We*, 17.
61. Chemers, *Staging Stigma*.

POSTSCRIPT

1. Gross, email to "friends," Subject: "News from the wilderness."
2. Healing Justice Toolkit, Dignity and Power Now, https://dignityandpowernow.org/wp-content/uploads/2019/05/Healing-Justice-Toolkit_PRINT_March-1.pdf; and Healing in Action: A Toolkit for Black Lives Matter Healing Justice and Direct Action, Decolonize Race Project, https://blacklivesmatter.com/wp-content/uploads/2024/05/blm-healing-action-r1.pdf. Thanks to Casey Golomski, who shared these with me.
3. Gross, "Intersex, Status and Law in South Africa and Africa in General," GALO121, C1.2, Academic papers: Sally Gross essays; and also on Gross's computer hard drive.

4. A friend and comrade of Sally, Charlene Smith writes that there are six genders referenced in Mishna, Talmud, midrash, and Jewish law codes from the first sixteen centuries: (1) Zachar: phallus, (2) Nekeivah: vagina, (3) Androgynos: a person with "male" and "female" sexual characteristics, (4) Tumtum: indeterminate sexual characteristics, (5) Ay'lonit: "female" at birth, develops "male" characteristics at puberty and is infertile, and (6) Saris: a person classified as "male" at birth who develops "female" characteristics at puberty and/or lacks a penis. Smith, "Neuroscience." A more precise, scholarly account can be found in Strassfeld's *Trans Talmud*.

5. Gross, "Life in the Shadow."

6. Gross, "Not in God's Image."

7. "In it the author describes an incident in a rural South African village in which a traditional healer, assisting with the delivery of a baby, witnessed how the baby was killed by family members when it was discovered that it had been born with ambiguous genitalia. They decided to lie to the mother and tell her that the child was stillborn. The author points out that this is an example of many cases of intersex infanticide that occur because of a belief that 'intersex babies are bad omens.' They are seen as a sign of witchcraft and a curse on the family and the community as a whole." Behrens, "Principled Ethical Approach."

8. National Dialogue on the Protection and Promotion of the Human Rights of Intersex People 2018 meeting report, 5. The report cites Carl Collision's "Intersex Babies Killed at Birth Because 'They're Bad Omens,'" *The Mail and Guardian Online*, January 24, 2018. In GALO121, C1.2, Academic papers, Sally Gross essays.

9. Behrens, "Principled Ethical Approach."

10. See Megan Goodwin's concept of contraceptive nationalism in *Abusing Religion*.

11. Danon, "Intersex Activists."

12. Danon, "Intersex Activists," 573. Danon claims, "Many Israeli scholars have highlighted the relationship between Israel's pronationalist culture, advanced reproductive technology, government subsidization of fertility treatment and pregnancy testing, and Israeli sociocultural norms that valorize family and the importance of the continued demographical growth of the Jewish people in Israel. I argue that the protonationalist culture in Israel and the advanced biotechnological fertility treatments are important and help many people to have families, but the same diagnostic tools threaten the existence of intersex bodies." "Intersex Activists," 573.

13. Greenberg, *Intersexuality*, 24.

14. Holmes, *Intersex*, 157.

15. "Public Statement by the African Intersex Movement," Astraea Lesbian Foundation for Justice, December 14, 2017, https://www.astraeafoundation.org/stories/public-statement-african-intersex-movement/.

16. March 1, 2017, South Africa, GALO121, G1, Memorabilia: memorial documents. Report on Human Rights of Intersex People in South Africa, April 11, 2018, https://sxpolitics.org/18375-2/18375, accessed November 18, 2024.

17. Gross, "Not in God's Image."

18. Behrens also states that this occurs in Uganda, Kenya, and China. Behrens, "Principled Ethical Approach."

19. Chui uses "s/he" pronouns.

20. Chui, interview.

21. There are a number of photographs of Hiker in this T-shirt in Sally's computer files, GALO121, F4.

22. Chui, interview.

23. According to the National Dialogue on the Protection and Promotion of the Human Rights of Intersex People 2018 meeting report, "Because IGM results in the forced sterilisation of intersex children, the Sterilisation Act can be used in combating non-medically necessary surgeries on intersex children" (17). Sally Gross and Rosemary Lennox, "Diversity in Nature," *Intersex South Africa*, October 1, 2017, intersex.org.za; National Dialogue on the Protection and Promotion of the Human Rights of Intersex People 2018 meeting report, 21.

24. Chui, interview.

25. "It was one of Sally Gross' great hopes that a modest directorate be set up to address intersex issues within the Department for Women, Children, and Persons with Disabilities with a mandate to engage with other Departments regarding the rights and needs of the intersex, [which] could achieve a great deal at minimal cost." Chui, interview.

26. Naidenov, interview.

27. Naidenov, interview.

28. Mokoena, interview.

29. In addition to my interview with Mokoena, they have publicly shared their story in a variety of publications: 2019 *National Intersex Meeting Report*, 6–7, GALO121, C1.5, Academic papers, Note, press clipping and posters?; "Celebrating Black History Month: Nthabiseng Mokoena," February 26, 2018, https://www.intersexequality.com/celebrating-black-history-month-nthabiseng-mokoena/; Mokoena, "Nthabiseng Mokoena"; "For Intersex Activist Nthabiseng Mokoena, the Shame Is Over," Interface Project, September 16, 2014, https://www.interfaceproject.org/nthabiseng-mokoena/; Mokoena, "Remembering Sally"; candidacy for the International Lesbian, Gay, Bisexual, Trans and Intersex Association. Jacobson, "Third Sex"; and others.

30. Jacobson, "Third Sex"; transcript on Sally Gross's computer hard drive provided by her brother Ray Schmidt-Gross.

31. Mokoena, "Remembering Sally."

32. Jacobson, "Third Sex."

33. Mokoena, interview.

34. Gross, "Not in God's Image."

35. Mokoena, interview.

36. Mokoena, interview.

37. Mokoena, "Remembering Sally." Nthabiseng Mokoena made similar claims in the 2018 *National Intersex Meeting Report*, 7.

38. Both films are on vhs tapes in the gala archives, galo121, f2; and the transcript from part 2 was on Sally's computer hard drive, provided by her brother Ray Schmidt-Gross. Gross also mentions this in her essay "Intersex and the Law in Post-Apartheid South Africa."

39. Mokoena, interview.

40. Mokoena, interview.

41. Mokoena, "Remembering Sally."

BIBLIOGRAPHY

Ahmed, Sara. *Complaint!* Durham, NC: Duke University Press, 2021.
Ahmed, Sara. *On Being Included: Racism and Diversity in Institutional Life*. Durham, NC: Duke University Press, 2012.
Ahmed, Sara. "Race as Sedimented History." *Postmedieval: A Journal of Medieval Cultural Studies* 6 (2015): 94–97.
Ahmed, Sara. "Sexism: A Problem with a Name." *New Formations: A Journal of Culture/Theory/Politics* 86 (2015): 5–13.
Ahmed, Sara. *Willful Subjects*. Durham, NC: Duke University Press, 2014.
Althaus-Reid, Marcella. *The Queer God*. New York: Routledge, 2003.
An, Yountae. *The Coloniality of the Secular: Race, Religion, and Poetics of World-Making*. Durham, NC: Duke University Press, 2024.
Annas, George. "Siamese Twins: Killing One to Save the Other." *Hastings Center Report* 17, no. 2 (1987): 27–29.
Anzaldúa, Gloria. *Borderlands/La Frontera: The New Mestiza*. San Francisco: Aunt Lute Books, 1987.
Armstrong, Amaryah. "Blackness and the Problem of Belonging: A Political Theology of Race and Reproduction." PhD diss., Vanderbilt University, 2019. https://ir.vanderbilt.edu/items/a41e2dce-c22a-4fae-9a44-64d53594e660.
Asad, Talal. *Formations of the Secular: Christianity, Islam, Modernity*. Redwood City, CA: Stanford University Press, 2003.
Awkward-Rich, Cameron. *The Terrible We: Thinking with Trans Maladjustment*. Durham, NC: Duke University Press, 2022.
Baratz, Arlene, and Katrina Karkazis. "Cris de Coeur and the Moral Imperative to Listen to and Learn from Intersex People." *Narrative Inquiry in Bioethics* 5, no. 2 (Summer 2015): 127–32. https://doi.org/10.1353/nib.2015.0030.
Beauvoir, Simone de. *The Second Sex*. Translated by Constance Borde and Sheila Malovany-Chevallier. New York: Vintage Books, 2011.
Behrens, Kevin. "A Principled Ethical Approach to Intersex Paediatric Surgeries." *BMC Medical Ethics* 21, no. 1 (2020). https://doi.org/10.1186/s12910-020-00550-x.
Belser, Julia Watts. *Rabbinic Tales of Destruction: Gender, Sex, and Disability in the Ruins of Jerusalem*. Oxford: Oxford University Press, 2018.
Berlant, Lauren. *Cruel Optimism*. Durham, NC: Duke University Press, 2011.

Bey, Marquis. *Cistem Failure: Essays on Blackness and Cisgender*. Durham, NC: Duke University Press, 2022.

Bordiss, Bradley. Interview by M. Wolff, Cape Town, South Africa, October 28, 2018.

Boum, Aomar. *Memories of Absence: How Muslims Remember Jews in Morocco*. Stanford, CA: Stanford University Press, 2013.

Boyarin, Daniel. "Freud's Baby, Fliess's Maybe: Homophobia, Antisemitism, and the Invention of Oedipus." *GLQ* 2, no. 1 (1995): 115–47.

Boyarin, Daniel. *A Radical Jew: Paul and the Politics of Identity*. Berkeley: University of California Press, 1994.

Boyarin, Daniel. *Socrates and the Fat Rabbis*. Chicago: University of Chicago Press, 2009.

Boyarin, Daniel. *Unheroic Conduct: The Rise of Heterosexuality and the Invention of the Jewish Man*. Oakland: University of California Press, 1997.

Boyarin, Daniel, Daniel Itzkovitz, and Ann Pellegrini, eds. *Queer Theory and the Jewish Question*. New York: Columbia University Press, 2003.

Brock, Helen. Interview by M. Wolff, Oxford, England, February 21, 2019.

Brock, Sebastian. Interview by M. Wolff, Oxford, England, February 21, 2019.

Brulmyer, Gracen. "Archival Assemblages: Applying Disability Studies' Political/Relational Model to Archival Description." *Archival Science* 18 (2018): 95–118.

Burich, Keith. *The Thomas Indian School and the "Irredeemable" Children of New York (The Iroquois and Their Neighbors)*. New York: Syracuse University Press, 2016.

Burnett, Scott. *White Belongings: Race, Land, and Property in Post-Apartheid South Africa*. Lanham: Rowman and Littlefield, 2022.

Cannon, Katie Geneva, Emilie M. Townes, and Angela D. Sims, eds. *Womanist Theological Ethics: A Reader*. Louisville, KY: Westminster John Knox Press, 2011.

Carpenter, Morgan. "The 'Normalization' of Intersex Bodies and 'Othering' of Intersex Identities in Australia." *Bioethical Inquiry* 15 (2018): 487–95.

Carter, J. Kameron. *The Anarchy of Black Religion: A Mystic Song*. Durham, NC: Duke University Press, 2023.

Castor, N. Fadeke. "Spiritual Ethnicity: Our Collective Ancestors in Ifá and Orisha Devotion Across the Americas." In Covington-Ward and Jouili, *Embodying Black Religions*.

Chemers, Michael M. *Staging Stigma: A Critical Examination of the American Freak Show*. New York: Palgrave Macmillan, 2008.

Chidester, David. *Empire of Religion: Imperialism and Comparative Religion*. Chicago: University of Chicago Press, 2014.

Chidester, David. *Savage Systems: Colonialism and Comparative Religion in Southern Africa*. Charlottesville: University of Virginia Press, 1996.

Chui, Hiker. Interview by M. Wolff, Zoom, September 25, 2018.

Clark, Elizabeth. *Reading Renunciation: Asceticism and Scripture in Early Christianity*. Princeton, NJ: Princeton University Press, 1999.

Coan, Stephen. Three-part series. *Natal Witness*. February 21–23, 2000, reprinted August 28, 2009.

Covington-Ward, Yolanda, and Jeanette S. Jouili, eds. *Embodying Black Religions in Africa and Its Diasporas*. Durham, NC: Duke University Press, 2021.

Covington-Ward, Yolanda, and Jeanette S. Jouili. "Introduction: Embodiment and Relationality in Religions of Africa and Its Diasporas." In Covington-Ward and Jouili, *Embodying Black Religions*.
Cox, Sharon. Interview by M. Wolff, Cape Town, South Africa, October 29, 2018.
Crawford, Jason. "Sabbath Reading." *Christianity and Literature* 70, no. 3 (2021): 202–11.
Crosby, Christina. *A Body, Undone: Living On After Great Pain*. New York: New York University Press, 2016.
Danon, Limor Meoded. "Intersex Activists in Israel: Their Achievements and the Obstacles They Face." *Journal of Bioethical Inquiry* 15, no. 4 (2018): 569–78. https://doi.org/10.1007/s11673-018-9877-2.
Dansky, Miriam. *Gateshead: Its Community, Its Personalities, Its Institutions*. Israel: Targum Press, 1992.
Davies, Andrew. Interview by M. Wolff, Cape Town, South Africa, October 30, 2018.
Daughtry, Herbert. *No Monopoly on Suffering: Blacks and Jews in Crown Heights*. Trenton, NJ: Africa World Press, 1997.
Davis, Georgian. *Contesting Intersex: The Dubious Diagnosis*. New York: New York University Press, 2015.
Douglas, Kelly Brown. "Black and Blues God-Talk/Body-Talk for the Black Church." In Cannon et al., *Womanist Theological Ethics*.
Dreger, Alice. *Hermaphrodites and the Medical Invention of Sex*. Cambridge, MA: Harvard University Press, 1998.
Dreger, Alice. "Intersex and Human Rights: The Long View." In *Ethics and Intersex*, edited by S. E. Sytsma. Dordrecht: Springer, 2006.
Dreger, Alice. "Losing Kiira." Alice Dreger (blog), November 4, 2012. http://alicedreger.com/losing_kiira.
Dreger, Alice. "Sex Typing for Sport." *Hastings Center Report* 40, no. 2 (2010): 22–24.
Driskill, Qwo-Li, Chris Finley, Brian Joseph, and Scott Lauria Morgensen, eds. *Queer Indigenous Studies: Critical Interventions in Theory, Politics, and Literature*. Tucson: University of Arizona Press, 2011.
Du Bois, W. E. B. *The Souls of Black Folk: Essays and Sketches*. Chicago: A. G. McClurg, 1903.
Estes, Nick. *Our History Is the Future: Standing Rock Versus the Dakota Access Pipeline, and the Long Tradition of Indigenous Resistance*. New York: Verso, 2019.
Ewing, Deborah. Interview by M. Wolff, Zoom, May 21, 2019.
Falkof, Nicky. *Worrier State: Risk, Anxiety, and Moral Panic in South Africa*. Manchester: Manchester University Press, 2022.
Fassen, Didier. *When Bodies Remember: Experiences and Politics of AIDS in South Africa*. Oakland: University of California Press, 2007.
Fausto-Sterling, Anne. *Sexing the Body: Gender Politics and the Construction of Sexuality*. New York: Basic Books, 2000.
Feder, Ellen. *Making Sense of Intersex: Changing Ethical Perspectives in Biomedicine*. Bloomington: Indiana University Press, 2014.
Fishkoff, Sue. *The Rebbe's Army: Inside the World of Chabad-Lubavitch*. New York: Schocken Books, 2003.

Flatman, Father Martin. Interview by M. Wolff, Oxford, England, February 23, 2019.
Flatman, Father Martin. Interview by M. Wolff, email, November 4, 2018.
Flatman, Frances. Interview by M. Wolff, Oxford, England, February 23, 2019.
Flatman, Samuel. Interview by M. Wolff, email, March 10, 2019.
Floyd-Thomas, Stacey. *Mining the Motherlode: Methods in Womanist Ethics*. Cleveland, OH: Pilgrim Press, 2006.
Foucault, Michel. *The Birth of the Clinic: An Archeology of Medical Perception*. Translated by A. M. Sheridan Smith. New York: Vintage Books, 1994.
Foucault, Michel. Introduction to *Herculine Barbin: Being the Recently Discovered Memoirs of a Nineteenth-Century French Hermaphrodite*. Translated by Richard McDougall. New York: Pantheon Books, 1980.
Friedman, Steven. Email message to M. Wolff, October 30, 2018.
Garber, Marjorie. "A Tale of Two Singers." In *Queer Theory and the Jewish Question*, edited by Daniel Boyarin, Daniel Itzkovitz, and Ann Pellegrini. New York: Colombia University Press, 2003.
Gebara, Ivone. *Longing for Running Water: Ecofeminism and Liberation*. Minneapolis, MN: Fortress Press, 1991.
Gill-Peterson, Jules. *Histories of the Transgender Child*. Minneapolis: University of Minnesota Press, 2017.
Goldschmidt, Henry. *Race and Religion Among the Chosen Peoples of Crown Heights*. New Brunswick, NJ: Rutgers University Press, 2006.
Goldschmidt, Henry. "Religion, Reductionism, and the Godly Soul: Lubavitch Hasidic Jewishness and the Limits of Classificatory Thought." *Journal of the American Academy of Religion* 77, no. 3 (2009): 547–72.
Gomez, Abel R. "Indigeneity." Political Theology Network, January 3, 2023. https://politicaltheology.com/indigeneity/.
Goodwin, Megan. *Abusing Religion: Literary Persecution, Sex Scandals, and American Minority Religions*. New Brunswick, NJ: Rutgers University Press, 2020.
Gossett, Reina, Eric A. Stanley, and Johanna Burton, eds. *Trap Door: Trans Cultural Production and the Politics of Visibility*. Cambridge, MA: MIT Press, 2017.
Greenberg, Julie A. *Intersexuality and the Law: Why Sex Matters*. New York: New York University Press, 2012.
Griffiths, David. "Queer Theory for Lichens." *UnderCurrents: Journal of Critical Environmental Studies* 19 (2015): 36–45.
Gross, S. Blackfriars Archive. Douai Abbey, Berkshire, United Kingdom.
Gross, Sally. "The Chronicle of an Intersexed Activist's Journey." In Tamale, *African Sexualities*.
Gross, Sally. "De-Gendering Unions: The Civil Union Act and the Intersexed." In *To Have and to Hold: The Making of Same-Sex Marriage in South Africa*, edited by Melanie Judge, Anthony Manion, and Shaun de Waal. Ann Arbor, MI: Jacanda Media, 2009.
Gross, S. "Jewish Responses: Neither the Same nor Different." In *Intellectual Traditions in South Africa: Ideas, Individuals and Institutions*, edited by Peter Vale, Lawrence Hamilton, and Estelle Prinsloo. Pietermaritzburg: University of KwaZulu-Natal Press, 2014.

Gross, Sally. "Life in the Shadow of Gender." *The Witness* (Pietermaritzburg), August 29, 2009.

Gross, Sally. "Not in God's Image: Intersex, Social Death, and Infanticide." Paper presented via Skype at the Intersex, Theology and Bible conference, University of Manchester, March 2013.

Gross, Sally. "Response on the Mistreatment of Caster Semenya." Intersex Initiative, 2018. http://www.intersexinitiative.org/media/castersemenya.html.

Gross, Sally. Sally Gross collection, GALA Queer Archive. University of Witwatersrand, Johannesburg, South Africa.

Harris, Melanie. "Ecowomanism: An Introduction." *Worldviews* 20, no. 1 (2016): 5–14.

Hatcher, Daniel. *The Poverty Industry: The Exploitation of America's Most Vulnerable Citizens*. New York: New York University Press, 2016.

Hayashi, Brian Masaru. *Democratizing the Enemy: The Japanese American Internment*. Princeton, NJ: Princeton University Press, 2004.

Henderson, Jennifer, and Pauline Wakeham. *Reconciling Canada: Critical Perspectives on the Culture of Redress*. Toronto: University of Toronto Press, 2013.

Heschel, Abraham Joshua. *The Sabbath: Its Meaning for Modern Man*. New York: Farrar, Straus and Giroux, 1951.

Holmes, Morgan. *Intersex: A Perilous Difference*. Selinsgrove, PA: Susquehanna University Press, 2008.

Horowicz, Edmund. "Intersex Children: Who Are We Really Treating?" *Medical Law International* 17, no. 3 (2017): 183–218. https://doi.org/10.1177/0968533217726109.

Hunter, Father Peter. Interview by M. Wolff, Zoom, March 13, 2019.

Imhoff, Sarah. *The Lives of Jessie Sampter: Queer, Disabled, Zionist*. Durham, NC: Duke University Press, 2022.

Jacobs, Daniel Malan. Interview by M. Wolff, Cape Town, South Africa, January 23, 2020.

Jakobsen, Janet. *The Sex Obsession: Perversity and Possibility in American Politics*. New York: New York University Press, 2020.

Jacobson, Lana. "The Third Sex." *Drum Magazine*. http://www.writerstudio.co.za/about-lana-jacobson/feature-writing/105-the-third-sex.html. Accessed December 2, 2024.

JanMohamed, Abdul. *The Death-Bound-Subject: Richard Wright's Archaeology of Death*. Durham, NC: Duke University Press, 2005.

Jiménez, Laura, Kierra Johnson, and Cara Page. "Beyond the Trees: Stories and Strategies of Environmental and Reproductive Justice." In *Radical Reproductive Justice*, edited by Loretta Ross, Lynn Roberts, Erika Derkas, Whitney Peoples, and Pamela Bridgewater. New York City: Feminist Press, 2017.

Joerstad, Mari. *The Hebrew Bible and Environmental Ethics: Humans, Nonhumans, and the Living Landscape*. Cambridge: Cambridge University Press, 2019.

Jütte, Robert. *The Jewish Body: A History*. Translated by Elizabeth Bredreck. Philadelphia: University of Pennsylvania Press, 2020.

Kafer, Alison. *Feminist, Queer, Crip*. Bloomington: Indiana University Press, 2013.

Kasrils, Ronnie. "Israel-Palestine Conflict: Declaration of Conscience." December 7, 2001. https://www.dws.gov.za/Communications/MinisterSpeeches/Kasrils

/2001/Israel%20Palestine%20Conflict%20Declaration%20of%20Conscience%20 speech%20by%20Minister%207%20Dec%2001.pdf. Accessed December 2, 2024.

Kauanui, J. Kēhaulani, ed. *Speaking of Indigenous Politics: Conversations with Activists, Scholars, and Tribal Leaders*. Minneapolis: University of Minnesota Press, 2018.

Kessler, Susan. "The Medical Construction of Gender: Case Management of Intersexed Infants." *Signs* 16, no. 1 (1990): 3–26.

Kim, Catherin Y., Daniel J Losen, and Damon T. Hewitt. *The School-to-Prison Pipeline: Structuring Legal Reform*. New York: New York University Press, 2012.

Kim, Hyjin. Interview by M. Wolff, Cape Town, South Africa, October 30, 2018.

Kimmerer, Robin Wall. *Braiding Sweetgrass: Indigenous Wisdom, Scientific Knowledge, and the Teachings of Plants*. Minneapolis: Milkweed Editions, 2013.

Lahood, Grant, dir. *Intersexion*. San Francisco: Frameline, 2012.

Le Roux, Gabrielle. Interview by M. Wolff, phone, Cape Town, South Africa, September 4, 2018.

Le Roux, Gabrielle. Interview by M. Wolff, phone, Cape Town, South Africa, September 11, 2018.

Le Roux, Gabrielle. Interview by M. Wolff, Johannesburg, South Africa, November 5, 2018.

Le Roux, Gabrielle. "A Tribute to Sally Gross." *The Feminist Wire*, February 23, 2014.

Löfgren-Måternson, Lotta. "'Hip to Be Crip?'": About Crip Theory, Sexuality and People with Intellectual Disabilities." *Sexuality and Disability* 31, no. 4 (2013): 413–24.

Long, Robyn. "Sexual Subjectivities Within Neoliberalism: Can Queer and Crip Engagements Offer an Alternative Praxis?" *Journal of International Women's Studies* 19, no. 1 (2018): 78–93.

Magaziner, Daniel. *The Law and the Prophets: Black Consciousness in South Africa, 1968–1977*. Athens: Ohio University Press, 2010.

Mahmood, Saaba. *Politics of Piety: The Islamic Revival and the Feminist Subject*. Princeton, NJ: Princeton University Press, 2011.

Malatino, Hil. *Queer Embodiment: Monstrosity, Medical Violence, and Intersex Experience*. Lincoln: University of Nebraska Press, 2019.

Malatino, Hil. *Trans Care*. Minneapolis: University of Minnesota Press, 2020.

Mars, Benjamin. Interview by M. Wolff, Cape Town, South Africa, January 21, 2020.

Masuzawa, Tomoko. *The Invention of World Religions: Or, How European Universalism Was Preserved in the Language of Pluralism*. Chicago: University of Chicago Press, 2005.

McClintock, Anne. *Imperial Leather: Race, Gender, and Sexuality in the Colonial Contest*. New York: Routledge, 1995.

McMahon, Father Malcolm. Interview by M. Wolff, Zoom, March 5, 2019.

Memmi, Albert. *The Colonizer and the Colonized*. Boston: Beacon Press, 1965.

Mignolo, Walter, and Catherine E. Walsh. *On Decoloniality: Concepts, Analytics, Praxis*. Durham, NC: Duke University Press, 2018.

Mitchell, Mani. "In Memory of Sally Gross ISSA-Intersex Society of South Africa." February 17, 2014. http://www.ianz.org.nz/2014/02/in-memory-of-sally-gross-issa-intersex-society-of-south-africa/.

Mitchell, Mani. Interview by M. Wolff, Zoom, December 28, 2018.

Mokoena, Nthabiseng. Interview by M. Wolff, Cape Town, South Africa, October 26, 2018.

Mokoena, Nthabiseng. "Nthabiseng Mokoena." Interface Project. https://www.interfaceproject.org/nthabiseng-mokoena/. Accessed August 15, 2019.

Mokoena, Nthabiseng. "Remembering Sally, and the Intersex Movement in South Africa." Intersex Day, October 22, 2015. http://intersexday.org/en/remembering-sally-south-africa/.

Morgan, Mogg. Interview by M. Wolff, WhatsApp recordings, September 9, 2018.

Morrison, Toni. *Beloved*. New York: Vintage Books, 2004.

Mosala, S. J., et al. "The National Democratic Revolution (NDR) in South Africa: An Ideological Journey." KOERS 84, no. 1 (2019): 1–16.

Moten, Fred. *In the Break: The Aesthetics of the Black Radical Tradition*. Minneapolis: University of Minnesota Press, 2003.

Mtshali, Mabongi. "Obituary. The Revd Victor Vivian Sipho Africander (1930–1990)." *Natalia* 20 (1990): 65–66. https://natalia.org.za/Files/20/Natalia%20v20%20obituaries%20Africander.pdf.

Muñoz, José Esteban. *Cruising Utopia*. New York: New York University Press, 2019.

Murray, Pauli. Genna Raae McNeil interview G-0044. Southern Oral History Program Collection 4007. University of North Carolina, Chapel Hill. February 13, 1976.

Naidenov, Pol. Interview by M. Wolff, Zoom, October 2, 2018.

Najmabadi, Afsaneh. *Women with Mustaches and Men Without Beards: Gender and Sexual Anxieties of Iranian Modernity*. Berkeley: University of California Press, 2005.

Ndebele, Nhlanhla, and Noor Nieftagodien. "The Morogoro Conference: A Moment of Self-Reflection." In *The Road to Democracy in South Africa*, vol. 1, 1960–1970, edited by Tsakani Ngomane and Constance Flanagan. Cape Town: Zebra Press, 2004.

Nofal, Justine. "Apla Blamed for Farm Murders." *Weekly Mail and Guardian*, October 23, 1997.

O'Connor, Flannery. "A Temple of the Holy Ghost." In *A Good Man Is Hard to Find*. San Diego, CA: Harcourt Brace Jovanovich, 1977.

Ozturk, Serkan. "Sally Gross Remembered as Fearless Intersex Leader." *Star Observer*, March 4, 2014. http://www.starobserver.com.au/news/international-news-news/sally-gross-remembered-as-fearless-intersex-leader/118968.

Paasonen, Susana. *Carnal Resonance: Affect and Online Pornography*. Cambridge, MA: MIT Press, 2011.

"Patricia." Interview by M. Wolff, Cape Town, South Africa, October 31, 2018.

Patterson, Orlando. *Slavery and Social Death: A Comparative Study*. Cambridge, MA: Harvard University Press, 1982.

Plemons, Eric. *The Look of a Woman: Facial Feminization Surgery and the Aims of Trans Medicine*. Durham, NC: Duke University Press, 2017.

Povinelli, Elizabeth. *Geontologies: A Requiem to Late Liberalism*. Durham, NC: Duke University Press, 2016.

Price, Margaret. *Crip Spacetime: Access, Failure, and Accountability in Academic Life.* Durham, NC: Duke University Press, 2024.

Puar, Jasbir K. "Coda: The Cost of Getting Better: Suicide, Sensation, Switchpoints." *GLQ* 18, no. 1 (2012): 149–58.

Qualtrough, Stuart. "Priest in Sex Swap." *The People*, August 4, 1994.

Radcliffe, Timothy. Interview by M. Wolff, Oxford, England, February 28, 2019.

Reis, Elizabeth. "Did Bioethics Matter? A History of Autonomy, Consent, and Intersex Genital Surgery." *Medical Law Review* 27, no. 4 (2019): 658–74. https://doi.org/10.1093/medlaw/fwz007.

Reynolds, Bryan, and Joseph Fitzpatrick. "The Transversality of Michel de Certeau: Foucault's Panoptic Discourse and the Cartographic Impulse." *Diacritics* 29, no. 3 (1999): 63–80.

Rogers, Sandy D. "Sabbath as Creation Care." *Review and Expositor* 119, nos. 3–4 (2022): 237–44.

Rosa, Hartmut. "The Idea of Resonance as a Sociological Concept." *Global Dialogue* 8, no. 2 (2018): 41–44.

Rothstein, Richard. *The Color of Law: A Forgotten History of How Our Government Segregated America.* New York: Liveright, 2017.

Rubin, David. *Intersex Matters: Biomedical Embodiment, Gender Regulation, and Transnational Activism.* New York: State University of New York Press, 2017.

Rubin, David. "Provincializing Intersex: U.S. Intersex Activism, Human Rights, and Transnational Body Politics." In *Reproductive Justice and Sexual Rights: Transnational Perspectives*, edited by Tanya Saroj Bakhru. New York: Routledge, 2019.

Said, Edward. *Orientalism.* New York: Vintage Books, 1979.

Salamon, Gayle. *Assuming a Body: Transgender and Rhetorics of Materiality.* New York: Columbia University Press, 2010.

Salamon, Gayle. *The Life and Death of Latisha King: A Critical Phenomenology of Transphobia.* New York: New York University Press, 2018.

Savoy, Lauret. *Trace: Memory, History, Race, and the American Landscape.* Berkeley, CA: Counterpoint, 2015.

Schmidt-Gross, Raymond (Ray). Interviews by M. Wolff, phone, September 20, 2018; phone, October 16, 2018; Boston, June 23, 2019.

Schmidt-Gross, Sharon. Interview by M. Wolff, Boston, June 24, 2019.

Schofield, Julian. "Israel and South Africa—Nuclear Collaboration." In *Strategic Nuclear Sharing.* London: Palgrave Macmillan, 2014.

Schotten, C. Heike. *Queer Terror: Life, Death, and Desire in the Settler Colony.* New York: Columbia University Press, 2018.

Shapiro, Edward. *Crown Heights: Blacks, Jews and the 1991 Brooklyn Riot.* Waltham, MA: Brandeis University Press, 2006.

Seshadri-Crooks, Kalpana. *Desiring Whiteness: A Lacanian Analysis of Race.* London: Routledge, 2000.

Smit, David. Interview by M. Wolff, Cape Town, South Africa, January 21, 2020.

Smith, Anna Deavere. *Fires in the Mirror: Crown Heights, Brooklyn and Other Identities.* New York: Dramatists Play Service, 1998.

Smith, Charlene. Interview by M. Wolff, Zoom, May 7, 2019.

Smith, Charlene. "What Neuroscience Tells Us About Transgender People." *Brainworld*, March 31, 2019. https://brainworldmagazine.com/what-neuroscience-tells-us-about-transgender-people/.

Spillers, Hortense. *Black, White, and in Color: Essays on American Literature and Culture*. Chicago: University of Chicago Press, 2003.

Springfield, Fran. Interview by M. Wolff, Vauxhall, England, February 19, 2019.

Stern, Jen. "Betwixt and Between." *South African Quaker News*, April, 2014, 36–40.

Stern, Jen. Interview by M. Wolff, Zoom, November 6, 2018.

Strassfeld, Max K. *Trans Talmud: Androgynes and Eunuchs in Rabbinic Literature*. Oakland: University of California Press, 2023.

Strings, Sabrina. *Fearing the Black Body: Racial Origins of Fat Phobia*. New York: New York University Press, 2019.

Stryker, Susan. "Ask a Feminist: Susan Stryker Discusses Trans Studies, Trans Feminism, and a More Trans Future with V Varun Chaudhry." *Signs*, February 2021. http://signsjournal.org/stryker/.

Stryker, Susan. *Transgender History: The Roots of Today's Revolution*. New York: Seal Press, 2017.

Styker, Susan, and Paisley Currah. Introduction to *Transgender Studies Quarterly* 1 (2014): 1–18. https://doi.org/10.1215/23289252-2398540.

Suzack, Cheryl, Shari M. Huhndorf, Jeanne Perreault, and Jean Barman, eds. *Indigenous Women and Feminism: Politics, Activism, Culture*. Vancouver: University of British Columbia Press, 2010.

Swarr, Amanda. Interview by M. Wolff, Zoom, October 16, 2018.

Sykes, Pam. Interview by M. Wolff, Cape Town, South Africa, October 31, 2018.

Tamale, Sylvia, ed. *African Sexualities: A Reader*. Cape Town: Pambazuka Press, 2011.

Tamale, Sylvia. *Decolonization and Afro-Feminism*. Quebec: Daraja Press, 2020.

Tamar-Mattis, Anne. "Exceptions to the Rule: Curing the Law's Failure to Protect Intersex Infants." *Berkeley Journal of Gender, Law and Justice* 21, no. 1 (2006): 59–110.

Theron, Liesl. Interview by M. Wolff, Zoom, September 4, 2018.

Tickell, Diana. Interview by M. Wolff, Oxford, England, February 25, 2019.

Tock, Eve, and K. Wayne Yang. "Decolonization Is Not a Metaphor." *Decolonization: Indigeneity, Education and Society* 1, no. 1 (2012): 1–40.

Townes, Emilie. "To Be Called Beloved: Womanist Ontology in PostModern Refraction." *Annual of the Society of Christian Ethics* 13 (1993): 93–115.

Townes, Emilie. *Womanist Ethics and the Cultural Production of Evil*. New York: Palgrave Macmillan, 2006.

Tuhkanen, Mikko. *The American Optic: Psychoanalysis, Critical Race Theory, and Richard Wright*. Albany: State University of New York Press, 2009.

van der Kolk, Bessel A. *The Body Keeps the Score: Brain, Mind, and Body in the Healing of Trauma*. New York: Penguin, 2015.

van Huyssteen, Wessel, dir. *The 3rd Sex*. Johannesburg: Tin Rage Production for the South African Broadcasting Company (SABC3).

van Rooyen, Eugene. Interview by M. Wolff, Cape Town, South Africa, October 26, 2018.

van Rooyen. Justine. Interview by M. Wolff, Cape Town, South Africa, November 3, 2018.

Vásquez, Manuel A. *More Than Belief: A Materialist Theory of Religion*. Oxford: Oxford University Press, 2010.

Weaver, Harlan. "The Tracks of My Tears: Trans* Affects, Resonances, and *Pit Bulls and Parolees*." *Transgender Studies Quarterly* 2, no. 2 (2015): 345–52.

Weglin, Michi Nishiura. *Years of Infamy: The Untold Story of America's Concentration Camps*. Seattle: University of Washington Press, 1996.

Weiss, Meria. *The Chosen Body: The Politics of the Body in Israeli Society*. Stanford, CA: Stanford University Press, 2004.

Westermann, Edward. *Drunk on Genocide: Alcohol and Mass Murder in Nazi Germany*. Ithaca, NY: Cornell University Press, 2021.

Williams, Delores. *Sisters in the Wilderness: The Challenge of Womanist God-Talk*. New York: Orbis Books, 1993.

Williams, Jennifer. Interview by M. Wolff, Cape Town, South Africa, October 26, 2018.

Wolff, M. "Conversation Partners." *Political Theology* 23, no. 5 (2022): 498–505.

Wolff, M. "A Diptych Reading of Christ's Transfiguration: Trans and Intersex Aesthetics Reveal Baptismal Identity." *Theology and Sexuality* 25, no. 1–2 (2019): 1–12.

Wolff, M. "Intimate Life Together: A Decolonial Theology." PhD diss., Duke University, 2017. ProQuest, https://hdl.handle.net/10161/14426.

Wolff, M. "Madonna and Child of Soweto: Black Life Beyond Apartheid and Democracy." *Political Theology* 19, no. 7 (2018): 572–92. https://doi.org/10.1080/1462317X.2018.1450468.

Wolff, M. "Sally Gross: Mother of Transnational Intersex Activism Died Alone." Paper presented at the annual meeting of the National Women's Studies Association, San Francisco, 2019.

Wolff, M. "Trans Embodiment Beyond Entrapment, or, an Invitation to Cultivate Compassionate Curiosity." Wabash Center for Teaching and Learning in Theology and Religion, June 26, 2023.

Wolff, M., David Rubin, and Amanda Swarr. "Creating Intersex Justice: Interview with Sean Saifa Wall and Pidgeon Pagonis of the Intersex Justice Project." "The Intersex Issue," special issue, *Transgender Studies Quarterly* 9, no. 2 (2022): 187–95. https://doi.org/10.1215/23289252-9612823.

Wolff, M., David Rubin, and Amanda Swarr, eds. "The Intersex Issue." Special issue, *Transgender Studies Quarterly* 9, no. 2 (2022).

Worsnip, Michael. Interview by M. Wolff, Maropeng, South Africa, November 6, 2018.

Zaaiman, Andre. Interview by M. Wolff, Cape Town, South Africa, November 1, 2018.

Zuijderduijn, Jaco and Roos van Oosten. "Breaking the piggy bank: What can historical and archaeological sources tell us about late-medieval saving behavior?" *Working Papers 65*, Utrecht University, Centre for Global Economic History, 2015, 1–46.

INDEX

Italic page numbers refer to figures

abbeys: Douai, 6, 34, 37, 206, 254n19, 258n14, 265n3, 284n12, 287n1; Westminster, 36, 204
ableism, 111, 116, 139, 199
Africander, Vivian Sipho, 132
African Intersex Movement, 237
African National Congress (ANC), 3, 20, 96, 123–25, 131, 142, 250n3, 251n12, 273n19, 280n21; attacks on, 104, 129; Freedom Charter, 122; Gross's work with, 3, 30, 56, 110, 112, 127, 129, 177, 182, 185, 187, 205, 217, 258nn18–19, 27n5; and IFP's Boipatong Massacre, 210–11; treason trials, 128; unbanning of, 20, 129, 204–5; Youth League, 122
African Resistance Movement (ARM), 273n5
Afrikaans language, 104–5, 122, 270n21
Afrikaner Broederbond, 112
Afrikaner Resistance Movement, 129
Afrikaners, 56, 104, 108, 112, 142, 184, 258n19
agitation, 20, 86, 170, 174, 232; and activism, 9–10, 17, 48, 50, 101, 113, 115–17, 124, 128–29, 192, 211, 214; agitator kinship, 133; and bodies, 3, 5, 8, 10, 45, 83, 115–17, 137–38, 163
Ahmed, Sara, 115, 213
AIDS Foundation of South Africa, 138, 154
Allison (landlord's wife), 73, 76, 262n37
Alteration of Sex Description Bill (2003), 217–19, 248n17, 248n22, 280n25
Althaus-Reid, Marcella, 3, 247n13
androgen insensitivity syndrome (testicular feminization syndrome), 277n21
Anglicanism, 53, 131–32, 140
Annas, George, 83

anti-apartheid activism, 51, 53–54, 60, 120, 122–23, 127–32, 140, 142, 194, 196, 210, 250n3, 273n8; and Communism, 20
antibodies, 214; activists as, 115–16
Antifa, 130
antiracism, 3, 189
antisemitism, 20, 39–40, 46, 49, 55, 61, 83, 116, 155, 174, 182–86, 194–95, 196, 200, 205, 212
anti-Zionism, 54, 60, 120, 126–27
Anzaldúa, Gloria, 99
apartheid, 53, 100, 108, 125–26, 155, 174, 183, 185, 188, 190, 206, 221; and Christianity, 15, 112, 122, 142, 194; and Communism, 20; end of, 56, 58, 103–6, 112, 138–39, 151, 216, 258n19; and Israel, 120, 140; and Judaism, 16, 122–24, 194–96, 251n5, 252n17; pass laws, 102, 113, 203; and patriarchy, 26, 120–21; and racism, 15, 26, 103–4; and Zionism, 15, 45, 49, 101. *See also* anti-apartheid activism
Apartheid Museum, 3, 248n17
Aquinas, Thomas, 35, 52, 132, 193, 201
Arab Students' Committee, 119
Aramaic language, 132, 192, 214
architecture, 23, 45, 193; of domination, 156
art, 222–23. *See also* portraits, of Gross
asexuality, 25–27, 36, 46, 59–60, 161, 178, 195, 215, 253n37
asylum, 41, 117, 124, 131, 197
atheism, 106–7, 112, 197, 201, 203, 208
Atlantic Philanthropies, 154
Australia, 100–101, 148
Awkward-Rich, Cameron, 295n60

Baby Suggs (character), 2, 5, 166, 171–72, 214
Baddiel, Dovid, 24
bans: on ANC, 20, 129; in apartheid, 120; on CPSA, 273n19; on Gross's visitation, 259n26; literature, 122
baptism, 51, 58, 135, 175–76, 196, 230
Baratz, Arlene, 248n19
Barbin, Adélaïde Herculine, 95
Battle of Blood River (1838), 130
Bavli Gittin, 100
Beauvoir, Simone de, 45
Beck, Max, 133, 158, 248n16, 275nn51–52
Behrens, Kevin, 207n18, 235–36
Belser, Julia Watts, 82, 100, 156
Benedictine Order, 52
Berlant, Lauren, 42, 256n49
Bernstein, Hilda, 16, 122, 250n3
Bernstone, Zachariah, 23
Biko, Steve, 122
Black Americans, 102, 184–88
Black Consciousness Movement (BCM), 122
Blackfriars (journal), 52
Blackfriars (Order of Preachers), 4, 41, 51, 54–55, 73, 161, 182, 189, 197, 203, 205, 209, 254n19; archives, 6, 34–40; Cambridge House, 37–38, 56–58, 69, 129, 192–93, 200, 206, 211, 287n1; and embodiment, 62; history of, 51–52; Oxford House, 35, 37–39, 52–53, 56–59, 62, 67, 70, 127–28, 175, 258n4, 258nn6–7, 258n19, 291n72
police surveillance of, 128; Women's Theology Group, 32
Black hermit figure, 102, 113, 203
Black nationalism, 20
Black Panther Party, 130
Black South Africans, 20, 122, 129
bodies as problems, 1, 3, 8, 9, 45, 80, 86, 88, 114, 163, 174
bodies of land, 3, 9, 49–50, 99–114
bodies of paperwork, 9, 49–50, 86–98, 113
bodiliness, 8, 10, 26, 29, 31, 37, 48, 163, 165–67, 204, 214, 232
Boipatong Massacre (1992), 210–11
Boraine, Alex, 131
Bordiss, Bradley, 140–41, 160, 277n13, 277n16
Botswana, 41, 89, 120, 124, 197, 274n35; Bontleng, 125; Mochudi, 125
Boyarin, Daniel, 39–40, 285n30

breaks, 1–2, 8, 42, 49–50, 114, 198; breakdowns, 135, 283n1; creating clearings, 4–5, 10, 163, 169–71, 173–90, 195; and resonance, 192, 214, 232; and sutures, 166, 171, 195, 209, 212, 214, 232
British Mandate for Palestine, 18
Brock, Helen, 97, 147, 157, 209–10, 258n19, 281n40, 291n77, 292n78
Brock, Sebastian, 97, 157, 209, 281n40, 292n78
Buddhism, 3–4, 49, 51, 106–8, 148, 151, 161, 189, 207, 209, 291n62; Theravada, 175, 202, 206, 208
Bulgaria, 239–40
Bullough, Edward, 192
Bullough, Enrichetta, 192
Buthelezi, Ronald, 110, 272n51

Call the Midwife, 77
Calvinism, 108, 112
Cambridge House, 37–38, 56–58, 69, 129, 192–93, 200, 206, 211, 287n1
canon law, 35, 56, 62, 77–78, 80, 89
Cape Talk Radio, 136
Cape Town, South Africa, 6, 11, 25, 110, 121, 123, 126, 132, 239, 249n1, 253n38, 273n5; District Six, 101, 106, 108; Observatory, 140, 146, 152, 214; Wynberg, 102
capitalism, 3, 42, 94, 122, 153, 160
care, 38, 44, 57, 62, 99, 103, 128, 137–38, 162, 172, 215, 257n54, 281n28; as debt, 149; health-, 5, 47, 79, 80–86, 89, 139, 156, 160, 162–63, 184–85, 236, 237, 240–41, 244, 277n21, 279n19; palliative, 157, 159; pastoral, 53; self-, 2, 145, 147, 156, 243; spiritual, 234, 249n23
Carmelite nuns, 35, 258n3
Carole (friend), 70
Carpenter, Morgan, 148
Castor, N. Fadeke, 247n8
categorization, 72, 106, 170, 221, 295n44; colonial, 101; failures of, 4–5, 29; gender, 8, 45, 48–50, 75, 94, 152, 160–61, 224–25, 228, 231, 262n42; racial, 16, 103, 185, 286n32; religious, 185, 203, 291n66, 291n76
Catholicism, 55, 68, 73, 92, 108, 123, 129, 140–41, 163, 231, 258n19; and antisemitism, 46; and embodiment, 8; and gender, 39, 53, 57, 78, 88, 89, 176, 215, 222, 228–29, 265n3; Gross's, 4, 6, 9, 29, 31, 46, 49–51, 54,

57, 61, 88–89, 110–11, 127, 148, 161, 174–77, 182, 193–207, 210–11, 215, 225, 228, 240; and intersexuality, 6, 57, 78, 80, 176, 222, 228–29; and Judaism, 34, 193–206, 289n24; laicization in, 38, 57, 80, 89, 176, 255n30; priesthood, 4, 8–9, 29, 31, 49–50, 53–54, 56–57, 62, 76, 78, 88–89, 104, 175, 182, 194, 203, 210, 228–29, 240, 265n3. *See also* Blackfriars (Order of Preachers); Carmelite nuns; Dominicans; Franciscans
Cato, Gavin, 184–85
Cedara, South Africa, 38, 129–30
celibacy, 25, 36, 55, 71, 79, 195, 222, 253n38, 253nn37–38
Charing Cross Hospital: gender identity clinic, 66
Chase, Cheryl (Bo Laurent), 135, 248n16, 275n3, 276n58. *See also* Intersex Society of North America (ISNA)
Chohan-Khota, Fatima, 217–18
chosen people, 184, 286n47
Christianity, 3–4, 36, 52, 127, 136, 140, 186, 229, 247n13, 284n8, 288n15, 292n85; and apartheid, 15, 112, 122, 142, 194; and atheism, 106; baptism in, 175–76; and Buddhism, 208; Christian community, 54, 55, 123, 204; and colonialism, 234; and embodiment, 55; forgiveness in, 131; fundamentalist, 107; Gross's, 30–31, 61, 155, 163, 174–76, 196, 215; Gross's Jewish-Christian sermons, 193–206, 289n24; and intersexuality, 151, 239; and nature, 170. *See also* Anglicanism; Blackfriars (Order of Preachers); Calvinism; Catholicism; Protestantism; Quakers
chromosomes, 68–69, 71, 93, 121, 144, 261n15
Chui, Hiker, 233, 237–39, 294n25, 294n28, 297n21
circumcision, 11–13, 39–40, 84, 141, 176, 225, 229
cisgender people, 21, 48, 193, 221, 224–25, 285n30
citizenship, 4, 8, 96, 174, 193, 228; bio-, 143; British, 268n49; Israeli, 126; naturalized, 56; South African, 129
Civil Cooperation Bureau (CCB), 129
Civil Union Bill (2006), 85
classism, 37, 241
clearings, 2–6, 10, 43, 45, 48, 50, 163, 169–73, 193, 214, 221, 232

clergy, 7, 38, 49, 54, 61, 127, 192, 195, 206, 222, 259n24, 261n7, 263n52, 265n2
Coan, Stephen, 81, 97, 215, 258n18, 269n63
Code of Practice, 90
Cohen, Judith, 218–20, 294n24
Cold War, 124
Collins, John, 129
colonialism/imperialism, 3–4, 7, 17, 50, 101, 116, 125, 273n19; Australian, 101; and body regulation, 82, 100, 264n72; British, 102, 184; Dutch, 102; Israeli, 18, 49, 119–20, 140, 155, 185, 189, 272n2; and religion, 122, 184, 198, 203, 234, 264n72, 291n66; settler colonialism, 100–102, 120
Coloured, category of, 16, 101, 103–6
Commission on Gender Equality, 237, 273n8
Communism, 20, 23, 54, 112, 119, 122, 124, 125, 197, 221, 250n3, 273n19
Communist Party of Israel (Maki), 119
Communist Party of South Africa, 20, 122, 221, 250n3, 273n19
Communist Youth League, 119
community building, 137–48
complaints, 89–93, 259n26, 266n8. *See also* Press Complaints Commission
congenital adrenogenital hyperplasia (CAH), 138, 249n2
Congregation for the Doctrine of Faith, 61
Conrad, Richard, 62, 70
consent, 47, 82, 85, 134, 144, 211
Convention for a Democratic South Africa (CODESA), 210–11
conversion, 31, 53, 68, 140, 175–76, 194, 199
"corrective" surgery, 49, 74, 91
Council for the Advancement of the South African Constitution (CASAC), 129
covenants, 13, 172, 176, 189, 198, 201, 206
Coventry, Martha, 275n51
COVID-19 pandemic, 6, 284n12, 286n31
Covington-Ward, Yolanda, 166
Cox, Sharon, 144–45
Crawford, Jason, 172
crip theory, 138, 257n1, 257n63. *See also* disability
Crosby, Christina, 45, 87–88
cross (Christian), 193, 195, 200, 204
crucifixion/crucifixes, 74, 131, 194–95, 204
cure discourse, 59, 71, 82

Daaboul, Jorge, 74
dance, 2, 166, 172, 178, 181–82, 214, 232
Danon, Limor, 236, 264n87, 296n12
Dansky, Miriam, 23–24
Davies, Andrew, 152
Davis, Georgiann, 95, 143
debility, 42–43
debt, 4, 43, 149, 154, 172
Declaration of Geneva (1948), 85
Declaration on Relations with Non-Christian Relations (Nostra Aetate), 175, 206
decolonization, 171, 173
Defiance Campaign Against Unjust Laws, 123
deism, 175
Democratic Republic of the Congo, 141
diagnosis, 45–46, 49, 65, 71, 75, 84, 93, 113, 143, 147, 236, 264n71, 296n12; mis-, 9, 48, 50, 68, 91, 95, 225, 261n11, 267n22
Diamond, Milton, 80–81, 277n21
dignity, 2, 43–45, 75–76, 147, 158–63, 204, 218–19, 280n26
Dingane (king), 130
disability, 5, 50, 75, 89, 100, 154, 156, 161, 222, 257n63, 279n9, 280n22, 295n60, 297n25; and ablebodiness, 232; and bodies as problems, 45–46; care for, 89, 110, 149, 163, 240; in Christianity, 199; creation of, 87–88; intersex as, 242, 276n1; social anxiety about, 83; social model of, 138
Disability Labour, 75
disambiguation, 82, 97, 134, 217, 238, 268n53
discipline, 4–5, 9, 23, 25–26, 48, 59, 74, 82, 93, 102, 205
discourse, 4, 40, 49, 82, 92–96, 116, 166, 184, 229, 262n42, 281n2
District Six, 101, 106, 108
Divine Law (Talmud Torah), 24
docile bodies, 10, 48, 82
domestic violence, 19–20, 33, 222, 254n10
Dominic, Hugh, 192
Dominicans, 4, 7, 31, 36, 55, 58, 72–73, 177, 196, 202, 203; and activism, 54, 205; on intersex and trans embodiment, 49, 61–62; relationship with Gross, 76, 88–90, 127, 129, 174, 291n63; way of life, 52, 56, 258n4. *See also* Blackfriars (Order of Preachers)
Dowd, Mark, 35
Dreger, Alice, 93, 248n19, 255n35, 267n29
Dryan, Dovid, 23

Du Bois, W. E. B., 1, 5, 22
Durban, South Africa, 58, 130
Dutch Reformed Church, 112

ecologies, 4, 6, 10, 48, 100, 192, 213, 257n63, 283n1, 292n3; diverse, 3, 5, 8, 114, 117, 137, 163, 169–70, 212, 232; of good relations, 3, 50; political, 10, 50, 113; social, 2
ecumenism, 38, 177, 199
Edendale, South Africa, 130
election, religious, 141, 183, 190, 196, 198, 200–201, 206
endocrines, 76, 78, 84, 90, 142, 277n21
endocrinology, 76, 78, 84, 90, 142, 277n21
Engender, 218, 248n22, 293n16
England, 4, 6, 29, 50, 53, 104, 128–29, 138, 141, 192, 245, 246, 249n1, 249n23, 263n54, 278n23; Eastbourne, 60, 68, 72–73, 75–77, 88, 92, 215, 262n37; English law, 85; Gateshead, 22–24, 171; London, 35, 38, 69, 75, 77, 127, 265; Newcastle, 23–24. *See also* Cambridge House; Great Britain; Oxford priory; United Kingdom
epistemology, 65, 99, 101, 173
ethics, 56, 70, 74, 84, 114, 135, 173, 182, 221–22; bio-, 235; Christian, 247n13; medical, 132, 248n19; monster approach to, 83; womanist, 3
Eucharist, 131, 197, 199, 206, 210–11
Eurocentrism, 190
Ewing, Deborah, 43, 138, 151
exile, 124–25, 128, 142
Exodus, 183–84, 223
"Eyes Left," 122

Facebook, 43, 145, 155, 161, 238, 240, 285n30
Fanon, Frantz, 132
Fantastic Hegemonic Imagination, 40
Fascism, 20, 185. *See also* Nazis
Fassin, Didier, 116
fatness, 1, 9, 37–38, 40, 46, 50, 111, 139
fatphobia, 37–38, 111, 139
Fausto-Sterling, Anne, 82, 94
Feder, Ellen, 83–85, 144, 264n75
Federal Theological Seminary, 132
The Felicia Show, 149, 217, 293n14
female genital cutting (FGC), 82–83
femininity, 32, 39–40, 69, 71, 141, 220, 238, 254n16

312 INDEX

feminism, 82, 262n42
Flatman, Frances and Martin, 53–54, 155, 258n7, 258n9, 281n27
flourishing, 4, 10, 45, 48, 82, 137, 156–57, 169, 192, 214
Forced Removals Group Areas Act (1950), 106, 108, 113
Foucault, Michel, 93–95, 162, 267n42
Franciscans, 52, 258n3
freaks, 150, 151, 230–31, 295n60
Free State, South Africa, 104
Friedman, Steven, 285n30
Futerfas, Berel, 178–79

Gaddafi, Muammar, 187
Gahal, 119
Gandhi, Mahatma, 130
Gay and Lesbian Memory in Action archives (GALA), 6, 264nn65–66, 265n2, 266n8, 268n53, 268n57, 269n63, 275n51, 281n36, 291n62
gaze, 48, 93, 133, 223, 238
Gebara, Ivone, 191
gender agony, 34, 48
Gender Dynamix, 139, 146
gender dysphoria, 21–22, 30, 34, 61, 67–68, 78, 90, 121–22, 229
Gender Dysphoria Trust, 68
gender euphoria, 41
gender identity, 31, 34, 41, 47–48, 66, 74, 92, 121, 138, 219, 221, 224, 255n25
gender nonbinary people, 48, 77, 82, 85, 92, 100, 109, 153, 159, 189, 203, 220–21
genital reassignment surgery, 44, 65–68, 75–76, 78, 225, 256n51, 268n53, 295n50
gender transition, 48–49, 62, 68, 70–71, 75, 97, 139, 225, 229
genocide, 185, 188–89. *See also* Holocaust
gentiles, 57–58, 155, 175, 183–89, 196, 199–200, 204–5, 229, 286n32
Germany, 17, 20, 23, 39, 85
Gill-Peterson, Jules, 83, 254n18
Gnosticism, 165
Go (game), 19, 152–53
GoFundMe, 147, 159
Goldschmidt, Henry, 179, 183, 185, 284n12, 285n18, 285n20
Gomez, Abel R., 165
good relations, 3–4, 50, 99–101, 110, 117, 171–72, 212

gossip, 61–63, 153
Gould, Len, 90, 92
Great Britain, 18, 56, 127, 129, 131, 268n49, 268n50; British colonialism, 18, 102, 184. *See also* England; United Kingdom
Greek language, 132, 147
Greenberg, Julie, 81–82, 96–97, 236, 268n53
Griffiths, David, 11
Griqua, Shaine, 235
Gross, Jacob (Jack) Henry, 112, 206, 249n1, 251n11, 274n21, 279n19; and Gross's birth, 11–13; in Israel, 54, 111, 125, 251n13; in Israeli military, 17–18, 251n9, 274n25; politics of, 18–20; violence of, 19–20, 33; will of, 162–63, 282nn65–66
Gross, Mildred, 17, 18, 54, 154, 206, 249n1, 251n9, 274n21, 279n19; and Gross's birth, 11–13; and Jack's violence, 19; politics of, 20; will of, 162–63, 282n65

Haganah: Palmach, 17–18
Haggadah, 141
Halakha, 84
Hanekom, Derek, 104
Hashomer Hatzair, 17–18
hate mail, 243
Healing in Action: A Toolkit for Black Lives Matter Healing Justice and Direct Action, 234
Healing Justice Toolkit, 234
Health Act (2003), 220, 248n22, 280n25
healthcare, 5, 47, 79, 80–86, 89, 139, 156, 160, 162–63, 184–85, 236, 237, 240–41, 244, 277n21, 279n19
Hebrew Bible (Tanakh), 2, 58, 124, 170, 223, 283n4; Hebrew Scripture, 201, 230, 289n24. *See also* Torah
Hebrew language, 41, 119, 132, 147, 175, 179, 192, 202, 223–24, 286n32, 291n77
Hebrew people (biblical), 102, 183, 198, 223–24
Hermaphrodites Speak!, 215, 248n16
Hermetic Order of the Golden Dawn, 175
Herzlia Highlands, 25
Heschel, Abraham Joshua, 171–72
heteronormativity, 215, 236
heterosexuality, 82, 85, 161, 178, 260n30
Hinduism, 106, 108, 151, 290n61
Hitler, Adolf, 186. *See also* Holocaust

HIV/AIDS, 75, 116, 138, 154, 294n21
Holmes, Morgan, 40, 93–94, 143, 236, 278n23
Holocaust, 15, 23, 45, 83, 116, 122, 194–96, 200
Holy Spirit (Paraclete), 198–99, 230–31
homophobia, 21, 36
homosexuality, 21, 82
hormones, 66, 70, 78, 85, 111, 144, 151, 229, 267n22
Horowicz, Edmund, 85
Human Rights Law Conference, 97
Hunter, Peter, 58–59, 77–78, 259n27

identity documents, 87, 90, 96–98, 177, 216–17, 249n1, 252n27, 268n50, 268n53, 268nn49–51, 269n63
incarnate, 197, 229–30
India, 102
Indian South Africans, 16, 104, 130
Indigenous people, 1–3, 99–101, 103, 165, 234, 237, 283n4
inequity, 1, 3, 9, 15, 185
infertility, 144, 239, 240, 296n4
injustice, 1, 5, 9, 55, 102, 113, 114, 116–17, 120, 137–39, 145, 154, 156, 189, 192, 197, 202, 214, 232; racial, 103–4, 113, 195; systemic, 40, 211
Inkatha Freedom Party (IFP): Boipatong Massacre (1992), 210–11
instigation, 4, 10, 115, 214
Institute for Democratic Alternatives in South Africa (IDASA), 142
Institutional Review Board, 7
Intellectual Traditions in South Africa, 16
interfaith commitments, 55, 193–206
Internal Security Act (1976), 122
International Defence and Aid Fund for Southern Africa, 38, 128
International Intersex, 220
interreligious commitments, 29, 31, 45, 58, 60, 145, 176, 189, 192–93, 197, 199–200, 202–3, 208, 212, 214, 221, 228
intersex activism, 4–10, 44, 80–82, 113, 134, 145, 158–59, 215, 220, 233–34, 237–38, 239, 240–44, 248n16, 264n87, 275n51. *See also individual organizations and activists*
Intersex International Australia, 148
intersex medicine, 83, 85, 132
intersex scholars, 3, 40–41, 80, 93–94, 143, 236
Intersex Society of North America (ISNA), 81, 135, 215, 248n16, 275n51

Intersex South Africa (ISSA), 3, 81, 109–10, 113, 134–35, 138, 153–55, 159, 218, 220, 243, 275n51, 276n58, 281n44
Intersex Trust Aotearoa, New Zealand, 133
Iranti, 237
Islam, 108, 140, 147, 151, 185, 197, 201–3, 222
Israel, 25, 61, 101, 111, 141, 176–77, 184, 199, 201, 223, 268n50, 279n19, 284n12; alliance with South Africa's National Party, 15; citizenship, 126; Gross in, 26–27, 97, 102, 116, 125–27, 154, 163, 185, 195, 197, 201; Gross's family's relationship to, 20, 29, 54, 119–21, 124, 125, 162–63, 282n65; Gross's military service in, 66, 126, 251n9; intersexuality in, 236, 264n87, 296n12; Israeli colonialism, 18, 49, 119–20, 140, 155, 185, 189, 272n2; Jerusalem, 123, 127, 178, 200; Knesset, 185; Negev, 18; settlements in Palestine, 18, 120, 272n2; special election of, 196, 206; Tel Aviv, 279n19. *See also* Israel Defense Forces; Zionism
Israel Defense Forces, 18, 25, 126, 251n9
Israelites, 22, 184, 284n8, 288n15

Jackson, Jesse, 185
Jacobs, Daniel Malan, 105, 107–8, 112, 250n1, 270n23, 271n37, 272n67, 272nn53–54, 276n57, 282n44
Jansen, Beverly, 113
Jarrett, Bede, 52
Jempson, Mike, 90–92
Jesus Christ, 58, 62, 74, 139, 172, 201–2, 228, 284n10, 289n24, 292n85; arrest and trial, 127; crucifixion of, 131, 166, 194, 204; divinity of, 229–30; as Jewish, 57, 174, 193–200, 205–6; as priest, 56; in Protestantism, 197; resurrection of, 195, 203, 209
Jeter, Jon, 140
Jewish–Christian relations, 194–206, 288n15
Jewish Defense League, 185
Jewish studies, 82, 100
Jimpa, 206
Joerstad, Mari, 2, 113, 170–71, 283n4
Johannes, George, 128
Johannesburg, South Africa, 6, 16, 19, 223; Linksfield, 102, 203
John (landlord), 76, 262n37
John, Victoria, 235
John/Joan case, 81

John Paul I (pope), 38
John Paul II (pope), 38
John the Baptist (biblical), 203
Jouili, Jeannette S., 166
Judaism, 35, 58, 70, 75, 108, 111, 137, 147, 160, 229–30, 264n72, 284n8, 288n15, 290n61; and antisemitism, 15–16, 20, 23, 39–40, 45–46, 49, 55, 61, 83, 116, 122, 155, 174, 182–86, 194–96, 200, 205, 212; and apartheid, 16, 122–24, 194–96, 251n5, 252n17; baptism in, 175–76; and Buddhism, 207; burial practices of, 44; and conditional whiteness, 9, 16, 20, 86, 101, 103, 188, 194; and embodiment, 100, 255n35, 264n72; gender in, 39–40, 252n31, 296n4; Gross's, 3–4, 30–31, 34, 39–40, 46, 51, 55, 61, 101, 112, 140–42, 194–99, 206–7, 211, 271n37, 285n30; and Gross's childhood, 22–25, 225; Gross's Jewish-Christian sermons, 193–206, 289n24; Gross's parents', 54; and interfaith identity, 4; and intersexuality, 83–85, 151; and Israel, 17–18, 119–20, 296n12; of Jesus Christ, 57, 174, 193–200, 205–6; and nature, 170; non-Jewish Jews, 16, 251n7; Orthodox, 6, 23–25, 36, 61, 84, 102, 176, 177–89, 194, 209, 252n31, 284n12, 285nn17–19, 286n32; and racism, 46, 122–24, 174, 177–89
juntas, 119–20
justice, 10, 17, 19, 101, 122, 124, 140, 142, 158, 172, 203, 205; gender, 32; intersex, 237; racial, 9, 50, 121, 178, 188; social, 3, 5, 31, 49, 113, 117, 128, 146, 156, 171, 189–90, 194, 196–97, 205, 212, 223, 276n2. *See also* injustice

Kach, 185
Kahan, Havav Eliezer, 23
Kahana, Meirke, 185
Karkazis, Katrina, 248n19
Kasrils, Ronnie, 140, 157, 160, 251n12, 280n21
kehillah, 23
Kessler, Suzanne, 81
Khoikhoi people, 102, 234
kibbutzim, 18, 51, 119, 251n13
Kim (friend), 70
Kim, Hyjin, 153, 279n15
Kimmerer, Robin Wall, 169
King, Martin Luther, Jr., 130
King David Day School, 21

Kirsten, Lex, 139
Kittay, Eva, 83
Kollapen, Jody, 218
Kollel HaRabbonim, 23
Krikler, Bernice, 67, 70
Ku Klux Klan, 187

Lahood, Grant: *Intersexion*, 139, 222, 224, 250n3, 258nn18–19, 263n63, 275n51, 276n58
laicization, 38, 57, 78, 80, 89, 176
land, 119–21, 152, 165, 169, 172–74, 183–84, 203, 232, 283n1; bodies of, 3, 9, 49–50, 99–114
Land Claims Court, 108
Land Reform (Labor Tenants) Act 3 (1996), 108
Landynski, Dovid, 23
Lapsley, Michael, 130–31
Latin language, 232
Law of Moses, 22, 289n24
League of Nations, 18
Lebanon, 189
Leeson, K. E., 90
Le Roux, Gabrielle, 158, 221–28, 263n38, 295n36, 295n43
Lesbian and Gay Equality Project, 217
Lesotho, South Africa, 130–31
Letish, Yoself, 184
LGBTQI+ activism, 4, 137, 152, 243, 248n22
liberation, 3, 22, 26, 51, 102, 121–22, 139, 142, 146, 171–72, 183–84, 197, 273n7
Libya, 187
Likotsi, Mofihli, 104
Lithuania, 252n29
Low, Joanna, 91
Lubavitch Hasidic community, 177–89, 284n12, 285nn17–18, 286n32
Luthuli, Albert, 122–23

Magaziner, Daniel, 122
Maimonides, Moses, 201
Malan, Daniel François, 15, 112
Malan, Rian, 104
Malatino, Hil, 1, 74, 95, 96, 149
Mandela, Nelson, 58, 104, 129–30, 136, 204–5, 293n14
Mars, Benjamin, 105–8, 110–11, 270n23, 271n27, 271n35, 271n37, 272n58
Marx, Karl, 132
Marxism, 32, 51, 54, 153

Mary Magdalene (biblical), 230
masculinity, 9, 25, 32–33, 36, 40, 70, 285n30
Mashinini, Teboho "Tsietsi," 128, 274n35
Massachusetts, 17
Mayson, Cedric, 129
Maytham, John, 136
Mbeki, Thabo, 56, 258n19
McCabe, Herbert, 35, 259n26
McGreal, Chris, 274n22
McMahon, Malcolm, 57, 59–61, 73, 76–80, 88, 175, 208, 228–30, 256n44, 259n26, 260n30, 291n71
medical bodies, 9, 49–50, 65–86, 192
medical gaze, 48, 93
medicalization, 80, 236
meditation, 51, 106–7, 148, 175, 189, 194, 206–8, 223, 225, 291n62
Memmi, Albert, 7
menstruation, 39–40
mental illness, 42, 61–62
Messiah, 176, 180, 195, 200, 228, 289n23
methodology of book, 6–8; archival research, 34–40
Michalowski, Zvi, 200
Mills, John, 88–89, 91, 263n52, 265n2, 266n8
misogyny, 39–40
misrecognition, 230
Mitchell, Mani, 97, 133–34, 158–59, 220, 248n16, 275nn51–52, 281n42, 282n51, 282n53
Mogoba, Stanley, 104
Mokoena, Nthabiseng, 233, 240–44, 297n29, 298n37
Money, John, 74–75, 80, 262nn41–42, 263n63
monstrance, 230, 232
monstrosity, 62, 83, 106, 150–51, 155, 215, 223, 232
moral panics, 236
Morgan, Mogg, 175
Morogoro Conference, 125
Morrison, Toni: *Beloved*, 2–3, 10, 166, 169, 214 (*See also* Baby Suggs (character))
Moses (biblical), 22, 102, 183, 203, 223–4, 289n24
Moten, Fred, 173–74
Muñoz, José Esteban, 115
music, 10, 17, 19, 54, 147, 150, 182, 214
Muslims. *See* Islam
mystery, 55, 167, 191, 229–30
myth, 33, 39, 40, 144, 179

Nachala settlement movement, 272n2
Nachman, Harav, 23
Naidenov, Pol, 233, 239–40
Naidoo, Lawson, 129
Nash, Daphne, 32
Natal Witness, 81
National Dialogue on the Protection and Promotion of the Human Rights of Intersex People, 219, 235, 248n22, 297n23
National Endowment for the Humanities, 81
National Geographic: "The Third Sex," 243, 253n2, 263n63
National Health Insurance Policy, 220, 280n25
nationalism, 276n3; Afrikaner, 184; contraceptive, 296n10; gendered, 17, 45; Jewish, 196, 272n2, 296n12; neo-Nazi, 274n39. *See also* Zionism
National Party (South Africa), 15–16, 20, 251n5. *See also* apartheid
National Union of South African Students (NUSAS): Wages Commission, 121, 124
Natives Land Act (1913, South Africa), 108
naturalization, 56
Nazis, 20, 122, 183, 186–87, 200; neo-, 274n39
Nelson, Lemrick, 184
Netherlands: Dutch colonialism, 102; Nijmegen, 79
Netherlands Culture and Health Program, 154
neurodivergence, 49
New Communist List (Rakach), 119
New Testament, 56, 199, 201; 1 Corinthians 1:23, 204; Acts, 205; Galatians 3:28, 58
New York City: Brooklyn, 6, 102, 185, 192, 284n12, 285n17; Crown Heights, Brooklyn, 35, 177–89, 254n19, 284n12, 285n18, 286n31
New Zealand, 133–34
Nichols, Aidan, 35, 69, 287n1
Nolan, Albert, 133, 194
nongovernmental organizations (NGOs), 109–10, 138–39, 146–47, 153, 160, 218, 243, 248n22; NGO industrial complex, 243. *See also individual organizations*
nonhuman bodies, 100–102, 113, 117, 138, 166–67
non-Jewish Jews, 16, 251n7
Norma (Fran Springfield's partner), 68, 77, 261n14

North Africa, 17
North Carolina, US: Asheville, 133, 158
Northern Cape, South Africa, 235
Northern Ireland, 51
Not in My Name, 140, 142
Nuremberg Code (1947), 85

obituaries, 215, 293n6
O'Connor, Flannery, 230–31
Old Testament, 201, 288n15; Exodus, 183–84, 223; Leviticus 18:28, 99; Psalm 23, 72–73, 123; Psalm 69:1, 41
Olympic athletes, 92
onah tradition, 84
ontology, 101, 207
ordination, 35, 49, 56, 176, 211, 258n19; of women, 38, 89, 229
Orme, John, 78
Orthodox Judaism, 23–24, 61, 84, 102, 194, 209, 285n19; baptism in, 176; celibacy in, 25; gender roles in, 36, 252n31; Lubavitch Hasidic community, 177–89, 284n12, 285nn17–18, 286n32
Overlander, Gershon, 177, 284nn13–14
Overlander, Sarah Leah, 284n14
Oxford Academics Against Apartheid, 51
Oxford Anti-Apartheid Group, 51, 127, 128
Oxford House, 35, 52, 62, 67, 70, 128, 258nn6–7; founding of, 258n4; Gross at, 37–39, 53, 56–59, 127, 175, 258n19, 291n72
Oxford University, 8, 56, 98, 182, 209, 249n26, 250n3, 251n14, 258n4, 259n26
Ozinsky, Max, 140

Paasonen, Susana, 292n3
Page, Cara, 165
Pagonis, Pidgeon, 248n16
Palestine, 17, 101, 119, 121, 140, 185, 194, 195, 277n17; Gaza, 184; Hebron, 120; Israeli settlements in, 18, 120, 272n2; Jerusalem, 123, 127, 178, 200; West Bank, 113, 120
Pan African Congress (PAC), 104
Parliamentary Portfolio Committee, 109, 217
Parliament on National Health Insurance, 220
pass laws, 102, 113, 203
Passover, 183, 197, 206, 209–10, 221
pastors, 2, 147, 171–72, 241, 249n23
pathologization, 43, 71, 121, 242, 247n14

patriarchy, 3, 25–26, 32–33, 114, 190, 229
Patricia (pseudonym), 142–44, 277n20
Patterson, Orlando, 42, 257n52
Paul VI (pope), 175
Pearson, Peter-John, 123
The People, 90
performance, 82, 84, 108, 173, 193, 231, 253n34
Persian Gulf, 68
phalloplasty, 97, 268n53
Pharaoh (biblical), 102, 183–84, 223
philosophical dualism, 165
Pietermaritzburg, South Africa, 130, 132, 249n1
Pityana, Sipho, 129
Plemons, Eric, 166, 191
pogroms, 184
Poland, 186
police, 20, 43, 75, 103–4, 123, 126, 128, 150, 185–86, 210–11
pornotroping, 40, 256n37
portraits, of Gross, 221–28, 295n43
post-traumatic stress disorder, 89, 92
poverty, 5, 37, 95, 117, 159, 162, 172, 228, 243; clerical vows to, 52; death from, 43–45, 156; financial precarity, 154–56; racialized, 3, 104, 144
Povinelli, Elizabeth, 100–101, 103
preaching, 2, 36, 52, 58, 62, 160, 166, 175–76, 187, 193–206, 229–30, 289n24
premature death, 4, 7, 10, 43, 45–46, 114
Press Complaints Commission, 90–92, 266n8
Pretoria, South Africa, 222
Promotion of Equality and Prevention of Unfair Discrimination Act (PEPUDA, 2000), 217–20, 248n17, 248n22, 280n25
protest, 15, 19, 53–54, 122–23, 127–31, 141, 211
Protestantism, 106, 108, 231; Evangelical, 197
providence, 23, 57, 184
psychoanalysis, 47, 67, 70, 95, 267n42
Puar, Jasbir, 42–43
Public Safety Act (1953), 15

Quaker Peace Centre, 214, 293n4
Quakers, 147–48, 208–10, 214–15, 253n38, 293n4
Qualtrough, Stuart, 88–90, 91, 210, 266n8
Queen's Council, 109

INDEX 317

queerness, 1, 3, 5, 75, 115, 214, 224, 241, 247n14, 253n1, 257n63
queer theory, 11

rabbis, 22–23, 25–26, 31, 40, 100, 140, 171, 175, 177–815, 197–98, 201–2, 207, 264n72, 284nn13–14, 285n17, 286n36. *See also individual rabbis*
racialization, 16, 103, 174, 237, 278n34
racial justice, 9, 50, 121, 178, 188
racism, 2–3, 114, 116, 139, 178, 186–87, 194, 196, 212; and apartheid, 15, 26; in Catholicism, 46; and intersexuality, 144; and Jewish–Black relations, 174, 177–89; and Jewish contingent whiteness, 101. *See also* antisemitism; apartheid; Zionism
Radcliffe, Timothy, 6, 34–35, 55, 69, 79, 121, 127, 198, 208, 213, 265n2, 265n5; and activism, 54, 127–28; and Gross's intersexuality, 59–60, 77, 121; and Gross's suicidal ideation, 89–90, 256nn44–45, 257n53; on Jewish converts to Catholicism, 175, 176; relationship with Gross, 57–58, 59–60, 157, 205
Ramatlhodi, Ngoako, 131
Rebbe Rebbe Menachem Mendel Schneerson, 178–85, 285n20
redlining, 102
refugees, 119–20, 124, 126, 156; Iraqi, 240; Jewish, 23; South African, 132
Regional Land Claims Commission, 49, 103, 105, 108–10, 112–13, 138, 152, 154, 271n39
regulation, 1–10, 45–50, 74–75, 80, 82–83, 86, 94, 100–101, 103, 114–15, 120–21, 166, 172, 192, 212, 224, 236
Reid, Russell, 74, 76
Reis, Elizabeth, 85
religiosity, 3, 5, 10, 106, 114, 147, 189, 212; *vs.* theism, 106
religious bodies, 2, 4, 9, 41, 44, 48–63, 180, 192, 211, 232
religious discrimination, 185–86, 205. *See also* antisemitism
religious studies, 80, 106
resonance, 3, 5, 10, 163, 166, 171, 174, 189, 192, 212–32, 247, 292n3
Restitution of Land Rights Act 22 (1994), 108
resurrection, 8, 59, 131, 191, 195, 202–3, 208–9
Revisionist movement, 20

Rick (therapist), 67
Roberts, Oliver, 250n3
Roberts, Sue, 91
Rogers, Sandy D., 172
Roman Catholic Church. *See* Catholicism
Rosa, Hartmut, 213
Rosenbaum, Yankel, 184–85
Rosh Hashanah, 181
Routledge, Jeremy, 293n4
Rubidge, Lloyd, 153
Rubin, David, 74, 82, 94–95, 139, 143, 173, 262n42
Russia, 17

Sabbath, 11–12, 23, 171–72, 198, 205, 250n3; Shabbat, 24, 141, 189
Safrin, Rabbi, 181
Salamon, Gayle, 47, 87–88, 254n17
salvation, 107, 157, 198–99
Sampter, Jessie, 253n1, 290n61
Sanders, David, 69–70
scars, 100, 103, 192, 209, 211, 215, 232
schisms, 174–76, 198
Schmidt-Gross, Raymond (Ray), 18–20, 24, 111–12, 249n1, 251n13, 252n20, 252n28; and book research, 6, 17, 155, 249n1, 250n3, 251n13, 251nn9–11, 252n20, 257n57, 274n21; financial troubles of, 162; and Gross's death, 43–44, 103, 155, 257n57; and Gross's gender identity, 155, 272n58; and Jack's violence, 19–20, 254n10; marriage of, 279n19; and parents' death, 163, 282nn65–66
Schmidt-Gross, Sharon, 155, 279n19, 281n28
Schneerson, Rebbe Menachem Mendel. *See* Rebbe Menachem Mendel Schneerson
Scott, Geoffrey, 35
Second Vatican Council (Vatican II), 51, 175, 206
secularism, 10, 22, 24, 39, 102, 160, 177, 190, 196, 203, 233, 236, 287n55
Seder, 141–42, 175, 206, 209–10, 277n16
Seligson, Michael, 285n17
Semenya, Caster, 92
Senegal: Dakar, 30, 56, 142, 258nn18–19
sermons, Gross's, 193–206, 289n24
sexism, 26, 116, 121, 139, 212
Sex Status Act 49 (2003), 219, 248n17, 248n22
sexual violence, 104, 145, 149, 183, 187
sex work, 75, 229

318 INDEX

Shemini Atzeret, 177–78
Shoval, 18
Sigmundson, Keith, 80–81
Simons, Ray Alexander, 16, 250n3
slavery, 2, 102, 183, 188, 223, 257n52, 271n40
slow death, 42
Smit, David, 105–7, 109–11, 113, 272n51, 272n53
Smit, Estian, 138, 217
Smith, Charlene, 145–46, 296n4
social death, 42, 161, 257n52
socialism, 17, 20, 120, 122, 125, 243, 252n17
social justice, 3, 5, 31, 49, 113, 117, 128, 146, 156, 171, 189–90, 194, 196–97, 205, 212, 223, 276n2
Society of Young Africa (SOYA), 124–25
Soskice, Janet, 72, 262n33
soul, 72, 166, 176, 195, 254n17; godly, 183, 286n32
Soundarajan, Santhi, 256n48
South African Constitution (1996), 97, 108, 220, 248n22, 280n25, 294n21; Equality Clause, 216–19
South African Defense Force, 292n81
South African Department of Education, 122
South African Department of Health, 97
South African Department of Home Affairs, 96, 268n49
South African Human Rights Commission (SAHRC), 80, 218, 237, 248n17, 248n22, 256n51, 293n18
South African Special Branch, 126
South African Student Organization, 122
South African Truth and Reconciliation Commission, 131, 163, 282n65
South African Zionist Federation, 126, 163
Soviet Union, 17, 20, 119, 273n19
Soweto Uprising (1976), 123, 128
Spillers, Hortense, 256n37, 268n46
Springfield, Fran, 67–72, 75–78, 91, 225, 255n24, 261nn14–16, 262n37, 263n45, 290n48
St. Albert the Great, 52
Stalin, Joseph, 17
State University of New York, 81
Stern, Jen, 214–15, 253n38
St. Joseph's Theological Institute, 129, 211
St. Michael and All Angels Church, 150
St. Michael's Catholic Church, 195
Stock, Benjamin (Benjy), 178, 181, 285n17, 285n19

Stock, Martha, 178, 188, 285n17
Stock, Shimshon, 178–79, 181–82, 185–88, 285n17
Sukkot, 177–78, 181
suicidal ideation, 9, 40–43, 95, 256n48
supersessionism, 174, 194
superstition, 203, 234–37
Suppression of Communism Act (1950), 122
sutures, 2, 5, 10, 50, 163, 166, 169, 190–212, 214, 232
Sykes, Pamela, 44, 161, 282n60
synagogues, 6, 19, 23, 140, 178–82, 187, 200, 205
Syria, 119
Syriac language, 209

Taiwan, 237–39
Talmud, 23–24, 40, 141, 296n4
Teriso, Tunchio, 235
terminology, 247n14
testicular feminization syndrome (androgen insensitivity syndrome), 277n21
theism, 106, 175, 208
Theron, Liesl, 138–39, 146–47, 276n5
Third Reich, 23
Thomas, Grafton, 286n36
Tickell, Diana, 128–29, 274n35
Tjipel, 100–101
Torah, 13, 23, 24, 177, 181–82, 187, 194, 199, 201, 230, 253n31, 283n4; Lithuanian method of study, 23
Townes, Emilie, 3, 5, 40, 247n13
transgender activism, 239, 243
Transgender Intersex Alliance, 242
transgender medicine, 65, 67, 72, 74, 83, 85–86, 240
transgender people, 1, 75–77, 138–39, 149, 193, 222, 230, 239, 252n25, 255n24, 290n48; and Gross's gender identity, 9, 21, 48, 49–50, 59, 62, 65, 67–71, 90, 97, 122, 221, 225; legal treatment of, 97, 217; and maladjustment, 295n60; and multispecies affective politics, 292n3; relation to intersex people, 72, 83, 97, 217, 242, 243, 254n18; and sex as property, 47; violence against, 238, 241
transnationalism, 15, 17, 45, 82–83, 116, 119–36, 143, 193, 228
transphobia, 62, 75
transsexual people, 34, 36, 61–62, 68, 71, 78, 89, 97

trauma, 7, 41, 81, 89, 92, 116, 133, 186, 190, 192, 215, 248n21, 291n77
Triangle Project, 144
Triea, Kiira, 275nn51–52
Trinity, 106, 198
Truth and Reconciliation Commission. *See* South African Truth and Reconciliation Commission
Tsadok, Rabbi, 100, 264n72
Turner, Rick, 122
Tutu, Desmond, 130–33, 293n14. *See also* South African Truth and Reconciliation Commission
Tyne River, 23

Union of Orthodox Synagogues, 140
Union Party, 75
United Kingdom, 22, 29, 68, 79, 88, 127, 129, 142, 158, 177, 268n50, 274n35, 277n21. *See also* England; Great Britain; Northern Ireland
United Nations Convention Relating to the Status of Refugees, 126
University Buddhist Society, 207
University Catholic Society, 194–95
University of Cape Town, 121, 126, 273n5; Jewish Association, 123; *Strike!*, 123–24
University of Haifa, 119

vaginoplasty, 97, 268n53
Vallie, Shamiella, 150
van der Kolk, Bessel, 116
van Ooijen, David, 79, 263n58
van Rooyen, Eugene, 43, 110
van Rooyen, Justine, 138, 151–52
Vásquez, Manuel A., 143
Viljoen, Sean, 123
Viloria, Hilda, 248n16
vocation, 61–62, 67, 78–79, 92, 148, 163, 232
Voortrekkers, 130
Voss, Suzanne, 131
Vredehoek Synagogue, 19

Wall, Sean Saifa, 248n16
Wannsee Conference, 200
Waring, Lauren, 150

Weaver, Harlan, 292n3
Weiss, Daniella, 272n2
West, Angela, 32
whiteness, 19, 130, 131, 143, 187, 190, 215, 234, 241; classed, 243; conditional Jewish, 9, 16, 20, 86, 101, 103, 188, 194; and land redistribution, 103–8; white privilege, 44, 50, 101–2, 106, 145, 190
white supremacy, 183, 184, 190, 274n39
Wilkes, Kathy, 72, 259n26, 262n33
Williams, Jennifer, 43, 109, 142, 147, 163, 207, 257n54, 258n19, 271n45; on Gross's cats, 257n54
Women's Media Watch, 222
Woods, Richard, 67
World War I, 18
World War II, 15–17, 45, 83–85, 122, 271n40
Worsnip, Michael, 105, 107, 109, 130–33, 142, 271n31, 275n41

xenophobia, 20, 189, 212
Xhosa language, 105, 241

Yentl, 253n34
Yesh, 119
yeshiva, 22–24, 46, 54, 171, 252n28, 253n34, 285n17
Yiddish language, 179, 181
Yiddishkeit (Jewishness), 23
Yishuv, 18
Yom Kippur, 181
Young, Gordon, 273n5
Youngsfield Military Base, 123
Yutar, Percy, 16

Zaaiman, Andre, 130, 142
Zionism, 126, 163, 183–84, 196, 282n65; and antisemitism, 20; and apartheid, 15, 45, 49, 101; and colonialism, 18, 49, 119–20, 140, 155, 185, 189, 272n2; Gross's relationship to, 25–26, 45, 49, 54, 60, 101, 120, 127, 137, 190, 252n17; socialist, 17, 122. *See also* anti-Zionism
Zulu people, 130, 210
Zuma, Jacob, 131

www.ingramcontent.com/pod-product-compliance
Lightning Source LLC
Chambersburg PA
CBHW021849230426
43671CB00006B/321